Weak Elements,
Weak Flesh

Weak Elements, Weak Flesh

Reading Galatians in Conversation with Philo and Greek Medical Discourse

Ernest P. Clark

LEXINGTON BOOKS / FORTRESS ACADEMIC
Lanham • Boulder • New York • London

Published by Lexington Books/Fortress Academic
Lexington Books is an imprint of The Rowman & Littlefield Publishing Group, Inc.
4501 Forbes Boulevard, Suite 200, Lanham, Maryland 20706
www.rowman.com

86-90 Paul Street, London EC2A 4NE, United Kingdom

Copyright © 2024 by The Rowman & Littlefield Publishing Group, Inc.

All rights reserved. No part of this book may be reproduced in any form or by any electronic or mechanical means, including information storage and retrieval systems, without written permission from the publisher, except by a reviewer who may quote passages in a review.

British Library Cataloguing in Publication Information Available

Library of Congress Cataloging-in-Publication Data

Names: Clark, Ernest P., 1976– author.
Title: Weak elements, weak flesh : reading Galatians in conversation with Philo and
   Greek medical discourse / Ernest P. Clark.
Description: Lanham : Lexington Books/Fortress Academic, [2024] |
   Includes bibliographical references and index. | Summary: "In Weak Elements,
   Weak Flesh, Ernest Clark reinvigorates an ancient interpretation overlooked since the
   fourth century. Clark argues that when Paul writes 'we too were enslaved under the
   elements of the world,' he is describing sin's enslavement of all people through the
   material elements that compose and compromise their flesh"—Provided by publisher.
Identifiers: LCCN 2023037021 (print) | LCCN 2023037022 (ebook) |
   ISBN 9781978713956 (cloth) | ISBN 9781978713963 (epub)
Subjects: LCSH: Bible. Galatians--Criticism, interpretation, etc. | Philo, of Alexandria--
   Criticism and interpretation. | Bible. Epistles of Paul—Criticism, interpretation, etc. |
   Jewish philosophy.
Classification: LCC BS2685.52 C53 2024 (print) | LCC BS2685.52 (ebook) | DDC
   227/.406—dc23/eng/20231011
LC record available at https://lccn.loc.gov/2023037021
LC ebook record available at https://lccn.loc.gov/2023037022

♾️™ The paper used in this publication meets the minimum requirements of American
National Standard for Information Sciences—Permanence of Paper for Printed Library
Materials, ANSI/NISO Z39.48-1992.

To Tiffany
who with valiant faith withstood the elements' fiercest weakness
and received Ἀναστασία

Contents

Tables	ix
Foreword	xi
Acknowledgments	xv
List of Abbreviations	xix
Introduction	1
1: The Term "Στοιχεια Του Κοσμου" in Ancient Greek and Early Jewish Works	31
2: The Concept of Enslavement under "Στοιχεια Του Κοσμου" in Ancient Greek and Early Jewish Works	59
3: The Argument for Redemptive Nomism in Philo's Philosophy According to the "Στοιχεια Του Κοσμου"	95
4: The Flesh and Sin: Enslaved Under the Στοιχεια Του Κοσμου	125
5: The Law Against the Στοιχεια and the Flesh	149
6: The Son and the Spirit Against the Στοιχεια and the Flesh	187
Conclusion	211
Bibliography	217
Subject Index	245
Scriptures Index	253
Ancient Sources Index	261
About the Author	275

Tables

Table I.1: Senses of Στοιχεῖον in Blinzler's Study	12
Table 1.1: √Στοιχεω by Category in Extant Early Jewish Sources	33
Table 1.2: Uses of Στοιχεῖον in Disputably Early Jewish Sources	50
Table 2.1: Combinations of Elemental Qualities in Humors and Seasons	69
Table 4.1: Two Sorts of Being "Under" in Gal 3.19–4.7	136
Table 5.1: Philo's and Paul's Allegories	174

Foreword

Skeptical onlookers sometimes ask biblical scholars how on earth they can find anything new to say. Have not these texts been studied to death, pored over, crawled over, scrutinized under the magnifying glass, to the point where all we can now attempt is the odd slight rearrangement of the furniture in an all-too-well-known room?

Ernest Clark's remarkable work, now transposed from a striking doctoral dissertation into this clear and carefully argued book, provides as good an answer as we are likely to find. As Thomas Kuhn pointed out a generation ago in *The Structure of Scientific Revolutions*, sometimes a fresh—and often young—pair of eyes, looking at evidence that older eyes had been long accustomed to see from one particular angle, suddenly notices a new aspect which had previously been missed.[1] Sometimes, as in this case, it was because those younger eyes, not quite satisfied with the data-base so frequently worked through, decided to cast the net just a bit wider.

Dr. Clark was studying the well-known question of the *stoicheia*, the "elements," in Paul—specifically in his letter to the Galatians. (We may hope that he will go on to broaden his study to consider the similar passages in Colossians, for which there was no space in the original research.) Many, including the present writer, had been more or less satisfied with one or other of the traditional explanations for this initially obscure language. In my case, I had gone along with the idea that Paul regarded the *stoicheia* (the root meaning of which is a "row" or "line") as the guardian spirits of the nations, lined up as it were, doing their job of looking after the pagan nations—with Torah being the equivalent for the people of Israel. But Ernest Clark's exhaustive survey of all the known ancient uses of the term led him in a very different direction: from the Jewish philosopher Philo, who uses term more frequently, and thence to the medical literature of the period. It seems that nobody who was interested in Galatians had been studying the ancient medical literature; and nobody who was interested in the ancient medical literature had been thinking of Galatians. Dr. Clark was the first one (since apparently the fourth century) to put two and two together.

Three things stand out initially from this. First, despite the popularity of various other theories (including the one I had myself earlier espoused), there is overwhelming evidence that the *stoicheia tou kosmou*, "the elements of the world," must refer to the four "elements" of which both the world as a whole and the human being are composed, namely (for most ancient philosophers) earth, air, water, and fire. The fact that this presses upon us more urgently the question, "So why were the Galatians, or Paul, interested in that?" is irrelevant. That's the basic meaning of the phrase.

Second, Dr. Clark makes a strong case for the proposition, repeated by many scholars over the last two centuries but still regularly ignored, that Philo has not been used half enough in the study of Paul. His presentation of the possibility that the "agitators" were offering the Galatians a theological worldview not unlike that of the great Jewish philosopher must be taken more seriously than I, and most others, have been inclined to do.

But the third point is the important one, forming the "aha" moment which distinguishes a truly exciting new proposal from a merely competent piece of research. In the medical literature, human sickness is the result of a person's *stoicheia* being in some way out of balance. What the doctor will then do is to prescribe a medical "regime," including various kinds of treatment ranging from herbal medicine to recommendations for exercise and so on. But—and here is the link with Galatians, the point at which the spark jumps from one source to another—such a "regime" would naturally be referred to in Greek as a *nomos*, a "law"; and such a law, when doing its job, would be playing the role of a *paidagôgos*, the household slave whose task was to keep the youngster in order and make sure he got to school on time. Anyone familiar with Galatians will have known all along how important for Paul's argument in chapter 3 is the point about the *nomos* acting as a *paidagôgos* until the coming of the Messiah, and of *pistis*, "faith/faithfulness." But until now nobody for sixteen centuries has seen this as (perhaps among other things) medical language. From now on, it will be just as impossible for serious readers of Galatians to ignore this as it would have been for Paul's original hearers. Dr. Clark is to be congratulated both on his ferreting out of the relevant texts and for his lucid, clear analysis and display of highly complicated sources.

We then face the question: how does this surprising insight, for so long unnoticed by Pauline scholars, help us in interpreting the letter as a whole, not least Paul's reference to the *stoicheia*? Here there are, no doubt, several possible ways forward. Dr. Clark advances what might appear to be the most obvious one: the Galatians are being told by the "agitators" that they need the Torah to be their medical "regime," to lead them, like a household slave, to the moral health that they presently lack. But this, Paul insists, will not work.

Foreword xiii

What they need instead, and what Paul "prescribes" for them in the body of the letter, is the twofold medicine of the Anointed (Clark's regular way of referring to "Christ" or "Messiah") and the Spirit. A good deal of the letter then appears to fall into place, not least the bracing ethical instructions of the last two chapters.

This is undoubtedly attractive, not to say powerful. But—as with all good research—we are thereby pointed to further questions. Reviewers and subsequent scholars will no doubt raise them more fully. Here I mention simply two, not at all as criticisms of the basic insight about the *stoicheia* and the medical terms associated therewith, but as questions of interpretation which take up these themes and see how they might work.

First, are we really sure that the problem which faced the Galatian converts was primarily one of moral behavior? Granted that many in the non-Jewish world were attracted to the Jewish way of life because of its theological simplicity and its moral rigor, was that really the main thing that was going on? And was Paul's main object in the letter to address that concern? If so, how does this analysis avoid the appearance of saying (to oversimplify for the moment) that the Jewish way of life can't solve your moral problem but that the Christian way of life can do so? Is not that a train of thought of which most have now learned to be wary?

Second, how do the medical "echoes"—if that is how we should characterize them—help with what appears to many of us the foundational argument of the letter, that those who belong to the Messiah really are Abraham's "seed," without needing to be circumcised? I and others have offered analyses of this argument (my most recent attempt being in my *Galatians*[2]) which try to ground the problem, and Paul's solution to it, in the swirling combination of theology, exegesis, sociology, and culture which we glimpse through a historical analysis of the situation of Jewish communities in the non-Jewish world. Jews, so far as we can tell, were normally exempt from pagan worship; what would happen when, quite suddenly, a group which included non-Jews claimed to be followers of Israel's Messiah and therefore to share the normal Jewish exemption?

If we make the latter approach fundamental, then the medical overtones of Paul's language must certainly still be heard, but perhaps more as a vivid ancillary metaphor than as the primary thrust of Galatians 3 and 4. Perhaps, rather than (or alongside?) highlighting the Galatians' moral impotence and the impossibility of solving this problem through Torah, Paul is insisting that Israel as a whole, in the long history from Moses to the present day, has been under a medical regime. But the household slave has not been the one to bring health—to see the young "son" through to maturity. That has come—as Dr. Clark rightly stresses—through the Messiah and the Spirit. The "healing" which was needed was not just anthropological and moral. It was both cosmic and ecclesial.

Such discussions are for the future. The present book, the fruit of so much careful and patient research laid out with exemplary clarity, will generate many more. For that, and for the sheer excitement of a fresh and unexpected set of insights into a notoriously difficult text, we are all in the debt of Dr. Ernest Clark.

N. T. WRIGHT
Wycliffe Hall, Oxford
June 2023

NOTES

1. Thomas S. Kuhn, *The Structure of Scientific Revolutions* (Chicago: University of Chicago Press, 1962).
2. N. T. Wright, *Galatians*, Commentaries for Christian Formation (Grand Rapids: Eerdmans, 2021).

Acknowledgments

This book is a slightly revised version of my thesis "Enslaved Under the Elements of the Cosmos," which the University of St. Andrews accepted for the degree of PhD in 2018. Prof. N. T. Wright supervised my research, and Profs. Paul Foster and James Davila examined my work in the *viva voce*. For their guidance and critical engagement I am thankful.

This book is also the fruit of diligent labor enabled and encouraged by many friends. To them all I am deeply grateful.

My professors modeled devoted scholarship for me, inspiring a love for scripture and equipping me with tools for historical study. Chief among these are Dan Estes, Floyd Elmore, Chris Miller, Tim Laniak, and Rollin Grams.

Four years of life in Scotland was a daunting prospect. Vance and Patty Woodyard were reassuring. Gifts from Mike and Mindy Denigan, Louis and Lucy Hamilton, and Rick and Sherri Wojick gave us confidence to begin. Later gifts from others enabled us to finish: Brian and Cara Bergeron, Bill and Karen Berry, Debi Burns, George and Meg Cook, Ben and Melinda Clark, Ernest Clark, Don and Drue Hamilton, Tim and Callie Hamilton, Trent Hamilton, Troy and Beth Hamilton, Tressa Garrison Hasty, Doug and Joanne Hayward, Mike and Judy Hogan, Craig and Gwen Kenton, Matt and Laurie Kuiper, Robert and Judy Levy, Van and Kelley Linn, Dave and Whitney Martineau, Walter and Judy Mills, Richard and Carey Moore, Mike and Wanda Robinson, Joe and Hanna Robson, Mike and Chris Ruff, Chan Sims and the Korean Ladies Bible Study Group, Josh and Alyssa Stanley, Christy Tanusaputra, Chris and Gileah Taylor, Jeremy and Abigail Toyer, Heather Denigan Trowell, David and Kayla Williams, Scott and Kathy Young, and Trinity Church.

The University of St. Andrews' 600th Anniversary Scholarship and grants from Mylne Trust and Sola Trust were a substantial help. Awards from the School of Divinity's Donald Baillie Memorial Fund and Fondation Catholique Ecossaise enabled interaction with German and French scholars. And the University Library was both generous and astonishingly prompt in acquiring new books. My thanks to them for sharing so graciously what they had received.

Dear friends in St. Andrews proved that Scots are as warm and bright as their weather is cold and dark. Saleem and Catriona Bhatti and their children welcomed foreign vagabonds as though they were long-lost cousins. The saints at St. Andrews Scottish Episcopal Church lived out what it means to be children of one Father: Eric and Clare Priest were instant uncle and aunt, and Anne Tynte-Irvine, grandmother; Trevor (and Rachel) Hart, Rosemary Bishop-White, and Diana Hall were faithful shepherds; Jill Anderson, a compassionate source of weekly manna from Prêt à Manger; and Martin Passmore (and the New Park Educational Foundation), a gracious source of accommodation.

Fellow students in St. Mary's College were stalwart companions on the pilgrimage through constant self-doubt to the PhD. I got to walk with Matt Ketterling and Tim Fox through the MLitt and then accompanied Tim to the Howie room, where we joined Isaac Blois, Jen Gilbertson, Tommi Karjalainen, Kim Euichang, and later Jared Van Tine. And the ever-cheerful Rachel Harris maintained the Roundel as an ideal environment for focused study.

In the Roundel, fellow Wright student Esau McCaulley shaped our growing understanding of Galatians; David Johnston was a wise sounding board for my ideas on Paul's view of the flesh; and the invitation from Eric Covington to co-chair the Ancient Cosmology and New Testament Interpretation section at the European Association of Biblical Studies Annual Meeting was a real boon.

Feedback there and at other conferences honed my argument. My thanks to the chairs of the New Testament Research Seminar at the University of St. Andrews, the Muted Voices Conference at the University of Durham, Doktorclub at South Asia Institute of Advanced Christian Studies (SAIACS), and the Pauline Epistles and Pauline Theology sections of the Society of Biblical Literature. My thanks also to Richard Bauckham and Eddie Adams who were gracious and affirming in their response to my critique of their work on 2 Peter.

At St. Andrews, I thank Scott Hafemann and Jim Davila, who taught me and engaged my developing thinking. Prof. Davila's benevolent razing of my six-month portfolio cleared the ground and drove me on to do proper scholarship.

I completed the thesis while Classics Consultant in the Department of New Testament at South Asia Institute of Advanced Christian Studies in Bengaluru, India. My thanks to Ian Payne, the principal, and Idicheria Ninan, the head of New Testament, for allowing me extensive time for research and writing. Thanks also to my colleagues Roji George, Varughese John, and Mary Varughese for affirming conversations along the way.

Acknowledgments xvii

Tom Wright was a faithful guide throughout. His challenge prompted me to investigate the mystery of the στοιχεῖα τοῦ κόσμου, his method of prayerful, rigorous historical study showed me how, and his model of supervision—equal parts demanding and inspiring—set me a pattern for guiding my own students.

Finally, my thanks go to my family. Catherine, Ben, and Ana agreed to a move to Scotland, endured the meager life of a postgraduate family, and filled our home with joy. Tiffany was a devoted companion and constant champion. She carried our family as I stumbled toward and over the finish line, and her patient kindness has helped me find my feet again on the Spirit's path of love.

Most days of research for this book began with the opening prayer from St. Andrews' graduation ceremonies. Now as my work has reached its completion it is only fitting to thank the almighty and eternal God whose help I sought and to pray again that this work *sanctum nomen eius glorificet.*

List of Abbreviations

PRIMARY SOURCES

ACT   Ancient Christian Texts

ANF   *The Ante-Nicene Fathers*, ed. Alexander Roberts, James Donaldson, et al. 10 vols. Edinburgh: T&T Clark, 1885.

AV   Authorized Version, 1769 [1611]

ASV   American Standard Version, 1901

BGU   *Aegyptische Urkunden aus den Königlichen Staatlichen Museen zu Berlin, Griechische Urkunden*. 15 vols. Berlin, 1895–1983.

BHS   *Biblia Hebraica Stuttgartensia*, ed. Karl Elliger and Wilhelm Rudolph. 5th ed. Stuttgart: Deutsche Bibelgesellschaft, 1997 [1967].

CD   Cairo Genizah copy of the *Damascus Document*

CCSL   Corpus Christianorum: Series Latina. Brepols: Turnhout, 1953–.

CMG   Corpus Medicorum Graecorum. Various publishers, currently Berlin: de Gruyter, 1927–.

CMG   Suppl. Or. Corpus Medicorum Graecorum Supplementum Orientale. Various publishers, currently Berlin: de Gruyter, 1963–.

CSEL   Corpus scriptorum ecclesiasticorum latinorum. Various publishers, currently Berlin: de Gruyter, 1864–.

DK   Hermann Diels and Walther Kranz, *Fragmente der Vorsokratiker*. 6th ed. 3 vols. Zurich: Weidmann, 1952.

ESV   *The Holy Bible: English Standard Version*. Wheaton, IL: Crossway, 2016.

FC   Fathers of the Church. Washington, D.C.: Catholic University of America Press, 1947–.

GCS   Die griechischen christlichen Schriftsteller. Berlin: Akademie, 1891–.

List of Abbreviations

LCL   Loeb Classical Library. Various publishers, currently Cambridge, MA: Harvard University Press, 1911–.

LXX   *Septuaginta: Id est Vetus Testamentum Graece iuxta LXX interpres*, ed. Alfred Rahlfs and Robert Hanhart. Rev. ed. 2 vols. in 1. Stuttgart: Deutsche Bibelgesellschaft, 2006 [1935].

NA   *Nestle-Aland: Novum Testamentum Graece*, ed. Barbara Aland, Kurt Aland, Johannes Karavidopoulos, Carlo M. Martini, and Bruce M. Metzger. 28th ed., rev. Stuttgart: Deutsche Bibelgesellschaft, 2012 [1898].

NET   *The NET Bible, New English Translation*. Richardson, TX: Biblical Studies, 2006.

NETS   *A New English Translation of the Septuagint and the Other Greek Translations Traditionally Included Under that Title*. Oxford: Oxford University Press, 2007.

NIV   *The Holy Bible: New International Version*. Colorado Springs, CO: Biblica, 2011.

NLT   *Holy Bible: New Living Translation*. Carol Stream, IL: Tyndale, 2013.

NRSV   *The Holy Bible: New Revised Standard Version*. Nashville: Thomas Nelson, 1989.

NPNF   *A Select Library of the Nicene and Post-Nicene Fathers of the Christian Church*, ed. Philip Schaff et al. 13 vols. Edinburgh: T&T Clark, 1886–98.

NT   New Testament

OECT   Oxford Early Christian Texts, ed. H. Chadwick. Oxford: Clarendon, 1970–.

OG   Old Greek translations of the Hebrew scriptures

OTP   *The Old Testament Pseudepigrapha*, ed. James H. Charlesworth. 2 vols. Peabody, MA: Hendrickson, 1983.

     PLondon Greek Papyri in the British Museum, 1893–.

PVTG   Pseudepigrapha Veteris Testamenti Graece. Leiden: Brill, 1964–.

RSV   Revised Standard Version, 1977

RV   Revised Version, 1885

SC   Sources chrétiennes. Paris: Cerf, 1943–.

SBLGNT   *The Greek New Testament: SBL Edition*, ed. Michael W. Holmes. Atlanta: SBL, 2011–13.

SVF   *Stoicorum Veterum Fragmenta*, ed. Hans F. A. von Arnim. 4 vols. Leipzig: Teubner, 1903–24.

TLG   *Thesaurus Linguae Graecae: A Digital Library of Greek Literature*. Irvine, CA: University of California Press. stephanus.tlg.uci.edu.

SECONDARY SOURCES

AB	Anchor Bible
ABD	*Anchor Bible Dictionary*, ed. David N. Freedman. 6 vols. New York: Doubleday, 1992.
ACNT	Augsburg Commentaries on the New Testament
AGJU	Arbeiten zur Geschichte des antiken Judentums und des Urchristentums
ALGHJ	Arbeiten zur Literatur und Geschichte des hellenistischen Judentums
AnBib	Analecta biblica
BA	*Biblical Archaeologist*
BAGD	*A Greek-English Lexicon of the New Testament and other Early Christian Literature*, ed. William F. Arndt, F. Wilbur Gingrich, and Frederick W. Danker. 2nd ed., based on Walter Bauer's *Griechisch-Deutsch Wörterbuch zu den Schrift en des Neuen Testaments und der Übrigen Urchristlichen Literatur*, 4th ed. Chicago: University of Chicago Press, 1979 [1957].
BBR	*Bulletin for Biblical Research*
BDAG	*A Greek-English Lexicon of the New Testament and other Early Christian Literature*. 3rd ed., rev. and ed. Frederick W. Danker, based on Walter Bauer's *Griechisch-Deutsch Wörterbuch zu den Schrift en des Neuen Testaments und der Übrigen Urchristlichen Literatur*, 6th ed., and on previous English eds. by William F. Arndt, F. Wilbur Gingrich, and Frederick W. Danker. Chicago: University of Chicago Press, 2000 [1957].
BECNT	Baker Exegetical Commentary on the New Testament
BibOr	Biblica et orientalia
BJS	Brown Judaic Studies
BNTC	Black's New Testament Commentary
BSac	*Bibliotheca sacra*
BTB	*Biblical Theology Bulletin*
BZ	*Biblische Zeitschrift*
BZNW	Beihefte zur Zeitschrift für die neutestamentliche Wissenschaft und die Kunde der älteren Kirche
CBET	Contributions to Biblical Exegesis and Theology
CBQ	*Catholic Biblical Quarterly*
CBQMS	Catholic Biblical Quarterly Monograph Series
ConBNT	Coniectanea biblica: New Testament Series

CQ	*Classical Quarterly*
CRINT	Compendia rerum iudaicarum ad Novum Testamentum
DSD	*Dead Sea Discoveries*
EDEJ	*The Eerdmans Dictionary of Early Judaism*, ed. John J. Collins and Daniel C. Harlow. Grand Rapids: Eerdmans, 2010.
EvQ	*Evangelical Quarterly*
ExpTim	*Expository Times*
GE	*Brill Dictionary of Ancient Greek*, by Franco Montanari, edited by Madeleine Goh and Chad Schroeder. Leiden: Brill, 2015.
GCS	Die griechische christliche Schriftsteller der ersten [drei] Jahrhunderte
HNT	Handbuch zum Neuen Testament
HTKNT	Herders theologischer Kommentar zum Neuen Testament
HTR	*Harvard Theological Review*
IBS	*Irish Biblical Studies*
ICC	International Critical Commentary
JAAR	*Journal of the American Academy of Religion*
JBL	*Journal of Biblical Literature*
JETS	*Journal of the Evangelical Theological Society*
JSJS	Supplements to the Journal for the Study of Judaism
JSNT	*Journal for the Study of the New Testament*
JSNTSup	Journal for the Study of the New Testament: Supplement Series
JSP	*Journal for the Study of the Pseudepigrapha*
JTS	*Journal of Theological Studies*
KEK	Kritisch-exegetischer Kommentar über das Neue Testament (Meyer-Kommentar)
LEH	*A Greek-English Lexicon of the Septuagint*, ed. Johan Lust, Erik Eynikel, and Katrin Hauspie. Rev. ed. Stuttgart: Deutsche Bibelgesellschaft, 2003.
LNTS	Library of New Testament Studies
LSJ	*The Online Liddell-Scott-Jones Greek-English Lexicon*, ed. Thesaurus Lingaue Graecae. Irvine, CA: University of California, 2011. stephanus.tlg.uci.edu/lsj. Digitization of *A Greek-English Lexicon*, ed. H. G. Liddell, R. Scott, and H. S. Jones. 9th ed., rev. Oxford: Clarendon, 1996.
MNTC	Moffatt New Testament Commentary
NAC	New American Commentary
NICNT	New International Commentary on the New Testament
NIGTC	New International Greek Testament Commentary
NIVAC	NIV Application Commentary
NovT	*Novum Testamentum*

NovTSup	Supplements to Novum Testamentum
NTL	New Testament Library
NTOA	Novum Testamentum et Orbis Antiquus
NTP	Novum Testamentum Patricum
NTS	*New Testament Studies*
OECS	Oxford Early Christian Studies, ed. Gillian Clark and Andrew Louth. Oxford: Oxford University Press, 1993–.
OED	*OED Online.* Oxford: Oxford University Press. Updated March 2017. oed.com. Digitization of the *Oxford English Dictionary.* 3rd ed. Oxford: Oxford University Press, 2014.
PHA	Philosophia Antiqua
Phil	*Philologus*
PNTC	Pillar New Testament Commentary
PRSt	*Perspectives in Religious Studies*
RB	*Revue Biblique*
RTR	*Reformed Theological Review*
SBL	Society of Biblical Literature
SBLDS	Society of Biblical Literature Dissertation Series
SC	Sources chrétiennes. Paris: Cerf, 1943–
SEÅ	*Svensk exegetisk årsbok*
SEL	*Studies in English Literature 1500–1900*
SHR	Studies in the History of Religions (supplement to *Numen*)
SNTSMS	Society for New Testament Studies Monograph Series
SP	Sacra pagina
SPhilo	*Studia philonica*
SR	*Studies in Religion/Sciences Religieuses*
ST	*Studia theologica: Nordic Journal of Theology*
SUNT	Studien zur Umwelt des Neuen Testaments
SVTP	Studia in Veteris Testamenti pseudepigraphica
TDNT	*Theological Dictionary of the New Testament*, trans. and ed. Geoffrey W. Bromiley. 10 vols. Grand Rapids: Eerdmans, 1964–76. Trans. of *Theologisches Wörterbuch zum Neuen Testament*, ed. Gerhard Kittel and Gerhard Friedrich. 10 vols. Stuttgart: Kohlhammer, 1933–76.
THKNT	Theologischer Handkommentar zum Neuen Testament
THNTC	Two Horizons New Testament Commentary
TSAJ	Texts and Studies in Ancient Judaism
TU	Texte und Untersuchungen. Various publishers, ultimately Berlin: de Gruyter, 1883–1962.

TUGAL	Texte und Untersuchungen zur Geschichte der altchristlichen Literatur
VC	*Vigiliae christianae*
VTSup	Supplements to Vetus Testamentum
WBC	Word Biblical Commentary
WMANT	Wissenschaftliche Monographien zum Alten und Neuen Testament
WUNT	Wissenschaftliche Untersuchungen zum Neuen Testament
ZECNT	Zondervan Exegetical Commentary on the New Testament
ZNW	*Zeitschrift für die neutestamentliche Wissenschaft und die Kunde der älteren Kirch*

Introduction

Scholars could not find what the poet could not flee. For three centuries early Christian scholars understood that when Paul wrote "we too . . . were enslaved under τὰ στοιχεῖα τοῦ κόσμου," he meant that Jews, like humans from every other nation, were enslaved under the cosmic elements that compose and compromise the flesh of the human body.[1] But this understanding was buried by Jerome's influential commentary in 386 and then lost to history for centuries. Yet, in 1635, while biblical scholars continued to insist that the elements were the law of Moses, the true physiological nature of the elements surfaced surprisingly in one of John Donne's Holy Sonnets.[2]

> I am a little world made cunningly
> Of Elements, and an Angelike spright,
> But black sinne hath betraid to endlesse night
> My worlds both parts, and (oh) both parts must die.
> You which beyond that heaven which was most high
> Have found new sphears, and of new lands can write,
> Powre new seas in mine eyes, that so I might
> Drowne my world with my weeping earnestly,
> Or wash it if it must be drown'd no more:
> But oh it must be burnt; alas the fire
> Of lust and envie have burnt it heretofore,
> And made it fouler; Let their flames retire,
> And burne me ô Lord, with a fiery zeale
> Of thee and thy house, which doth in eating heale.

In an age of cosmic discovery and global exploration, Donne's plea is not to understand the cosmic elements beyond heaven or on the other side of the sea but to address the corruption of those same elements in his body.[3] Following a millennia-old tradition, Donne identifies himself as "literally . . . a 'little world' . . . made up of four elements and possessing an immortal soul."[4] As Jeanne Shami explains, Donne identifies "man and the universe in order to show how man participates in the sickness and mutability of the cosmos."[5] The elements compose and compromise the flesh of the human body, exposing it to both biological and ethical disease. Donne draws these

2   *Introduction*

ideas from "Hypocrates" and Galen, but he finds them also in scripture (see his sermon on Ps 38.3), and he employs them again and again to express to God his heart's anguish over his body's weakness and susceptibility to sin.[6] In "I am a little world," he describes the solution to his problem in elemental terms. Since the great men of his day cannot pour "new seas" into his eyes so that he might drown his world with tears of contrition (see Ps 119.136), he asks the Lord to burn him with a fiery zeal that overtakes and renews him. Similarly, in the first four verses of "A Litany," Donne requests the Father to recreate him and purge his heart made of "red earth," implores the Son to be nailed to his heart "and crucified again," asks the Holy Ghost by flame and tears to reconstruct the "mud walls" of his body into his temple, and entreats the Trinity that he might be "elemented" of the Trinity's power, love, and knowledge.

Whether Donne read στοιχεῖα τοῦ κόσμου in Gal 4 (or Col 2) from the perspective of his elemental cosmology and physiology is uncertain. Primary sources do not answer the question, and secondary sources have not considered it.[7]

Nonetheless, John Donne's Holy Sonnet expresses in compressed elegance several of the essential components of this study: the composition of the human body from the four cosmic elements; the moral corruption of the flesh made of those elements (as posited in Greek medical discourse); and faith in the Trinity to empower a liberated life of holiness and love even while one lives within the body's "mud walls." As the literature review will show, these ideas slipped from Pauline scholarship in the late fourth century and, despite extensive investigation into the στοιχεῖα, have not been considered again until now.

A. INTERPRETING THE "ELEMENTS OF THE COSMOS" IN THE FIRST CENTURIES

While the phrase "the elements of the cosmos" sounds alien to modern readers, Christian writers for three centuries after Paul instinctively understand the στοιχεῖα as the material components of which the world and its bodies, including human bodies, are made. Section A shows how some of the earliest Christian writers understand the term στοιχεῖον in that way, sometimes quoting from and commenting on Gal 4.3, 9 and Col 2.8. This survey leads up to the 360s and the oldest surviving commentary on Galatians, by Marius Victorinus, who presents a full picture of the dynamics of the elements and the ways in which they cause human behaviors.

1. Second-Century Writers

Four themes emerge in Gerhard Delling's summary of second-century Christian uses of στοιχεῖον.[8] First, as Hermas mentions in about 125, "the κόσμος is held together through four στοιχεῖα" (*Vis.* 3.13.3). This theme occurs also in Clement of Alexandria (c. 150–c. 215; see *Ecl.* 26.2; *Exc.* 3.48; *Strom.* 2.6.31; 2.11.51; 5.6.32).[9]

Second, as Aristides argues in his *Apology* (c. 125), humans are made of the στοιχεῖα (7.3). This theme, overlooked by most modern scholars, appears as a standard Christian idea in Justin Martyr (c. 100–165; see *Dial.* 62.2), Clement (*Paed.* 3.12.100), and *Resurrection* (2.5; 3.2), a work attributed disputably to Athenagoras.

Third, according to Athenagoras's *Plea* (c. 177), the πτωχὰ καὶ ἀσθενῆ στοιχεῖα are "passible matter" moved by God (*Leg.* 16.3, quoting Gal 4.9). Clement too "knows the nature of the στοιχεῖα to be capable of change and production (γενητός)" (*Strom.* 1.11.52; see 6.148.2; *Protr.* 1.5).

Fourth, for this reason, Athenagoras and Clement argue that the στοιχεῖα should not be worshipped as gods (*Leg.* 16.1–5; see 19.4; 22.1–12; *Strom.* 1.11.50; *Protr.* 5.65, quoting Gal 4.9). This last theme is prevalent, appearing as early as Aristides (*Apol.* 3.2–3; 4.1; 7.3–4) and continuing in Justin's student Tatian (*Ad Graec.* 21.3). However, the sources make it plain that the στοιχεῖα themselves are material components, not spirits or gods.[10]

A fifth, "allegorical" use of στοιχεῖα τοῦ κόσμου escapes Delling's notice and eludes Joseph Blinzler's and Dietrich Rusam's studies as well.[11] According to Clement, "the most elementary (στοιχειωτική) instruction of children embraces the interpretation of the four στοιχεῖα" (*Strom.* 5.8.46). From this perspective, then, Paul can speak "allegorically" of "Hellenic philosophy" itself as "στοιχεῖα τοῦ κόσμου" (*Strom.* 6.8.62).

2. Origen

Origen Adamantinus (185–254) accepts and then develops second-century Christian ideas about the στοιχεῖα. The first three themes above appear in his *Commentary on the Gospel according to John*. Origen states that τὰ τέσσαρα τοῦ κόσμου στοιχεῖα are earth, water, air, and fire, and that "every material body," including human bodies, is made of στοιχεῖα and is thus "mutable and subject to variation and change" (*Comm. Jo.* 10.262; 13.127). Further, Origen, like Clement, identifies the philosophy κατὰ τὰ στοιχεῖα τοῦ κόσμου in Col 2.8 as "the ideas of those who have founded philosophical sects" (*Cels.* pref.5; see 4.56, 63; 8.72; and *Strom.* 5.8.49; 6.15.117).

Origen also develops earlier Christian understandings of the στοιχεῖα. Preaching in about 240, he seems to be the first Jew or Christian to use the term στοιχεῖον to label an ἄγγελος appointed over each of the four elements and "also for the sun and another for the moon, another also for the stars" (*Hom. Jer.* 10.6, commenting on Jer 12.4).

In the absence of Origen's work on Galatians, though, we cannot know how he interprets the στοιχεῖα there. J. B. Lightfoot thought that he sees them as "the physical elements."[12] Martin Meiser argues from *Comm. Rom.* 7.2 and *Hom. Num.* 24.1.1 that Origen sees Paul's "Elementarmächte als erziehende Geister," but neither of those works even uses the lemma στοιχεῖον.[13] Since these assertions are ambiguous and the evidence they cite is scant, Origen's interpretation of στοιχεῖα τοῦ κόσμου in Gal 4 will remain unknowable until further evidence surfaces. However, this much is clear: the standard second-century Christian concept that the human body was composed of the four material στοιχεῖα, and compromised by their passibility, continued in Origen. It will reach its high point in the fourth century with Victorinus.

3. Victorinus and Other Fourth-Century Writers

Gaius Marius Victorinus (280s–c. 366) expounds Paul's reference to the στοιχεῖα τοῦ κόσμου more deeply and fully than most of his predecessors and, frankly, most of his successors as well. As a renowned professor of rhetoric and a lifelong student of Plato and Greek philosophy, Victorinus has the mature perspective to discuss with native fluency the *elementa mundi* and the "necessities" that their "motions" cause in and upon humans.[14] He identifies the elements as "fire, water, earth, and air," and he lists four pagan misconceptions about the elements: (1) that the "elements are gods," (2) that "the gods are the originators of the elements," (3) that gods (i.e., idols) may be made from the elements, and (4) that daemons are associated with earth, water, air, and fire (145). But Victorinus's real insight comes in showing how it is that Jews, like Greeks, are "under the elements of the world": the elements of the world, he says, have natural motions that create necessities, that is., that cause certain actions (138).

> The elements of the world bring with them their own motions and create certain necessities, so to speak, from these motions. We see this in regard to the stars, by whose rotation the life of human beings is drawn into necessity: thus human beings serve the elements, doing as the stars have commanded and the course of the world has ordained. (138–139)

The world's course and the stars' rotation cause necessities that the elements' natural motions mediate to humans as virtual commands.

These processes are the natural causes and effects attendant on the qualities and forces of material bodies within the cosmos. They operate in a

Introduction 5

physiological, not a conceptual, mode (contra Clement, *Strom.* 1.11.53), and, as Stephen Cooper affirms, they should be understood within the field of cosmology, not of pagan worship.[15] But they relate to more than just astrology,[16] for, as Cooper clarifies, Victorinus is not "just making the uncontroversial claim that human lives are structured according to a calendar which itself is determined by the forces of the universe around us."[17] Victorinus is arguing that the natural motions of the elements cause effects within human flesh that precipitate particular behaviors.[18]

In Victorinus's view, the flesh, like the elements, has motions and powers. Commenting on Gal 4.9, he connects the "beggarly" elements with the flesh, which "always goes begging," "longing to be" sustained "with foods, drinks, and its desires" (145). At Gal 5.17—"the flesh lusts against the spirit"—he explains that the flesh has its own motions and "powers of sense perception" (165). These motions cause desires apart from the soul and against the leading of the spirit. The motions and powers of the flesh work like those of the elements: each has its own impulses and powers, as do water, fire, and earth. However, just as Victorinus states that mixtures arise from these elements, the surviving text breaks off. The trajectory of his discussion suggests that he is about to explain that the flesh is one such mixture of elements and that the impulses and powers of the elements are contributing factors in the motions and desires of the flesh. As Cooper explains, "the general sense is that lust comes from the material nature of flesh, . . . whence it can arise independently of the soul's initiative."[19] But certainty about Victorinus's precise meaning is lost in the lacuna.

From Victorinus's perspective, Paul's answer to the problem of the elements' necessities and forces is Christ and the Spirit. Though Jews teach that "circumcision and the other observations based on Jewish teaching" oppose the flesh (165), Victorinus presents the Spirit as liberator: "from all of these things are released all those who, having faith in Christ, have received the Spirit as Lord of their life from Christ, so as to escape and evade every necessity of the world and every elemental force and avoid serving the world. Serving Christ instead, they have liberty in their actions under the Spirit's ruling" (139). "The view," says Cooper, "that faith in Christ frees believers from the 'elemental forces' was a well-worn path in early Christianity."[20]

Victorinus's work is the high-water mark of extant ancient scholarship on the στοιχεῖα τοῦ κόσμου.[21] He follows earlier writers by identifying the στοιχεῖα as the material components of the world and of human bodies, and he fills out their view of elemental compounds as "mutable and subject to change" by describing the physiology of elements, their natures, motions, and necessities.

6 *Introduction*

Within a few years, however, Ambrosiaster says that the world is formed by the elements and that "all corporal birth is from the elements" (190, 192). And he calls the elements *gubernacula* (rudders) for the world and the human race (79, 192), but his simple identification of the *elementa mundi* as "new moons and the sabbath" seems to restrict the elements' directive effect to the calendar and its times (43, 46).[22]

The fullness of Victorinus's knowledge recedes further in the commentaries of Augustine (394) and Chrysostom (c. 395). Augustine seems perplexed. On the one hand, in Gal 4.3, only the Gentiles are under the elements, apparently in their worship of them. But then in 4.10, he notes, "the Jews also slavishly observe days, months, years, and times in their carnal observance of the sabbath and new moon, the month of new corn, and the seventh year."[23] In Meiser's opinion, Augustine requires an "exegetisch Kunstgriff" to hold the two parts of Abraham's one seed together.[24] Chrysostom's interpretation is simpler still: the elements are the sun and the moon, whose courses "regulate" the new moons and sabbaths.[25]

But in 386 Jerome had already proposed a new interpretation: the elements are letters, he says, signifying "the Law and the prophets."[26] He dismisses both Victorinus's commentary and the man himself, and Victorinus's learned interpretation is soon obscured.

B. MISREADING THE "ELEMENTS OF
THE COSMOS" SINCE JEROME

With Jerome's commentary on Galatians, the physiological identity of the στοιχεῖα τοῦ κόσμου as the material elements that compose and compromise the flesh of the human body is forgotten. From his understanding of Paul's broader theology, Jerome argues that when Paul writes "στοιχεῖα τοῦ κόσμου" he must mean "the law." For centuries to follow, through the medieval period and the Reformation, though a material reading of the στοιχεῖα remains possible, for scholars influenced by Jerome, it seems implausible in context. Only with the innovative proposals of Albrecht Ritschl and Otto Everling in the nineteenth century does Jerome face any real challenge. Yet their contention, that the στοιχεῖα τοῦ κόσμου are elemental spirits, leads back not to Christian understandings of the first and second centuries but rather to an intricate hypothesis that proves hollow when probed.

1. Jerome

Jerome's interpretation of the στοιχεῖα τοῦ κόσμου in Gal 4.3 as "the Law of Moses and the prophets" paved the path that would attract the majority

Introduction 7

of scholars for the next 1500 years (107). His reading includes several new data. First, though he cites "others" who "interpret the basic elements of this world as the Law of Moses and the utterances of the prophets," he does not identify them. In his preface, Jerome names his main sources—Origen chief among them—but this interpretation is unattested in the surviving witnesses to their commentaries.

Second, the only alternative interpretation that Jerome lists—"some are of the opinion that these are angels who preside over the four elements of the world" (106)—is also unattested in earlier extant sources. Origen did use the term στοιχεῖον to label an ἄγγελος over each of the elements, the sun, the moon, and the stars (*Hom. Jer.* 10.6), but Origen understood the στοιχεῖα in Col 2.8 to be the material elements (*Cels.* pref.5).

Third, Jerome nowhere mentions the possibility that the *elementa mundi* could be the four elements themselves. This reading was standard in the second century, present in Origen, and developed by Jerome's Latin predecessor Victorinus. But Jerome does not even mention it.

This oversight is symptomatic of the differences in Jerome's and Victorinus's hermeneutical methods. To explain a scripture within Paul, Jerome follows Origen's pattern of quoting scripture from outside Paul in a manner "reminiscent of rabbinic discussion."[27] In Gal 4.3, for example, the term *elementa* prompts Jerome to quote the *principium* of wisdom in Prov 1.7 and the *elementa principii* of God's word in Heb 5.12 (106). In contrast, Victorinus interprets "Paul on the basis of what Paul himself said," and to explain Paul's use of στοιχεῖα "to a contemporary audience" requires a simple summary of physiological ideas about the elements; "calling to mind other scriptures would distract from the immediate task."[28]

But Jerome disparages Victorinus's "learned" approach (*Vir. ill.* 101): "engrossed in secular learning as he was, . . . he was completely ignorant of Scripture, and nobody—no matter how eloquent he may be—is able to discuss competently what he does not know" (6). Perhaps then it was because Jerome found Victorinus's commentary so inadequate—and Ambrosiaster's so intimidating—that he could lie so brazenly in his preface: "I shall undertake a work that no Latin writer before me has attempted" (6).[29]

But Jerome's confidence in his method fails him on Gal 4.3, 9. There is precious little other scripture with which to illustrate στοιχεῖα in Gal 4; one is compelled to consider the term and concept in secular usage (as Victorinus does). Thus Jerome's appeal to other scripture disorients him, and in that error he is confirmed by his understanding of Paul's theology.

> In everything that the Apostle wrote or said in person, he tirelessly taught that the burdensome obligations of the old Law have been abolished and that everything that had preceded in types and symbols (the Sabbath rest, injurious

8   *Introduction*

circumcision, the recurring cycle of new moons and of the three annual feast, the dietary laws, and the daily ablution, after which one would become defiled again) ceased to have validity with the arrival of evangelical grace, which is fulfilled by the faith of the believing soul and not by the blood of animal sacrifices. (7)

Closer attention to Origen's full understanding of the στοιχεῖα might have reoriented Jerome (see *Comm. Jo.* 10.262, 266; 13.127), as could his own understanding of "the dominion of the flesh" (180–181). But Jerome is too entrenched in his interpretation to be recalled, even when he can offer only a feeble response to the objections he himself raises (106–107, 114–115, 118–119). Onward he digs his wayward canal, and out rushes the secular learning of the forebear he spurned.

In retrospect, both Jerome's interpretation and his method come to be paradigmatic. To the present day, scholars who argue that the στοιχεῖα are elementary principles appeal to scriptures that nowhere use the term στοιχεῖον, impose a general understanding of Paul's theology upon the reading of the particular point of the στοιχεῖα, and then end up labeling the law a στοιχεῖον.

2. Aquinas, Luther, and Calvin—and now Longenecker

Little changes for the next 1400 years. Driven by the term's use in its Pauline contexts, scholars continue to read στοιχεῖα as the law. They remain aware that στοιχεῖα τοῦ κόσμου could refer to earth, water, air, and fire, but the physical quality of the law's practices and the materiality of the cosmos, and even the flesh, fade slowly from view.

In his commentary on Galatians, Thomas Aquinas (1225–1274) identifies the στοιχεῖα as the law's "corporeo-religious usages, . . . such as days of the moon, new moons and the Sabbath."[30] By saying that, unlike "the pagans who served the elements of this world," the Jews "served and worshipped God" under the elements, Aquinas sorts out Augustine's ethnic conundrum (how could Jews be "under the elements" as the Gentiles are?). He also recognizes that the law's harmony with nature has pedagogical potential. "It was necessary that the Jews serve God under the elements of this world, because such an order is in harmony with human nature which is led from sensible to intelligible things." The elements, "the literal observance of the law," are "weak, because they do not bring to perfection by justifying . . . and needy, because they do not confer virtues and grace or offer any help of themselves."[31] Aquinas describes at some length a material reading of the elements. The elements are "needy, because they need God and one another to fill out the universe." The sun and moon determine "the distinction of days, months, years and times," which some people observe as "auspicious" or "inauspicious,"

Introduction 9

and they are "the cause of certain effects, namely, bodily." But he argues that the elements must be read instead as "the legal observances," for this corresponds "with the Apostle's intention."[32]

According to Martin Luther's 1525 commentary on Galatians, Paul has a "peculiar manner of speech," by which he uses the term "elements" to refer to "the law of God" and not to "those corporal elements, the fire, the air, the water, and the earth."[33] Luther recognizes that humans are "weak and beggarly of themselves," but, echoing Aquinas, he takes these adjectives as comments on the law's inability to justify. The "ceremonial laws" in particular "consist only in outward things, as meat, drink, apparel, places, times, the temple, the feasts, washings, the sacrifices, etc., which be but mere worldly things, and ordained of God only for the use of this present life, but not to justify or save before God."[34] Luther argues by analogy that "the laws and decrees of the Pope" are even more "weak and unprofitable to justification."[35] "It is all one thing," he says, whether a believer fall from grace and "turn again to the law, or to the worshipping of idols; it is all one whether he be called a monk, a Turk, a Jew, or an Anabaptist."[36]

Twenty years later, John Calvin explains that the στοιχεῖα are "rudiments" of the world because "we did not . . . enjoy the truth in a simple form, but involved in earthly figures."[37] Leaving aside Luther's focus on justification, Calvin notes that, for "the fathers," "the ceremonies . . . were not only profitable exercises and aids to piety, but efficacious means of grace." However, in response to "the false apostles" who "oppose the ceremonies to Christ, as if Christ alone were not sufficient," Paul calls the ceremonies "beggarly elements."[38] Pointing to "the observance of days" as "one description of 'elements,'" Calvin denies that Paul is concerned with times as set by the sun and moon, as Chrysostom argued. Paul "reproves" instead the "observation" of days "as if it were necessary to the worship of God" and to regarding "holy days" as "a part of divine worship."[39]

The interpretation of the στοιχεῖα τοῦ κόσμου as elementary principles, specifically the law, persists to the present.[40] Richard Longenecker, for example, identifies the στοιχεῖα τοῦ κόσμου as "elemental teachings."[41] He acknowledges Delling's conclusion that "a man of NT days would take στοιχεῖα τοῦ κόσμου to refer to the 'basic materials' of which everything in the cosmos, including man, is composed,"[42] and that conclusion could have led him to see the basic materials in the flesh of the human body.[43] But, following Bo Reicke's suggestion, Longenecker asserts that Paul gives the phrase "a new twist" by connecting "the view of τὰ στοιχεῖα as being 'first principles'" with "κόσμος in an ethical sense."[44] Σάρξ too is more an ethical concept than a material substance. In this ethical cosmos, Jews were enslaved under the "worldly elemental teachings" of "the Mosaic Law" (Gal 4.3).[45]

10   *Introduction*

Thus, the Mosaic law comes "under the same judgment" as paganism "when seen from the perspective of being 'in Christ.'"[46]

Like Jerome, Luther and Calvin see in the law's ceremonies enough of an outward materiality that they can refer to them, and thus to the law in general, as "the elements of the world." Distracted by Paul's strong words against the law, they associate the στοιχεῖα τοῦ κόσμου with issues related to worship, ritual, and justification. However, with time, their theological heirs lose even this connection of the law's "elemental teachings" with physical practices in the material cosmos.[47] As a result, they not only fail to see that Paul's concern lies at a deeper level—the weakness of the elemental flesh as enslaving—but, in some cases, they also approve of approaches to the elements that this study will call into question.[48]

Jerome's commentary detached the meaning of στοιχεῖα τοῦ κόσμου from the earliest Christian interpretation, a separation that persisted through medieval and early modern interpreters. Novel proposals in the late nineteenth century extended the distance to another realm.

3. Ritschl and Everling—and now Betz

With their arguments that the στοιχεῖα τοῦ κόσμου in Gal 4, and in Col 2, are "persönliche Geistwesen," Albrecht Ritschl and Otto Everling introduce and establish the interpretation that becomes the consensus opinion through the twentieth century.[49] Ritschl works step by step through Paul's argument to posit three premises: (1) the Jews who were ὑπὸ νόμον were also δεδουλωμένοι ὑπὸ τὰ στοιχεῖα τοῦ κόσμου; (2) the angels surrounded God as (meteorological) elements of a storm when he gave the law at Sinai (Ps 104.4; see Exod 20); and (3) in Gal 4.2, the "Aufseher und Verwalter" are persons, as are the στοιχεῖα τοῦ κόσμου in Col 2.8, where Paul confronts the Essenes who impose the law on Gentiles.[50] Thus, "ich finde es demnach nicht zweifelhaft, daß mit den 'Weltelementen' die Engel bezeichnet sind, welche das Gesetz gegeben haben."[51] In 1888, Everling expects his readers will be astonished to find that he has included the "vielbesprochenen 'στοιχεῖα τοῦ κόσμου'" in a work entitled *Die paulinische Angelologie und Dämonologie.*[52] But, beginning with Ritschl's argument that the στοιχεῖα in Gal 4 are "persönliche Geistwesen," drawing on August Dillmann's exposition of Enoch, and then quoting Albert Klöpper's assertion that the στοιχεῖα in Col 2.20 are "persönliche Himmelsgewalten," Everling concludes that it is "unumgänglich" to include a discussion of the στοιχεῖα τοῦ κόσμου in his exposition of Paul's *Gedankwelt.*[53] By 1899, Hermann Diels too is convinced that the στοιχεῖα τοῦ κόσμου in Gal 4.3 are "persönliche Geistwesen," and by 1946 the RV's and ASV's "rudiments of the world" becomes the RSV's "elemental spirits of the universe."[54]

Introduction 11

The interpretation of the στοιχεῖα τοῦ κόσμου as spirits has been the consensus opinion of scholars for several decades.[55] For Hans Dieter Betz, the στοιχεῖα τοῦ κόσμου are "demonic forces which constitute and control 'this evil aeon.'"[56] According to first-century "Greco-Roman (and Jewish) syncretism," he says, the "four or five 'elements'" that compose the world "are not simply material substances, but demonic entities of cosmic proportions and astral powers which were hostile towards man."[57] These forces work "inside of man"—indeed, "they make up the body"—and outside of him, in "terrible and traumatic experiences" caused by Fate.[58] "*All* Christians, whether Jewish or Gentile in origin," were enslaved under "angelic beings" and "demonic forces," because they devoted themselves to "cultic requirements" that would "soothe and pacify" the spirits.[59] In this way, "being 'under them' is not different from being 'under the Law.'"[60] From Paul's "enlightened" perspective, Betz says, believers who would take on the law's "ritual requirements" are "superstitious."[61]

Despite Betz's many references to first-century Jewish and Greek worldviews and religious practices, including a statement that the elements "make up the body" and work "inside of man," he fails to recognize the material elements as the substantial cause of the weakness of the flesh and its corruption by sin. Instead, with no evidence at all, he identifies the στοιχεῖα as demons. This move is confusing: would any first-century writer say that demons "make up" the human body? Nonetheless, Betz's instinct is on target when he suggests that the ancients used "cultic measures" to moderate the force of the elements (however understood). But then, Betz fails to see the role of the law in restraining the rule of the elements. Instead, the inertia of historical interpretation compels him, like most scholars in any camp, to perceive enslavement under the στοιχεῖα τοῦ κόσμου as enslavement under the Law, to mistake the treatment for the disease.[62]

C. REDISCOVERING THE "ELEMENTS OF THE COSMOS" SINCE BLINZLER

The quest for the meaning of "enslaved under the στοιχεῖα τοῦ κόσμου" changes definitively in 1963. Josef Blinzler demonstrates lexically that "στοιχεῖα κόσμου" always refers to the material elements of the cosmos.[63] Though many ignore his evidence,[64] in time scholars have accepted his conclusion and seek to make sense of that meaning in its context in Galatians. Martinus de Boer associates the στοιχεῖα τοῦ κόσμου with "a complex of religious beliefs and practices centered around the four elements of the physical cosmos."[65] De Boer's work then becomes the ground plan within which John Barclay constructs his argument.[66] None, however, recovers the physiological

12 *Introduction*

identity of the στοιχεῖα τοῦ κόσμου as the elements that compose and compromise the flesh of the human body, and Peter Leithart's monograph moves the discussion back toward Jerome.[67]

1. Blinzler and Rusam

Josef Blinzler and Dietrich Rusam focus narrowly on the term στοιχεῖον and the phrase στοιχεῖα κόσμου. Their findings expose the frequency of στοιχεῖον's various senses and identify the single sense of στοιχεῖα κόσμου. Blinzler analyzes 175 occurrences of στοιχεῖον in early Jewish and Christian writing, including 99 of 109 occurrences in early Jewish sources.[68] Table I.1 summarizes his findings.[69]

Table I.1: Senses of Στοιχεῖον in Blinzler's Study

Sense	Buchstaben	Grundstoffe	Grundlagen	Gestirne
Percent	17.7	78.3	3.4	0.6

Two of Blinzler's results are critical. First, he finds no instance before T. Sol. in which στοιχεῖον has the meaning "Elementargeister."[70] Second, he observes that in every one of the eleven places in ancient Greek literature where στοιχεῖον is modified by the genitive (τοῦ) κόσμου, the combination refers always to material elements.[71]

Thirty years later, Rusam's search of the TLG canon discovers ten more instances of στοιχεῖα κόσμου in five sources from the second and third centuries.[72] Of these, nine refer to earth, water, air, and fire, and one hints that "die Pythagoräer die Zahlen als στοιχεῖα τοῦ κόσμου ansahen" (*Pyr.* 3.152).[73] Agreeing further with Blinzler, Rusam concludes that Eduard Lohse's and Heinrich Schlier's "Vermutung" that στοιχεῖα τοῦ κόσμου refers to "belebte Geister" "entbehrt lexikalisch jeder Grundlage, da sich für diese Wortverbindung dafür kein einziger Beleg findet." Στοιχεῖα τοῦ κόσμου means the four physical elements.[74]

But even clear proof finds it hard to unseat self-assured tradition, especially when the proof cannot show how the necessary sense makes sense in context.

2. Schweizer and Martyn

Two distinguished attempts to implement Blinzler's findings have won few followers.[75] Eduard Schweizer presents a range of ancient texts to show that early Christians worried that the harmony of the material elements "might turn to disharmony" and that "the soul might not be able to pierce through the elements to heaven after death."[76] Thus, he asserts, they were attracted

Introduction 13

to the early Jewish idea that "the high priest guarantees the harmony of the universe," preserving the equilibrium of the στοιχεῖα as seasons and weather change.[77] In the end, though, Schweizer's texts show that the destination of a soul is contingent not on the relative harmony of the elements but on the guilt or purity of the individual soul.[78]

Louis Martyn uses a complex argument to work from the στοιχεῖα τοῦ κόσμου as earth and water, and air and fire to the elements as "the religious pairs of opposites, circumcision/uncircumcision, Jew/Gentile, Law/Not-Law."[79] Beginning with Blinzler's, Schweizer's, and Rusam's evidence that the στοιχεῖα τοῦ κόσμου are "elemental substances," Martyn states that some ancients arranged the elements "in pairs of opposites."[80] Thus, Martyn posits the "reasonable hypothesis" that by στοιχεῖα τοῦ κόσμου Paul means "the elemental pairs of opposites listed in 3:28, emphatically the first pair, Jew and Gentile, and thus the Law and the Not-Law."[81] Galatian believers who "*turn* to the law" honor at least two elemental pairs: Law/Not-Law and holy times/profane times, the latter set by "astral elements." In this way, "they in fact *return* to the worship of the falsely deified elements (4.9–10)."[82] From Martyn's perspective, "for Gentiles Law observance" is "nothing other than" "the slavery that characterizes all *religion* as such."[83]

Though Martyn does not identify the στοιχεῖα in the flesh, he acknowledges several ways in which the Galatians or the Teachers may have seen a physiological connection between the flesh and evil actions.[84] Martyn cites Schweizer for the Greek "medical and philosophical thought" that the flesh affects actions.[85] He sees the danger of "the Impulsive Flesh" in Philo's explanation of πάθη (*Spec. Laws* 4.79). He reads ἐπιθυμίαι σαρκὸς as the "Greek rendering" of בשׂר יצר.[86] He explains τὰ ἔργα τῆς σαρκός subtly as "'*the effects* of the Flesh,' deeds accomplished in a significant sense *by* the Flesh," but then he conflates the παθήμτα and the ἐπιθυμίαι of the flesh.[87] Finally, Martyn suggests that the Teachers would have promoted the Law both as the "antidote" to the problem of the flesh and as the path to the "perfection of virtue,"[88] a program remarkably similar to Philo's redemptive nomism (see chapter 3). In the end, though, Martyn insists that Paul thinks of the flesh, like its new opposite the Spirit, as an "apocalyptic power" external to the individual.[89] For this reason, "the opposition between the Spirit and the Flesh cannot be grasped . . . in the image of an infection and a medicinal antidote. . . . On the contrary, that opposition is a genuine conflict, an apocalyptic war."[90]

Despite his erudition, Martyn is mistaken on two points. First, by failing to recognize that the elements are within the flesh of each human body, he misses the fundamental nature of the slavery: sin has corrupted the flesh and enslaved all humans. As a result, Martyn misrepresents the role of the law, mistaking Paul's restraining παιδαγωγός for a prison guard. Nevertheless, Martyn's scholarship provides a strong warrant that validates two tasks

14   *Introduction*

fundamental to this study: (1) comparing Paul with Greek medical philosophy in order to examine more closely the physiology of the σάρξ and its παθήματα, ἐπιθυμίαι, and ἔργα; and (2) comparing Paul with Philo to sketch the features of an early Jewish Christian appropriation of teaching similar to Philo's redemptive nomism.

3. de Boer and Barclay

In contrast to Schweizer and Martyn, de Boer and Barclay extend Blinzler's research in a more productive direction. De Boer builds on Blinzler, Schweizer, and Rusam and, with discerning creativity, introduces a critical distinction into the argument.[91] He distinguishes between the referential meaning of στοιχεῖα τοῦ κόσμου—"a technical expression" for "the four elements of the physical universe"—and the "beliefs and practices" associated with those elements.[92] As de Boer explains, Paul uses στοιχεῖα τοῦ κόσμου as a "metonym" for "the religion of the Galatians before they became believers in Christ."[93] While the στοιχεῖα τοῦ κόσμου *per se* are earth, water, air, and fire, they are also worshipped by pagans as gods (Gal 4.8; see Wis 13.1–3; *Contempl. Life* 3–5), and they and their "associated phenomena (the movements of sun, moon, planets, stars)" are "linked" to "calendrical observances" (Gal 4.10; see Jub. 2.8–9; 1 En. 82.7–9; Wis 7.17–19).[94] Echoing Aquinas and Augustine, de Boer notes that it is here, in their calendars set by the heavenly lights, that the pagans' "veneration of τὰ στοιχεῖα τοῦ κόσμου is functionally and conceptually equivalent to the observance of the Law."[95]

De Boer's work represents the most constructive application of Blinzler's findings. By distinguishing between στοιχεῖα κόσμου's referential meaning and its associated beliefs and practices, he holds onto the term's necessary sense while also making sense of the "not gods" in 4.8 and calendar observance in 4.10. However, despite his nuanced views of the στοιχεῖα and the σάρξ, de Boer fails to see that the στοιχεῖα compose the σάρξ. This oversight only exacerbates his invariably negative view of the law, and he joins others in mistaking enslavement under τὰ στοιχεῖα τοῦ κόσμου as enslavement under the law. Nonetheless, his perspective on the στοιχεῖα lays the ground plan according to which Barclay and Leithart have sketched their construction of Paul's argument.

In *Paul and the Gift*, Barclay makes both actual and potential contributions to the quest for the στοιχεῖα. On an actual level, he affirms de Boer's "fine analysis" and goes on to explain that "Paul represents both Torah-observance and pagan religious practice—hugely different though they were—as beholden to the natural order of the cosmos through alignment to its elemental, physical components."[96] Thus, "from the perspective of the Christ-event," both "idolatry and Torah-allegiance . . . are variant forms of a common

Introduction 15

'slavery' to the 'elements of the world.'"[97] Specifically, "Paul characterizes the Jewish calendar, in its alignment to the physics of the cosmos, as *another* symptom of entrapment within the domain of the cosmic elements."[98] For this reason and others, Paul argues that "the Torah is . . . no advantage or aid, no positive framework for 'living to God.'"[99] In sum, the Torah can "neither liberate people from the dominance of sin, nor give life to the dead."[100]

On a potential level, though Barclay admits that he does not show *how* the στοιχεῖα enslave, he provides much of the data needed to connect the weak στοιχεῖα with the weak σάρξ.[101] First, by quoting Philo several times to illustrate the sort of view of the law that Paul opposes in Galatians, he implies that Philo is pertinent to Paul.[102] This study realizes that potential by citing *Rewards* 118–124, where Philo asserts that the minds of those who follow the holy laws will be redeemed by God from slavery to the body, its elementally induced πάθη, its lusts, and its vices. Second, Barclay notes that Marius Victorinus "associated the physical elements with the stars, the calendar, and the force of necessity in the cosmos."[103] This study has noted already that Victorinus also saw the motions of the infirm elements in the flesh of the human body, arousing lust and beggarly action even apart from the soul. Third, in his comments on Rom 7, Barclay identifies the dominion of flesh as within the physical body and "in the physical deployment of its 'organs.'"[104] From this perspective, Barclay clearly exhibits the human condition, the limited function of the law, and the physicality of the implications of salvation.

> The "law" that is at work in the organs (7:23) is a set of predispositions and orientations too deep to be altered by the instructions of the Torah, however much the mind may approve of them. What is needed is "rescue from this body of death" (7:24)—a new φρόνημα of cognitive and practical schemas operative in physical deportment, corporeal practice, and bodily appetites.[105]

Alongside Barclay, this study affirms that the στοιχεῖα τοῦ κόσμου are the "physical elements of the world."[106] Then, picking up where he leaves off, it shows (1), from Philo, that some early Jews practiced the law in order to be redeemed from slavery to a body weakened by the στοιχεῖα and (2), following Victorinus, that Paul says the Son and the Spirit liberate believers from "every necessity of the world and every elemental force" (139).

But first the study must review a recent work that takes deliverance from the elements of the world as its central motif.

4. Leithart

Leithart identifies the στοιχεῖα τοῦ κόσμου as "primarily the organized parts that constitute the system and order of the physical universe."[107] He

16 *Introduction*

appreciates de Boer's "clear, careful treatment" of the phrase, but he construes Paul's use of στοιχεῖα in a very different direction.[108] Leithart asserts that "Paul is more sociologist than scientist, more priest than philosopher," with "little interest in the natural world." "This is nowhere more obvious," Leithart states, "than in his knack for 'humanizing' and 'socializing' terms borrowed from Greek philosophy and science.[109] So Leithart makes it his "principal aim" in the book "to show that Paul gives a socioreligious meaning to the phrase 'elements of the world.'"[110]

Leithart's intentional preclusion of "normal" meanings of Greek scientific terms, including στοιχεῖα τοῦ κόσμου, blinkers his theological perspective on the flesh, the law, and redemption. Leithart sees a "clear" "connection between the *stoicheia* and *sarx*," but he fails to see that the flesh is composed of στοιχεῖα.[111] He is correct: "humanity's fleshly condition is the presumption behind Paul's talk about 'the elements of the world,'" and "being 'born' of *stoicheia* is being born of flesh."[112] Nevertheless he maintains that the elements and the flesh are not the same: "the elements are institutions and practices for human beings who exist under conditions of flesh, sin and death."[113]

Since Leithart denies that human flesh is actually the στοιχεῖα, he does not see that Paul understood the elements as the media of physiological processes that cause ethical effects. Instead, his "socio-religion as science" hermeneutic leads him to offer a psychological explanation of life "according to the flesh."[114]

Leithart's socio-cultural view of the flesh also affects his understanding of the law and deliverance. He is right that Torah "partially overcomes the effects of flesh" but "cannot deliver from flesh" and thus "cannot justify."[115] However, for Leithart, the flesh that Torah addresses is primarily socio-cultural, not physical. Further, he reads "under Torah" and "'under *ta stoicheia tou kosmou*' as parallel descriptions of Israel's childhood," not labels for the prescription and the problem.[116] For by "elements," "clearly" Paul "does not mean what Aristotle or Greek scientists meant. He does not claim that the gospel announces a change in the constitution of the physical world."[117] But here Leithart missteps. Paul may not say that the Son's death and resurrection change "the constitution of the physical world," but Paul certainly does say that the answer to sin's corruption of the weak physical flesh is the sending of God's Spirit into believers' hearts. The Spirit bears the fruit of righteousness (i.e., love) in their lives as they live in fleshly bodies in the physical world.

Further, Leithart's socio-religious cosmology obstructs him from seeing what Philo promotes in the law. Leithart asserts that "for Jews like Philo, . . . it was *unthinkable* that human beings could outgrow subjection to *ta stoicheia* or the practices that express that subjection."[118] But that is precisely what Philo promotes in his redemptive nomism. For Philo, the function of

Introduction 17

the elements within the body exacerbates its necessities and desires, which in turn enslave the mind and make it "incapable of guiding the course of its own life aright" (*Rewards* 121).[119] But God promises those who obey the "holy laws" a healthy body (*Rewards* 119–122). He breaks "asunder the miseries of its slavery" to the body's "many lusts" and "redeems" it "into freedom" (*Rewards* 124).

In the end *Delivered from the Elements* offers an abundant theology of the atonement but meager pickings on the elements. Leithart insists that "atonement theory . . . has to be a theory of everything," but while his "everything" includes culture and religion, it intentionally precludes science, especially physiology.[120] Yet the humans that make cultures and practice religions are humans made of flesh, and the issue of flesh, as Leithart recognizes, constitutes the heart of the problem.[121] Leithart's socio-cultural emphasis would have lost little had he attached the labels *stoicheia* and *stoicheic* to his robust theology of the flesh rather than to his equally robust theology of the law, culture, and religion. For, even when viewed in their bare, physiological simplicity, the four material στοιχεῖα τοῦ κόσμου are critical components of a socio-religious analysis of the human problem.

Paul's elusive reference to enslavement under "τὰ στοιχεῖα τοῦ κόσμου" has led scholars on an exciting chase for 1600 years. Though early Christian writers understand Paul to be referring to the elements that compose the physical body, that sense is obscured when Jerome removes the στοιχεῖα from their place in the body and attaches them instead to the law. Much later, scholars no longer see the physical quality either of the flesh or of the law's practices. While Ritschl and Everling's proposal that the στοιχεῖα are personal spirits regains a tinge of the στοιχεῖα's physicality, their interpretation, now the majority opinion, has been unable to produce any lexical warrant from before AD 240. Blinzler's research proves that στοιχεῖα τοῦ κόσμου must refer to the material elements, but forty years pass before de Boer offers a reasonable explanation for why Paul would caution new believers about earth, water, air, and fire. This study now pushes one step further, and it reconnects στοιχεῖα τοῦ κόσμου's necessary ancient meaning with its meaningful sense in that ancient context.

18   Introduction

D. DIAGNOSING AND TREATING THE
WEAK ΣΤΟΙΧΕΙΑ IN HUMAN FLESH

1. Thesis

As this study joins the conversation on the στοιχεῖα τοῦ κόσμου, it extends recent developments in the discourse by reinvigorating Victorinus's ancient perspective. Victorinus argued that the flesh made of elements has its own motions and powers. In line with Victorinus's thinking, I thus accept Blinzler's foundational conclusion that the στοιχεῖα τοῦ κόσμου are the four material elements, earth, water, air, and fire. And I work within de Boer's ground plan of distinguishing between στοιχεῖα's referential and associated meanings. As such, I, like de Boer, am able to affirm some of the conclusions of scholars like Longenecker, without accepting their identification of the στοιχεῖα with elementary principles.

But my distinct contribution is to specify the στοιχεῖα τοῦ κόσμου as the material elements that compose and compromise the human body and to explicate the implications of that identity for Paul's conception of the flesh and the law. Betz and Longenecker (citing Delling) have stated already that the elements compose the body; they simply didn't consider that sense of στοιχεῖα when reading Gal 4. This understanding of the στοιχεῖα was (as we have seen) a standard view in the early church and was the personal experience of Donne. However, no recent scholar has suggested that when Paul mentions being "enslaved under the στοιχεῖα τοῦ κόσμου" he is referring to the dominion of sin in the vulnerable flesh of a body composed of weak elements. This is what I shall now do.

2. Method

In pursuit of that objective, the study shapes its research and argumentation in accord with Emma Wasserman's concept of "discourse."[122] Together with N. T. Wright's concept of "engagement" and Dean Fleming's analysis of "contextualization," Wasserman's "discourse" offers a robust framework for considering the significance of terms, concepts, and arguments in one text in comparison with those in other texts while avoiding the "perils of parallels."[123]

Wasserman defines "discourse" as "a set of shared concepts, language, motifs, metaphors and assumptions about their relationships that enable and constrain intellectual production."[124] Her definition develops Stanley Stowers's use of "discourse" while also appreciating the significance of "human practices" as analyzed by Pierre Bourdieu and Theodore Schatzki.[125] From this nuanced perspective, her concept of "discourse" "accounts for

Introduction   19

continuity and discontinuity" in speech, that is, the repeated use of specific terms, concepts, and premises in arguments that not only differ from, but indeed compete with, each other.[126] In this way, Wasserman's concept of discourse accepts "creative elaboration" as "an ordinary feature of language."[127]

Wasserman's "discourse" provides a theoretical foundation for Wright's analysis of Paul's "engagement" and Fleming's study of contextualization. Wright uses engagement as "a deliberately vague term . . . to involve . . . borrowing, parallel thought, and the rich mixture of affirmation, denial, derivation, confrontation, subversion, transformation, and a whole range of possible 'yes-but' and 'no-but,' or perhaps 'yes-and' and 'no-and,' relations."[128] As he says, "Paul was quite capable of using language and ideas from the world of pagan philosophy in order to bring them, as it were, on side with his own project" (2 Cor 10.5).[129] Fleming concurs. Paul "intentionally uses the philosophical language of his audience, not simply to stake out common ground, but in order to transform their worldview. . . . Familiar terminology is, therefore, co-opted and infused with new meaning."[130]

These perspectives affirm the inevitable complexity in Paul's letters as he engages contemporary discourses in other contexts. As the Anointed's apostle to the nations,[131] Paul's message is both necessarily intercultural and explicitly reconciliatory.[132] Following a pattern discernible in some texts in Israel's scriptures, Paul's prophetic speech, even when it involves reproach, builds on an informed approach, a careful familiarity with the world of his audience.[133] This sort of apostolic communication then expresses itself along a continuum from retaining to rejecting. On the one hand, Paul accepts, and indeed gains from, the Greek concept that the human body is composed of the four στοιχεῖα κόσμου; on the other, he opposes any sort of early Jewish redemptive nomism. The most "creative elaboration," though, falls somewhere in between, in what could be called reappropriating. Thus, for example, Paul adapts the παιδαγωγός motif to label the law of Moses.

As a heuristic, the concept of "discourse" can be applied objectively and subjectively. From an objective perspective, it must be significant that all four of the earliest extant uses of the phrase "στοιχεῖα κόσμου" occur in early Jewish documents (three in Philo) and that each refers to the material elements of the cosmos (see chapter 1). From a subjective perspective, scholars read two texts in conversation with each other and assess their mutual intelligibility. Are their uses of specific terms and concepts in their own arguments meaningful within a given discourse? In Dale Martin's estimation, for example, "Paul's argument" in 1 Cor 15.36–38 "would strike the philosophically educated as familiar and completely acceptable."[134]

The norm of mutual intelligibility thus legitimates the adduction of a particular discourse to illuminate a text that seems to engage that discourse. To do so, it need not imply that one author had direct knowledge of another.[135]

20 *Introduction*

Short of recovering an identifiably Pauline letter and finding in it a citation of Plato or Philo (which, in itself, would make most scholars doubt its authenticity), no one can prove that Paul read either of them.[136] But the shared terms and concepts in the arguments they contributed to ancient medical discourse illuminate in demonstrably meaningful ways the sense and significance of Paul's diagnosis of the effects of the material composition of the body on human behavior and his prescription for a faithful life in the new creation.

3. Content

The structure of the study conforms to its method. It investigates the term στοιχεῖον in ancient Greek and early Jewish sources, considers the concept of weak elements in ancient medical theory, and examines the role of the στοιχεῖα κόσμου in Philo's redemptive nomism in order to illuminate the meaning of Paul's phrase "enslaved under τὰ στοιχεῖα τοῦ κόσμου." In this light, Paul's theology of the flesh, the law, the Son, and the Spirit represents, among other things, an intelligible contribution to ancient discourse on the constraints of the elemental body on human behavior.

Chapter 1 investigates the term "στοιχεῖα τοῦ κόσμου" in ancient Greek and early Jewish works. It shows (1) that while στοιχεῖον can refer to either a material or an immaterial element, the term's referent is consistently clear in context, (2) that the phrase "στοιχεῖα κόσμου" appears in extant sources as an early Jewish innovation to refer unambiguously to the material elements of which the cosmos and its bodies are made, and (3) that scholars have yet to show that anyone in the first or second centuries used στοιχεῖον to refer to a spirit.

Chapter 2 explores the concept of enslavement to the στοιχεῖα τοῦ κόσμου in ancient Greek and early Jewish works. Finding in Galen the phrasing most similar to Paul's reference to enslavement, it follows him as a guide through earlier literature. The survey shows that Greek and Jewish scholars analyze the human body as both composed of and compromised by the material στοιχεῖα. It shows also that the στοιχεῖα mediate παθήματα (or πάθη) that provoke ἐπιθυμίαι which overcome weak bodies and enslave souls. Further, scholars in Greek medical discourse prescribe various regimens (including νόμος) as παιδαγωγοί to guide the person to wholeness.

Chapter 3 examines the argument for "redemptive nomism" in Philo's philosophy according to the "στοιχεῖα τοῦ κόσμου." It exhibits the functional role of στοιχεῖον and its cognates in Philo's work, and it shows that Philo promotes observance of the law as the effective way (1) to be "redeemed from slavery" to the flesh, (2) to attain righteousness, and (3) to live in harmony with the cosmos.

Introduction 21

Chapter 4 exposes the theology of flesh and sin that underlies Paul's reference to being "enslaved under the στοιχεῖα τοῦ κόσμου" (Gal 4.3). It expounds, in turn, Paul's concepts in physiology, pathology, and epidemiology: (1) that weak στοιχεῖα compose the weak σάρξ, (2) that the στοιχεῖα mediate the sinful παθήματα, ἐπιθυμίαι, and ἔργα τῆς σαρκός, and (3) that children and childish people are most susceptible to the disease of sin.

Chapter 5 analyzes Paul's views on the use of the law, as a παιδαγωγός, to guard against the στοιχεῖα that compose and compromise the flesh. With due attention to Barclay's cautions on "mirror-reading," it argues that Philo's works, and especially his redemptive nomism, correspond to many points in the agitation in the Galatian assemblies.[137] For Paul, such misuse of the law leads not to life and righteousness but rather back to enslavement to "the weak and miserable στοιχεῖα," as though Abraham, the recent monotheist, were to return to the pantheism and polytheism of the Chaldeans.

Chapter 6 presents crucifixion with the Anointed and new life with the Spirit as the cure for sin's infection of the flesh made of weak στοιχεῖα.

Finally, the conclusion reviews the way in which applying Wasserman's concept of "discourse" to Paul's phrase "enslaved under the στοιχεῖα τοῦ κόσμου" frames it as an intelligible contribution to ancient medical discourse on the στοιχεῖα, the weakness of the body, and the regulation of human behavior. This observation, newly restored from Victorinus, then corrects misperceptions of the flesh and the law in Galatians scholarship and offers fresh insight on the physiological nature of the παθήματα τῆς σαρκός, on the narrative implicit in returning to enslavement to the στοιχεῖα, and on the role of καιρός in the new creation.

NOTES

1. Within this book I use *element* and its cognates as technical terms. I reserve *element* as a translation for στοιχεῖον or as a referent to something denoted by στοιχεῖον. I use *elemental* to mean "of or pertaining to the 'four elements,' earth, air, fire, and water, or to any one of them," and *elementary* to refer only to "the nature of elements or rudiments; rudimentary" (*OED*).

2. John Donne, *Complete English Poems*, ed. C. A. Patrides, 2d ed., Everyman Library (London: J. M. Dent, 1994).

3. Kimberly Anne Coles, "The Matter of Belief in John Donne's Holy Sonnets," *Renaissance Quarterly* 68 (2015): 921–23, https://doi.org/10.1086/683855.

4. Joseph A. Mazzeo, "Notes on John Donne's Alchemical Imagery," *Isis* 48 (1957): 104–5; see Asloob Ahmad Ansari, "Two Modes of Utterance in Donne's Divine Poems," in *Essays on John Donne: A Quarter Centenary Tribute*, ed. Asloob Ahmad Ansari (Aligarh: Aligarh Muslim University, 1974), 341. See also Donne, "The Second Anniversarie. Of the Progres of the Soule," lines 263–66 (Donne,

22   *Introduction*

Complete English Poems) and John Donne, *The Sermons of John Donne*, ed. Evelyn
Mary Simpson and George Reuben Potter, 10 vols. (Berkeley: University of California Press, 1953), 2.78–79; 3.299; 4.359; 9.51, 69, 173, 230, 305).

5. Jeanne Shami, "John Donne: Geography as Metaphor," in *Geography and Literature: A Meeting of the Disciplines*, ed. William E. Mallory and Paul Simpson-Housley (Syracuse: Syracuse University Press, 1987), 162.

6. Donne, "Expostulation 22"; Donne, *The Sermons of John Donne*, 2.88–89; see Ramie Targoff, *John Donne, Body and Soul* (Chicago, Ill: University of Chicago Press, 2008), 150–151; Anne Coles, "The Matter of Belief in John Donne's Holy Sonnets," 922–23. Scholars have analyzed Donne's view of body and soul in light of the Hippocratic Corpus and Galen (Michael Carl Schoenfeldt, *Bodies and Selves in Early Modern England: Physiology and Inwardness in Spenser, Shakespeare, Herbert, and Milton*, Cambridge Studies in Renaissance Literature and Culture 34 (Cambridge; New York: Cambridge University Press, 1999), 11–20; Nancy Selleck, "Donne's Body," *Studies in English Literature* 41 (2001): 150, 168; Erica Nicole Daigle, "Reconciling Matter and Spirit: The Galenic Brain in Early Modern Literature" (University of Iowa, PhD diss., 2009); Margret Fetzer, *John Donne's Performances: Sermons, Poems, Letters and Devotions* (Manchester: Manchester University Press, 2010), 34–39; Richard Sugg, *The Smoke of the Soul: Medicine, Physiology and Religion in Early Modern England* (Houndmills: Palgrave Macmillan, 2013), 141–45).

7. Donne, *The Sermons of John Donne* includes no sermon on Gal 4.3, 9 or Col 2.8, 20.

8. Gerhard Delling, "Στοιχέω, Συστοιχέω, Στοιχεῖον," *TDNT* 7:677–78.

9. Josef Blinzler, "Lexikalisches zu dem Terminus τὰ στοιχεῖα τοῦ κόσμου bei Paulus," in *Studiorum Paulinorum Congressus Internationalis Catholicus 1961: simul Secundus Congressus Internationalis Catholicus de Re Biblica: completo undevicesimo saeculo post S. Pauli in urbem adventum*, vol. 2 of *Analecta biblica* 17–18 (Rome: Pontifical Biblical Institute, 1963), 435–36 n. 5 argues cogently against Otto Stählin, ed., *Clemens Alexandrinus*, Die griechischen christlichen Schriftsteller der ersten drei Jahrhunderte 39 (Leipzig: Hinrichs, 1936), showing that στοιχεῖα in *Exc.* 3.48 (as in 4.81 and in *Strom.* 6.148.2) refers to material elements and not to elemental spirits.

10. Meiser claims misleadingly that Irenaeus (c. 130–c. 202) "die στοιχεῖα als die heidnischen Götter benennt" (Martin Meiser, *Galater*, Novum Testamentum Patricum 9 (Göttingen: Vandenhoeck & Ruprecht, 2007), 196, citing *Haer.* 3.12.6). However, Rousseau and Doutreleau's "Tableau des Fragments Grecs" shows no Greek witness for *Haer.* 3.12.6, and even their retroversion from the Latin uses lemma στοιχεῖον nowhere in 3.12.6! See François Sagnard, Adelin Rousseau, and Louis Doutreleau, eds., *Irénée de Lyon: Contre les hérésies, Livre 3*, 2 vols., *Sources chrétiennes* 210–211 (Paris: Cerf, 1974), 210:53–55.

11. Blinzler, "Lexicalisches"; Dietrich Rusam, "Neue Belege zu den Στοιχεῖα τοῦ Κόσμου (Gal 4,3.9; Kol 2,8.20)," *ZNW* 83 (1992): 119–25.

12. J. B. Lightfoot, *Saint Paul's Epistle to the Galatians: A Revised Text with Introduction, Notes, and Dissertations* (London: Macmillan, 1887), 167; contrast Stephen Andrew Cooper, *Marius Victorinus' Commentary on Galatians*, Oxford Early

Christian Studies (Oxford University Press, 2005), 219, http://www.oxfordscholarship.com/view/10.1093/0198270275.001.0001/acprof-9780198270270.

13. Meiser, *Galater*, 197, see n. 684.

14. John M. G. Barclay, *Paul and the Gift* (Grand Rapids: Eerdmans, 2015), 410 n. 47; Cooper, *Marius Victorinus' Commentary on Galatians*, 17–18; R. P. C. Hanson, *The Search for the Christian Doctrine of God: The Arian Controversy 318–381* (London: T&T Clark, 2005), 532.

15. Cooper, *Marius Victorinus' Commentary on Galatians*, 220. Victorinus explains these physiological processes as distinct from the laws and social mores that govern the lives of both Jews and Greeks "under the elements of the world" (138).

16. Contra Meiser, *Galater*, 199.

17. Cooper, *Marius Victorinus' Commentary on Galatians*, 220; see 303 n. 32.

18. Cooper, *Marius Victorinus' Commentary on Galatians*, 222.

19. Cooper, *Marius Victorinus' Commentary on Galatians*, 336 n. 187.

20. Cooper, *Marius Victorinus' Commentary on Galatians*, 303 n. 32; citing David Amand de Medieta, *Fatalisme et Liberté Dans l'antiquité Grecque* (Amsterdam: Hakkert, 1973).

21. Cooper, *Marius Victorinus' Commentary on Galatians*, 219, 222.

22. Meiser, *Galater*, 198.

23. See Eric Plumer, ed., *Augustine's Commentary on Galatians*, Oxford Early Christian Studies (Oxford: Oxford University Press, 2003), 176–77, 184–87, http://www.oxfordscholarship.com/view/10.1093/0199244391.001.0001/acprof-9780199244393; Cooper, *Marius Victorinus' Commentary on Galatians*, 218–25; John Riches, *Galatians Through the Centuries*, Wiley-Blackwell Bible Commentaries (Oxford: Wiley-Blackwell, 2013), 216–17.

24. Meiser, *Galater*, 199.

25. *NPNF* 13.30, 284.

26. Cooper, *Marius Victorinus' Commentary on Galatians*, 221.

27. Cooper, *Marius Victorinus' Commentary on Galatians*, 107; see Alexander Souter, *The Earliest Latin Commentaries on the Epistles of St. Paul: A Study* (Oxford: Clarendon, 1927), 22.

28. Cooper, *Marius Victorinus' Commentary on Galatians*, 107.

29. Cooper, *Marius Victorinus' Commentary on Galatians*, 104, see 28; Andrew Cain, trans., *St. Jerome: Commentary on Galatians*, FC 121 (Washington, D.C.: Catholic University of America Press, 2010), 32–33.

30. Thomas Aquinas, *Super Epistolam B. Pauli ad Galatas Lectura: Commentary on Saint Paul's Epistle to the Galatians*, ed. Joseph Kenny, trans. Fabian R. Larcher, online, Aquinas Scripture Series 1 (Albany: Magi, 1966), http://dhspriory.org/thomas/SSGalatians.htm, at Gal 4.3.

31. Aquinas, *Ad Galatas Lectura*, at Gal 4.3. See also Q61, A4; Q62, A6; Q103, A2 in *Summa Theologica* (Thomas Aquinas, *Summa Theologica*, trans. the Fathers of the English Dominican Province, 1947, sacred-texts.com/chr/aquinas/summa/index.htm).

32. Aquinas, *Ad Galatas Lectura*, at Gal 4.9.

24   *Introduction*

33. Martin Luther, *Die Epistel S. Paul an die Galater* (Wittenberg: Steiner, 1525); see Martin Luther, *A Commentary on Saint Paul's Epistle to the Galatians* (Philadelphia: John Highland, 1891), 355–56.

34. Luther, *Galatians*, 357.

35. Luther, *Galatians*, 399.

36. Luther, *Galatians*, 388.

37. John Calvin, *Commentarii in Quatuor Pauli Epistolas: Ad Galatas, Ad Ephesios, Ad Philippenses, Ad Colossenses* (Geneva: Jean Gérard, 1548); see John Calvin, *Commentaries on the Epistles of Paul to the Galatians and Ephesians*, trans. William Pringle (Edinburgh: Calvin Translation Society, 1854), 117.

38. Calvin, *Galatians and Ephesians*, 123.

39. Calvin, *Galatians and Ephesians*, 124.

40. Scholars since Blinzler holding this view include W. Carr, *Angels and Principalities*, SNTSMS 42 (Cambridge: Cambridge University Press, 1981); Walter Wink, *Naming the Powers* (Philadelphia: Fortress, 1984); Linda Belleville, "'Under Law': Structural Analysis and the Pauline Concept of Law in Galatians 3.21–4.11," *JSNT* 26 (1986): 53–78; R. Y. Fung, *The Epistle to the Galatians*, NICNT, ed. F. F. Bruce (Grand Rapids: Eerdmans, 1988); D. R. Moore-Crispin, "Galatians 4:1–9: The Use and Abuse of Parallels," *EQ* 60 (1989): 203–23; Richard Longenecker, *Galatians*, WBC 41 (Dallas: Word, 1990); D. R. Bundrick, "Ta Stoicheia tou Kosmou (Gal. 4:3)," *JETS* 34 (1991): 353–64; Frank J. Matera, *Galatians* (Collegeville, MN: Liturgical, 1992); Ben Witherington III, *Grace in Galatia: A Commentary on St. Paul's Letter to the Galatians* (Grand Rapids: Eerdmans, 1998); Ben Witherington III, *The Letters to Philemon, the Colossians, and the Ephesians: A Socio-Rhetorical Commentary on the Captivity Epistles* (Grand Rapids: Eerdmans, 2007); Marianne Meye Thompson, *Colossians and Philemon*, THNTC (Grand Rapids: Eerdmans, 2005). The most substantial earlier work in this camp is Andrew J. Bandstra, *The Law and the Elements of the World: An Exegetical Study in Aspects of Paul's Teaching* (Kampen: Kok, 1964).

41. Longenecker, *Galatians*, 165–66.

42. Delling, "Στοιχέω," 7:684, quoted by Longenecker, *Galatians*, 165.

43. P. Vielhauer, "Gesetzesdienst und Stoicheiadienst im Galaterbrief," in *Rechtfertigung. Festschrift für Ernst Käsemann zum 70. Geburstag*, ed. J. Friedrich, W. Pöhlmann, and P. Stuhlmacher (Tübingen: Mohr, 1976), 553 also acknowledges this sense but fails to connect it to Gal 4.3.

44. Longenecker, *Galatians*, 165–66, citing Bo Reicke, "The Law and This World According to Paul: Some Thoughts Concerning Gal 4:1–11," *JBL* 70 (1951): 261.

45. Longenecker, *Galatians*, 164–65.

46. Longenecker, *Galatians*, 181.

47. A semblance of this connection persists in Lightfoot, *Galatians*, 167; Ernest De Witt Burton, *A Critical and Exegetical Commentary on the Epistle to the Galatians*, ICC (Edinburgh: T&T Clark, 1921), 515–18.

48. Consider Aquinas: "It is lawful to consider" "the influence of the stars" and their "bodily" effects (Aquinas, *Ad Galatas Lectura*, at Gal 4.9).

Introduction 25

49. Albrecht Ritschl, *Die christliche Lehre von der Rechtfertigung und Versöhnung*, vol. 2: Der biblische Stoff der Lehre (Bonn: Adolph Marcus, 1874); Otto Everling, *Die paulinische Angelologie und Dämonologie: ein biblisch-theologischer Versuch* (Göttingen: Vandenhoeck & Ruprecht, 1888).

50. Albrecht Ritschl, *Rechtfertigung und Versöhnung* (Bonn: Adolph Marcus, 1882), 2.249–51.

51. Ritschl, *Rechtfertigung und Versöhnung*, 2.251.

52. Everling, *Die paulinische Angelologie und Dämonologie: ein biblisch-theologischer Versuch*, 65.

53. Everling, *Angelologie und Dämonologie*, 68–101; see August Dillmann, *Das Buch Henoch* (Leipzig: Vogel, 1853), 235; Albert Klöpper, *Der Brief an die Colosser. Kritisch untersucht und in seinem Verhältnisse zum paulinischen Lehrbegriff exegetisch und biblisch-theologisch erörtert* (Berlin: Reimer, 1882), 455.

54. Hermann Diels, *Elementum: Eine Vorarbeit zum Griechischen und Lateinischen Thesaurus* (Leipzig: Teubner, 1899), 50–54, archive.org/stream/elementumeinevo02dielgoog#page/n6/mode/2up, citing Everling, *Angelologie und Dämonologie*, 70ff.

55. Scholars since 1963 holding this view include Albrecht Oepke, *Der Brief des Paulus an die Galater*, ed. Joachim Rohde, 3d ed., THNT 9 (Berlin: Evangelische Verlagsanstalt, 1973); E. P. Sanders, *Paul and Palestinian Judaism* (Philadelphia: Fortress, 1977); Hans Dieter Betz, *Galatians: A Commentary on Paul's Letter to the Churches in Galatia*, Hermeneia (Philadelphia: Fortress, 1979); F. F. Bruce, *The Epistle to the Galatians*, NIGTC (Grand Rapids: Eerdmans, 1982); C. B. Cousar, *Galatians*, Interpretation (Louisville, Ky: John Knox, 1982); E. Krentz, *Galatians, Philippians, Philemon, 1 Thessalonians*, Augsburg Commentaries on the New Testament (Minneapolis: Augsburg, 1985); Hans Hübner, "Paulusforshung seit 1945. Ein Kritischer Literaturbericht," *ANRW* 25.4:2691–94; J. Rohde, *Der Brief des Paulus an die Galater*, THNT 9 (Berlin: Evangelische Verlagsanstalt, 1989); J. Becker, *Paul: Apostle to Gentiles*, trans. O. C. Dean, Jr. (Louisville, KY: Westminster/John Knox, 1993); In-Gyu Hong, *The Law in Galatians*, JSNTSup 81 (Sheffield: JSOT Press, 1993); Bruce Longenecker, *The Triumph of Abraham's God: The Transformation of Identity in Galatians* (Edinburgh: T&T Clark, 1998); Thomas R. Schreiner, *Galatians*, ZECNT, ed. Clinton E. Arnold (Grand Rapids: Zondervan, 2010); N. T. Wright, *Paul and the Faithfulness of God*, Christian Origins and the Question of God 4 (London: SPCK, 2013); Robert Ewusie Moses, *Practices of Power: Revisiting the Principalities and Powers in the Pauline Letters* (Minneapolis: Fortress, 2014).

56. Betz, *Galatians*, 204.

57. Betz, *Galatians*, 204–5.

58. Betz, *Galatians*, 205.

59. Betz, *Galatians*, 204–5; italics Betz's.

60. Betz, *Galatians*, 205.

61. Betz, *Galatians*, 217–18.

62. See Peter J. Leithart, *Delivered from the Elements of the World: Atonement, Justification, Mission* (Downers Grove, IL: IVP Academic, 2016), 37 n. 32.

63. Blinzler, "Lexicalisches."

26   Introduction

64. Betz, *Galatians* and Longenecker, *Galatians* cite Blinzler nowhere.

65. Martinus C. de Boer, *Galatians: A Commentary*, NTL (Louisville, KY: Westminster John Knox, 2011), 256.

66. Barclay, *Paul and the Gift*.

67. Leithart, *Delivered from the Elements of the World*.

68. By "early Jewish sources" I mean texts that Jews wrote in Greek before AD 135.

69. See Blinzler, "Lexicalisches," 440.

70. Blinzler, "Lexicalisches," 434–36, disputing Martin Dibelius, *Die Giesterwelt im Glauben des Paulus* (Göttingen: Vandenhoeck & Ruprecht, 1909), 229.

71. Blinzler, "Lexicalisches," 440–41. His eleven instances are Philo, *Eternity* 109; *Heir* 134, 140; Sib. Or. 2.206–207; 3.79–82; 8.337–338; Galen, *HNH*, 1.39; Pseudo-Lucian, *Amores* 9; *Hymn. Orph.* 5.4; Irenaus, *Haer.* 1.5.4; Clement of Alexandria, *Exc.* 48.3. Blinzler misses Clement, *Strom.* 6.8.62 (see section A.1. above), as too does Rusam. This text represents a critical exception to their totalizing conclusions. However, the preponderance of their evidence still supports their claim in general.

72. Rusam, "Neue Belege" presents Marcus Aurelius, *Med.* 1.18.1; Galen, *Hipp. Elem.* 1.55, 456, 472; *HNH* 15.58; Sextus Empiricus, *Pyr.* 3.152; Oracula Chaldaica 39; Alexander of Aphrodisias, *Comm. Mete.* 2.1; *Comm. Metaph.* 802–3; *Fat* 203.22.

73. Rusam, "Neue Belege," 124.

74. Rusam, "Neue Belege," 125, confirming Blinzler, "Lexicalisches"; Delling, "Στοιχέω"; Eduard Schweizer, "Die 'Elemente Der Welt' Gal. 4, 3.9; Kol. 3, 8.20," in *Verborum Veritas: Festschrift Für Gustav Stählin Zum 70. Geburtstag*, ed. Otto Böcher and Klaus Haacker (Wuppertal: Brockhaus, 1970), 160–61; Eduard Schweizer, "Slaves of the Elements and Worshipers of Angels: Gal 4:3, 9; Col 2:8, 18, 20," *JBL* 107 (1988): 466; Vielhauer, "Gesetzesdienst und Stoicheiadienst," 550.

75. For example, de Boer, *Galatians*, 256 n. 382 allots James Louis Martyn, *Galatians: A New Translation with Introduction and Commentary*, AB 33A (New York: Doubleday, 1997), 402–6 only a footnote.

76. Schweizer, "Slaves of the Elements," 466–67.

77. Schweizer, "Slaves of the Elements," 460, citing *Moses* 2.121, 125, 133; *Spec. Laws* 2.190–192, 255; *Heir* 146–152; *Contempl. Life* 3–4; *Eternity* 109–111; see *QE* 2.118.

78. See Empedocles 11/115, Cicero, *Tusc.* 18–19, 42–45, Alexander Polyhistor DK 1.58b1.

79. Martyn, *Galatians*, 389.

80. Martyn, *Galatians*, 394–95, 403.

81. Martyn, *Galatians*, 404.

82. Martyn, *Galatians*, 396–401, 414–18, italics his.

83. Martyn, *Galatians*, 369, italics his.

84. Martyn, *Galatians*, 290–92, 526–27.

85. Martyn, *Galatians*, 290, citing Eduard Schweizer, Friedrich Baumgärtel, and Rudolf Meyer, "Σάρξ, Σαρκικός, Σάρκινος," in *TDNT*, 7:102–3. But Martyn, like Schweizer, does not make the connection that the elements that compose the flesh are the same elements that weaken Paul's flesh and enslave all humans (Gal 4.9, 13). For

Introduction 27

Martyn, the "elements of religious differentiation" are weak because they are "impotent to grant life" or "to redeem from the state of enslavement" (412).

86. Martyn, *Galatians*, 526–27, especially nn. 162, 166. See also the "guilty impulse" and its "foreskin" in CD 2.14–16 and 1QS 5.5.

87. Martyn, *Galatians*, 527, 532.

88. Martyn, *Galatians*, 292–93, 527–28.

89. Martyn, *Galatians*, 528. For a review of Martyn's "apocalyptic Paul" see N. T. Wright, *Paul and His Recent Interpreters: Some Contemporary Debates* (London: SPCK, 2015), 155–86; J. P. Davies, *Paul Among the Apocalypses?: An Evaluation of the 'Apocalyptic Paul' in the Context of Jewish and Christian Apocalyptic Literature*, LNTS 562 (London: Bloomsbury T&T Clark, 2016), chap. five.

90. Martyn, *Galatians*, 530.

91. de Boer, *Galatians*, 253 considers their conclusions "demonstrated beyond any reasonable doubt."

92. de Boer, *Galatians*, 253.

93. de Boer, *Galatians*, 256, italics his.

94. de Boer, *Galatians*, 253–57, 273–77.

95. Martinus C. de Boer, "The Meaning of the Phrase τα Στοιχεια του Κοσμου in Galatians," *NTS* 53 (2007): 222, see 201, 257–58.

96. Barclay, *Paul and the Gift*, 409.

97. Barclay, *Paul and the Gift*, 426.

98. Barclay, *Paul and the Gift*, 410, see 334.

99. Barclay, *Paul and the Gift*, 410.

100. Barclay, *Paul and the Gift*, 407.

101. Barclay, *Paul and the Gift*, 409–10.

102. Barclay, *Paul and the Gift*, 374, 392, 395, 400–401 (citing *Rewards* 126), 404, 409, 414.

103. Barclay, *Paul and the Gift*, 410 n. 47; Cooper, *Marius Victorinus' Commentary on Galatians*, 302–3, 312–14, 336.

104. Barclay, *Paul and the Gift*, 505–6.

105. Barclay, *Paul and the Gift*, 508.

106. Barclay, *Paul and the Gift*, 409.

107. Leithart, *Delivered from the Elements of the World*, 36.

108. Leithart, *Delivered from the Elements of the World*, 36–39 nn. 28, 32, 33, 36, 37, quoting de Boer, "The Meaning of the Phrase τα Στοιχεια του Κοσμου in Galatians."

109. Leithart, *Delivered from the Elements of the World*, 25.

110. Leithart, *Delivered from the Elements of the World*, 26.

111. Leithart, *Delivered from the Elements of the World*, 78 n. 5.

112. Leithart, *Delivered from the Elements of the World*, 78, 194.

113. Leithart, *Delivered from the Elements of the World*, 211 n. 25; disagreeing with Vielhauer, "Gesetzesdienst Und Stoicheiadienst," 533, though for Vielhauer the Fleisch is a "'Welt' qualifizierende Größe," not the substance of the physical body (see n. 43 above).

114. Leithart, *Delivered from the Elements of the World*, 81–84.

28 *Introduction*

115. Leithart, *Delivered from the Elements of the World*, 126.

116. Leithart calls this "a truism of exegesis" on Gal 4.1–11 (*Delivered from the Elements of the World*, 37 n. 32).

117. Leithart, *Delivered from the Elements of the World*, 38.

118. Leithart, *Delivered from the Elements of the World*, 42.

119. See *Spec. Laws* 3.9–10; 2.202; 4.91; *Rewards* 124; *Alleg. Interp.* 1.69.

120. Leithart, *Delivered from the Elements of the World*, 17–20, 25.

121. See Leithart, *Delivered from the Elements of the World*, chap. four.

122. Emma Wasserman, "Paul among the Philosophers: The Case of Sin in Romans 6–8," *JSNT* 30 (2008): 393–95, https://doi.org/10.1177/0142064X08091441.

123. See Wright, *Paul and the Faithfulness of God*, 44–45; Dean Fleming, *Contextualization in the New Testament: Patterns for Theology and Mission* (Downers Grove, IL: InterVarsity, 2005); and Davila, "The Perils of Parallels: 'Parallelomania' Revisited," summarized in Bankole P. Davies-Browne, "The Significance of Parallels between the Testament of Solomon and Jewish Literature of Late Antiquity (between the Closing Centuries BCE and the Talmudic Era) and the New Testament" (University of St Andrews, PhD thesis, 2004), 17–20, interacting with Samuel Sandmel, "Parallelomania," *JBL* 81.1 (1962): 1–13.

124. Wasserman, "Paul among the Philosophers," 393.

125. Wasserman, "Paul among the Philosophers," 393 n. 7, 395. See Stanley Kent Stowers, *A Rereading of Romans: Justice, Jews, and Gentiles* (New Haven, CT: Yale University Press, 1994); Pierre Bourdieu and J. D. Wacquant, *An Invitation to Reflexive Sociology* (Chicago: University of Chicago Press, 1992); Pierre Bourdieu, *The Field of Cultural Production: Essays on Art and Literature*, ed. Randal Johnson (New York: Columbia University Press, 1993); Theodore R. Schatzki, "Practiced Bodies: Subjects, Genders, and Minds," in *The Social and Political Body*, ed. Theodore R. Schatzki and Wolfgang Natter (New York: Guilford, 1996), 49–77; Theodore R. Schatzki, *Social Practices: A Wittgensteinian Approach to Human Activity and the Social* (Cambridge: Cambridge University Press, 1996); Theodore R. Schatzki, *The Site of the Social: A Philosophical Account of the Constitution of Social Life and Change* (University Park, PA: Penn State University Press, 2002).

126. Wasserman, "Paul among the Philosophers," 393–94.

127. Wasserman, "Paul among the Philosophers," 395.

128. Wright, *Paul and the Faithfulness of God*, 44, citing Dale B. Martin, "Paul and the Judaism/Hellenism Dichotomy: Toward a Social History of the Question," in *Paul Beyond the Judaism/Hellenism Divide*, ed. Troels Engberg-Pedersen (Louisville, KY: Westminster John Knox, 2001), 29–62; Wayne A. Meeks, "Judaism, Hellenism, and the Birth of Christianity," in *Paul Beyond the Judaism/Hellenism Divide*, ed. Troels Engberg-Pedersen (Louisville, KY: Westminster John Knox, 2001), 17–28.

129. Wright, *Paul and the Faithfulness of God*, 614, citing Christopher Gill, "The School in the Roman Imperial Period," in *The Cambridge Companion to the Stoics*, ed. Brad Inwood (Cambridge: Cambridge University Press, 2003), 49; Michael J. White, "Stoic Natural Philosophy (Physics and Cosmology)," in *The Cambridge Companion to the Stoics*, ed. Brad Inwood (Cambridge: Cambridge University Press,

Introduction 29

2003), 136, http://universitypublishingonline.org/cambridge/companions/chapter.jsf ?bid=CBO9780511998874&cid=CBO9780511998874A009.

130. Fleming, *Contextualization in the New Testament*, 79; see also Gregory K. Beale, "Other Religions in New Testament Theology," in *Biblical Faith and Other Religions: An Evangelical Assessment*, ed. David W. Baker (Grand Rapids: Kregel, 2004), 79–105.

131. I use "Anointed" to translate both מָשִׁיחַ and Χριστός, normally rendered "Messiah" or "Christ."

132. To analyze Paul's intercultural communication, both Martin and George appeal to Bakhtin's concepts of dialogic and heteroglossia. See Dale B. Martin, *The Corinthian Body* (New Haven, CT: Yale University Press, 1995), 133, citing Mikhail M. Bakhtin, *Speech Genres and Other Late Essays* (Austin: University of Texas Press, 1986); Tzvetan Todorov, *Mikhail Bakhtin: The Dialogical Principle* (Minneapolis: University of Minnesota Press, 1984); Michael Holquist, *Dialogism: Bakhtin and His World* (London: New Accents, 1990). Roji T. George, *Paul's Identity in Galatians: A Postcolonial Appraisal* (New Delhi: Christian World Imprints, 2016) builds on Mikhail M. Bakhtin, *The Dialogic Imagination: Four Essays*, ed. Michael Holquist, trans. Caryl Emerson and Michael Holquist (Austin: University of Texas Press, 1981); Holquist, *Dialogism: Bakhtin and His World*; see Barbara Green, *Mikhail Bakhtin and Biblical Scholarship: An Introduction*, SBL Semeia Studies (Atlanta: SBL, 2000); and Homi K. Bhabha, *The Location of Culture* (London: Routledge, 1994); Homi K. Bhabha, "Culture's In-Between," in *Questions of Cultural Identity*, ed. Stuart Hall and Paul du Gay (London: Sage, 1996), 53–60 to construct Paul's "hybrid cultural identity" from a postcolonial perspective.

133. See Daniel I. Block, "Other Religions in Old Testament Theology," in *Biblical Faith and Other Religions: An Evangelical Assessment*, ed. David W. Baker (Grand Rapids: Kregel, 2004), 43–78.

134. Martin, *The Corinthian Body*, 125.

135. This is a leading concern in Sandmel, "Parallelomania."

136. Martin, *The Corinthian Body*, xiii thinks Paul "surely didn't read" Greek medical texts. Jason Zurawski, "Mosaic Torah as Encyclical Paideia: Reading Paul's Allegory of Hagar and Sarah in Light of Philo of Alexandria's," in *Wisdom & Apocalypticism* (SBL Chicago, presented at the SBL, 2012) cannot deny that Paul read Philo.

137. John M. G. Barclay, "Mirror-Reading a Polemical Letter: Galatians as a Test Case," *JSNT* 31 (1987): 73–93.

1

The Term "Στοιχεια Του Κοσμου" in Ancient Greek and Early Jewish Works

When Paul told the assemblies in Galatia, "We also were enslaved under the 'στοιχεῖα τοῦ κόσμου,'" he selected a term that had recognizable meaning (4.3). Greek writers had used the term and discussed the concept for centuries, and Jewish writers had enlisted the term to expound their tradition in conversation with Greek philosophy. As mysterious as the term στοιχεῖα—let alone στοιχεῖα τοῦ κόσμου—may seem to us in the twenty-first century, it actually meant something in the first century, and that meaning is rather more mundane than the adjective *cosmic* might suggest. Paul was referring to the material elements that compose and compromise the human body.

Paul chose that term in order to discuss a distinct concept and engage critically with a particular discourse. Chapter 1 focuses on the term, the development of its various meanings, and the definite sense of the phrase στοιχεῖα τοῦ κόσμου. It builds on Gerhard Delling's *TDNT* entry (still the best exhibition of στοιχεῖον and its meanings), fills in gaps in his work, and addresses the places where I differ from him.[1] The chapter is both corrective and constructive. It corrects common misperceptions of the term στοιχεῖον and it constructs a full understanding of first-century use of the term along five lines. (1) A στοιχεῖον is an element, a component of a compound, whether material or immaterial. (2) Though στοιχεῖον's referent may be either material or immaterial, in each case, its sense is clear in context. (3) Early Jews employ the term στοιχεῖον within their representations of a scriptural view of the cosmos. (4) The phrase στοιχεῖα κόσμου appears in extant literature as an early Jewish innovation to refer unambiguously to the material elements which compose the cosmos and its bodies. (5) Στοιχεῖον does not come to refer to a star before AD 100 or to a spirit before AD 240. Though scholars as respected and varied as Bousset and Bruce, Betz and Wright advocate a

32   *1*

"spiritual" reading, there is no evidence that anyone in Paul's lifetime or for centuries after used στοιχεῖον to denote a spirit.[2]

A. ΣΤΟΧΕΙΟΝ MAY REFER TO A MATERIAL
OR AN IMMATERIAL ELEMENT

For centuries before Empedocles, the term στοιχεῖον does not refer to the material elements of the cosmos. As Delling explains, its meaning, "member of a series" (στοῖχος), develops from its original sense, "sound" or "letter," to "element" and then to "principle."[3] Plato disdains to stretch the meaning of the term further and pin it to Empedocles's concept of four elements, but Aristotle acquiesces shortly thereafter, and his definition holds for 450 years. In extant sources, Jews begin to use στοιχεῖον and its cognates after Aristotle. As their works show, they adopt the term, integrate it naturally in a scriptural worldview, and use it to refer clearly either to an immaterial element (a sound, letter, or principle) or to a material one (earth, water, air, or fire).

1. The Developing Meaning of the Term Στοιχεῖον in Ancient Greek Sources

The term στοιχεῖα comes to refer to earth, water, air, and fire only in the third century BC. Though the sixth-century Milesian philosophers appreciated "the four great cosmic masses," it is Empedocles (c. 490–430 BC) who "focussed exclusively upon the four forms earth, air, fire and water . . . and established these four as the canonical tetrad."[4] However, he calls these four substances of all things "ῥιζώματα," not "στοιχεῖα."[5] Plato (428/7–348/7 BC) accepts Empedocles's four-element theory, but he scorns the idea that those elements would be termed "στοιχεῖα."[6] For him, the four materials are, as the Milesians called them before, ἀρχαί (*Tim.* 48b).[7]

Within decades, Aristotle (384–322 BC) acknowledges that the four elements of the cosmos are popularly called στοιχεῖα and, with some nuanced disclaimer, uses the term with that sense throughout his works.[8] Material elements appear naturally in his definition of στοιχεῖον.

> "Στοιχεῖον"[9] means (*a*) the primary immanent thing, formally indivisible into another form, of which something is composed. . . . (*b*) Those who speak of the στοιχεῖα of bodies similarly mean the parts into which bodies are ultimately divisible, . . . (*c*) The term is applied with a very similar meaning to the "στοιχεῖα" of geometrical figures, and generally to the "elements" of demonstrations; . . . (*d*) The term "στοιχεῖον" is also applied metaphorically to any small unity which is useful for various purposes; and so that which is small or simple or indivisible is called a "στοιχεῖον." (*Metaph.* 5.3, 1014a–b)

The Term *"Στοιχεία Του Κόσμου"* in Ancient Greek and Early Jewish Works   33

Thus a στοιχεῖον is basically a "part" (*a*), whether material (*b*), immaterial (*c*), or, specifically, simple (*d*). For Lagercrantz, this definition is "kanonisch und zwar nicht nur für das Altertum."[10]

Aristotle seems to find the term στοιχεῖον so fitting for the concept element that he substitutes it for earlier authors' original terms. Thus, he summarizes Empedocles's theory of four ῥιζώματα as "Empedocles says that Fire, Water, Air, and Earth are four στοιχεῖα" (*Gen. corr.* 1.1, 314a), and he represents Plato similarly in 2.1, 329a.

With Aristotle, term weds concept, and what he joins together no one separates for centuries to follow. For the next 450 years, στοιχεῖον remains "the primary thing of which something is composed," whether that thing is immaterial (a letter in the alphabet, a sound in a word, a premise in an argument, a plane face of a solid) or material (earth, water, air, or fire). However, the material sense comes to be the more common.[11] Both the immaterial sense and the material sense, and the prevailing frequency of the latter, are present in early Jewish sources.

Table 1.1: √Στοιχεω by Category in Extant Early Jewish Sources

στοιχεῖον (στοιχεῖα) – *element*		
Material		Immaterial
1. Sib. Or. 3.80	40. *Heir* 134	Sound
2. Wis 7.17	41. *Heir* 140	1. *Sacrifices* 74
3. Wis 19.18	42. *Heir* 152	2. *Agriculture* 136
4. *Moses* 1.96	43. *Heir* 197	3. *Planting* 10
5. *Moses* 1.97	44. *Heir* 226	4. *Heir* 210
6. *Moses* 1.155	45. *Heir* 226	5. *Prelim. Studies* 150
7. *Moses* 1.156	46. *Heir* 226	6. *Prelim. Studies* 150
8. *Moses* 1.216	47. *Heir* 227	7. *Ἀριθμῶν* 73a
9. *Moses* 2.53	48. *Prelim. Studies* 117	Letter
10. *Moses* 2.65	49. *Dreams* 1.21	8. Sib. Or. 11.142
11. *Moses* 2.88	50. *Dreams* 1.212	9. Sib. Or. 11.154
12. *Moses* 2.121	51. *Contempl. Life* 3	10. Sib. Or. 11.190
13. *Moses* 2.121	52. *Contempl. Life* 4	11. Sib. Or. 11.196
14. *Moses* 2.148	53. *Flaccus* 125	12. *Creation* 126
15. *Moses* 2.154	54. *Embassy* 80	(= *Ἀριθμῶν* 73a)
16. *Moses* 2.251	55. *Providence* 2.45	13. *Creation* 127
17. *Moses* 2.267	56. *Providence* 2.53	(= *Ἀριθμῶν* 74)
18. *Moses* 2.286	57. *Eternity* 6	14. *Alleg. Interp.* 1.14
19. *Creation* 38	58. *Eternity* 29	(= *Ἀριθμῶν* 73b)
20. *Creation* 52	59. *Eternity* 61	15. *Alleg. Interp.* 3.121
(= *Ἀριθμῶν* 27a)	60. *Eternity* 74	16. *Heir* 282
21. *Creation* 84	61. *Eternity* 78	17. *Names* 61
22. *Creation* 131	62. *Eternity* 82	18. *Names* 61
23. *Creation* 131	63. *Eternity* 90	19. *Names* 77
24. *Creation* 146	64. *Eternity* 103	

34   *I*

25. *Abraham* 162	65. *Eternity* 107	20. *Abraham* 81
26. *Decalogue* 31	66. *Eternity* 109	21. *Eternity* 113
(= Ἀριθμῶν 99)	67. *Eternity* 111	22. *Flaccus* 55
27. *Spec. Laws* 1.208	68. *Eternity* 116	23. Sib. Or. 5.15
28. *Spec. Laws* 1.266	69. *Eternity* 123	
29. *Spec. Laws* 1.294	70. *Eternity* 144	Logical Component
30. *Spec. Laws* 1.328	71. Gal 4.3	24. *Worse* 7
31. *Spec. Laws* 2.151	72. Gal 4.9	25. *Worse* 8
32. *Spec. Laws* 2.255	73. Col 2.8	26. *Heir* 190
33. *Virtues* 73	74. Col 2.20	(= Ἀριθμῶν 5a)
34. *Rewards* 44	75. 2 Pet 3.10	27. *Heir* 209
35. *QG* 4 fragment 51b	76. 2 Pet 3.12	28. *QG* 4 fragment 8b
36. *Cherubim* 127	77. *J.W.* 1.377	(= Ἀριθμῶν 21a)
37. *Worse* 8	78. *J.W.* 6.47	29. Heb 5.12
38. *Giants* 22	79. *Ant.* 3.183	
39. *Unchangeable* 46	80. 4 Macc 12.13	

ἀναστοιχειόω *resolve matter into its elements*	μεταστοιχειόω *change the elementary nature of a thing*
Material Components	1. *Moses* 1.78
1. *Posterity* 5	2. *QG* 4 fragment 51b
2. *Heir* 29	3. *Migration* 83
3. *Heir* 184	4. *Dreams* 2.118
4. *Heir* 200	
5. *Abraham* 43	
6. *Eternity* 94	
Other Constituent Components	
1. *Moses* 2.288	
(= Ἀριθμῶν 4h)	

στείχω (στίχω) *walk, march, in line*	στιχίζω *be arranged in a row*	καταστείχω *return from exile*
1. *Moses* 2.251	1. Ezek 42.3	1. *Good Person* 7
2. *Eternity* 135		
3. *Names* 179		
4. *Sobriety* 48 (participle)		

στοιχέω *be drawn up in a line,* *correspond, be satisfactory*	συστοιχέω *stand in the same rank, correspond*	περιστοιχίζω *surround*
1. Eccl 11.6	1. Gal 4.25	1. *Ant.* 17.33
2. Gal 5.25		2. *Ant.* 17.192
3. Gal 6.16		
4. Rom 4.12		
5. Phil 3.16		
6. Acts 21.24		

The Term "Στοιχεια Του Κοσμου" in Ancient Greek and Early Jewish Works 35

ἀστοιχείωτος *ignorant of first elements*	στοιχειώδης *elementary*	στοιχείωσις *fashion of elements, elementary teaching*
1. *Planting* 52	Material: "elemental" 1. *Giants* 7 2. *Migration* 180 3. *Unchangeable* 104 Immaterial: "elementary" 1. *Agriculture* 181 2. *Heir* 102 3. *Spec. Laws* 2.177 (= Ἀριθμῶν 103, 103, 131)	1. 2 Macc 7.22 2. *Agriculture* 140

στίχος (διστιχία, τριστιχία, τετράστιχος) *row or file; line*		στοῖχος (τριστοίχος, τετραστοιχεί, ἀντίστοιχος) *row in an ascending series*
στίχος	διστιχία	στοῖχος
1. Exod 28.17	1. *Ant.* 8.78	1. *Moses* 2.124
2. Exod 28.17		2. Moses 2.133
3. Exod 28.18	τριστιχία	3. *Creation* 141
4. Exod 28.19	1. *J.W.* 2.173	4. *Joseph* 217
5. Exod 28.20	2. *Ant.* 3.172	5. *Spec. Laws* 2.1
6. Exod 36.17	3. *Ant.* 8.136	6. *Spec. Laws* 3.162
7. Exod 36.17		7. *Dreams* 2.139
8. Exod 36.18	τετράστιχος	8. *Contempl. Life* 66
9. Exod 36.19	1. Exod 28.17	9. *Ant.* 15.413
10. Exod 36.20	2. Exod 36.17	
11. 1 Kgs 6.36	3. Wis 18.24	τριστοίχος
12. 1 Kgs 6.36	4. *Alleg. Interp.* 1.81	1. *J.W.* 5.131
13. 1 Kgs 7.6		2. *Ant.* 15.418
14. 1 Kgs 7.6		
15. 1 Kgs 7.6		τετραστοιχεί
16. 1 Kgs 7.28		1. *Moses* 2.112
17. 1 Kgs 7.39		
18. 1 Kgs 7.40		ἀντίστοιχος
19. 1 Kgs 7.49		1. *Ant.* 15.413
20. 1 Kgs 7.49		
21. *Alleg. Interp.* 1.81		
22. *Alleg. Interp.* 1.81		
23. *Alleg. Interp.* 1.81		
24. *J.W.* 7.312		
25. *Ant.* 3.120		
26. *Ant.* 3.146		
27. *Ant.* 3.167		
28. *Ant.* 3.168		
29. *Ant.* 15.415		
30. *Ant.* 20.267		

36 *1*

ἀκροστιχίς—*acrostic*	στοιχηδόν—*in a row; line by line*
1. Sib. Or. 11.17	1. *Joseph* 160
2. Sib. Or. 11.23	2. *Spec. Laws* 4.203
	3. *Flaccus* 92
	4. *Flaccus* 156

2. Immaterial and Material Στοιχεῖα in Early Jewish Sources

Στοιχεῖον and its cognates occur in more than a dozen early Jewish sources, from 2 Maccabees in the mid-second century BC to Josephus, Sibylline Oracle 11, and 4 Maccabees in the late first or early second century AD. As the excerpts in this section show, Jews, like non-Jews, use the term to denote clearly either an immaterial element or, more commonly, a material element. Their adoption of the phrase is natural and, of itself, is not a sign of assimilation.[12] Indeed, √στοιχεω is first employed in the midst of an anti-Hellenistic tirade to express a concept from the Hebrew scriptures (2 Macc 7.22). The excerpts show also that Philo's use of the term and concept στοιχεῖον is representative of the diverse ways in which στοιχεῖον was used by Jews through these centuries and around the Mediterranean world. This last point warrants relying on Philo to fill out at least one strand of early Jewish thinking about the στοιχεῖα τοῦ κόσμου.

a. Στοιχεῖον as an Immaterial Element

Sibylline Oracles 5 and 11, Philo, and Hebrews use στοιχεῖον to refer to an immaterial element. In each case, the immaterial referent of the term is clear. And the quotations from the other three sources show that Philo's use of στοιχεῖον is typical, not atypical, of early Jews, for each of their distinct senses has an analogue in Philo's corpus.

(1) Sibylline Oracles 5 and 11. Writing in Egypt perhaps around the turn of the era, Sib. Or. 11 uses gematria to identify "diverse men" in history.[13] "I will tell the numbers and name them in acrostics (ἀκροστιχίδες)," the Sibyl says (15–17). She then cites the first letter or στοιχεῖον of four names: Agamemnon (141–142), Aeneas (153–154), Philip of Macedon (189–190), and Alexander (195–196). This use of στοιχεῖον to refer to a letter in a word or in a name is similar to Philo's use in *Creation* 127; *Ἀριθμῶν* 73a.r and in *Abraham* 81; *Names* 61, 77, respectively.[14]

Writing most likely in Egypt in the late first or early second century AD, Sib. Or. 5 also uses gematria to identify world rulers as it "reviews history from Alexander to Hadrian."[15] While the Sibyl views the cosmos as made of elements (51–53, 115–134, 294–305, 377–380, 447–450), her one use of the

The Term *"Στοιχεῖα Τοῦ Κοσμου"* in Ancient Greek and Early Jewish Works 37

term στοιχεῖον refers to the letters of the alphabet (στοιχεῖα . . . γράμματος) (13–15). This use of στοιχεῖον to refer to the letters of the alphabet mirrors Philo's as well.

(2) Philo. Like Aristotle, Philo (c. 20 BC–c. AD 50) sees a basic similarity between material and immaterial στοιχεῖα. An immaterial στοιχεῖον may be a part of speech (*Sacrifices* 74; *Agriculture* 136; *Heir* 210; *Prelim. Studies* 150; *Ἀριθμῶν* 73a), a letter (*Creation* 126, 127; *Abraham* 81–83; *Alleg. Interp.* 1.14; 3.121; *Heir* 282; *Names* 61, 77; *Flaccus* 55; *Eternity* 113), or a conceptual source (*Worse* 7–8; *Heir* 190),[16] but each immaterial στοιχεῖον is analogous to a material στοιχεῖον since both are components of ordered compounds (*Planting* 10; *Heir* 209; *Eternity* 113). The analogy may be as simple as naming the five parts of Alexandria "after the first στοιχεῖα of the alphabet" (*Flaccus* 55) or as complex as Philo's double-harmony of earth with heaven and the cosmos with the law, but στοιχεῖον is the fulcrum on which the analogy turns.

Philo's use of the term στοιχεῖον is clear and follows a distinct pattern. In most of his extant works, Philo uses στοιχεῖον to refer overwhelmingly to material elements.[17] But in the Allegory of the Law (especially outside *Heir*) Philo reserves στοιχεῖον as a term for immaterial elements. In some of those passages, Philo uses a term other than στοιχεῖα to identify the material elements. Thus alongside an immaterial στοιχεῖον, Philo refers to a material element (1) with μέρος in *Planting* 10, (2) with ἀρχή in *Heir* 281–282 (see *Worse* 153–155), and (3) with δύναμις in *QG* frag. 4.8b;[18] *Heir* 281–282; *Eternity* 107–108 (see *Posterity* 5–6).[19]

(3) Hebrews. The letter to the Hebrews warns its hearers against the peril of "regression" to spiritual immaturity. "For though by this time you ought to be teachers, you need someone to teach you again the στοιχεῖα of the beginning of God's oracles" (5.12). Commentators agree that the στοιχεῖα refer to immaterial elements, that is "elementary principles" or "elementary truths."[20] This use of στοιχεῖον to refer to rudimentary knowledge is similar to Philo's use in *QG* frag 4.8b, and the pairing with ἀρχή is similar to *Heir* 209.

The data from these four sources demonstrate three points. First, early Jews can use στοιχεῖον with an immaterial referent. Second, when they do, the context makes it clear that the referent is indeed immaterial. Third, while the other sources incorporate στοιχεῖον in distinct arguments, their uses of στοιχεῖον find corresponding uses in Philo's corpus. Thus we see that Philo's use of the term στοιχεῖον with an immaterial referent is representative of early Jewish usage. However, both in Philo and in other early Jewish writings, references to στοιχεῖον as an immaterial element are outnumbered by references to the material elements of the cosmos, whether a material substance or a material space.

38   *1*

b. Στοιχεῖον as a Material Elemental Substance

Wisdom of Solomon, Philo, and Josephus use στοιχεῖον to refer to an element as a material substance. As with immaterial referents above, in each case the context makes it clear that στοιχεῖον refers to a material element. The quotations in this section make three further points. First, Wisdom is like Philo in seeing a material στοιχειον as analogous to an immaterial στοιχεῖον, for each is a component of a composite. Second, early Jews often use the term στοιχεῖον when they are retelling scripture, especially the creation, flood, and exodus narratives. Third, the congruence of the conceptual frameworks within which Wisdom, Philo, and Josephus use στοιχεῖον suggests that many Jews in the first century shared a similar scripturally-sourced, philosophically-shaped perspective on the στοιχεῖα within the κόσμος.

(1) *Wisdom of Solomon.* Probably written by a Jew in Alexandria sometime between 30 BC and AD 40,[21] Wisdom of Solomon identifies the material elements of the cosmos and marvels at the elements' unnatural behavior during the exodus. The author writes to persuade "his fellow Jews . . . that *their* way of life, rooted in the worship of the One true God, is of an incomparably higher order than that of their pagan neighbors."[22]

In his discussion of the "nature and benefits of wisdom" and his "quest" for her, "Solomon" details the knowledge of creation that God taught him by wisdom.[23] "The structure of the κόσμος and the activity of the στοιχεῖα" head the list of this "unerring knowledge" (7.15–22 NRSV). The term "κόσμος" may allude to the OG's translation of צבאם as "ὁ κόσμος αὐτῶν" (Gen 2.1).[24] Michael Kolarcik identifies two further sources for this list: "the traditional knowledge attributed to Solomon" in the scriptures and "technical and popular Hellenistic ideas on the universe."[25] Among many references to the latter, David Winston points rightly to Plato's *Timaeus*, but he states wrongly that Plato used στοιχεῖα to label Empedocles's ῥιζώματα.[26] The text's terms and its congruence with Gen 1 also confirm that the στοιχεῖα are the material components of the structure of the cosmos.

The elemental motif recurs as Wis 11–19 retells the wonders of the exodus. The earth produced gnats, not land animals; "the river spewed out . . . frogs," not fish; hail and fire fell together, without melting or being quenched (16.22; 19.10, 18–20; see Exod 7–9; Ps 105.29–32). The author explains the dynamic of these marvels by analogy. "For the στοιχεῖα changed places with one another, as on a harp the notes vary the nature of the rhythm, while each note remains the same" (Wis 19.18). The context makes it clear that the στοιχεῖα are material elements. They are analogous to immaterial elements, but they are clearly distinct from them.[27] Here again, this early Jewish use of στοιχεῖον is a sign of acculturation, but not of assimilation. It comes naturally and clearly in a Greek language retelling of Israel's scriptures.

The Term "Στοιχεῖα Τοῦ Κοσμου" in Ancient Greek and Early Jewish Works   39

(2) Philo. Philo normally uses στοιχεῖον to refer to a material element of the cosmos. In an extended philosophical treatise against Stoic cosmic destruction, Philo identifies the στοιχεῖα explicitly: "there are four στοιχεῖα, earth, water, air and fire, of which the κόσμος is composed" (*Eternity* 107; see *Eternity* 6, 61, 74, 78, 82, 90, 103, 109, 111, 116, 144). On the identity of the στοιχεῖα and in "most of the major themes" of his philosophy, Philo shares much in common with Wisdom. Winston notes that both were "steeped" in the "philosophical tradition so influential at that time in Alexandria" and "have virtually identical theories of creation."[28] Like Wis 7.17, when Philo describes creation, whether in Mosaic or Greek concepts, he identifies the στοιχεῖα as the components of the cosmos (*Creation* 38, 52; *Decalogue* 31; *Spec. Laws* 1.328; 2.151; *Cherubim* 127; *Heir* 133–134, 140, 152). Finally, in each author, these ideas about the elements contribute to a paradigm that promotes Israel's heritage of God-given instruction as an example of "living in harmony with the cosmic principle of order."[29]

(3) Josephus. Josephus, a priest and leading political figure in first-century Judea, wrote his records of the Judean War in Aramaic in Rome in the late 70s, translating them into Greek shortly thereafter.[30] In *J.W.*, Herod admits that a deadly earthquake could have been daimonic "blows," but he assures his soldiers that it was rather an instance of "physical causes" producing "accidents (πάθη) to which the στοιχεῖα are subject" (1.373, 377).[31] The identity and function of the στοιχεῖα are clear: they are material substances subject to physical πάθη. They are explicitly not δαιμόνια.

In *Antiquities*, published in the early 90s, Josephus also sees the four στοιχεῖα symbolized in the temple. "The pieces of cloth woven of four materials indicate the nature of the στοιχεῖα" (*Ant.* 3.183). Here Josephus echoes his earlier explanation in *J.W.* 5.212–513, where he names the individual elements—fire, earth, air, and sea—but does not identify them as στοιχεῖα.

In each of these three sources, the context makes it clear that στοιχεῖον refers to a material element—just as each context pointed clearly to an immaterial referent in section (1) above. But section *b* goes beyond section *a*: it shows not only that Philo's use of στοιχεῖον is similar to use by other early Jews but also that they use the term within similar conceptual frameworks. This similarity suggests that many Jews in the first century may have shared a biblically-sourced, philosophically-shaped perspective on the στοιχεῖα within the κόσμος. Section *c* displays a similar elemental cosmology in two further sources, even though those sources disagree with Philo's eschatology, and in Israel's scriptures themselves.

40   *1*

c. Στοιχεῖον as a Material Elemental Space

Though they assert very different eschatologies, Sibylline Oracle 3, Philo, and 2 Peter use στοιχεῖον in a material sense to refer to an elemental space. Commentaries on these texts have not noted the distinction between a material στοιχεῖον as a substance and as a space, but the contexts in which Sib. Or. 3 and 2 Peter (and often Philo) use the term clearly identify the στοιχεῖον as a space rather than a substance. Recognizing this particular referent helps solve persistent hermeneutical puzzles, and it confirms the scriptural roots of a Jewish elemental cosmology.

(1) Appendix to Sibylline Oracle 3. Sibylline Oracle 3.75–92 prophesies the bereaving of the στοιχεῖα κόσμου in a great fiery judgment.[32] These lines fall in a patchwork of texts probably added to Sibylline Oracle 3 by Jews around the turn of the era or perhaps by Christians in the late first or early second century AD. The Sibyl identifies στοιχεῖα κόσμου explicitly as heaven, earth, and sea.

> Then all στοιχεῖα . . .
> κόσμου will be bereft, when God who dwells in the sky
> rolls up the heaven as a scroll is rolled,
> and the whole variegated vault of heaven falls
> on the wondrous earth and ocean. An undying cataract
> of raging fire will flow, and burn earth, burn sea,
> and melt the heavenly vault . . . (3.80–86)

Jane Lightfoot misses the Sibyl's explicit identification of στοιχεῖα κόσμου as three elemental spaces: heaven, earth, and ocean (or sea). Citing Richard Bauckham, she says that the term στοιχεῖα in Sib. Or. 3.80, as in 2 Pet 3.10, "seems to be used in its then-current sense of heavenly bodies to interpret the δυνάμεις of Isa 34:4."[33] If these lines date to the second century, "heavenly body" would be a "current sense" of στοιχεῖον, but I argue below that the στοιχεῖα in 2 Pet 3 are elemental spaces, not heavenly bodies.[34]

(2) Philo. In his cosmology, Philo thinks of the elements both as substances and as the spaces characterized by those substances. Philo can use the alternate term μέρος to specify his particular meaning. He also discerns suitable inhabitants in each of the spaces.

Sometimes Philo uses μέρος to sharpen the distinction between elemental substances and elemental spaces. When thinking of the elements as substances, Philo may list the four as earth, water, air, and fire and call them στοιχεῖα (*Creation* 131, 146, see 147), but when thinking of the spaces characterized by those substances, he may list them as earth, sea, air, and heaven and call them μέρη (*Virtues* 73; *Giants* 7–8; see *Moses* 2.37; *Spec. Laws* 2.45; 3.111, 151–152; *Rewards* 36; *Dreams* 1.39; *Flaccus* 123, 125).

In *Eternity* 115–116 Philo asserts that the μέρη—earth, water, air, and fire—cannot be transposed, even though the στοιχεῖα interchange (see *Eternity* 123–129). But the difference between στοιχεῖα and μέρη all but disappears a few lines later when Philo calls the στοιχεῖα the μέρη of the cosmos (*Eternity* 143–144). Philo's perspective is clearest, though, when he calls earth, sea, air, fire, and heaven the "elementary divisions," στοιχειώδη μέρη, of the cosmos (*Giants* 7–8).

In the Exposition of the Law, Philo shows from Genesis that there are three sublunar elemental regions, each populated by creatures fit for it: land creatures, water creatures, and air creatures, including angels (*Moses* 2.121; *Creation* 84; see *Eternity* 131).[35] It is according to these elemental spaces that Moses proscribes the eating of certain creatures in order to guard Jews against "insatiate desire" (*Spec. Laws* 4.100, 118, 129; *Providence* 2.69).[36]

Philo's explanation of his cosmology betrays inconsistencies, especially between the Exposition and the Allegory, but the referent of στοιχεῖον—whether immaterial or material, substantial or spatial—is consistently clear in context. And Philo finds suitable inhabitants within each of the elemental spaces.

(3) 2 Peter.[37] In early Jewish sources, the distinct sense of στοιχεῖον as material space, rather than as material substance, finds its greatest significance in 2 Pet 3. Reading the στοιχεῖα as material elemental spaces makes better sense of 2 Peter's argument, and it reveals the letter's coherence with the content and mode of ancient Israelite prophecies.

Most scholars follow Bauckham in reading 2 Peter as a pseudonymous, late first-century, Jewish-Christian testament, written perhaps from Rome.[38] Presenting himself as "Simeon Peter," the author describes the coming of the day of the Lord.

> The heavens will pass away with a loud noise, and the στοιχεῖα will be dissolved with fire (καυσόω), and the earth and everything that is done on it will be disclosed. . . . The heavens will be set ablaze and dissolved, and the στοιχεῖα will melt (τήκω) with fire (καυσόω). (3.10, 12)

Bauckham established the consensus view that the στοιχεῖα that dissolve and melt with fire are "heavenly bodies."[39] Other scholars associate spirits closely with these bodies.[40] Opposing the majority view, Jerome Neyrey, Edward Adams, and Gene Green read στοιχεῖον in its most common sense as a material element of the cosmos.[41] At least two reasons support this reading. First, Adams notes that in Greek physics, the four elements are associated with the earth, not with the celestial realm, whose bodies are composed of ether.[42] Second, it would seem unusual, if not impossible, to suggest that fire could melt heavenly bodies composed of fiery ether. The only earlier extant collocation of στοιχεῖα and τήκω denies that fire can "melt" fire: in *Eternity* 110 Philo explains that melting is the transition from an earthen to a watery state. Thus, in 2 Pet 3, "στοιχεῖα" cannot refer to heavenly bodies.

However, the στοιχεῖα can be material spaces, and taking them that way clarifies two things. First, it illuminates what 2 Peter actually prophesies. Reading the στοιχεῖα as material substances leads Green to say that the earth will be destroyed,[43] but "Simeon" does not mention the earth's destruction. Rather, in the great fire, heaven and the στοιχεῖα will be dissolved, exposing the earth such that it is "found."[44] Thus Adams is correct to say that "the eschatological dissolution will expose all the deeds of human beings to divine scrutiny," but he is incorrect to assert that the whole earth will be dissolved and consumed, something taught explicitly nowhere in 2 Pet 3.5–13.[45] Taking στοιχεῖα as spaces precludes such a misreading.

Second, a spatial reading of στοιχεῖον highlights how 2 Pet 3 coheres with prophetic warnings in older scriptures. Though Bauckham and others cite Isa 34.4 as a definitive perspective for identifying the στοιχεῖα and interpreting Simeon's warning as a whole—"heaven shall roll up like a scroll, and all the stars shall fall"—2 Pet 3 coheres more closely with Isa 63.19–64.1, which Bauckham also cites.[46] There the prophet says that if God were to open heaven, the mountains would melt (τήκω) like wax, and God's adversaries would be burned up (κατακαίω). Other scriptures also describe mountains, valleys, domains, and nations melting when the Lord comes as judge (Ps 96 [97].3–6; Mic 1.3–4; Nah 1.5–6; Hab 3.6; see Isa 24.23).

Finally, 2 Pet 3's use of στοιχεῖον is a window onto Simeon's apostolic communication. He uses terms and concepts that resonate meaningfully with the Stoic concept of a cosmic conflagration, but he does so to issue a Jewish-style prophetic warning that corrects the thought and practice of early Christians.[47] Adams suggests that 2 Pet 3 is relying more on Stoic precedent than on scriptural, because it says (1) that the earth was formed out of and through water and (2) that the flood destroyed the cosmos (3.5–6).[48] On review, though, the first statement coheres neatly with the creation of earth through the double separation of the waters and the formation of dry land (Gen 1.6–7, 9–10). And Simeon's second statement is an accurate summary of the earth being flooded by water from two other elemental spaces: the abyss and heaven (Gen 7.11–12).[49] Further, though 2 Peter (like Sib. Or. 3.75–92) shares several nouns with the Stoic discussions of conflagration—οὐρανοι, πῦρ, γῆ, and, distinctively, στοιχεῖα—the standard terms ἐκπύρωσις and ἀναλύω are curiously absent in either the Petrine or the Sibylline tradition, though they figure prominently throughout *Eternity*.[50] While Simeon's (like Paul's) selection of στοιχεῖον is an example of acculturation, the way Simeon (like Paul) uses the term and the end to which he puts it are better categorized as adaptation: a

The Term *"Στοιχεῖα Τοῦ Κοσμου"* in Ancient Greek and Early Jewish Works   43

creative, intelligent, intentional "yes-but" response to a Greek concept. This is lively discourse. Simeon is no Stoic (and Paul no Middle Platonist) if he finds in Greek philosophy terms and concepts that he can use as tools to build a different argument on a different foundation for quite a different purpose. He is rather an apostle (2 Pet 1.1; see Gal 1.1).

Thus we see that Simeon uses στοιχεῖα to refer clearly to material elements. Close attention to his words shows those elements to be spaces, and it shows that his concept of the στοιχεῖα is profoundly scriptural. Indeed, 2 Peter—and Wisdom, the Sibyl, Philo, and Josephus—are simply doing what Aristotle did before them: using the term στοιχεῖον to identify a concept that their predecessors did not call "στοιχεῖον." For early Jews like Paul, an elemental cosmology is firmly scriptural.

3. Conclusion

Set side by side with the origins of the term στοιχεῖον and the concept "element" in ancient Greek philosophy, the review of στοιχεῖον in early Jewish sources makes five points. First, Jews and other Greek-speakers can use the term στοιχεῖον with an immaterial or a material referent. Second, when they do, the context makes the immateriality or materiality of the referent clear. Third, a material στοιχεῖον may refer to a substance (earth, water, air, or fire) or a space (earth, sea, sky, or sometimes heaven). Fourth, Philo's uses of στοιχεῖον are typical of early Jewish uses. Fifth, the roots of the similar cosmologies within which some early Jews refer to a material στοιχεῖον can be traced to the elemental structuring of the creation narrative in the Hebrew scriptures.

But if στοιχεῖον can refer to a material or an immaterial element, is its meaning in context actually that clear? The contexts in which Philo refers to a material στοιχεῖον within a few lines of an immaterial one, or even to a material στοιχεῖον as analogous to an immaterial one, show that it is.

B. THE MATERIAL OR IMMATERIAL REFERENT OF ΣΤΟΙΧΕΙΟΝ IS CONSISTENTLY CLEAR

Blinzler's survey is instructive in laying out the general pattern of usage of στοιχεῖον in early Jewish and Christian texts. However, though the material use of στοιχεῖον was "die bei weitem geläufigste" in his survey, even a frequency as high as 78.3 percent is an inadequate reason to read στοιχεῖα in Gal 4 as "Grundstoffe."[51] In any given occurrence of στοιχεῖον, it is the context, and not the frequency of usage, that will specify the sense of the term. Philo, for example, uses στοιχεῖον to refer to material elements three times as often

44   *1*

as to immaterial elements, but it is the context of each usage that specifies his particular referent. Such precision is especially evident in his proximate and analogous uses of στοιχεῖον with material and immaterial referents.

Within the space of a few lines, Philo refers clearly to an immaterial στοιχεῖον as analogous to a material στοιχεῖον. In *Worse* 7–8, Philo is explaining Joseph's "treatment of the three kinds of good things, those pertaining to the outside world, to the body, and to the soul."

> These, though indeed parts (μέρη) or στοιχεῖα of good things, are not good things in perfection. He points out that neither fire nor earth nor any of the four elements, out of which the universe was formed, is a κόσμος, but the coming together and blending of the στοιχεῖα into one; and argues that in precisely the same way happiness is found to be neither a peculiar property of the things of the outside world, nor of the things pertaining to the body, nor of those pertaining to the soul, taken by themselves. He argues that each of the three classes mentioned has the character of a part (μέρη) or στοιχεῖα and that it is only when they are all taken together in the aggregate that they produce happiness. (*Worse* 7–8)

In this obscure argument about the nature of goodness, the referent of each instance of στοιχεῖα is clear. The first στοιχεῖα's referent is immaterial (the three parts of good things), the second's is material (fire, earth, and the others of the four), and the third is immaterial again (the three parts of good things). These two sorts of στοιχεῖον are clearly distinct, the very thing that, in Philo's view, Joseph fails to see because he conflates three kinds of things that are "separated from each other by complete diversity of nature" (*Worse* 7).[52]

This excerpt from Philo corrects at least three common misconceptions of the term στοιχεῖον. First, some studies of στοιχεῖον, like Walter Bauer's, make it seem as though στοιχεῖον's three meanings (immaterial, material, and "spiritual"[53]) are unconnected.[54] However, the excerpts here and above show that while στοιχεῖον's immaterial and material senses are distinct, both of them relate to στοιχεῖον's basic meaning: member of a series, component.

Second, many writers assume that if στοιχεῖον is associated with something (usually a spirit) in a particular context, then it may reasonably be identified with that thing. In his extensive study, Blinzler showed that association does not establish identification.[55] Delling argues the same in his exasperated review of Lawrence Scheu's "spiritual" reading of στοιχεῖον.

> The misleading or wrong interpretations of many passages adduced for this sense, or for "spiritual beings," can hardly be discussed here. One striking example may be given. Acc. to Scheu, 52 στοιχεῖον is used for stellar gods in Simpl. in Aristot. *De Caelo Comment.*, I, 3, 49b. But here στοιχεῖα does not mean stars. It means the elements of which living creatures are begotten and in

The Term "Στοιχεῖα Τοῦ Κόσμου" in Ancient Greek and Early Jewish Works 45

which they dissolve again acc. to Simpl. The στοιχεῖα are not called gods; the ref. is to the gods set over them.[56]

Yet, thirty years later, BDAG still cites Simplicius for a "spiritual" reading.[57]

Third, many writers also assume that the term στοιχεῖον is ambiguous, either hopelessly or plenteously so. James Dunn, for one, seems delighted with στοιχεῖον's bounteous potential. "Does it denote 'the elemental substances' . . . or 'the elementary forms' of religion . . . or 'the heavenly bodies, the stars' understood as divine powers? . . . The answer is probably 'All three!' Or more precisely, that Paul did not have such distinctions in mind."[58] Yes, the semantic range of στοιχεῖον is ambivalent, but the use of the term in context is not, and I have encountered few, if any, ancient sources that use στοιχεῖον with the almost witless ambiguity that Dunn purports to find in Paul.

Across the literature, the ambiguous, even "shadowy," identity of the στοιχεῖα suggests that the meaning of the term in a given text is as likely found by a stab in the dark as by a sensitive reading of the context.[59] But attentive review of text after text—across the centuries and among various peoples—shows that the specific referent of a given instance of στοιχεῖον is either clearly immaterial or clearly material. (But certainly not "spiritual" until the third century!) This precision is true of the term by itself. The addition of the phrase τοῦ κόσμου only sharpens the clarity further.

C. THE PHRASE ΣΤΟΙΧΕΙΑ ΚΟΣΜΟΥ REFERS UNAMBIGUOUSLY TO THE MATERIAL ELEMENTS OF THE COSMOS

Blinzler's and Rusam's lexical research concluded that the phrase στοιχεῖα κόσμου refers to material elements.[60] A second look at their data shows that, in the full corpus of extant Greek texts, στοιχεῖα κόσμου appears first in Jewish sources as a way to refer unambiguously to the material elements of which the cosmos and its bodies are made.

Blinzler found στοιχεῖα κόσμου in only two sources that can be dated before Paul. Both sources are Jewish: Philo (*Heir* 134, 140; *Eternity* 109) and Sib. Or. 3.79–82. Having discussed the appendix to Sib. Or. 3 above, I present the other instances here.[61] The data show that στοιχεῖα κόσμου refers unmistakably to the material elements.

For Philo, the στοιχεῖα κόσμου are the substances from which God formed the cosmos and its bodies, and by which they are sustained.

> The great Artificer . . . made two sections, heavy and light. . . . Then again He divided each of these two, the rare into air and fire, the dense into water and land,

46

1

and these four He laid down as first foundations, to be ἃ καὶ στοιχεῖα αἰσθητὰ αἰσθητοῦ κόσμου (the sensible elements of the sensible world). (*Heir* 133–134)

Thus God sharpened the edge of his all-cutting Word, and divided universal being, which before was without form or quality, and the four τοῦ κόσμου στοιχεῖα which were formed by segregation from it, and the animals and plants which were framed with them as materials. (*Heir* 140)[62]

Philo sees the interchange of the elements—earth to water to air to fire and back—as evidence of their eternity. "Τὰ στοιχεῖα τοῦ κόσμου in their mutual interchanges seem to die, yet, strangest of contradictions, are made immortal as they ever run their race backwards and forwards and continually pass along the same road up and down" (*Eternity* 109).

I present these data in full because, despite the conclusiveness of Blinzler's and Rusam's analyses, many scholars continue to read στοιχεῖα τοῦ κόσμου in Gal 4 as referring to immaterial elements.[63] Yet the data show explicitly that the στοιχεῖα τοῦ κόσμου are the four material elements: earth, water, air, and fire. The data show further—and very significantly, though no one, to my knowledge, has made this observation—that *the phrase στοιχεῖα κόσμου appears in extant sources as a first-century Jewish innovation to refer unambiguously to the material elements of which the cosmos and its bodies are made.*

Even more consistently the consensus of scholars continues to assume or insist, in the absence of any actual data, that "elemental spirit" was a common sense of the term στοιχεῖον in the first century and is the referent intended by στοιχεῖα (τοῦ κόμσου) in Gal 4 (as in Col 2). So far, this chapter has shown what στοιχεῖον *can* mean (immaterial or material element) and what στοιχεῖα κόσμου *must* mean. I show next what it *cannot* mean (star or elemental spirit) before explaining what it *does* mean in Gal 4 (the elements that compose and compromise the flesh of human bodies).

D. ΣΤΟΙΧΕΙΟΝ DOES NOT COME TO REFER TO STARS UNTIL ABOUT AD 100 AND TO SPIRITS UNTIL THE THIRD CENTURY

Though the consensus of scholars posits "elemental spirits" as the referent of στοιχεῖα τοῦ κόσμου in Gal 4, neither that meaning nor the meaning "star" is attested in extant sources from before the second century AD.[64] The meaning "star" appears first around AD 100. The meaning "spirit" does not appear until the third century, despite conjectures and claims to the contrary.[65] While Paul could certainly have been the first to label a spirit a στοιχεῖον, the data as

The Term *"Στοιχεια Του Κοσμου"* in Ancient Greek and Early Jewish Works   47

we have them now require not only that Paul would thus have used στοιχεῖον with a new meaning but also that, apart from verbatim quotations of Galatians or Colossians, no one used the term again with that meaning for 200 years.

In this section, I present the strongest arguments for each of these readings, and I show how the arguments fall short of proving their point.

1. The Sense "Star" Appears around AD 100

While stars appear often in earlier cosmological discussions replete with the term στοιχεῖον, a star itself is not labelled στοιχεῖον until about AD 100. The first extant instance is found in *PLondon* 1.130, which mentions στοιχείῳ Διός, normally taken as a reference to the planet Jupiter as a στοιχεῖον.[66] As Delling notes, by the early 160s when Justin writes his Second Apology, this meaning is "familiar" (see *2 Apol.* 5.2).[67] Given the imprecision of dating ancient papyri, it is possible that some people in Paul's day did use στοιχεῖον on occasion to refer to a star. However, no data suggest that that sense was common in the first century. The data show rather that στοιχεῖα κόσμου refers consistently to the material elements of which the cosmos and its bodies are made.

2. Scholars Argue that the Sense "Elemental Spirit" Coheres with Paul's "Apocalyptic" Jewish Worldview

In the decades following Ritschl and Everling, scholars have presented several reasons why the στοιχεῖα τοῦ κόσμου in Gal 4 are spirits.[68] Most of their reasons relate to the worldview and religious practices of ancient Jews and pagans.

a. Scholars Observe that Early Jews Associated Angels and Spirits with the Elements

Israel's scriptures and early Jewish writings mention spirits or angels and the elements and the stars in the same contexts. In a psalm with a recognizably elemental cosmology, the Lord makes his messengers wind and his ministers fire (Ps 104.4; see 148.2–4, 8). Isaiah describes seraphim as flaming attendants who praise the Lord (6.1–6). 2 Baruch pictures God ruling the holy beings—"who are flame and fire"—that stand around his throne (21.6). At God's command, angels "are changed to wind and fire" (4 Ezra 8.22) and "flames . . . into winds" (2 Bar. 48.8). In a list of spirits God created on the first day, Jubilees includes angels associated with "the spirit of fire, . . . the spirit of the winds, . . . the spirit of" wet weather, and the spirits of the seasons

48 *1*

(2.2). And Jubilees frag. *a* refers to τὰ στοιχεῖα within a context that "conceives of the elements as governed by angels."[69]

Angels and spirits are associated with stars. In his first response to Job, the Lord sets the morning stars and angels in synonymous parallel, each celebrating the foundation of the earth (38.7). God created "the army of luminaries, the support of the spirits, the control of the holy ones" (1QM War Scroll X 11–12). "The Astronomical Book, best known through the Book of the Luminaries," details an angel and four leaders over 360 stars that "rule the firmament" and separate seasons, months, and days (1 En. 75.3).[70] The Lord set the angel Uriel "over all the heavenly luminaries," "the sun, the moon, the stars, and all the heavenly powers which revolve in their circuits" (75.3; 82.8).

Some stars act as persons. Stars fight against Sisera from their courses in heaven (Judg 5.20). Sun and moon threaten to strike pilgrims (Ps 121.5–6; see σεληνιάζομαι in Matt 4.24; 17.15). Conversely, in 4Q88 Psalms[f] X, "all the stars of dusk . . . rejoice" (5–6). The light responds to God with trembling and the stars with gladness (Bar 33–34). The sun, moon, and stars give ear when they are sent (Ep Jer 60). And Philo identifies "the stars" as "souls divine," which Moses called ἄγγελοι and philosophers call δαίμονες (*Giants* 7–8). As scholars have shown, evidence abounds for the close association of the elements with angels and spirits.

b. Scholars Observe that Stars and Spirits Rule Over and Oppress the Nations

Israel's scriptures and early Jewish writings associate stars and spirits and describe each as rulers over the nations. Moses warns the Israelites against serving the sun, moon, stars, and all the host (κόσμος) of heaven. They are "things that Yahweh your God has allotted to all the peoples under all the heavens" (Deut 4.19–20). Similarly the Most High "apportioned the nations" and "established the boundaries of the peoples according to the number of the sons of God" (Deut 32.8–9).[71] The Lord appointed "a ruler for every nation" (Sir 17.17). When the gods judge unjustly, God confronts them in the Council of El (Ps 82.1; see Ps 58). Jubilees presents this misrule as God's intention: God "caused spirits to rule" over all nations and people "so that they might lead them astray from following him" (15.31–32). Pseudo-Moses fragments threaten Israel with even worse rule; they show God handing Israel over to the rule of "the angels of destruction" (4Q388 Pseudo-Moses[c] 1 6–7; 4Q390 Pseudo-Moses Apocalypse[e] 1 11; 2 I 3–7). As scholars have shown, early Jewish sources present the stars and spirits as oppressive rulers.

The Term "Στοιχεία Τοῦ Κοσμοῦ" in Ancient Greek and Early Jewish Works 49

c. Scholars Assert that Στοιχεῖον Occurs with a Spiritual Referent in Later Works Whose Traditions Reach into the First Century and Earlier

While in the sources just cited the term στοιχεῖον is present only in Philo and Jub. frag. *a*, it is present as well in other works whose traditions, scholars allege, may reach into the first century or earlier.

(1) Greek Magical Papyri. Clint Arnold works closely with extensive evidence for how people really thought, spoke, and acted in Asia Minor. He finds that "in the Greek Magical Papyri, the term *stoicheia* is used most commonly in connection with the stars and/or the spirit entities, or gods, they represent."[72] According to Arnold, though "each of the papyrus texts postdates the first century," "most of the traditions incorporated into the magical papyri are much earlier, including the astrological terms and concepts."[73] Thus, "one may safely conclude that in the context of magic and astrology, even in Jewish and early Christian circles, the term *stoicheia* was indeed used of personalized spiritual forces. . . . Furthermore, these traditions (including the demonic use of *stoicheia*) reach into the first century A.D. and even earlier."[74]

(2) 2 Enoch. The longer recension of the Slavonic 2 Enoch, whose "primitive form" likely dates to the first century AD, includes "elements" (*stikhii*) in a list between "the bodiless armies" and "the army of the cherubim" (1a.5–6).[75] Citing Bousset and Gressmann, Arnold states that the most probable retrojection of the text in Greek would be "*pneumata, stoicheia, angeloi.*"[76]

(3) Testament of Solomon. In T. Sol. 18, whose original form is alleged to date to the second century BC, στοιχεῖον "appears twice . . . to refer to the 36 astral decans which it also calls 'demons.'"[77] The spiritual identity of the στοιχεῖα is unmistakable. "We are thirty-six στοιχεῖα, the world rulers of the darkness of this age" (18.2).

d. Scholars Argue that Spirits and Angels Feature Significantly in Paul's "Apocalyptic" Worldview

Following Martyn, scholars argue that Paul was an "apocalyptic" early Jew and that his letters show the significant role that spirits and angels played in his worldview.[78] Paul foregrounds a two-age chronology in his letter to the Galatians (1.4), identifies angels as the arrangers of the law (3.19), and mentions angels in 1.8 and 4.14.

However, despite the widespread acceptance of these arguments, these scholars' conclusions far over-reach their evidence.

50   *1*

3. The Term Στοιχεῖον is Missing from Most of the Cited Texts

Lagercrantz's critique of Diels's argument applies as well to most later proponents of reading στοιχεῖον as spirit. "In den Belegen, . . . hören wir zwar von Engeln des Feuers, der Wasser, von Geistern des Himmels und der Erde, aber nichts von στοιχεῖα οὐράνια oder στοιχεῖα überhaupt."[79] In the texts cited in *a.* and *b.* above, στοιχεῖον appears in only two sources: Jubilees fragment a, whose early Jewish provenance is disputable, and Philo, who, though indisputably a first century Jew, never uses στοιχεῖον to refer to a spirit.

Table 1.2: Uses of Στοιχεῖον in Disputably Early Jewish Sources

Text	Sense	Dispute
1. Sib. Or. [2].206	Material: "air, earth, sea"	Second century[80]
2. *Ant.* 1.p	Material	Later descriptive heading[81]
3. Jub. frag. a.20	Indiscernible	Later summary introduction[82]
4. Jub. frag. a.113	Immaterial: letter	Later explanatory note?
5. T. Sol. 18.1	Spirit	Third or fourth century
6. T. Sol. 18.2	Spirit	Third or fourth century

4. Texts Containing Στοιχεῖον Attain First-Century Provenance Only by Conjecture

While στοιχεῖον may have a "rich tradition" of "widespread use . . . in pagan magic, astrology, and mystery cults," Arnold's data establish that tradition only to the third century.[83] He and others may allege a long, antecedent tradition of the term στοιχεῖον itself, but their hypothesis remains just that until confirmed by actual evidence from the first century or earlier. The same applies to the retrojection of the Slavonic *stikhii* to the Greek στοιχεῖα. Andersen himself is uncertain (1) whether *stikhii* refers to "angelic beings" or to "physical elements" and (2) "how close this is to the *stoikheia* of the NT."[84]

In scholarship on στοιχεῖον, T. Sol. 18.1, 2 is probably the most cited text outside scripture. The claim is simple: στοιχεῖον occurs in chapter 18, which circulated independently as early as the second century BC. The facts are rather more complex. Preisendanz, Daniel, and Schwarz suggest from external and internal evidence that 18.1–3 was not part of the oldest section: 18.4–40.[85] McCown, Gundel, and Duling suggest that the oldest section, written in Hebrew, was not translated into Greek until the third century.[86] Davila, Davies-Brown, and Schwarz question whether T. Sol. 18 is demonstrably Jewish.[87] And Busch says that it is not at all but rather "a genuinely Christian text from the 4th century."[88] In the end, the fragmented state of current scholarship cautions against using the paucity of ancient textual evidence as the

The Term "Στοιχεια Του Κοσμου" in Ancient Greek and Early Jewish Works 51

basis for arguing anything more than the slight possibility that some early Jews may have used στοιχεῖον to refer to stars or spirits.

5. Scholars who Interpret Galatians as "Apocalyptic" Identify the Στοιχεῖα as Material Elements

While angels play a significant role in Jewish thought and appear at key points in Galatians, associating στοιχεῖον with an angel does not identify στοιχεῖον as an angel. Philo describes angels at length within an elemental cosmology, but he never calls an angel a στοιχεῖον.[89] Further, Martyn and de Boer, the two leading "apocalyptic" commentators on Galatians, read στοιχεῖα τοῦ κόσμου as the material elements, not as spirits.[90]

On careful review, there is not a shred of actual evidence that στοιχεῖα τοῦ κόσμου in Gal 4 could have referred to spirits.[91] Yes, certainly Paul might have introduced a "novel" meaning of στοιχεῖον,[92] but *the data would require not only that Paul would have used στοιχεῖον with a new meaning but also that, apart from verbatim quotations of Galatians or Colossians, no one used the term again with that sense for 200 years.* And that is most improbable.

E. CONCLUSION

This chapter has shown that the στοιχεῖα τοῦ κόσμου in Galatians 4 and Colossians 2 must refer to the material elements: earth, water, air, and fire. It offers actual textual evidence that extends Blinzler's data and confirms his conclusions. It shows that ancient Greek and early Jewish sources can use the term στοιχεῖον to refer clearly to an immaterial or a material element and that early Jews integrate the concept of the material στοιχεῖα into a worldview grounded in Israel's scriptures. Finally, the chapter shows that Jews in the first century use the phrase στοιχεῖα κόσμου to refer unambiguously to the material elements of which the cosmos and its bodies are made.

Nevertheless Scott's objection remains: Blinzler's data are "convincing," but "neither this nor any other interpretation of the στοιχεῖα τοῦ κόσμου seems to satisfy the context" of Gal 4.[93] The pressing question is, in a letter to new believers, why in the world would Paul be bothered by earth, water, air, and fire?

NOTES

1. Delling, "Στοιχέω."

2. Wilhelm Bousset and H. Gressmann, *Die Religion des Judentums im Späthellenistischen Zeitalter*, 3d ed., Handbuch zum Neuen Testament 21 (Tübingen: Mohr, 1966); Betz, *Galatians*; Bruce, *Galatians*; F. F. Bruce, *Epistles to the Colossians, to*

52   *1*

Philemon and to the Ephesians, NICNT (Grand Rapids: Eerdmans, 1995); Wright, *Paul and the Faithfulness of God*, 382.

3. Delling, "Στοιχέω," 7:670–79. Delling's sequence agrees with Diels's in his landmark *Elementum* and with Burkert (Diels, *Elementum*, 14–24; Walter Burkert, "Στοιχεῖον. Eine semasiologische Studie," *Philologus* 103 (1959): 167–97). Otto Lagercrantz, *Elementum: Eine lexikologische Studie*, Skrifter utgifna af K. Humanistiska Vetenskaps-Samfundet i Uppsala XI.1 (Uppsala: Akademiska Bokhandeln, 1911), 3–38 and W. Vollgraff, "Elementum," *Mnemosyne* 2 (1949): 89–115 argue that στοιχεῖον came to mean "element" earlier on.

4. James Longrigg, "Elements and After: A Study in Presocratic Physics of the Second Half of the Fifth Century," *Apeiron: A Journal for Ancient Philosophy and Science* 19.2 (1985): 93.

5. "Contra Gallavotti in his edition, fragment 1, line 5" (Brad Inwood, ed., *The Poem of Empedocles*, revised ed., Phoenix Pre-Socratics 3 (Toronto: University of Toronto Press, 2001), 37 n. 80; see Carlo Gallavotti, *Empedocle: Poema Fisico e Lustrale* (Milan: Mondadori, 1975), 7).

6. Wigodsky thinks that Plato's words in *Tim.* 32b "confirm" Eudemus's assertion that Plato "was himself the first to call" "the elemental first principles (τὰς στοιχειώδεις ἀρχὰς) . . . στοιχεῖα" (fr. 31 Wehrli = Simpl. *in Phys.* 7.10–14; see Michael Wigodsky, "Homoiotetes, Stoicheia and Homoiomereiai in Epicurus," *The Classical Quarterly* 57 (2007): 525, followed by Leithart, *Delivered from the Elements of the World*, 31). However, of the 65 times lemma στοιχεῖον occurs in Plato's extant corpus, none refers to earth, water, air, or fire as a material component (see Delling, "Στοιχέω," 7:673). See, e.g., 25 occurrences in *Theat.* 201e–208c.

7. Edward Adams, "Graeco-Roman and Ancient Jewish Cosmology," in *Graeco-Roman and Ancient Jewish Cosmology*, ed. Jonathan T. Pennington and Sean M. McDonough, LNTS 355, ed. Mark Goodacre (London: T&T Clark, 2008), 9. Properly speaking, the στοιχεῖα are the two triangles that compose the solid forms of earth, water, air, and fire (*Tim.* 54d, 55b) (see further D. R. Lloyd, "Symmetry and Asymmetry in the Construction of 'Elements' in the Timaeus," *The Classical Quarterly* 56 (2006): 459–74).

8. Timothy J. Crowley, "Aristotle's 'So-Called Elements,'" *Phronesis* 53 (2008): 242, https://doi.org/10.1163/156852808X307061.

9. I leave untranslated all uses of στοιχεῖον in ancient sources. Remaining references to "element" in English translations of ancient sources usually express the antecedent reference of τό, as in definition *c*, or of αὐτό, τουτό, etc. Sometimes this protocol requires changing *an element* to *a στοιχεῖον*, as in *d*.

10. Lagercrantz, *Elementum: Eine lexikologische Studie*, 18.

11. Blinzler, "Lexicalisches," 431.

12. John M. G. Barclay, *Jews in the Mediterranean Diaspora: From Alexander to Trajan (323 BCE – 117 CE)* (Edinburgh: T&T Clark, 1996) describes "assimilation" as "social integration (becoming 'similar' to one's neighbours)" (92). He contrasts this with acculturation, which relates to the "linguistic, educational and ideological aspects of a given cultural matrix" (92).

The Term "Στοιχεῖα Τοῦ Κόσμου" in Ancient Greek and Early Jewish Works 53

13. John J. Collins, "Sibylline Oracles," in *The Old Testament Pseudepigrapha*, ed. James H. Charlesworth (Peabody, MA: Hendrickson, 1983), 430–32 calls the dating "tentative."

14. Similarly, in the only occurrence of στοιχεῖον in extant Egyptian papyri from before AD 200—στοιχ(είου) ε κολ(λήματος) ιζ (BGU 3.959)—στοιχεῖον refers to the serial number (17) of a papyrus roll.

15. Collins, "Sibylline Oracles," *OTP*, 390 considers Sib. Or. 5 Jewish, but James R. Davila, *The Provenance of the Pseudepigrapha: Jewish, Christian, or Other?*, JSJSup 105 (Leiden: Brill, 2005), 186–89 assesses the data as inconclusive: the author may be a Jew, a Jewish-Christian, or "a devout gentile God-fearer." Davila, *Provenance of the Pseudepigrapha*, 186–89; Collins, "Sibylline Oracles," *OTP*, 390.

16. From this sense of στοιχεῖον the cognates στοιχείωσις, στοιχειώδης, and ἀστοιχείωτος get their "elementary" sense (*Spec. Laws* 2.177; *Agriculture* 140, 181; *Planting* 52; *Heir* 102).

17. Contra Delling's assertion that in Philo "the main ref. is to spoken parts of words" (Delling, "Στοιχέω," 7:671); see Blinzler, "Lexicalisches"; Rusam, "Neue Belege."

18. Philo discusses the elements at great length in Questions and Answers. However, Q & A survives as a whole only in an Armenian translation of the Greek original, of which only fragments remain. Marcus is confident that his proposed reconstructions of various Armenian terms are "probably correct," but I do not cite instances of στοιχεῖον in his reconstructed Greek text, and I refer to Q & A only for significant conceptual insights (Ralph Marcus, ed., *Philo*, Loeb Classical Library (London: Heinemann, 1953), supplement 1:vi).

19. See also the four ῥίζαι in *Planting* 120. Van Kooten notes that δυνάμεις can "denote the *qualities* of the four elements, i.e., the forces (δυνάμεις) dry, wet, cold, and hot" (Geurt H. van Kooten, *Cosmic Christology in Paul and the Pauline School: Colossians and Ephesians in the Context of Graeco-Roman Cosmology, with a New Synopsis of the Greek Texts*, WUNT 2.171 (Tübingen: Mohr Siebeck, 2003), 102, emphasis his). See *Heir* 152–153; *Sacrifices* 108; *Eternity* 21.

20. Gareth Lee Cockerill, *The Epistle to the Hebrews*, NICNT (Grand Rapids: Eerdmans, 2012), 256. For arguments about the term's referent and about advancement through a Greek or Jewish pedagogical sequence see Harold W. Attridge, *The Epistle to the Hebrews: A Commentary on the Epistle to the Hebrews*, Hermeneia, ed. Helmut Koester (Philadelphia: Fortress, 1989), 162; William L. Lane, *Hebrews 1–8*, WBC 47A (Dallas: Word, 1991), 137; Craig R. Koester, *Hebrews: A New Translation with Introduction and Commentary*, AB 36 (New York: Doubleday, 2001), 308–9; Peter T. O'Brien, *The Letter to the Hebrews*, PNTC (Grand Rapids: Eerdmans, 2010), 207–8, 212 n. 10; Cockerill, *The Epistle to the Hebrews*, 257 n. 15.

21. Most recent scholars follow David Winston, ed., *The Wisdom of Solomon: A New Translation with Introduction and Commentary*, AB 43 (Garden City, NY: Doubleday, 1979), 3, 20–25; "Solomon, Wisdom of," *ABD* 6:120–23. However, Davila, *Provenance of the Pseudepigrapha*, 218–25, 230–35, is wary. While Wisdom is "fairly likely to be of Jewish origin," it could have been written "by a Hellenistic

54

Jew, a God-fearer, or a Jewish Christian any time in the Hellenistic period up to the second half of the first century" (225, 234).

22. Winston, *The Wisdom of Solomon*, 63.

23. Randall D. Chesnutt, "Solomon, Wisdom of," *EDEJ*, 1242.

24. See Susan Brayford, *Genesis*, Septuagint Commentary (Leiden: Brill, 2007), 225. Κόσμος refers to the ordered parts of the heavens and the earth in six places in the OG; in five of those it stands for צבא (Gen 2.1; Deut 4.19; 17.3; Isa 24.21; 40.26; Isa 13.10.).

25. Michael Kolarcik, "The Book of Wisdom: Introduction, Commentary, and Reflections," in *The New Interpreter's Bible* (Nashville: Abingdon, 2000), 502.

26. Winston, *The Wisdom of Solomon*, 173–74.

27. Kolarcik, "Wisdom," 598 traces the analogy of cosmic order and musical harmony to Plato, Aristotle, the Pythagoreans, and others. See Plato, *Resp.* 7.12, 530d; Aristotle, *Metaph.* 1.5, 986a.

28. Winston, *The Wisdom of Solomon*, 3, 59–63; see Kolarcik, "Wisdom," 439.

29. Chesnutt, "Solomon, Wisdom Of," 1244.

30. Louis H. Feldman, "Josephus Flavius," *Encyclopedia of the Dead Sea Scrolls* 1:427–31.

31. Philo expresses similar ambiguity, but with subtler complexity, in his discussion of the causation of natural events. See *Providence* 2.45, 53 in chapter 4 below.

32. Scholarly consensus agrees that 3.1–92 are a later addition to the main corpus of Sib. Or. 3 (John J. Collins, "Sibylline Oracles," *ABD* 6:4; Rieuwerd Buitenwerf, *Book III of the Sibylline Oracles and Its Social Setting: With an Introduction, Translation, and Commentary*, SVTP 17 (Leiden: Brill, 2003), 134, 387; Davila, *Provenance of the Pseudepigrapha*, 182; Lorenzo DiTommaso, "Sibylline Oracles," *EDEJ*, 1227). Collins, "Sibylline Oracles," *OTP*, 360–61 places lines 46–62 + 75–92 after the Battle of Actium in 31 BC. Against Collins, Jane L. Lightfoot, ed., *The Sibylline Oracles: With Introduction, Translation, and Commentary on the First and Second Books* (Oxford: Oxford University Press, 2007), 484 suggests that 3.84–87 is similar to Sib. Or. 2.194–213 and may also be a Christian composition.

33. Lightfoot, *The Sibylline Oracles*, 487, citing Richard Bauckham, *Jude, 2 Peter*, WBC 50 (Waco: Word Books, 1983), 315–16.

34. Sib. Or. 2.196–213 uses very similar terms to foretell a similar fiery judgment. However, Lightfoot has convinced me that Sib. Or. 1–2 was "through-composed" by "a Christian living in the second century AD or later" (Lightfoot, *The Sibylline Oracles*, 149–50). Thus I consider Sib. Or. 1–2 only secondarily pertinent to exhibiting an early Jewish use of the term and concept στοιχεῖον with which Paul might be familiar.

35. See Brayford, *Genesis*, 209, 215, citing William P. Brown, *Structure, Role, and Ideology in the Hebrew and Greek Texts of Genesis 1:1–2:3*, SBLDS, ed. David L. Petersen (Atlanta: Scholars, 1993), 36–37; and see Richard Bauckham, "Humans, Animals and the Environment in Genesis 1–3," in *Genesis and Christian Theology*, ed. Nathan MacDonald, Mark W. Elliott, and Grant Macaskill (Grand Rapids: Eerdmans, 2012), 176–77. In the Allegory, Philo catalogues creatures in five στοιχειώδη μέρη: earth, sea, fire ("fire-born" creatures, "which are said to be found especially in

The Term *"Στοιχεια Του Κοσμου"* in Ancient Greek and Early Jewish Works   55

Macedonia"), air (birds and angels), and heaven (stars) (*Giants* 6–7, 16, 22; *Planting* 12, 14; *Dreams* 1.137).

36. See Lev 11; Deut 14.4–20; G. Geoffrey Harper, "Time for a New Diet? Allusions to Genesis 1–3 as Rhetorical Device in Leviticus 11" (SBL International Meeting St Andrews, Scotland, 2013); and chapter 3 below.

37. I presented this argument in a paper, with Bauckham attending (Ernest P. Clark, "'What Sort of Persons Ought You to Be?': Early Christian Identity and the Dissolution of the Elements in 2 Peter" (Muted Voices, University of Durham, 2015)). For Bauckham's response, see n. 50.

38. Bauckham, *Jude, 2 Peter*, 132, 159–62; see Kevin B. McCruden, "2 Peter and Jude," *The Blackwell Companion to the New Testament*, 599, 609. However, Gene L. Green, *Jude and 2 Peter*, BECNT (Grand Rapids: Baker, 2008), 149 observes, "2 Peter does not follow the conventions of the testamentary genre and is quite dissimilar to known testaments" (see 165–66; cf. Jerome H. Neyrey, ed., *2 Peter, Jude: A New Translation with Introduction and Commentary*, AB 37C (New York: Doubleday, 1993), 111). Ellis and Moo have argued for composition in the early 60s (E. Earle Ellis, *History and Interpretation in New Testament Perspective*, Biblical Interpretation 54 (Leiden: Brill, 2001), 51 n. 82; Douglas J. Moo, *2 Peter and Jude*, NIVAC (Grand Rapids: Zondervan, 1996), 24–25).

39. Bauckham, *Jude, 2 Peter*, 315–16; Pieter W. van der Horst, "'The Elements Will Be Dissolved with Fire': The Idea of Cosmic Conflagration in Hellenism, Ancient Judaism, and Early Christianity," in *Hellenism, Judaism, Christianity: Essays on Their Interaction*, 2d enlarged ed., Contributions to Biblical Exegesis and Theology 8 (Leuven, Belgium: Peeters, 1998), 288; Peter H. Davids, *The Letters of 2 Peter and Jude*, PNTC (Grand Rapids: Eerdmans, 2006), 283–86; Duane F. Watson, "Comparing Two Related Methods: Rhetorical Criticism and Socio-Rhetorical Interpretation Applied to Second Peter," in *Reading Second Peter with New Eyes: Methodological Reassessments of the Letter of Second Peter*, ed. Robert L. Webb and Duane F. Watson, LNTS 382 (London; New York: T & T Clark, 2010), 48–49; see ESV, NET.

40. Anders Gerdmar, *Rethinking the Judaism-Hellenism Dichotomy: A Historiographical Study of Second Peter and Jude*, Coniectanea Biblica 36 (Stockholm: Almqvist & Wiksell International, 2001), 180; Ryan P. Juza, "Echoes of Sodom and Gomorrah on the Day of the Lord: Intertextuality and Tradition in 2 Peter 3:7–13," in *Emerging Scholarship on the New Testament* (IBR Annual Meeting, Chicago, 2012), ibr-bbr.org/files/pdf/2012/Juza_Echoes_Day_IBR_Emerging_NT_2012.pdf.

41. Neyrey, *2 Peter, Jude*, 243; Edward Adams, *The Stars Will Fall from Heaven: Cosmic Catastrophe in the New Testament and Its World*, LNTS 347, ed. Mark Goodacre (London: T&T Clark, 2007), 223; Green, *Jude and 2 Peter*, 330.

42. Adams, *Stars Will Fall*, 223.

43. Green, *Jude and 2 Peter*, 329–30; see Adams, *Stars Will Fall*, 207 n. 30.

44. Here I follow most scholars and English translations in preferring the reading in NA27 (cf. SBLGNT) (εὑρεθήσεται) to that in NA28 (οὐχ εὑρεθήσεται). See Bauckham 1983, 320; Davids 2006, 286–87, for this interpretation.

45. Adams, *Stars Will Fall*, 228–29.

46. NETS; Bauckham 1983, 304–5, 315–16. See van der Horst, "Elements Will Be Dissolved"; Gerdmar, *Rethinking the Judaism-Hellenism Dichotomy*; Green, *Jude and 2 Peter*; Juza, "Echoes of Sodom."

47. Neyrey, *2 Peter, Jude*, 132, 241; see Green, *Jude and 2 Peter*, 323.

48. Adams, *Stars Will Fall*, 211–16.

49. Bauckham, *Jude, 2 Peter*, 297.

50. I have found no scholar who observes these data. See ἐκπύρωσις in *Eternity* 4, 9, 47, 54, 76, 77, 82, 87, 88, 89, 90, 95, 99, 104, 105, 107, and ἀναλύω in 6, 8, 85, 87, 99, 102, 105, 107. Scholars have also failed to observe (1) that the key verbs in 2 Peter (καυσόω, πυρόω, τήκω) and in the Oracles (φλέγω, ῥέω, χωνεύω) differ from each other, and (2) that they are rare in Philo's discussion of the conflagration (*Eternity* 88, 110). In conversation following Clark, "What Sort of Persons Ought You to Be?," Bauckham suggested that the poetic meter of the Oracles may have constrained the Sibyls' word choice.

51. Blinzler, "Lexicalisches," 439–40.

52. See also Philo's reference to the three lines in the immaterial στοιχεῖον I (*Eternity* 113) in the midst of references to the material στοιχεῖα in *Eternity* 103, 107, 109, 111, 116.

53. I use "spiritual" to refer to the interpretation of στοιχεῖα (κόσμου) as spirits, whether elemental or otherwise.

54. Thus BAGD more than BDAG.

55. Blinzler, "Lexicalisches," 436.

56. Delling, "Στοιχέω," 7:682 n. 84, criticizing Lawrence E. Scheu, *Die "Weltelemente" beim Apostel Paulus (Gal. 4,3.9 und Kol. 2,8.20)*, Universitas Catholica Americae 37 (Washington: Catholic University of America, 1933), 52. For another example see Clinton Arnold, *The Colossian Syncretism: The Interface Between Christianity and Folk Belief at Colossae*, WUNT 2/77 (Tübingen: Mohr Siebeck, 1995), 179.

57. BDAG 946.

58. James D. G. Dunn, *The Epistle to the Galatians*, BNTC (London: A & C Black, 1993), 212–13.

59. For "shadowy," see Wright, *Paul and the Faithfulness of God*, 480.

60. Blinzler, "Lexicalisches"; Rusam, "Neue Belege."

61. Other, very relevant, evidence are the two uses of στοιχεῖα τοῦ κόσμου in Col 2.8, 20. This study prioritizes a careful analysis of the term and the concept στοιχεῖα (κόσμου) in the Mediterranean world before Paul, a thorough review of the philosophy within which Philo used the term, and a sensitive reading of Paul's use of the term in his letter to the Galatians. Consistent diligence in these tasks will inform later interpretation of the use of the term in the argument of Colossians.

62. See στοιχεῖον further in *Heir* 197, 226 (thrice), 227.

63. Carr, *Angels and Principalities*; Wink, *Naming the Powers*; Belleville, "Under Law"; Fung, *Galatians*; Moore-Crispin, "Galatians 4:1–9: The Use and Abuse of Parallels"; Longenecker, *Galatians*; Bundrick, "Ta Stoicheia tou Kosmou (Gal. 4:3)"; Matera, *Galatians*; Witherington, *Grace in Galatia*; Witherington, *Colossians*; Thompson, *Colossians and Philemon*.

The Term *"Στοιχεῖα Τοῦ Κοσμου"* in Ancient Greek and Early Jewish Works   57

64. See Oepke, *Galater*; Sanders, *Paul and Palestinian Judaism*; Betz, *Galatians*; Bruce, *Galatians*; Cousar, *Galatians*; Krentz, *Galatians, Philippians, Philemon, 1 Thessalonians*; Hübner, "Paulusforschung"; Rohde, *Der Brief des Paulus an Die Galater*; Becker, *Paul*; Hong, *The Law in Galatians*; Longenecker, *Abraham's God*; Schreiner, *Galatians*; Wright, *Paul and the Faithfulness of God*; Moses, *Practices of Power*.

65. The earliest such use I have found is Origen, *Hom. Jer.* 10.6 in about 240.

66. Blinzler, "Lexicalisches," 433; LSJ.

67. Delling, "Στοιχέω," 7:681.

68. Ritschl, *Rechtfertigung und Versöhnung*, vol. 2: Der biblische Stoff der Lehre; Everling, *Angelologie und Dämonologie*.

69. Arnold, *Colossian Syncretism*, 179.

70. See George W. E. Nickelsburg and James C. VanderKam, *1 Enoch 2: A Commentary on the Book of 1 Enoch Chapters 37–82*, ed. Klaus Baltzer, Hermeneia (Minneapolis: Fortress, 2012), 403.

71. Reading 4QDtj's אלוהים בני against MT's ישראל בני. See Michael S. Heiser, "Deuteronomy 32:8 and the Sons of God," *BSac* 158 (2001): 52–74; Longenecker, *Abraham's God*, 51.

72. Clinton Arnold, "Returning to the Domain of the Powers: 'Stoicheia' as Evil Spirits in Galatians 4:3,9," *NovT* 38 (1996): 57–58.

73. Arnold, *Colossian Syncretism*, 170.

74. Arnold, *Colossian Syncretism*, 173.

75. C. Böttrich, *Weltweisheit, Menschheitsethik, Urkult: Studien zum Slavischen Henochbuch*, WUNT 2/50 (Tübingen: Mohr, 1992), 52; Arnold, "Powers," 59.

76. Bousset and Gressmann, *Religion des Judentums*, 323; Arnold, "Powers," 59.

77. Arnold, "Powers," 58; see Wilhelm Gundel, *Dekane und Dekansternbilder: Ein Beitrag zur Geschichte der Sternbilder der Kultervölker*, Studien Der Bibliothek Warburg 19 (Glückstadt und Hamburg: J. J. Augustin, 1969), 45, 56–57; Todd Klutz, *Rewriting the Testament of Solomon: Tradition, Conflict, and Identity in a Late Antique Pseudepigraphon*, Library of Second Temple Studies 53 (London: T&T Clark, 2006), 109.

78. See Martyn, *Galatians*, 97–105.

79. Lagercrantz, *Elementum: Eine lexikologische Studie*, 44.

80. See n. 34 above.

81. Eusebius includes a prologue to Joesphus's *Ant*. Few, if any, scholars regard "*Ant*. 1.p" as original to Josephus, but Blinzler counts its mention of the στοιχεῖα as one of Josephus's four uses of στοιχεῖον (Josef Blinzler, "Lexicalisches zu dem Terminus τὰ στοιχεῖα τοῦ κόσμου bei Paulus," in *Studiorum Paulinorum Congressus Internationalis Catholicus 1961: simul Secundus Congressus Internationalis Catholicus de Re Biblica: completo undevicesimo saeculo post S. Pauli in urbem adventum*, vol. 2 of *Analecta biblica* 17–18 (Rome: Pontifical Biblical Institute, 1963), 440).

82. Lines 1–23 of Jub. frag. *a* seem to be an introduction, summarizing the work as a whole. Denis notes points of correspondence between frag. *a* and the better preserved Ge'ez translation of the Greek text. The topics, but not the terms, mentioned in lines 1–23 correspond, in this order, to Jub. 48.1; 2.1, 14; 5.20; 10.24; 1.1; 2.8; 4.17.

The reference to the angel Gabriel teaching Moses about τὰ στοιχεῖα comes in line 20. However, beginning with line 24, the words correspond quite closely with Jub. 2.2–20 in Wintermute's *OTP* translation from the Ge'ez. Lines 1–23 thus appear to be a summary introduction appended to Jub. 2 by a later editor. This reconstruction coheres with Segal's assessment of Jubilees manuscripts: "no direct Greek textual evidence is known today" (Michael Segal, "Jubilees, Book Of," *The Eerdmans Dictionary of Early Judaism*, 844).

83. Arnold, *Colossian Syncretism*, 184, 189.

84. F. I. Andersen, "2 (Slavonic Apocalypse of) Enoch," in *OTP*, 1:104.

85. K. Preisendanz, "Ein Wiener Papyrusfragment zum Testamentum Salomonis," *Eos* 48 (1956): 162–64; Robert W. Daniel, "The Testament of Solomon XVIII 27–28, 33–40," in *Festschrift zum 100-Jährigen Bestehen der Papyrussammlung der Öster-reichische Nationalbibliothek: Papyrus Erzeherzog Rainer* (Vienna: Brüder Holinek, 1983), 294–95; Sarah L. Schwarz, "Demons and Douglas: Applying Grid and Group to the Demonologies of the Testament of Solomon," *JAAR* (2012): 15 n. 19, https://doi.org/10.1093/jaarel/lfs072.

86. C. C. McCown, *The Testament of Solomon* (Leipzig: Hinrichs, 1922); Gundel, *Dekane und Dekansternbilder*, 56; Dennis C. Duling, "Testament of Solomon," in *OTP*, 1:941–42.

87. Davies-Browne, "The Significance of Parallels," 14, 230–31; Davila, *Provenance of the Pseudepigrapha*, 20, 61, 65–69; Sarah L. Schwarz, "Reconsidering the Testament of Solomon," *JSP* 16 (2007): 233–37, https://doi.org/10.1177/0951820707077166; Schwarz, "Demons and Douglas," 14.

88. Peter Busch, *Das Testament Salomos. Die älteste christliche Dämonologie, kommentiert und in deutscher Erstübersetzung*, TUGAL 153 (Berlin: de Gruyter, 2006).

89. Contra Gregory E. Sterling, "A Philosophy according to the Elements of the Cosmos: Colossian Christianity and Philo of Alexandria," in *Philon d'Alexandrie et le langage de la philosophie: actes du colloque international organisé par le Centre d'études sur la philosophie hellénistique et romaine de l'Université de Paris XII-Val de Marne (Créteil, Fontenay, Paris, 26–28 octobre 1995)*, ed. Carlos Lévy, Monothéismes et philosophie (Turnhout: Brepols, 1998), 349–73. See chapter 3.

90. Martyn, *Galatians*, 393–405; de Boer, *Galatians*, 253–56.

91. Walter Wink, "The 'Elements of the Universe' in Biblical and Scientific Perspective," *Zygon* 13.3 (1978): 226–27.

92. So Charles H. Cosgrove, *The Cross and the Spirit: A Study in the Argument and Theology of Galatians* (Sweet & Maxwell, 1988), 76, citing Delling, "Στοιχέω," 7:685.

93. James Scott, *Adoption as Sons of God*, WUNT 2/48 (Tübingen: Mohr, 1992), 159–60.

2

The Concept of Enslavement under "Στοιχεια Του Κοσμου" in Ancient Greek and Early Jewish Works

Chapter 1 examined the term στοιχεῖα (τοῦ κόσμου) in ancient Greek and early Jewish works. It showed that the στοιχεῖα τοῦ κόσμου in Gal 4.3 must refer to the material elements: earth, water, air, and fire. But it left the real question unanswered: what is it about earth, water, air, and fire that bothers Paul? What concepts do Greek-speakers in the first century associate with the material elements? And how could lifeless substances that Paul calls "weak" enslave anyone (Gal 4.3, 9)?

The answer to this question lies in Greek medical discourse. For Greek thinkers since Empedocles, for Philo, and, I argue, for Paul, the material elements compose and compromise the human body. That is *what*—and importantly, *where*—the στοιχεῖα τοῦ κόσμου are and *why* Paul is so concerned about them.

But the medical tradition in Greek philosophy is almost entirely overlooked by biblical scholars. Philipp Vielhauer and Hans Dieter Betz recognize that the elements compose the body.[1] Gerhard Delling says straight out: "a man of NT days would take στοιχεῖα τοῦ κόσμου to refer to the 'basic materials' of which everything in the cosmos, including man, is composed."[2] Andrew Bandstra identifies the στοιχεῖα τοῦ κόσμου as "the Law and the Flesh," but he, like Richard Longenecker and Peter Leithart, construes the σάρξ as an ethical concept, not a substantial reality.[3] Eduard Schweizer and Louis Martyn cite Greek "medical and philosophical thought" and Philo for the idea that the πάθη, ἐπιθυμίαι, and ἔργα τῆς σαρκός are physical processes of the flesh that affect the person (*Spec. Laws* 4.79).[4] Troy Martin argues that "ancient medical texts . . . provide a productively coherent context in which to read Paul's statements about the Spirit."[5] And Emma Wassermann examines

59

60   *2*

Rom 7 from the perspective of Greek psychology.[6] But no one joins these dots up to show that Paul's picture of the στοιχεῖα and the σάρξ is readily recognizable from the perspective of Greek medical discourse. The material στοιχεῖα τοῦ κόσμου (4.3) are the miserable στοιχεῖα (4.9) that compose and weaken the σάρξ (4.13) by mediating the παθήματα, ἐπιθυμίαι, and ἔργα τῆς σαρκός (5.16–24) through which sin enslaves the person (3.19–4.3).

That summary of Paul's theology of the στοιχεῖα τοῦ κόσμου may leave some modern readers scratching their heads in bewilderment, but many ancient writers would simply nod their heads and say, "Well then, Paul, what regimen or νόμος will you prescribe as a παιδαγωγός to address this slavery under the στοιχεῖα?"

To make sense of that summary statement, chapter 2 traces the concept of enslavement to the elements through Greek and Jewish works from Empedocles and Plato through Philo and early Christian writers to Galen. The texts will show (a) that the material στοιχεῖα compose human bodies; (b) that the material στοιχεῖα compromise the body and enslave the person by mediating the παθήματα, ἐπιθυμίαι, and ἔργα τῆς σαρκός; and (c) that a regimen (or νόμος) of nourishment and exercise for body and soul can work as a sort of παιδαγωγός to rehabilitate the person. Chapter 4 will show that Paul agrees with Israel's scriptures and some early Jewish writings on point *a* and shares their concern about point *b*. Indeed, analyzing the flesh at the elemental level may help Paul explain how the weak σάρξ becomes a wicked σάρξ. However, chapter 5 argues that Paul differs strongly with those who, as chapter 3 will show from Philo, propose that careful practice of the law of Moses can redeem people from such enslavement.[7] Rather, as chapter 6 demonstrates, Paul uses the phrase στοιχεῖα τοῦ κόσμου to engage philosophical ideas about the body and human behavior in order to present God's Son and his Spirit as the only effective cure for the common human disease.

We will take the argument one premise at a time. First, the material στοιχεῖα compose human bodies.

A. THE MATERIAL ΣΤΟΙΧΕΙΑ
COMPOSE HUMAN BODIES

1. The Four-Element Theory Always Identifies the Cosmic Elements as the Material Components of the Human Body

Right from the beginning, when the "four-element theory" makes its first appearance in Empedocles's poem, discussions about the four elements of the cosmos lead as a matter of course into descriptions of those same elements as

The Concept of Enslavement under *"Στοιχεῖα Τοῦ Κοσμου"* 61

the components of the human body. The connection is direct and simple: the human body and the cosmos are made of the same stuff—earth, water, air, and fire. Empedocles, Plato, the Hippocratic Corpus, and Aristotle all subscribe to this concept.[8]

a. Empedocles

Empedocles writes his poem as a philosopher and as a medical practitioner. He narrates the formation of sun, earth, moon, wind, rain, and sea and then describes in similar terms the blending of mortals from the same elements.[9]

> Pleasant earth in her well-built channels
> received two parts of gleaming Nestis out of the eight
> and four of Hephaistos; and they become white bones
> fitted together with the divine glues of harmony. (62/96)[10]
> From the blending of water and earth and aither and sun
> the forms and colours of [all the] mortals came to be. (74/71)

Empedocles sees the four elements of the cosmos as the elements in the human body, and, according to James Longrigg, that insight helps him explain how the human body works.[11]

b. The Hippocratic Corpus

Similarly, the Hippocratic tradition, which accreted to the legacy of Hippocrates (c. 460–c. 370 BC), finds the causes of health and disease in the relative mixture of the elements in and around a body. *The Nature of Man* denies that the human person is made entirely of "air, or fire, or water, or earth" (1). Rather, "each of the elements contributing to his formation preserves in the body the power (δύναμις) which it contributed" (3). These δυνάμεις—"heat, cold, dryness and moisture"—combine to form the four humors: "blood, phlegm, yellow bile and black bile" (4–5). A body is healthy when "these constituent substances are in the correct proportion to each other, both in strength (δυνάμιος) and quantity, and are well mixed. Pain occurs when one of the substances presents either a deficiency or an excess, or is separated in the body and not mixed with the others" (4). Like the body, "the year has its share of all the elements: heat, cold, dryness and wetness" (7). Thus, meteorology and astronomy play "a very important part in medicine since the changes of the seasons produce changes in diseases" (*Aër.* 2). So too the qualities of air, water, and land in a place affect the health of elemental human bodies.

c. Plato

Plato details the elemental anatomy and physiology of the human body in *Timaeus*, arguably "the most important philosophical text of antiquity."[12] After the creator makes the cosmos from all that is of earth, water, air, and fire (32b–c), he charges the gods to make mortals. "They took the immortal principle of the mortal living creature, and imitating their own Maker, they borrowed from the κόσμος portions of fire and earth and water and air, . . . and the portions so taken they cemented together" (42e–43a).

However, one implication of the body's composition from the cosmic elements is the susceptibility of the elements inside the body to the effects of the same elements outside the body. "When heat and cold, and all things which have violent potencies (δυνάμεις) surround a composite body from without and collide with it they dissolve it unduly and make it to waste away by bringing upon it ailments and age" (33a). When earth, water, air, or fire collides with a creature's body—as, for example, when nourishment enters the body—the παθήματα (or stimuli) cause motions that "rush through the body" and "impinge upon the Soul" as "sensations" or αἰσθήσεις (43c). These παθήματα cause each of the four kinds within the body to change places (57c). The interchanges of the elements, then, along with excess or deficiency of the elements, cause "countless diseases and corruptions" (82b).

> The origin of disease is plain, of course, to everybody. For seeing that there are four elements of which the body is compacted,—earth, fire, water and air,— when, contrary to nature, there occurs either an excess or a deficiency of these elements, or a transference thereof, . . . then these and all similar occurrences bring about internal disorders and disease. (82a)

Thus, centuries before Paul, in "the only Greek prose work that . . . every educated man could be assumed to have read,"[13] Plato makes two concepts clear: (1) the human body is made of the same four things that compose the cosmos, and (2) the body's elemental composition makes it susceptible to παθήματα which cause disease.

d. Aristotle

Like Plato, Aristotle identifies reciprocal activity and susceptibility as essential to the nature of the στοιχεῖα. "But the 'στοιχεῖα' must be reciprocally active and susceptible (ποιητικὰ καὶ παθητικά), since they 'combine' and are transformed into one another" (*Gen. corr.* 2.2, 329b).

N. T. Wright is correct to say that Stoics in the first century would view themselves as "creatures composed, as is the whole world, of a mixture of the elements."[14] But our review of sources suggests that many, many other

The Concept of Enslavement under "Στοιχεῖα Τοῦ Κοσμου"   63

Greek-speakers would think the same. By Paul's day, the composition of the human body from the four cosmic elements had been established and accepted within Greek philosophies for half a millennium. Ancient texts available to us suggest that Greek-speakers in the first century would read "στοιχεῖα τοῦ κόσμου" naturally and easily as earth, water, air, and fire, the material components of the cosmos and its bodies. They would be no less likely to think of those elements in the human body than in the stars. And, as the late first- or early second-century medical notebook *Anonymus Londinensis* shows, many would know that doctors diagnosed and treated diseases of body and soul with reference to the four στοιχεῖα (see 4.20–21.9).

2. Early Jews Used √Στοιχεω to Express the Hebrew Concept that God Made Humans from Earth

Though many scholars seem to think that the Greek term στοιχεῖον fits awkwardly within a Jewish worldview, early Jewish sources find in √στοιχεω a set of terms that convey naturally in Greek a concept from the foundational chapters of the Hebrew scriptures: the elemental composition of the human body. The scriptural background for this concept is evident in 2 Maccabees and Philo, and the concept itself is present in Paul, Josephus, and 4 Maccabees.

a. 2 Maccabees

The first nominal occurrence of στοιχεω in a Jewish source is στοιχεῖωσις in 2 Maccabees.[15] Alluding to Gen 2, the martyrs' mother states that the Creator made her sons' bodies from the element earth. Speaking "in the language of their ancestors," she encourages her sons:

> A It was not I who gave you life and breath,
>> B nor I who set in order the στοιχεῖωσις within each of you.
>> B' Therefore the Creator of the world, who shaped the beginning of humankind (ὁ πλάσας ἀνθρώπου γένεσιν) and devised the γένεσις of all things,
> A' will in his mercy give life and breath back to you again. (7.22–23 NRSV)

The meaning of στοιχεῖωσις in this context is obscure. LSJ's "teaching; elementary exposition" (cf. *Agriculture* 140) won't fit. And translations since the Vulgate have rendered στοιχεῖωσιν as plural, *membra*, perhaps following στοιχεῖα in the retelling in 4 Macc 12.[16]

However, read side by side with Gen 2.7, the passage's chiastic structure identifies the sons' στοιχεῖωσις as the earth from which their bodies were formed. Lines A and A' repeat the phrase τὸ πνεῦμα καὶ τὴν ζωὴν (life and

64   2

breath), which van Henten traces to Gen 2.7.[17] There the second line reads, "God . . . breathed into his face πνοὴν ζωῆς, καὶ ἐγένετο ὁ ἄνθρωπος εἰς ψυχὴν ζῶσαν" (NETS). While the phrase is not identical with 2 Macc 7.22, the terms and the concept are remarkably similar. In the same way, lines B and B' repeat the idea of God arranging στοιχείωσις and shaping (πλάσσω) ἄνθρωπος. These two terms are present in the first line of Gen 2.7 (ἔπλασεν ὁ θεὸς τὸν ἄνθρωπον χοῦν ἀπὸ τῆς γῆς). Further, the narrator's reference to earth and sea in 2 Macc 5.21—Antiochus thought "in his arrogance that he could sail on the land and walk on the sea" (NRSV)—suggests that he would identify Gen 2's γῆ as a στοιχεῖον. These data imply what scholars have not yet observed: when 2 Maccabees uses the term στοιχείωσις it is referring to earth, from which God shaped the first human, and air, by which God made him alive.

This observation implies that Greek discourse may have offered this Jewish writer terms and concepts appropriate for conveying the scriptural concept that humans are made of one or several elements. As Wright might say, "Here, in a book which we know to have been in circulation in the first century, is a powerful statement of one regular form of the Jewish world-view": אדם is made from the element אדמה.[18]

b. Philo

Within his program of reading Moses through Plato, Philo explains that humans, like all creatures, are compounds of the cosmic στοιχεῖα and there-fore susceptible to weakness. Following his Exposition of Gen 1–2, and with clear allusions to *Tim.* 42e–43a, Philo describes the human body as "a com-pound made from the same things" as "the entire κόσμος": "earth and water and air and fire, each of the στοιχεῖα making the required contribution for the completion of an entirely sufficient material" (*Creation* 146).[19] He says much the same in a philosophical and an apologetic treatise (*Eternity* 29; *Contempl. Life* 4). In the Allegory, which appears to have a high view of the στοιχεῖα and a low view of the human body, Philo describes the first man Adam as simply "moulded out of the earth" (*Planting* 34; *Dreams* 2.70). Philo also describes death in elemental terms, specifically as dissolution (ἀναστοιχειόω) (*Posterity* 5; *Migration* 3; *Heir* 29, 282; see Gen 18.27).

For Philo, human composition from the elements has physiological and ethical implications. First, the physiological implications: elemental compo-sition makes humans susceptible to physical weakness. Since the στοιχεῖα from which the cosmos was formed are associated with powers "which produce ἀσθένειαι" (*Eternity* 74), creatures compounded from the elements are susceptible to ἀσθένεια (*Spec. Laws* 1.294).[20] Indeed, creatures of earth and water "are naturally liable to far greater ἀσθένεια than the creatures of

The Concept of Enslavement under "Στοιχεῖα Τοῦ Κόσμου" 65

the upper world, since they in largest measure partake of the lowest form of substance": earth (*Cherubim* 89).[21]

Second, the ethical implications: recognition of their elemental composition should instill humility and humanity.[22] Before a person is "worthy of offering sacrifices," he must infer "from the στοιχεῖα of which he is composed that he is nothing worth" (*Dreams* 1.212). Further, humans should treat each other as equals. "If the Creator and Maker of the universe . . . has regard to your ἀσθένεια, . . . how ought you to treat other men, your natural kinsfolk, seedlings from the same στοιχεῖα as yourself?" (*Spec. Laws* 1.294)

As these excerpts show, Philo consistently thinks of the human body as composed of στοιχεῖα, whether one (earth) or all four. Elemental composition makes humans susceptible to weakness, but it also instils in them humility and a sense of shared humanity.

c. Paul

Paul too follows Gen 2.7 in seeing humans as made of earth. He does not use στοιχέω in 1 Corinthians, but he does "consciously" construct his discussion of the resurrection body "around Genesis 1 and 2."[23] After mentioning different sorts of flesh among creatures of the earth (1 Cor 15.39), Paul quotes Gen 2.7 (1 Cor 15.45) and then says that the first man was made "of dust from the earth" (1 Cor 15.47). For Paul, as for 2 Maccabees and Philo, Gen 2 teaches the composition of the human body from earth.[24]

d. Josephus

In Josephus, the idea that the human body and soul are made of elements proceeds from the mouth of Titus, a Roman general. Titus emboldens his soldiers by reminding them that the ether accepts the souls of soldiers slain in battle. "For what brave man knows not that souls released from the flesh by the sword on the battlefield are hospitably welcomed by that purest στοιχεῖον, the ether, and placed among the stars?" (*J. W.* 6.47) Titus's psychology is similar in some ways to Philo's (*Heir* 282–283). However, Josephus's narration does not reveal what he himself thought about the human body and soul or whether Philo's thought influenced him at this point as well.

e. 4 Maccabees

Fourth Maccabees develops the idea of the elemental composition of the human body, present in 2 Maccabees, in the ethical direction advanced by Philo.[25] The book is a cross-cultural apologetic for Torah. As David deSilva notes, it promotes "the Jewish way of life" as "the surest path to fulfill the highest ideals prized even among Greco-Roman ethical philosophers."[26]

66   *2*

According to Jan Willem van Henten, these philosophical ideals may include Jewish variants of the Stoic concepts of συμπάθεια within the cosmos and of "life lived in harmony" with nature.[27] (Chapter 3 shows each of these ideas in Philo.)

This agenda actuates development from 2 Maccabees. Terms change: the elemental arrangement (στοιχείωσις) of the human body, presumably from the one element earth, becomes composition from στοιχεῖα, plural. And intention changes: whereas the mother argued from the body's στοιχείωσις that God could raise her sons from the dead, the seventh brother now argues from the common στοιχεῖα for a common human ethic. "As a man, were you not ashamed, you most savage beast, to cut out the tongues of men who have feelings like yours and are made of the same στοιχεῖα as you?" (12.13)

The quote from 4 Maccabees shows both continuity with earlier sources in the Maccabean tradition—the composition of the human body is elemental— and development along lines similar to Philo—common elemental composition implies a common human ethic.

3. Conclusion

Careful review of Greek and Jewish concepts about the elements begins to show why Paul is concerned about earth, water, air, and fire. For 500 years before Paul, Greek philosophies propound the composition of the human body from the four cosmic elements. For 200 years before Paul, Jewish sources use στοιχεω and related concepts to represent the Hebrew scriptural doctrine that humans are made of the element earth. Further, for Greek philosophers and for Philo, the body's composition from the elements makes it susceptible to weakness. While the weakness of his flesh bothers Paul, he is concerned primarily by the way that physical weakness compromises moral capacity. Indeed, in stark terms he describes humans as "enslaved under the στοιχεῖα τοῦ κόσμου." This moves us to the second premise in the argument: the material στοιχεῖα which (a) compose human bodies (b) compromise the body and enslave the person.

B. THE MATERIAL ΣΤΟΙΧΕΙΑ COMPROMISE THE BODY AND ENSLAVE THE PERSON

Though the phrase στοιχεῖα τοῦ κόσμου was readily intelligible to Greeks and Jews in the first century, Paul's sentence in Gal 4.3 remains curious: ἡμεῖς . . . ὑπὸ τὰ στοιχεῖα τοῦ κόσμου ἦμεθα δεδουλωμένοι. The syntax is peculiar: the TLG canon shows that, apart from verbatim quotations of Gal 4.3 (Clement, *Paed.* 1.6.33; *Strom.* 1.11.53), no one before Paul and no one

The Concept of Enslavement under *"Στοιχεία Του Κοσμου"*   67

for centuries after sets στοιχεῖον in the accusative as the object of ὑπό. And the semantics are idiosyncratic: no one before Paul puts στοιχεῖα as the active subject of a δουλ verb. But no scholar has noticed that someone after Paul does.[28] The medical philosopher Galen (AD 129–c. 216) writes: whether the soul is "mixed with the substances of the body" or "(merely) takes up residence in bodies, it is subservient (δουλεύει) to their natures, which are, as I have said, derived from some mixture of the four στοιχεῖα" (*Prop. plac.* 15). Galen quotes Hippocrates, Plato, Aristotle, and the Stoics to show that their philosophies state, or at least imply, that the soul is enslaved to the mixtures of the στοιχεῖα. That idea is evident as well in Philo. And, to my knowledge, these data have yet to appear in scholarly literature on the στοιχεῖα in Gal 4 or Col 2.

1. The Most Proximate Text with a Similar Construction is Galen's

In Galen's massive collection of works, he puts his own ideas gained from medical practice into conversation with the Greek medical tradition since Hippocrates. His corpus includes over 600 uses of the lemma στοιχεῖον. In *The Elements According to Hippocrates*, to which he refers frequently in other works, Galen, like Aristotle, uses the term στοιχεῖον to expound elemental theories that did not originally use the term.

Galen's statement about the soul's enslavement to the elements comes near the end of *My Own Doctrines*. Citing his earlier work *Mixtures*, he explains that the four elements combine to form nine possible mixtures or temperaments (*Prop. plac.* 5; 15). Human "bodies are a mixture of 'hot, cold, dry, and wet,' . . . in other words the actual στοιχεῖα: air, fire, water, and earth" (*Temp.* 1.1, 510). These elemental mixtures produce the bodies' natures, to which the soul is enslaved (*Prop. plac.* 15).

Galen mounts a full-scale defense of this hypothesis in *That the capacities* (δυνάμεις) *of the soul depend on the mixtures of the body* (*QAM*). The treatise's title is its thesis, and its aim is clear: if it's the soul you want to treat, come see a philosopher-physician like me. Galen builds his argument (1) by showing that his hypothesis holds true whether one adopts Plato's theories or Aristotle's, and (2) by citing cases of his own. Galen begins with the most common example of a substance affecting the soul's capacities; wine "relieves us of all distress and low spirits," aids digestion, and makes "our souls gentler, and braver, too" (3, 777–778). He then identifies other substances that alter the heat or coolness, moisture or dryness of the bodies' mixtures. For example, by heating or cooling the body excessively, drugs can cause death, derangement, distress, and melancholy (3, 779). Galen cites Plato to show that nourishment moistens the body and thereby dulls even the rational part of the soul, that is, the mind (*QAM* 4, 781, quoting *Tim.* 44a–b). When infancy and senility, drugs and bad humors cause loss of memory, mind, motion, or perception, they are "impeding" "the soul . . . from acting with the capacities which it has by nature." Thus, the soul "is dominated by and enslaved (δουλεύειν) to the body" (*QAM* 5, 787).[29]

Galen's prescription is straightforward. "Those who wish to improve their own souls" should attend to their bodies. Food, drink, and "daily practices" "bring about good mixture in the body" and thereby "achieve virtue for the soul" (*QAM* 1, 767–768). Indeed, in *Mixtures* Galen asserts that "the entire bodily condition" of someone well-balanced in body and soul "will manifest faultless physical as well as mental activities (ἐνεργείαι ψυχικὰς)" (*Temp.* 2.1, 576–577). So, interested patients should "come to me to learn what they should eat and drink." Galen's treatment will enhance the "philosophy related to their characters" and "the capacities of their rational souls," and it will improve intelligence, virtue, and memory. Galen will also teach them about "winds, mixtures of the ambient air," and places (*QAM* 9, 807–808).

As a source for reading Paul, Galen is problematic. On the one hand, no other extant source before Galen mentions "enslavement to the στοιχεῖα," and, read side by side with Gal 4, *Prop. plac.* 15 makes plain sense of Paul's unusual phrase. On the other hand, Galen is writing more than a century after Paul, and so his works cannot stand as the substance of an argument for reading Paul. However, his works, like any other secondary literature, can be a guide, something that points out the substance for us to analyze and assess. Galen's works point us back through the sources to see the grounds for the second premise in my argument: the elemental composition of the flesh weakens the body and enslaves the person.

2. The Proportions of the Elements in the Body Affect the Soul's Capacities

Right from the first postulation of the elements of the cosmos, Greek philosophers teach not only that the human body is composed of the elements of the cosmos but also that the elemental substance of the body affects the person's soul. Whether the soul is itself an elemental compound or whether it merely resides within the body, changes in the elements impede or enhance the soul's capacities. Greek medical discourse and Galen's engagement with it show how this problem was diagnosed in the centuries before and after Paul. It is remarkable that in previous scholarship this concept appears to have gone unnoticed.

a. Empedocles

Empedocles analyzes human physiology and psychology in terms of the elements. For him, human flesh, blood, and soul are formed from the juxtaposition of the elemental roots.[30]

> Earth happened to meet with these most equally,
> Hephaistos and rain and all-gleaming aither,
> anchored in the perfect harbours of Kupris [Aphrodite]. . . .
> From these blood came to be and the forms of other kinds of σάρξ.
> (98/98)[31]
> Blood then surrounded the heart and became the medium of its
> understanding (96/105).

Empedocles reasons further that humans can perceive the elements because we are made of the elements. "By earth we see earth; by water, water; by aither, shining aither; but by fire, blazing fire" (17/109). From this text, Aristotle and Galen understand Empedocles to mean that "the soul is composed of, or is identical with, all the στοιχεῖα" (*De an.* 1.2, 405b; see 1.2, 404b; *Gen. corr.* 2.6, 333b; *Prop. plac.* 7). And Theophrastus explains that Empedocles taught that the arrangement of the elements determines intelligence: "those in whom these mingled elements" are most proportionate "are most intelligent and keen of sense; . . . but those whose condition is the very reverse are the least intelligent" (*Sens.* 11).

Empedocles and his interpreters show that, from the first days of the four-element theory, philosophers understand the elemental substance of the body (here specifically blood) to affect the capacities of the soul.

b. The Hippocratic Corpus

The Hippocratic corpus teaches that elemental proportion in the body and the atmosphere affects the health of both body and soul. The four qualities—earth's dryness, water's wetness, air's cold, and fire's heat—produce humors by pairing, and each humor is associated with a season (*Nat. hom.* 1–7).

Elemental ratios in the seasons affect health. "Every disease occurs at all seasons of the year but some of them more frequently occur and are of greater

Table 2.1: Combinations of Elemental Qualities in Humors and Seasons

Elements	Qualities	Humors	Seasons
Air, water	Cool, wet	Phlegm	Winter
Water, fire	Wet, hot	Blood	Spring
Fire, earth	Hot, dry	Yellow bile	Summer
Earth, air	Dry, cool	Black bile	Autumn

70   2

severity at certain times" (*Aph.* 3.23). Most of the diseases affect the body only, but madness, melancholy, and epilepsy are listed as the first of spring's common diseases and the last of autumn's (*Aph.* 3.20, 22). So a good physician should be "familiar with the progress of the seasons and the dates of rising and setting of the stars," for "the changes of the seasons produce changes in diseases" (*Aër.* 2).

Elemental ratios in geography also affect health. "You will find, as a general rule, that the constitutions and the habits of a people follow the nature of the land where they live" (*Aër.* 24).[32] Since east-facing districts "do not experience such extremes of heat and cold," their inhabitants "are likely to be healthier" and "of better temperament and intelligence than those exposed to the north" (*Aër.* 5). On the same grounds, Europe's "variable climate" causes "distress of body and ψυχή" and so produces fierce, courageous inhabitants (*Aër.* 23). Asia's "equable blending of the climate" produces "milder and less passionate" inhabitants (*Aër.* 16). People who live in "bare, waterless and rough" land, "swept by the winter gales and burnt by the summer sun" are "hard and spare." "They are keener at their crafts, more intelligent and better warriors" (*Aër.* 24). Thus, the Hippocratic corpus agrees with Empedocles and his interpreters: the qualities of the elements influence the character of the soul in a variety of ways.

3. The Elements Mediate the Παθήματα and Ἐπιθυμίαι of Body and Soul

Beginning at least with Plato, Greek philosophers discuss the role of the elements (later termed "στοιχεῖα") in mediating—and thus affecting—various process of the body and the soul. Chief among these processes are πάθημα and πάθος, "that which happens to a person or thing," whether (1) an incident or experience or (2) an emotion, passion, or condition.[33] Translating either of these terms consistently is problematic. Is πάθος emotion, passion, affection, or feeling?[34] And semantic inconsistency in the Greek texts only complicates the problem. Some writers, like Aristotle, use the terms πάθημα and πάθος interchangeably. Here the ambiguity of the English word *passion* may suit well. However, other writers, like Philo, seem to distinguish between πάθημα and πάθος.[35] There the precision of *incident* or *stimulus* (for πάθημα) and *condition* or *emotion* (for πάθος) conveys the distinction. For clarity's sake, then, I leave each term untranslated throughout this section.

Such variety notwithstanding, two concepts are common to Plato, Aristotle, Chrysippus, and Philo. First, they agree that the material elements mediate and influence παθήματα, πάθη, ἐπιθυμίαι, and ἔργα. Second, all see a πάθημα and a πάθος as essentially passive phenomena. A third concept is common to

The Concept of Enslavement under *"Στοιχεῖα Τοῦ Κόσμου"*   71

Plato, Aristotle, and Philo: namely, that it is children who are most vulnerable to enslavement by passions and desires. As chapter 4 will show, these three perspectives are important for Paul as well, for these natural processes are the means through which a person, especially a child, is enslaved under the στοιχεῖα τοῦ κόσμου that compose the body (Gal 4.3; 5.16–24).[36]

a. Plato

Plato shows vividly how the elemental composition of the body exposes the soul to positive and negative influences. As Vivian Nutton explains, Plato assumes "a holistic somaticism, in which moral failings, e.g., excess pleasure and pain, can be ascribed to physical causes."[37] In Plato's own words, bodily appetites "attempt to enslave" the mind and heart (*Resp.* 4.442b).

Plato's contention that the body incapacitates the soul is built on his concept of the tripartite soul. When the gods made mortal bodies, they placed the "divine soul" in the head as the λογιστικόν; it uses reason to govern the body and the two parts of the mortal human soul (*Tim.* 42e–43a). The spirited soul or θυμοειδές is chambered in the heart between the lungs; it is characterized by passions like anger and courage (70a–d). The ἐπιθυμητικόν or desiderative soul sits in the liver and responds to the body's appetites for food, drink, and sex (70d–71d). The ἐπιθυμητικόν can "attempt to enslave (καταδουλόω) and rule" the others (*Resp.* 4.442b), but the λογιστικόν and θυμοειδές cooperate to compel its obedience (*Tim.* 70a). Thus "two desires naturally exist amongst men—the desire of food (τροφή) for the body's sake, and the desire of wisdom for the sake of the most divine part we have" (88a–b).

For Plato, while an ἐπιθυμία is something that the soul does, a πάθημα is something that happens to it. When someone desires, the soul "longs for what it desires (ἐπιθυμέω), or draws itself toward whatever it wishes to possess" (*Resp.* 4.437c). But the soul also experiences (πάσχω) elemental παθήματα and μέρη ("affections and particles") from outside that modify its ἐπιθυμίαι (*Tim.* 43a, 78a, 88a–d; *Resp.* 4.437e, 439d).[38]

These παθήματα are most prevalent in infancy, but less so later on. Plato comments, "Now as in the beginning, so often as the Soul is bound within a mortal body it becomes at the first irrational," subjected to παθήματα, a "stream of increase and nutriment" that collide with the soul's revolutions and master the soul (*Tim.* 44a–b). However, with time these παθήματα diminish, the soul's "revolutions are straightened out," and the person becomes "intelligent" (44b). Perhaps for this reason, Plato states elsewhere, "of all wild creatures, the child is the most intractable; for in so far as it, above all others, possesses a fount of reason that is as yet uncurbed, it is a treacherous, sly and most insolent creature" (*Leg.* 7.808d).[39]

72   *2*

Elemental παθήματα impinge on all three parts of the soul (*Tim.* 42e–43b).[40] From outside the body, the winds, sunshine, waters, and earth in a district's environment affect the condition of people's bodies and are "equally able to effect similar results in their souls as well" (*Leg.* 5.747c).[41] Within the body, the ἐπιθυμητικόν desires substances and sensations that affect body and soul. Wine, for example, heats "the soul as well as the body" (*Tim.* 60a; see *Leg.* 1.645d–e). And "acid and saline phlegms" or "bitter and bilious" humors "mingle their vapour with the movement of the soul" and plant all kinds of soul-diseases in all three regions of the soul (*Tim.* 86e–87a, 88a–b). Thus the elements of the παθήματα render the soul "irrational," for the body's "evil conditions" produce "all varieties of bad temper and bad spirits, . . . of rashness and cowardice, and of forgetfulness also, as well as of stupidity" (43a, 87a, 88a–b).

Pleasure and pain are the worst of the diseases "of the soul which are due to the condition of the body" (*Tim.* 86b). When someone experiences great pleasure or pain, "he is unable either to see or to hear anything correctly, and he is . . . wholly incapable of exercising reason" (86b–c). Thus, for example, when an excess of semen in the marrow makes a body disproportionately moist, a man

> becomes for the greatest part of his life maddened on account of these very great pleasures and pains, and keeps his soul diseased and senseless by the actions of his body, and is supposed to be voluntarily wicked and not diseased. But the truth is that this sexual intemperance has come about as a disease of the soul primarily through the condition of a single substance, which owing to the porousness of the bones floods the body with its moisture. (86d)[42]

In Dale Martin's opinion, "An Epicurean or Stoic could not have put it more 'materialistically.'"[43]

Though Plato may not think that the soul is made of elements, he describes clearly how the elements that compose both the body and the παθήματα that happen to the body can affect the soul's desires, especially so in a child, and direct its actions apart from its choice (see *Phaedr.* 245c).[44] For Plato, the material elements are the media of the soul's enslavement.

b. Aristotle

Aristotle describes both the soul's processes and the soul itself in material terms. As such, the material στοιχεῖα affect both a soul's capacities and its πάθη, and they mediate the bodily ἐπιθυμίαι to which children are most vulnerable.

For Aristotle, the soul is "the first actuality of a natural organic body" (*De an.* 2.1, 415b).[45] As such, the elemental qualities of a creature's blood are the

The Concept of Enslavement under *"Στοιχεῖα Τοῦ Κόσμου"* 73

cause of "the temperament of animals and their power of sensation" (*Part. an.* 2.4, 651a).[46] Hot, cold, dry, and wet are "the principles of the physical στοιχεῖα" (2.2, 648b). Blood that is cold and thin (or watery) makes an animal "conducive to sensation and intelligence"; hot, thin, clear blood makes it both courageous and intelligent (2.2, 648a; 2.4, 650b). Aristotle and Plato differ on moisture's effects on the soul—Plato thinks it renders the soul irrational; Aristotle says it enhances intelligence—but each agrees that elemental qualities in the body affect the capacity of the soul in one way or another.

According to Aristotle, the soul's πάθη (or παθήματα) are material and passive (*De an.* 1.1, 403a–b).[47] "The πάθη of the soul are formulae expressed in matter," and they "are associated with the body . . . ; for when they appear the body is also affected (πάσχει τι τὸ σῶμα)" (*De an.* 1.1, 403a).[48] Since a person's experience of πάθη is passive, πάθη are distinct from capacities (δυνάμεις) and dispositions. "The capacities are the faculties in virtue of which we can be said to be liable to the emotions (παθητικοί). . . . The dispositions are the formed states of character in virtue of which we are well or ill disposed in respect of the πάθη" (*Eth. nic.* 2.5.2). But πάθη are neither capacities nor dispositions. People do not choose πάθη, rather "we are said to be 'moved' by the πάθη" (*Eth. nic.* 2.5.4).

Children and profligates are most susceptible to such movements. Aristotle states, "the susceptibility to pleasure has grown up with all of us from the cradle (ἐκ νηπίου)" (*Eth. nic.* 2.3.6). "For children, like profligates, live at the prompting of ἐπιθυμία; and the appetite for pleasure is strongest in childhood" (*Eth. nic.* 3.12.6). "The young, as to character, are ready to desire (ἐπιθυμητικοί) and to carry out what they desire (ἐπιθυμέω). Of the bodily desires (αἱ περὶ τὸ σῶμα ἐπιθυμίαι) they chiefly obey those of sensual pleasure and these they are unable to control" (*Rhet.* 2.12.3, 1389a).[49] Profligates too are led by their ἐπιθυμία and πάθη (3.11.6; 4.5.3; 7.7.3, 8). Worse, if the "appetite for pleasure" is gratified intensely, the gratification "actually overpowers the reason" (λογισμός), and ἐπιθυμία leads the person and puts "the various parts of the body in motion" (3.12.7; 7.3.10).

Though Aristotle accepts that material πάθη happen to people and affect their elemental bodies and souls, he does not thereby excuse every one of their ἔργα.[50] Unlike Plato, Aristotle refuses to accept that "actions done as a result of appetite and emotion . . . fall outside the scope of the voluntary (and hence for him outside the scope of responsibility as well)."[51]

c. The Stoics

For Stoics, both the body and the soul are made of elements.[52] Consequently, as Teun Tieleman argues, "the soul's disposition, including its moral quality, depends on physiological processes in the body."[53]

74   2

Research in the last twenty-five years has brought to light the complexity and corporeality of the passions and their causes in Stoic thought. Following Diogenes Laertius's presentation of Zeno's classic definition of πάθος, scholars long maintained that for Stoics a πάθος is an expression of purely cognitive volition. As Zeno states, a πάθος is "an irrational and unnatural movement in the soul" or an "impulse in excess" (*Vit. philos.* 7.1.110). Simply put, falsehood perverts the διάνοια, and πάθη arise from that perverted mind, apparently apart from any material or external influence on the mind.

However, Christopher Gill's and Teun Tieleman's research adjusts our perspective on this definition.[54] First, Gill explains that, for Stoics, πάθη are both rational and irrational. They are rational in a functional sense, for, "as *hormai* (impulses or conations), they depend on assent (*sunkatathesis*) to impressions (*phantasiai*), which are 'rational' in the sense that their content can be expressed verbally by the adult herself."[55] On the other hand, πάθη are irrational in a normative sense: first, because "the beliefs which underlie the *pathos* are not those which a perfectly reasonable, wise person would hold," and second, because the "passionate 'impulse'" itself pushes on or moves the person.[56] So then, there is an irrationality and a passivity to Stoic πάθη.

Tieleman concurs, and he observes that Zeno's classic definition of πάθος is an "outline," the "preliminary step" taken "prior to the construction of a true definition."[57] To fill out a true Stoic definition of πάθος, Tieleman identifies within Chrysippus's theory two causes of πάθος: a sustaining cause and a preliminary cause. For Chrysippus, the material στοιχεῖα play an instrumental role in each cause.

The sustaining cause of a πάθος is "the (physical) condition of the intellect." According to Galen, the Stoics "hold that the soul, like nature (φύσιν), is a kind of breath (πνεῦμα)" (*QAM* 4, 45.5–46.1).[58] "Now this pneuma has two parts, στοιχεῖα, or states that are blended with one another through and through, the hot and the cold, or . . . air and fire; and it also takes some moisture from the bodies in which it dwells" (*PHP* 5.3.8).[59] The ratio of air to fire affects the person. Galen remarks that a "well-tempered blend of these two [elements]" made Chrysippus "intelligent," but that "boundless heat" made Hippocrates's sons "swinish" (*QAM* 4, 45.5–46.1). As Tieleman observes, for Stoics, "health resides in a good proportion between the four elemental qualities in body and soul alike," for "the corporeal soul is no less subject" to "physical realities . . . than the body."[60]

When the soul is weak from lack of tension, it is especially prone to a "mental appearance," the preliminary cause of a πάθος.[61] Chrysippus cites Euripides to illustrate how an external cause acting on a weak or slack soul gives rise to a πάθος, in this case ἐπιθυμία. Galen summarizes:

The Concept of Enslavement under *"Στοιχεῖα Τοῦ Κοσμου"*   75

> Menelaus had formed the judgment to kill Helen and had drawn his sword, but when he drew near he was struck by her beauty and, because of his soul's softness and weakness (ἀσθένεια) . . . he not only threw away the sword but also kissed the woman and, one might say, surrendered himself to be her slave (δοῦλος). (*PHP* 4.6.10; see Euripides, *Andr.* 629–630)[62]

Thus, in Chrysippus's words, "every such situation defeats and enslaves (δουλόω) us, so that by yielding to it we . . . offer ourselves up to many shameful acts after our former impetus has gone slack (ἐκλύω)" (*PHP* 4.6.8).

As Tieleman demonstrates, such "movements or processes, including those of the soul, are of a corporeal nature, since what moves or is moved are bodies."[63] Galen notes that Chrysippus quoted Homer, *Iliad* 18.108–110 to show that bile or gall effects anger: "gall which drives even the very sensible to harshness . . . rises in men's breasts like smoke" (*PHP* 3.2.12, 7.52). On Tieleman's reading, Chrysippus's assertion that "bodily factors . . . influence even the intellect of sensible people" is remarkably similar to the selection from Plato above (*Tim.* 86e–87a).[64] Indeed, Chrysippus describes the soul's subjection to the elements' effects as being "carried away," for "persons angered counter to their own reason . . . could not be said . . . to be moving in conformity with themselves but instead to be moving in conformity with some force external to themselves" (*PHP* 4.6.35).

For the Stoics then, the material στοιχεῖα are key ingredients in the condition of the body and of the soul (the sustaining cause of πάθη) and in the passive experience of mental appearances (the preliminary cause of πάθη), which can enslave the weak soul against its will. Both concepts bear on a medical reading of Gal 4–6. Paul too describes slackness (ἐκλύω) as a negative sustaining cause and παθήματα as preliminary causes (Gal 5.24; 6.9).

d. Philo

In keeping with other traditions in Greek medical discourse, Philo too states that the elemental body is weak, that its susceptibility to elemental πάθη and ἐπιθυμίαι subjects the mind to enslavement, and that this enslavement is most prevalent among children. Unlike some writers, though, Philo differentiates between παθήματα and πάθη. The term πάθημα is rare and usually designates a factor that affects something, especially the element air.[65] Πάθος, on the other hand, is far more common and is ambiguous. It refers at times to an affecting factor and at other times more to an affection.

Philo discusses πάθη as a Middle Platonist. He combines both "Platonic and Stoic terminology and conceptuality," he repudiates the πάθη as vile, and he presents the soul as sometimes passive and sometimes active.[66] Loren Kerns presents a detailed analysis of these Stoic and Platonic antecedents of Philo's view of the passions. For Kerns, Stoic emphasis is primary and Platonic is secondary.[67] Philo's "essentially Stoic" psychology is evident in his "unique" emphasis on "the passions' blameworthiness."[68]

Kerns is correct that Philo's renunciation of the passions is unprecedented, but his insistence that Philo's psychology is Stoic follows from two faulty assertions. First, Kerns states that, unlike the Stoics, Plato would not consider passion "blameworthy."[69] But Kerns overlooks *Tim.* 86b–e, where Plato blames "sexual intemperance" on a πάθος and not on the person.[70]

Second, Kerns declares that "Philo considered all passions to result from voluntary movements of the hegemon."[71] He admits that "on one occasion, Philo described *sense perception* as 'the cause of the passions' (ἡ παθῶν αἰτία)," and he identifies sense perception rightly as an "antecedent cause."[72] However, he dismisses sense perception as a real cause, for "though the external impression actuates the assent to action as the 'antecedent cause,' it cannot by itself necessitate the action without the mind's assent."[73] "Hence, when Philo attributed the cause of passion to sense perception, he was in no way contradicting the idea that passion has its origin in the mind, since he understood sense perception itself to be nothing other than the activation of a faculty and condition already dormant in the mind."[74] In support of his conclusion, Kerns cites *Alleg. Interp.* 2.22–24, 37, 40–41, 45. In those sections, Philo allegorizes on the happy service that sense-perception (the woman) offers to the mind (the man) "if Sense the inferior follow Mind the superior," for then "both of them will be Mind" (2.50). But that is not the scenario in which Philo identifies sense-perception as "the moving cause of the πάθη" (2.50). Rather, sense-perception becomes "the moving cause of the πάθη" when Mind "cleaves to and becomes one with sense-perception . . . so that the two of them become one flesh and one πάθος" (2.49). In that scenario, "when bodily sense is in command, the mind is in a state of slavery heeding none of its proper objects" (2.70). Furthermore, earlier in *Alleg. Interp.* 2, Philo's allegoresis of the beasts and birds depicts the πάθη as well out of the man's control, indeed wildly so. "The πάθη [Moses] likens to wild beasts and birds, because, savage and untamed as they are, they tear the νόος to pieces, and because like winged things they light upon the understanding; for the assault of the passions is violent and irresistible" (2.11).

Philo's view of the passions is more complex than Kerns makes it out to be. In these texts, Philo's thought does cohere with Stoic thinking on the passions, but only as now explained by Gill and Tieleman, whose arguments Kerns disregards.[75] In other texts, Philo's thought is more typically Platonic (see below).[76] Yet, with one exception, I find in Kerns's dissertation no engagement with the following texts, texts that would challenge his thesis.[77]

For Philo, the πάθη do enslave the soul—as *Alleg. Interp.* 2.49–50 makes clear—and this enslavement is mediated by the elements.[78] For example, the

The Concept of Enslavement under "Στοιχεῖα Τοῦ Κόσμου"   77

desire for copulation is mediated by moisture, and, since the body "contains a great amount both of fire and of moisture," "the blame in most of these cases rests less with the soul than with the body" (*Spec. Laws* 3.9–10). Similarly, the desire for food consumes like the element fire, and when it "takes hold of the region of the belly, it produces . . . base slaves (δοῦλοι) to strong drink and fish and dainty cakes" (*Spec. Laws* 4.91). Those who consume strong drink and various delicacies thus fan "the flame of the insatiable ever-greedy ἐπιθυμία," and they are "base slaves (δοῦλοι) not of one πάθος only, ἐπιθυμία, but of all" (*Spec. Laws* 4.113; see 3.9–10). For this reason, Philo says that the senses associated with these desires—taste, smell, and touch (along with hearing)—are "in slavery (δουλεύω) to σάρξ and the σαρκὸς πάθη" (*Abraham* 164).

Philo agrees with Plato and Aristotle that this slavery to πάθη is worst among children. "Nature has not yet trained" νήπιοι "to be rational," he says (*Alleg. Interp.* 3.210; see *Confusion* 21). Rather, "when the life of man begins, from the very cradle till the time when the age of maturity brings the great change and quenches the fiery furnace of the πάθη, folly, incontinence, injustice, fear, cowardice, and all the kindred maladies of soul are his inseparable companions" (*Sacrifices* 15).[79]

Philo's clearest use of πάθη to mean affecting factors or "sensations" comes in *Rewards* 121–124,[80] a passage whose terms and concepts resonate profoundly with Paul's in Galatians, yet whose argument is diametrically opposed. Philo states that people are "affected by . . . the troublesome πάθη which the necessities of the body engender, subjecting it to a domination unduly usurped by such πάθη" (*Rewards* 121).[81] Philo describes these πάθη according to the qualities of the four elements: "for if anything over-chills or over-heats it, the house becomes warped and dried up or contrariwise wet and damp, and all these make the mind incapable of guiding the course of its own life aright" (*Rewards* 121). However, for Philo, the law of Moses is God's gift to redeem people from such enslavement under the elemental πάθη.[82] As he notes, the mind (νοῦς) of the person who follows "the holy laws," though it lay recently "under the yoke of many pleasures and many ἐπιθυμίαι and the innumerable ἀνάγκαι which its vices and ἐπιθυμίαι entail, . . . has been redeemed (ἐξαιρέω) into freedom (ἐλευθερία) by God, who broke asunder the miseries of its slavery (δουλεία)" (*Rewards* 119, 124).[83]

It is hard to overstate the relevance of this first-century Jewish text for understanding Paul's argument in Galatians about the flesh, its παθήματα and ἐπιθυμίαι, and the law. Yet it is cited nowhere in Winston, "Philo on Emotions" or Kerns, "Passions in Philo" and is overlooked in most discussions.[84]

In exploring Philo's medical philosophy, we have wandered away from our tour guide Galen. However, Maren Niehoff assures us that Philo "follows" Plato and "anticipates" Galen as he builds his argument (*Tim.* 86c–e; *Spec.*

78   2

Laws 3.10).[85] And that is what the texts establish. Similar to Plato and others in the Greek medical traditions, Philo explains that the body's elemental πάθη "usurp domination" over the mind and provoke ἐπιθυμίαι and other vices, especially among children (*Rewards* 121). However, Philo promises that God redeems (ἐξαιρέω) from slavery (δουλεία) into freedom (ἐλευθερία) the minds of those who follow the holy laws (*Rewards* 124). John Barclay sees Philo's diagnosis of the human problem: "Philo . . . stands firmly in the Platonic tradition in which the passions and sense-impressions of the body ensnare and impede the soul."[86] But neither he nor any scholar for centuries has seen that the media of that ensnarement are the στοιχεῖα τοῦ κόσμου of Gal 4.3.[87]

e. Conclusion

Galen proves to be an able guide in the quest for Paul's "enslaving elements." Scholars may note Galen's "serious ambiguities,"[88] and they may still be working back and forth toward a more nuanced explanation of Galen's theory of complex, reciprocal influence of body and soul,[89] but they agree that Galen wrote *Capacities of the Soul* "to give some kind of statement (however strong, and however consistent) of the fundamental importance for the soul of what happens to the body, and of physical, bodily composition" and "to justify such a statement as being consistent with a range of authorities, above all that of Plato."[90] And this is what Galen has done. At each halt on the tour, he pointed out the concept of the soul's enslavement to the elements in the body. And we heard Paul's key terms as well: Plato's ἐπιθυμητικόν attempts to καταδουλόω the mind and heart, and his soul is crippled by elemental παθήματα; Aristotle's material στοιχεῖα alter blood and determine intelligence, and he and others are moved by physical πάθη that prompt ἔργα; Chrysippus's στοιχεῖα compose the soul itself and δουλόω the soul that is ἀσθενής or ἐκλυόμενα; (and Philo's people δουλεύω to σαρκὸς πάθη and ἐπιθυμίαι, but they can be ἐξαιρέω from δουλεία into ἐλευθερία if they follow the holy νόμοι). Author differs from author in the concepts he associates with some of the terms and in the arguments in which he uses them, but, read together, their texts form a coherent and intelligible discourse on the physical body and human behavior. Now, at the end of the tour, Galen states his conclusion again in his own words: the soul "is subservient (δουλεύει) to [the body's] natures, which are, as I have said, derived from some mixture of the four στοιχεῖα" (*Prop. plac.* 15). As James Hankinson remarks, this idea of the soul's enslavement to the body is "one of the few genuine commonplaces in ancient moral thought."[91]

The Concept of Enslavement under "Στοιχεῖα Τοῦ Κόσμου" 79

4. Other Early Jewish Sources Describe the Weakness of the Material Flesh as an Impediment to the Spirit

Though Galen ignores Jewish sources, aspects of this concept are evident not only in Philo, whose dependence on Plato is explicit, but in other sources as well. Old Greek translations of the Hebrew scriptures present the σάρξ as material and weak; Jesus of Nazareth identifies the weak σάρξ as an impediment to the spirit; and Paul describes the σάρξ as exposing him to enslavement to sin.

a. In the LXX, Σάρξ is the Weak Substance of the Body

The Old Greek translations of the Hebrew scriptures use σάρξ to identify the material substance of a body, and they characterize σάρξ more as weak than wicked.[92] Genesis introduces the composition of humans in 2.7. God forms the human with dirt from the earth and then enlivens or "ensouls" him with his own breath. The man later recognizes the substance that he shares with the woman as bone and σάρξ (2.23; see 21, 24).[93]

The OG presents human σάρξ more as weak than wicked. Genesis associates human σάρξ with mortality (6.3). The psalmist cries, "My heart and my σάρξ failed; God is the God of my heart and is my portion forever" (72[73].26, NETS). Other psalms pair σάρξ with καρδία or with ψυχή in their shared desire for and delight in God (15[16].9; 27[28].7; 62[63].2; 83[84].3). And Ezekiel presents a heart of σάρξ (as opposed to stone) as one of the blessings of the new covenant (11.19; 36.26).

Only two OG scriptures describe σάρξ as wicked. Prior to the flood, the Lord God saw that "all σάρξ had ruined his way upon the earth" (Gen 6.12, NETS). And Ezekiel uses σάρξ to label the unrestrained, animal-like lust of Jerusalem's paramours (23.20). Apart from these texts, as Schweizer observes, "the LXX shows no inclination to link σάρξ esp. with sexuality, but rather avoids this usage."[94]

However, each of these contexts also associates the sinful σάρξ with childhood.[95] After the flood, the Lord remarks that "the mind of humankind applies itself attentively to evil things from youth" (Gen 8.21, NETS). Ezekiel observes this youthful tendency to sin expressed throughout Israel's history (Ezek 23.3, 8, 19, 21; see Jer 3.25).[96] Further, in Ps 25 (24), a psalmist asks the Lord not to remember the sins of youth or of ignorance (7).[97]

In these verses, "youth" translates νεότης, not νήπιος, the term Paul uses in Gal 4.1, 3. The LXX prefers to use νήπιος only in "a positive sense."[98] In Pss 18.8; 114.6; 118.130, when √פתה has a positive sense, LXX translates it as νήπιος. But in Prov 1.22, 32, LXX stumbles over the Hebrew text's negative use of √פתה. Aquila's and Symmachus's second-century translations contest

80   *2*

this use of νήπιος. They correct the LXX to align with the MT, thus casting νήπιοι in a negative light. In their translations, Wisdom asks, "How long, νήπιοι, will you love νηπιότητα?" (1.22, A). And then Wisdom warns, "The νήπιοι's turning away will kill them" (1.32, Σ). Thus we see that some early Jews recognize that the νήπιος, like the νεότης, is also vulnerable to error.

The OG presents the σάρξ as the substance of creaturely bodies. Humans, as σάρξ, are weak and mortal. The σάρξ is a malleable agent; it can desire and delight in God, or it can give way to wickedness. Such corruption is especially typical of children and youths. These are the assumptions with which the OG equips readers of the writings collected in the New Testament.

b. Matthew, Mark, and Paul Present Weak Flesh as an Impediment to the Spirit

New Testament writings describe the body as weak and susceptible to both physical and moral weakness. More often than not, in the New Testament documents √ἀσθενεω describes bodily weakness or sickness.[99] Further, when √ἀσθενεω describes σάρξ, the collocation normally exposes the moral implications of bodily weakness.[100]

In Matthew's and Mark's gospels, Jesus contrasts the willingness of the spirit with the weakness of the flesh. He exhorts his sleeping disciples, "Stay awake and pray that you may not come into the time of trial; the spirit indeed is willing, but the σάρξ is ἀσθενής" (Matt 26.41, NRSV ‖ Mark 14.38). The disciples' ἀσθενὴς σάρξ—specifically the heaviness of their eyes (Matt 26.43 ‖ Mark 14.40)—prevents them from praying with Jesus despite their ardent devotion to him (Matt 26.35 ‖ Mark 14.31).

In Paul's discussion of sex and marriage, his terms resonate meaningfully with the elemental composition and function of the body. Here fire inflames sexual desire (see 1 Cor 7.36–37).[101] Since husbands and wives experience ἀκρασία, a "bad mixture" associated with "intemperance," Paul advises them to abstain from sex only for a short time, lest Satan tempt them (1 Cor 7.5). Similarly, if the unmarried or widows do not practice self-control (ἐγκρατεύομαι), it is better for them to marry than πυροῦσθαι, "blaze" (1 Cor 7.9).[102] As "Ambrosiaster" explains, "When the will gives in to the heat of the body, it is burned."[103]

Paul discusses the weakness of the flesh and its moral implications at more length in Rom 6–8. Paul goes beyond the OG's portrayal of the σάρξ as physically weak. He uses language that resonates throughout with Greek medicine to show how the weakness of the flesh allows sin to enslave people (6.19; see 5.6, 8; 8.3).[104] For Paul, the medium of sin's influence over a human is the σάρξ, the material substance of the physical body (6.17–19; 7.14–18, 23, 25; 8.13).[105] Paul is conflicted: with his σάρξ he is a slave (δουλεύω) to the law of sin, and in his mind he is a slave to God's law (7.25).[106] I will explore Paul's theology of flesh and spirit in chapters 4 and 6.

5. Conclusion

Galen's tour and his tips for our own explorations have proven fruitful. In the centuries leading up to Paul, ancient Greek and early Jewish sources show surprising support for the idea that a person (or a soul) is enslaved through the flesh. The sources we reviewed agree that the material στοιχεῖα compose the human body (though 2 Maccabees may imply composition from only two elements, earth and air). They agree that the σάρξ is the material substance of the body, and that it is weak, susceptible to other forces. They agree that the στοιχεῖα mediate παθήματα (or πάθη) that provoke ἐπιθυμίαι. And, most importantly for our reading of Galatians, they agree that the weakness of the flesh impedes the person or exposes them to enslavement. The primary differences between the sources are (1) whether the person is responsible for actions (ἔργα) that result from the πάθη of the body and (2) what someone should do about this enslavement.

But the essential point is this: on review of key, even authoritative, sources, the concept that the material στοιχεῖα compose the flesh, weaken the body, and allow the enslavement of the person proves to be no more "Greek" than "Jewish." This is precisely why Paul is so bothered about earth, water, air, and fire: their miserable weakness enslaves people to sinful stimuli and desires.

C. A REGIMEN (OR ΝΟΜΟΣ) OF NOURISHMENT AND EXERCISE FOR BODY AND SOUL CAN WORK AS A SORT OF ΠΑΙΔΑΓΩΓΟΣ TO REHABILITATE THE PERSON

In response to the common problem of enslavement under the weakness of the elemental flesh, the Hippocratic corpus, Plato, Aristotle, Philo, and Paul present a variety of regimens to guide the person.[107] Two of these soul-doctors prescribe a νόμος, and three call for the employment of a παιδαγωγός.

1. The Hippocratic Corpus Prescribes Νόμος to Instill Traits that People Do Not Have within Their Souls by Nature

The Hippocratic corpus asserts that νόμος can instill traits that people do not have within their souls by nature. For example, "bravery and hardihood are not an integral part of [the] natural characters" of people who live "in

82   *2*

low-lying, stifling lands" that receive "a larger share of warm than cold winds, and where the water is warm." However, "these traits can be created by training (νόμος)" (*Aër.* 24). Galen explains, "By νόμος here he evidently means the regular (νόμιμος) upbringing in each country, which we also refer to as nurture, education and local habituation" (*QAM* 8.801). Here the Hippocratic corpus prescribes the first remedy for the soul's compromise by the elements, and that remedy is νόμος. This cannot but be interesting for a reader of Galatians.

2. Plato Prescribes a Regimen to Παιδαγωγέω Diseases of the Soul

Plato is concerned as much with teleological ethics as he is with cosmology.[108] To address the madness that the elements in the body cause the soul, Plato prescribes a regimen for body and soul to παιδαγωγεῖν diseases (*Tim.* 89d). Plato's regimen will remedy the soul's incapacitation and lead it to harmony with the universe.

Plato prescribes a παιδαγωγός for slave-like adults as well as children. Since some adults have been diseased by the body's elementally mediated παθήματα and ἐπιθυμίαι, Plato advises them to use a regimen to παιδαγωγεῖν or "control" the disease (*Tim.* 86d, 88a–d, 89d).[109] Also, since "intractable" "παῖδες cannot live without a παιδαγωγός, nor slaves without a master," Plato instructs, that a child should be "bridled" with παιδαγωγοί to guide his childish ignorance (παιδίας καὶ νηπιότητος χάριν). They should treat him both "as becomes a freeborn child" and "as a slave" (*Leg.* 7.808d–e).

Though a regimen should begin at the earliest, it can also be used remedially (*Tim.* 87b; see *Leg.* 7.789a–e, 792e). If an adult has received "unskilled nurture" (ἀπαίδευτος τροφὴ), he "must endeavour, as best he can, by means of nurture and by his pursuits and studies to flee the evil and to pursue the good" (87b). "Remedial treatment of body and mind" is "the one means of salvation" (87c, 88c).

From Plato's perspective, the universe sets the pattern for the regimen (87c, 88b–e). When someone imitates the universe's constant movement, the exercise produces "moderate vibrations" that arrange "the παθήματα and particles . . . in their due reciprocal order," thus defending the body "in nature's way" and promoting "sound health" (88d–e). While ἐπιθυμίαι and contentions lead the soul toward mortality, the "congenial food [and] motion" for the soul—music, mathematics, philosophy, and astronomy—lead to "immortal and divine" thoughts (88c, 90b–c).[110] Those who learn "the harmonies and revolutions of the Universe" will make "the part that thinks like unto the object of its thought, in accordance with its original nature."[111] This likeness

The Concept of Enslavement under "Στοιχεῖα Τοῦ Κόσμου"   83

to the universe is the "goal of life" which "the gods" "set before men . . . as the most good both for the present and for the time to come" (90d).

Plato's *Timaeus* paints the bleakest picture of enslavement to the elements within a body, but it also prescribes, with real confidence, a regimen to guide (παιδαγωγεῖν) people, especially children, to the salvation of their souls and harmony with the universe.

3. Aristotle Compares the Rational Principle to a Παιδαγωγός for the Appetitive Element

Leaning heavily on Plato, Aristotle too prescribes a "παιδαγωγός" to restrain the body's ἐπιθυμία.[112] Aristotle's one extant use of παιδαγωγός comes in the middle of the paragraph we cited above.[113] He compares a licentious adult to a child, because each "is led (ἄγω) by his ἐπιθυμία' (*Eth. nic.* 3.11.6). His prescription for each is a παιδαγωγός, though of different sorts. "Just as a child should live according to his παιδαγωγός's command, so too should the ἐπιθυμητικόν according to reason" (3.12.8).[114] With reason as a παιδαγωγός, "the appetite for pleasure" must be brought under its rule, "'well-disciplined' and 'chastened'" (3.12.6–8).[115] Aristotle uses the term παιδαγωγός to describe the sort of prophylactic treatment that will prevent the ἐπιθυμητικόν and its ἐπιθυμία from overpowering a person's reason. Aristotle's and Plato's positive view of the παιδαγωγός and the Hippocratic prescription of a νόμος reappear in Philo's examination of the mind enslaved by the flesh and its elements.

4. Philo Presents the Law of Moses as God's Way to Lead the Mind in "Spiritual Exodus" to Freedom from Enslavement to the Flesh

When it comes to the question of the elements, the body, and the mind, Philo thinks that Plato diagnoses the problem and Moses prescribes the remedy. The problem is that the στοιχεῖα are ἀσθενῆ and the body's elemental qualities enslave the mind. The remedy is God and God's νόμος.

Johannes Woyke's study comes close to recognizing this problem and remedy in Philo, but he is misled by thinking that Paul "*klassifiziert* den νόμος unter die Rubrik der στοιχεῖα τοῦ κόσμου."[116] In Philo's writings, Woyke sees the remedy clearly, but he misses the problem. He recognizes that Philo promotes the law to deal with bondage to the σῶμα: the σάρξ and its πάθη. This solution leads eventually to death, the elemental resolution of the body, and the liberation of the soul, as Abraham's migration showed.[117] However, Woyke fails to see that the στοιχεῖα τοῦ κόσμου are the very factors that mediate the πάθη and compose and weaken the σάρξ. Instead, he asserts that Philo considers the στοιχεῖα weak because they have no "inherent creative

84 *2*

power and thus are unable to solve the anthropological problem of sin."[118] But neither Philo nor Paul nor any early Jewish source I have read locates the στοιχεῖα's weakness in their inability to deal with the problem of sin. Sustained attention to Philo's actual use of the terms στοιχεῖον and ἀσθενής would correct Woyke's analysis and strengthen his thesis that Paul and Philo are contesting opposing means of redemption from sin's work in the body.

In Philo's philosophy, God is the people's redeemer from slavery to desires, and God's law is a guide to life in harmony with the cosmos. The law addresses both mind and body in the cosmos. On the one hand, God rescues people from being δοῦλοι of creation by rebuking them, as παιδαγωγοί rebuke their charges. He does this "by sending forth into our mind His own word, that reproves and chastens" and heals it (*Worse* 145–146; see *Names* 217). Though Philo knows many incompetent παιδαγωγοί, their role, like that of νόμοι, is normally positive (*Virtues* 178; *Sacrifices* 15, see 51; *Heir* 295). They should use "reproaches, and sometimes . . . punishments" to "effect improvement in the souls of those whom they are educating (παιδευομένοι)" (*Migration* 116; see *Embassy* 115).[119] This is what Macro seeks to do for Gaius when he sees him "straying from the regular way and letting his impulses range unbridled anywhither and in any way" (*Flaccus* 14). And this is the ideal that Gaius himself twists as he speaks deceitfully to the chief officials about his cousin, Tiberius's grandson by blood: "'You see yourselves that he is still a mere νήπιος and needs ἐπιτρόποι and teachers and παιδαγωγοί. . . . And I,' he continued, 'will be more than ἐπίτροποι, παιδαγωγοί and a teacher. I will appoint myself to be his father and him to be my son'" (*Embassy* 26–27). As background for Gal 3.22–4.3, the collocation of the terms νήπιος, ἐπιτρόπος, and παιδαγωγός is remarkable—all the more striking for its near absence in the literature[120]—but so too is the superior valuation of the father-son relationship.

The law also has direct implications for the life of the body in the cosmos. God promises those who obey the "holy laws" a healthy body, completely free of disease, which will allow the mind the leisure to pursue wisdom and enjoy a happy life (*Rewards* 119–124).[121]

The law's effectiveness follows from a general κόσμος:νόμος harmony (*Moses* 2.47; *Creation* 3), which is often mediated by the στοιχεῖα. This harmony underlies the specific practices of the Mosaic calendar and circumcision. Observing the sabbath and the various festivals inculcates self-control, reason, and other virtues (*Spec. Laws* 2.56–175; *Migration* 91).[122] In particular, the timing of the feast of unleavened bread (on the fifteenth day of the first month during the spring season of the year) and its food (unleavened bread) assimilate the worshipper's life to the καιρός when the cosmos was created and the στοιχεῖα were "separated and placed in harmonious order" (*Spec. Laws* 2.150, 161). Following similar principles, Philo promotes both

The Concept of Enslavement under *"Στοιχεῖα Τοῦ Κοσμου"*   85

the symbol and the practice of circumcision as effective for cutting off excessive desires (*Spec. Laws* 1.9; *QG* 3.47; *Migration* 92).

Thus Philo presents the law of Moses—both its symbolic meaning and its physical practices—as the way "to accomplish the spiritual exodus" from the flesh and slavery to the mind and freedom.[123] Chapter 3 will expound Philo's philosophy with particular reference to the στοιχεῖα τοῦ κόσμου in Galatians.

5. Conclusion

Greek medical discourse prescribes a variety of regimens for body and soul to remedy the weakness of the flesh and rehabilitate the person. The Hippocratic Corpus calls such a regimen νόμος. Plato and Aristotle compare it to a παιδαγωγός. And Philo sees both these qualities in God's νόμος, which will liberate the mind to live in harmony with the cosmos. For centuries before Paul, these are the terms and concepts with which Greek (and later Jewish) sources have diagnosed and prescribed treatment for the enslavement of the soul under the weakness of the elemental flesh. Paul too describes the scripture's νόμος as a sort of παιδαγωγός to manage the problem of sin, but now that God has sent his Son and his Spirit, Paul will prescribe an entirely different cure for the disease.

D. CONCLUSION

Building on the survey of the term στοιχεῖον in chapter 1, this chapter considered the concept of enslavement under the στοιχεῖα. It found in Galen, the textual source most proximate to Paul's concept of enslavement. And, following Galen's lead, it presented textual evidence that

1. From the first proposition of the concept of the four elements of the cosmos and the application of the term στοιχεῖα to that concept, philosophers understand the human body to be composed of the cosmos's four elements—earth, water, air, and fire—and some Jews ground this idea in the foundational chapters of the Hebrew scriptures.
2. Greek writers opine that the elements that compose the body also mediate παθήματα (or πάθη) that provoke ἐπιθυμίαι, overpower the weak body, and enslave the soul. Similarly, the Hebrew scriptures and their Old Greek translations consistently present human flesh as weak, the Gospels' Jesus identifies the weak flesh as an impediment to the spirit, and Philo and Paul describe the person as enslaved to sinful desires on account of the weakness of the flesh.

86 *2*

3. Some Greek authorities and Philo promote a regimen (or νόμος in Hippocrates's words) of diet and exercise for body and soul (as a sort of παιδαγωγός) to remedy the soul's weakness.

Unlike many theories in the scholarly literature, these premises are neither reconstructions nor hypotheses. They are firm evidence for the actual use of the term στοιχεῖον in extant ancient texts. The presence of each of these ideas in Plato's *Timaeus* shows the long establishment and wide popularity of this medical tradition. Their presence in Galen shows how they are still being read a century after Paul. And their presence in Philo shows how a leading Jewish scholar in one of the centers of Jewish (and Mediterranean) learning in Paul's day works each of them into a philosophy according to the elements grounded in the law of Moses.

In Galatians, several of Paul's key terms correspond to, and several of his concepts cohere with, Greek medical discourse. This correspondence and coherence suggests that Paul uses the phrase στοιχεῖα τοῦ κόσμου to engage philosophical ideas about the body and human behavior in order to present God's Son and his Spirit as the only effective cure for the common human disease.

However, as scholars have long noted, the primary concern of Galatians is not medical theory but rather the misuse of the law by those who believe in the Anointed. The letter insists that practices like circumcision and calendar observance neither liberate the person from the flesh nor confer righteousness. Chapter 3 shows how Philo takes the opposite view: he not only promotes those practices for those very ends but does so within a philosophy structured according to the στοιχεῖα τοῦ κόσμου.

NOTES

1. Vielhauer, "Gesetzesdienst und Stoicheiadienst," 553; Betz, *Galatians*, 205.

2. Delling, "Στοιχέω," 7:684, cited by Longenecker, *Galatians*, 165.

3. Bandstra, *The Elements*, 60–61, 67, 70; Longenecker, *Galatians*, 164–66; Leithart, *Delivered from the Elements of the World*, 78, 81–84, 194.

4. Schweizer, Baumgärtel, and Meyer, "Σάρξ," 102–3, 122; Martyn, *Galatians*, 290; 526–27, especially nn. 162, 166; 532; see also 412.

5. Troy W. Martin, "Paul's Pneumatological Statements and Ancient Medical Texts," in *The New Testament and Early Christian Literature in Greco-Roman Context: Studies in Honor of David E. Aune*, ed. John Fotopoulos, NovTSup 122 (Leiden: Brill, 2006), 126; similarly Martin, *The Corinthian Body*, 3–37. In other work though, Troy Martin reads the στοιχεῖα in Gal 4.3, 9 as referring to the "present material world" and "connected with the Jewish law" (Troy W. Martin, "Pagan and

The Concept of Enslavement under "Στοιχεια Του Κοσμου" 87

Judeo-Christian Time-Keeping Schemes in Gal 4.10 and Col 2.16," *NTS* 42 (1996): 117, https://doi.org/dx.doi.org/10.1017/S0028688500017100).

6. Wasserman, "Paul among the Philosophers"; *The Death of the Soul in Romans 7: Sin, Death, and the Law in Light of Hellenistic Moral Psychology*, WUNT 2/256 (Tübingen: Mohr Siebeck, 2008); "The Death of the Soul in Romans 7: Revisiting Paul's Anthropology in Light of Hellenistic Moral Psychology," *JBL* 126 (2007): 793–816.

7. Martyn, *Galatians*, 292–93, 527–28 recognizes this view of the law in Philo.

8. Martin, *The Corinthian Body*, 16–18.

9. Barbara Böck and Vivian Nutton, "Medicine," in *Brill's New Pauly*, ed. Hubert Cancik and Helmuth Schneider (Leiden: Brill, 2006).

10. Nestis and Hephaestus represent water and fire, respectively.

11. James Longrigg, *Greek Medicine: From the Heroic to the Hellenistic Age: A Source Book* (London: Duckworth, 1998), 39.

12. Edward Adams, *Constructing the World: A Study in Paul's Cosmological Language*, Studies of the New Testament and Its World, ed. John M. G. Barclay, Joel Marcus, and John Riches (Edinburgh: T&T Clark, 2000), 64.

13. Roberto Radice and David T. Runia, *Philo of Alexandria: An Annotated Bibliography 1937–1986* (Leiden: Brill, 1988), 57.

14. Wright, *Paul and the Faithfulness of God*, 235.

15. Scholars dispute 2 Maccabees's origin and agree only that it is the source for 4 Maccabees (David Arthur deSilva, *4 Maccabees: Introduction and Commentary on the Greek Text in Codex Sinaiticus*, Septuagint Commentary Series (Leiden: Brill, 2006), xxx; Daniel R. Schwartz, "Maccabees, Second Book Of," *EDEJ*, 905; Jan Willem van Henten, "Maccabees, Fourth Book of," *EDEJ*, 909).

16. So RSV; NRSV; NETS; Daniel R. Schwartz, *2 Maccabees* (Berlin: Walter de Gruyter, 2008), 297; see "members" in AV.

17. Jan Willem van Henten, *The Maccabean Martyrs as Saviours of the Jewish People: A Study of 2 and 4 Maccabees*, JSJSup 57 (Leiden: Brill, 1997), 176.

18. N. T. Wright, *The New Testament and the People of God*, Christian Origins and the Question of God 1 (London: SPCK, 1992), 323, showing from 2 Macc 7 "the extremely physical nature of the anticipated resurrection."

19. See David T. Runia, *Philo of Alexandria and the Timaeus of Plato*, Philosophia Antiqua 44 (Leiden: Brill, 1986), 259–60.

20. See van Kooten, *Cosmic Christology*, 62–66.

21. Colson mistakenly renders περὶ τῶν χερσαίων ἢ καθ' ὕδατος as "the creatures of air and water."

22. van Kooten, *Cosmic Christology*, 63.

23. N. T. Wright, *The Resurrection of the Son of God*, Christian Origins and the Question of God 3 (London: SPCK, 2003), 346, see 273, 313.

24. While Martin, *The Corinthian Body*, 125–26 traces Paul's ideas to a "philosophical commonplace," Roy E. Ciampa and Brian S. Rosner, *The First Letter to the Corinthians*, PNTC (Grand Rapids: Eerdmans, 2010), 805 critique his suggestion and reinforce Wright's assertion with further references to Genesis (see Gordon D. Fee,

The First Epistle to the Corinthians, NICNT (Grand Rapids: Eerdmans, 1987), 783 n. 32).

25. van Kooten, Cosmic Christology, 63. Most scholars agree that 4 Maccabees is a product of the Jewish Diaspora sometime in the first or early second century AD (see Hugh Anderson, "Maccabees, Books of: Fourth Maccabees," The Anchor Bible Dictionary 4:453; van Henten, Maccabean Martyrs, 78–82; van Henten, "Maccabees, Fourth Book Of," 909; Davila, Provenance of the Pseudepigrapha, 231; deSilva, 4 Maccabees, xvii).

26. deSilva, 4 Maccabees, xxvi.

27. van Henten, Maccabean Martyrs, 276–78, esp. nn. 33–34.

28. Indeed, Billie Jean Collins, Bob Buller, and John F. Kutsko, eds., The SBL Handbook of Style, 2d ed. (Atlanta: SBL, 2014) do not even list Galen in their table of abbreviations for classical and ancient Christian writings (141–68).

29. Similarly, in Opt. med., Galen describes someone who is "continually drinking or eating or indulging in sex" as "to put it briefly, . . . a slave (δουλεύω) to genitals and belly" (59). I owe this reference to R. James Hankinson, "Galen's Anatomy of the Soul," Phronesis 36.2 (1991): 230.

30. James Longrigg, Greek Rational Medicine: Philosophy and Medicine from Alcmaeon to the Alexandrians (London: Routledge, 1993), 53, 71; Longrigg, Greek Medicine: Source Book, 27.

31. Hephaestus represents fire, Kupris, water.

32. Among Jewish sources, Let. Aris. 107–120 assumes a similar principle as the reason for the zeal of Judean farmers and the wantonness of Alexandrian citizens.

33. LSJ, s.v. "πάθημα," "πάθος."

34. Teun Tieleman, Chrysippus' On Affections: Reconstruction and Interpretation, Philosophia Antiqua 94 (Leiden: Brill, 2003), 15–16; John T. Fitzgerald, "The Passions and Moral Progress: An Introduction," in Passions and Moral Progress in Greco-Roman Thought, ed. John T. Fitzgerald, Routledge Monographs in Classical Studies (London: Routledge, 2008), 3–4.

35. And some, like Zeno, are not known to have used πάθημα at all. A TLG search finds no use of lemma πάθημα in SVF 1. Other occurrences of πάθημα in Stoic fragments do not show clearly that the Stoic philosopher himself used the term. See πάθημα in SVF 2.79, 695, 876, 1103; 3.463; Posidonius, Frag. 336b, 338b, 395b, 464.

36. See too Rom 6.12; 7.5–20.

37. Vivian Nutton, "Mental Illness," in Brill's New Pauly, ed. Hubert Cancik and Helmuth Schneider (Leiden: Brill Online, 2015).

38. In Tim. 61d–68a, Plato seems to use πάθος and πάθημα interchangeably, though a slight distinction may be discerned in 62b, 65b.

39. See David J. Lull, "'The Law Was Our Pedagogue': A Study in Galatians 3:19–25," JBL 105 (1986): 493, citing this text and Leg. 2.653b–c.

40. My reading of Plato's psychology accords with Galen's explanation (QAM 7). I do not see why Aristotle wrote, "like Empedocles, . . . Plato constructs the soul out of the στοιχεῖα" (De an. 1.2, 404b).

41. Galen quotes Leg. 5.747 in QAM 807.

The Concept of Enslavement under "Στοιχεια Του Κοσμου" 89

42. Galen quotes *Tim.* 86c–87a in *QAM* 789–90. I quote this selection from Longrigg, *Greek Medicine: Source Book*, 28.

43. Martin, *The Corinthian Body*, 12.

44. Plato goes on to absolve the person of guilt, since the man's reasoning soul, after all, has been detained in a state of senselessness. "For no one is voluntarily wicked, but the wicked man becomes wicked on account of some evil disposition of the body and an uneducated upbringing" (*Tim.* 86d–e).

45. Jonathan Barnes, "Aristotle," in *The Oxford Companion to the Mind*, 2d ed. (Oxford: Oxford University Press, 2004), oxfordreference.com/10.1093/acref/9780198662242.001.0001/acref-9780198662242-e-61; see Pierluigi Donini, "Psychology," in *The Cambridge Companion to Galen*, ed. R. J. Hankinson (Cambridge: Cambridge University Press, 2008), 197–98, http://universitypublishingonline.org/cambridge/companions/chapter.jsf?bid=CBO9781139001908&cid=CBO9781139001908A010.

46. Galen quotes *Part. an.* 2.2, 648a; 2.4, 650b–651a in *QAM* 791–95.

47. In *De an.* 1.1, Aristotle does not distinguish clearly between παθήματα and πάθη (which Hett translates "provocations"). Similarly, in *Eud. eth.* 2.2–3, παθήματα and πάθη are functionally interchangeable (so Burton, *Galatians*, 321).

48. Galen will describe "the unseemliness of behavior due to erotic desire, gluttony, drunkenness, and luxurious eating" as "*erga* and *pathē* of the desiderative power of the soul" (R. James Hankinson, "Actions and Passions: Affection, Emotion, and Moral Self-Management in Galen's Philosophical Psychology," in *Passions & Perceptions: Studies in Hellenistic Philosophy of Mind: Proceedings of the Fifth Symposium Hellenisticum*, ed. Jacques Brunschwig and Martha Craven Nussbaum (Cambridge: Cambridge University Press, 1993), 208 n. 77, citing *Aff. dig.* 27–28). As Hankinson explains, "gluttony and the like are indeed actions *of the desiderative soul*; but they are . . . at best *pathē* of [the whole man]" (Hankinson, 208).

49. See Lull, "Pedagogue," 493, citing this text and *Rhet.* 2.14.3, 1390b.

50. Hankinson, "Actions and Passions," 187.

51. Hankinson, "Actions and Passions," 194 n. 36.

52. Christopher Gill, "Galen and the Stoics: Mortal Enemies or Blood Brothers?," *Phronesis: A Journal of Ancient Philosophy* 52.1 (2007): 92–93; Wright, *Paul and the Faithfulness of God*, 214, 235.

53. Tieleman, *Chrysippus' On Affections*, 147, citing *PHP* 3.1.10; 5.2.31–33.

54. Gill and Tieleman differ most from Richard Sorabji. See Tieleman, *Chrysippus' On Affections*, 8; Gill, "Galen and the Stoics," 111–12; Christopher Gill, *Naturalistic Psychology in Galen and Stoicism* (Oxford: Oxford University Press, 2010), 343–44, responding to Richard Sorabji, *Emotion and Peace of Mind: From Stoic Agitation to Christian Temptation*, The Gifford Lectures (Oxford: Oxford University Press, 2000). See also Richard Sorabji, "Chrysippus—Posidonius—Seneca: A High-Level Debate on Emotion," in *The Emotions in Hellenistic Philosophy*, ed. Juha Sihvola and Troels Engberg-Pedersen, The New Synthese Historical Library 46 (Dordrecht: Kluwer, 1998), 149–70.

55. Christopher Gill, "Did Galen Understand Platonic and Stoic Thought on the Emotions?," in *The Emotions in Hellenistic Philosophy*, ed. Juha Sihvola and Troels

Engberg-Pedersen, *The New Synthese Historical Library* 46 (Dordrecht: Kluwer, 1998), 116.

56. Gill, "Did Galen Understand Platonic and Stoic Thought on the Emotions?," 116–17.

57. Tieleman, *Chrysippus' On Affections*, 94.

58. In this section, I quote *QAM* from Tieleman, *Chrysippus' On Affections*, 147–53.

59. Galen also identifies the elements as the definitive features of sustaining causes in the Stoic-based medicine of Athenaeus (*CC* 2.4). See Tieleman, *Chrysippus' On Affections*, 110–11.

60. Tieleman, *Chrysippus' On Affections*, 157.

61. Tieleman, *Chrysippus' On Affections*, 106–12, 168.

62. See Tieleman, *Chrysippus' On Affections*, 112–13.

63. Tieleman, *Chrysippus' On Affections*, 103; see Gill, "Galen and the Stoics," 92; contra Stanley Kent Stowers, "Paul and Self-Mastery," in *Paul in the Greco-Roman World: A Handbook*, ed. J. Paul Sampley (London: Continuum, 2003), 540.

64. Tieleman, *Chrysippus' On Affections*, 159–60, cf. 188. Tieleman notes that Gretchen J. Reydams-Schils, *Demiurge and Providence: Stoic and Platonist Readings of Plato's Timaeus*, Monothéismes et Philosophie 2 (Turnhout: Brepols, 1999), 65ff.; Christopher Gill, "Galen versus Chrysippus on the Tripartite Psyche in Timaeus 69–72," in *Interpreting the Timaeus–Critias: Proceedings of the IV Symposium Platonicum: Selected Papers*, ed. Tomás Calvo Martínez and Luc Brisson, International Plato Studies 9 (Saint Augustin: Academia, 1997), 267–73 have shown that "Chrysippus was influenced by the *Timaeus*" (160 n. 83).

65. As TDNT states, Philo uses πάθημα only 7 times: *Moses* 2.126; *Creation* 70; *Abraham* 2; *Spec. Laws* 1.210; *Cherubim* 88; *Giants* 10; *Confusion* 23 (Wilhelm Michaelis, "Πάσχω, Παθητός, Προπάσχω, Συμπάσχω, Πάθος, Πάθημα, Συμπαθής, Συμπαθέω, Κακοπαθέω, Συγκακοπαθέω, Κακοπάθεια, Μετριοπαθέω, Ὁμοιοπαθής, Πραϋπάθεια," in *TDNT*, 5.931). The distinction between πάθος and πάθημα is clearest in *Confusion* 23.

66. David Winston, "Philo of Alexandria on the Rational and Irrational Emotions," in *Passions and Moral Progress in Greco-Roman Thought*, ed. John T. Fitzgerald, Routledge Monographs in Classical Studies (London: Routledge, 2008), 202–5; see Loren Kerns, "Platonic and Stoic Passions in Philo of Alexandria" (Kings College London, Ph.D. diss., 2013), 20–21, 219–20, http://digitalcommons.georgefox.edu/gfes/6.

67. Kerns, "Passions in Philo," 27–31, 36, 127, 220.

68. Kerns, "Passions in Philo," 73, 119, 126, citing *Creation* 80; *Spec. Laws* 2.31; 4.79, 95; *Alleg. Interp.* 3.68, 75; *Agriculture* 123; *God* 71.

69. Kerns, "Passions in Philo," 31.

70. I can find no reference to *Tim.* 86b–e in Kerns, "Passions in Philo."

71. Kerns, "Passions in Philo," 126.

72. Kerns, "Passions in Philo," 57, citing *Alleg. Interp.* 2.50; italics his.

73. Kerns, "Passions in Philo," 57, citing Cicero, *Fat.* 42.

74. Kerns, "Passions in Philo," 57, citing *Alleg. Interp.* 2.37, 40, 45.

The Concept of Enslavement under "Στοιχεῖα Τοῦ Κοσμοῦ" 91

75. Kerns, "Passions in Philo," 21 n. 49. Wasserman, "Death of the Soul," 802; Hans Svebakken, *Philo of Alexandria's Exposition of the Tenth Commandment*, Studia Philonica Monographs 6 (Atlanta: Society of Biblical Literature, 2012), 47–48 also ignore Tieleman, but with the opposite effect, going on to deny Stoic influence on Paul and Philo, respectively.

76. John M. G. Barclay, *Obeying the Truth: A Study of Paul's Ethics in Galatians*, Studies of the New Testament and Its World (Edinburgh: T&T Clark, 1988), 186; Maren R. Niehoff, *Philo on Jewish Identity and Culture*, TSAJ 86, ed. Martin Hengel and Peter Schäfer (Tübingen: Mohr Siebeck, 2001), 96.

77. See *Spec. Laws* 4.91 in Kerns, "Passions in Philo," 110.

78. Ronald Williamson, *Jews in the Hellenistic World: Philo*, Cambridge Commentaries on Writings of the Jewish and Christian World, 200 BC to AD 200 I.2 (Cambridge: Cambridge University Press, 1989), 284.

79. See Lull, "Pedagogue," 492–93.

80. Thus F. H. Colson, trans., *Philo*, LCL, 8.387 n. b.

81. For ἀνάγκαι, Colson puts *distresses* in the text and *necessities* in a note (Colson, *Philo*, 8.387 n. a). See *Alleg. Interp.* 2.49–50; *Heir* 268. See Colson, *Philo*, 8:387 n. b.

82. James W. Thompson, *Moral Formation According to Paul: The Context and Coherence of Pauline Ethics* (Grand Rapids: Baker Academic, 2011), 141.

83. See also *Alleg. Interp.* 1.69; *Good Person* 159.

84. David Winston, "Philo of Alexandria on the Rational and Irrational Emotions," in *Passions and Moral Progress in Greco-Roman Thought*, ed. John T. Fitzgerald, Routledge Monographs in Classical Studies (London: Routledge, 2008), 201–20; Loren Kerns, "Platonic and Stoic Passions in Philo of Alexandria" (Kings College London, Ph.D. diss., 2013), http://digitalcommons.georgefox.edu/gfes/6. Niehoff, *Jewish Identity*, 254–55 discusses *Rewards* 121–124, but it is not listed in the indices in Betz, *Galatians*; Barclay, *Obeying the Truth*; Cosgrove, *The Cross and the Spirit*; Longenecker, *Galatians*; Dunn, *Galatians*; Martyn, *Galatians*; Longenecker, *Abraham's God*; Witherington, *Grace in Galatia*; Mark D. Nanos, *The Irony of Galatians: Paul's Letter in First-Century Context* (Fortress Press, 2002); Karl Olav Sandnes, *Belly and Body in the Pauline Epistles*, SNTSMS 120 (Cambridge: Cambridge University Press, 2002); Lorenzo Scornaienchi, *Sarx und Soma bei Paulus: Der Mensch zwischen Destruktivität und Konstruktivität*, NTOA/SUNT 67 (Göttingen: Vandenhoeck & Ruprecht, 2008); de Boer, *Galatians*; Douglas J. Moo, *Galatians*, BECNT (Grand Rapids: Baker, 2013); Wright, *Paul and the Faithfulness of God*; or Peter Oakes, *Galatians*, Paideia: Commentaries on the New Testament (Grand Rapids: Baker Academic, 2015). Though neither author cites *Rewards* 121–124, Orrey McFarland, "The God Who Gives: Philo and Paul in Conversation" (Durham University, Ph.D. thesis, 2013), 106 n. 218 (cf. 118), http://etheses.dur.ac.uk/9409/ mentions *Rewards* 119–120, and Barclay, *Paul and the Gift*, 236–37, 310, 401 discusses *Rewards* 119, 126.

85. Niehoff, *Jewish Identity*, 96. Runia, *Philo of Alexandria and the Timaeus of Plato*, 319–22 does not develop Philo's use of *Timaeus* at this point.

86. Barclay, *Obeying the Truth*, 186.

87. Barclay, *Obeying the Truth*, 210.

88. Donini, "Psychology," 200; Peter N. Singer, "The Capacities of the Soul Depend on the Mixtures of the Body," in *Galen: Psychological Writings*, ed. Peter N. Singer, Cambridge Galen Translations (Cambridge: Cambridge University Press, 2013), 358.

89. G. E. R. Lloyd, "Scholarship, Authority and Argument in Galen's Quod Animi Mores," in *Le Opere Psicologiche di Galeno: Atti del Terzo Colloquio Galenico Internazionale, Pavia, 10–12 Settembre 1986*, ed. Paola Manuli and Mario Vegetti, Elenchos 13 (Naples: Bibliopolis, 1988), 36–37 says Galen distances himself from "a straightforward physical determinist position" in order to preserve culpability. Hankinson, "Actions and Passions," 218 n. 99 finds instead "the hardest determinism you care to espouse" (see Donini, "Psychology," 201, 209 n. 101). Peter N. Singer, "General Introduction," in *Galen: Psychological Writings*, Cambridge Galen Translations (Cambridge: Cambridge University Press, 2013), 28 is the most nuanced.

90. Singer, "Capacities of the Soul," 344.

91. Hankinson, "Actions and Passions," 206; see Tieleman, *Chrysippus' On Affections*, 197.

92. See Douglas J. Moo, *The Epistle to the Romans*, NICNT (Grand Rapids: Eerdmans, 1996), 47.

93. See LEH, s.v. "σάρξ."

94. Schweizer, Baumgärtel, and Meyer, "Σάρξ," 108

95. See Scott J. Hafemann, "Paul and the Exile of Israel in Galatians 3–4," in *Exile: Old Testament, Jewish, and Christian Conceptions*, ed. James M. Scott, JSJSup 56 (Leiden: Brill, 1997), 338 n. 24.

96. In Ezek 16, νηπιότης refers to Jerusalem's childhood before her debauchery (Ezek 16.22, 43, 60).

97. See νεότητος ἁμαρτίαι as well in Job 13.26; cf. Jer 3.25.

98. I owe the following discussion to Georg Bertram, "Νήπιος, Νηπιάζω," in *TDNT*, 4:916–17.

99. Ἀσθένεια describes bodily weakness in 17 of its 24 occurrences, ἀσθενέω in 22 of 33 (or 34), and ἀσθενής in 12 of 26.

100. Matt 26.41; Mark 14.38; Rom 6.19; 8.3; Gal 4.13.

101. See fire burning as indignation in 2 Cor 11.29 and as anger in Est 5.1d; 2 Macc 4.38; 10.35; 14.45.

102. GE.

103. Ambrosiaster, *Commentaries on Romans and 1–2 Corinthians*, trans. and ed. Gerald L. Bray, ACT (Downers Grove, IL: IVP Academic, 2009), 150.

104. Wasserman, "Paul among the Philosophers."

105. Similarly, 1 Pet 2.11 describes τῶν σαρκικῶν ἐπιθυμίαι fighting as soldiers against the believers' ψυχή. (See 1 Pet 4.6.)

106. While the conflict between mind and flesh, inner self and bodily members, resonates with the tensions between the parts of Plato's soul, Paul, like Aristotle, differs from Plato in holding the person responsible for the actions of their flesh (Rom 6.20–23).

107. Chrysippus too promotes an elemental regimen to "influence one's mental and hence moral disposition through diet and exercise." For example, Zeno's "dry and

The Concept of Enslavement under *"Στοιχεῖα Τοῦ Κόσμου"*   93

cold soul" was warmed and "mellowed" by his drinking wine (Tieleman, *Chrysippus' On Affections*, 165–66).

108. Longrigg, *Greek Medicine: Source Book*, 148.

109. Lull, "Pedagogue" overlooks this text, but it is significant: of the thirty-four times Plato uses "παιδαγωγ," five appear in his discussion of soul-disease in *Tim.* 89d.

110. See Sorabji, *Emotion and Peace of Mind*, 256. LCL prints a typo here: "congenial food arid motion."

111. Plato promotes the study of the stars' periods not because the stars are elements or are made of an element (fire or ether) and the soul is diseased by the elements, but simply because when the soul studies astronomy, it tunes itself to the universe's motions.

112. Richard Longenecker, "The Pedagogical Nature of the Law in Galatians 3:19–4:7," *JETS* 25.1 (1982): 54; Moses, *Practices of Power*, 128. This reference too is curiously absent in Lull, "Pedagogue."

113. A search for lemma παιδαγωγός in the TLG canon finds no other occurrences in Aristotle's extant works (see *Div. Arist.* 18.1, 2).

114. Translation mine.

115. See *Eth. nic.* 3.12 in Betz, *Galatians*, 177; Longenecker, "The Pedagogical Nature of the Law in Galatians 3," 54; Longenecker, *Galatians*, 147.

116. Johannes Woyke, "Nochmals zu den 'Schwachen und Unfähigen Elementen' (Gal 4.9): Paulus, Philo und die Στοιχεῖα τοῦ Κόσμου," *NTS* 54 (2008): 231, https://doi.org/10.1017/S002868850800012X, italics his; see 221.

117. Woyke, "Elementen," 228–29, see *Heir* 276–283.

118. Woyke, "Elementen," 221.

119. Barclay, *Obeying the Truth*, 107–8.

120. Lightfoot, *Galatians*, 166; Norman H. Young, "Paidagogos: The Social Setting of a Pauline Metaphor," *NovT* 29 (1987): 155, 169 are exceptions.

121. See Lev 26.13.

122. Niehoff, *Jewish Identity*, 259–66.

123. Valentin Nikiprowetzky, *Le commentaire de l'Écriture chez Philon d'Alexandrie: son caractère et sa portée, observations philologiques*, ALGHJ 11, ed. Karl Heinrich Rengstorf (Leiden: Brill, 1977), 239, translation mine.

3

The Argument for Redemptive Nomism in Philo's Philosophy According to the "Στοιχεια Του Κοσμου"

Just as medical traditions in ancient Greek and early Jewish sources illuminate the meaning of the term and the concept στοιχεῖα τοῦ κόσμου in Gal 4, comparison with Philo's works explicates the concerns of the argument within which the term is used. Galatians denies the law's ability to help someone control the insatiety of the flesh or attain righteousness, whether by practicing circumcision or by observing the calendar. Chapter 3 shows that Philo's philosophy in general and his approach to some nomistic practices in particular promote the law for just those ends. The evidence in this chapter supports the hypothesis that, in Galatians, Paul opposes an amalgam of early Jewish ideas now most accessible to us in the massive extant corpus of Philo.

This chapter develops its argument in two stages. First, it argues, in principle, that Philo's works are relevant to the study of Paul. Second, it bears the principle out in practice by showing how the general shape of Philo's philosophy, its structural use of στοιχεῖα, and its specific features are congruent with errors Paul opposes in Galatians. Following his philosophical program and within the broad context of his cosmology, Philo promotes the law as the παιδεία that leads the human spirit in a spiritual exodus from enslavement to the flesh into true freedom, righteousness, and harmony with the cosmos. Paul, however, denies this power to the law and points to the Anointed and the Spirit as the only ones who can effectively oppose the flesh and lead believers to produce righteousness in the context of new creation.

96   *3*

A. RELEVANCE: PHILO'S PERTINENCE
TO GALATIANS 4

Philo's corpus is relevant to the study of Paul's epistles and to the New Testament generally, but, as Gregory Sterling complains, "Philo has not been used half enough."[1] It is hard to say why much Pauline scholarship ignores Philo. Perhaps his content is dull or his argumentation, especially his allegoresis, is esoteric. Perhaps he seems anomalous: his paradigm is philosophical, and we expect "real" early Jews to be covenantal or apocalyptic;[2] he is sophisticated, and New Testament writers are supposed to be "simple folk."[3] Or perhaps his extant corpus is simply immense and impenetrable.[4] But, as Sterling contends, Philo's writings help "us to understand the dynamics of early Christianity more adequately than any other corpus" from the early Jewish world.[5]

This section outlines five reasons why those who want to understand the meaning of στοιχεῖα τοῦ κόσμου in Gal 4 should read Philo. The first three reasons require us to read Philo. The fourth reason validates Philo's relevance. And the final reason confirms that reading Philo does indeed help make sense of στοιχεῖα τοῦ κόσμου in the arguments of Gal 4.

1. Philo's Use of the Term Στοιχεῖον Surpasses and Represents Other Early Jewish Uses

Other early Jewish sources use the term στοιχεῖον 19 times; Philo uses the term στοιχεῖον 90 times. Thus any credible survey of first-century use of the term στοιχεῖον must consider him carefully. But if Philo's abundant use of the term is idiosyncratic, his data would only skew the study's conclusions. Yet the survey in chapter 1 showed that Philo's usage of στοιχεῖον is representative of early Jewish usage. Philo appeared alongside other early Jewish sources in each category: στοιχεῖον as an immaterial element, as a material substance, as a material space, and in the human body. Philo's usage is typical, not deviant.

2. Of the Four Times "Στοιχεῖα Κόσμου" Occurs Before Paul, Three are in Philo

As chapter 1 showed, the phrase στοιχεῖα κόσμου appears in extant sources as a first-century Jewish innovation to refer unambiguously to the material elements of which the cosmos and its bodies are made. As with the simple term στοιχεῖον, most uses of the phrase στοιχεῖα κόσμου are found in Philo: *Heir* 134, 140; *Eternity* 109. These texts make the sense of στοιχεῖα κόσμου clear:

The Argument for Redemptive Nomism in Philo's Philosophy 97

they are material. But the use of στοιχεῖα κόσμου in *Heir* 134, 140 also makes its significance clear, for there Philo uses the phrase in an allegoresis of God's covenant with Abraham, the "heir of divine things"—makes its significance in Galatians clear. Read side by side with *Heir*, Paul's use of στοιχεῖα τοῦ κόσμου within a couple paragraphs of an allegoresis on Abraham, the covenant, and the inheritance appears patently intelligible, if not intentional.

3. Philo is the Leading Early Jewish Allegorist

Paul's explicit use of allegory in Gal 4.21–31 corresponds to nothing else in the New Testament, the Septuagint, or the Dead Sea Scrolls. But it, along with Josephus's mention of ἀλληγορέω in *Ant.* 1.24,[6] corresponds with 45 instances of √αλληγορεω in Philo. Further, Paul applies the hermeneutical method implicit in Philo's allegoresis to one of Philo's favorite subjects: Abraham, Sarah, and Hagar. These points of correspondence lend compelling weight to Jason Zurawski's argument that Paul may have used the tools of Alexandrian allegorical exegesis to subvert the very ends to which they were normally used: the promotion of Moses's law for the liberation of the soul. Zurawski follows Peder Borgen and argues, against C. K. Barrett and the scholarly consensus, that Paul's allegory in Gal 4 interacts with "a tradition akin to Philo's."[7] For Zurawski, the evidence is so strong that he does not "roundly dismiss the possibility" that "Paul was reading Philo."[8] Thus, Philo is *the* source to consider when analyzing first-century Jewish allegory, including Paul's allegory in Gal 4.

4. Philo is Relevant to the Study of Early Christian Theology in General

Philo's influence validates his unique relevance as a backdrop against which to read many sections of the New Testament. His works are known and read decades later across the Mediterranean world. Writing to a Roman in the first century, the (presumably) pagan author "Longinus" cites *Drunkenness* 198 in *On the Sublime* 44.1–5.[9] Writing from Rome forty years after Philo's death, Josephus identifies Philo as "the head of the delegation of the Jews, a man held in the highest honour, . . . and no novice in philosophy" (*Ant.* 18.259).[10] Sterling asserts that "Josephus certainly used *De opificio mundi* in his account of creation."[11] And David Runia, Louis Feldman, and others contend that aspects of Philo's philosophy influenced Josephus himself, especially as regards the cosmos and the elements.[12] Philo's influence continued into the second century. In Syria, Numenius of Apamea and Celsus show "knowledge of his works," and, in Greece, Plutarch may as well.[13]

98   3

5. Philo's "Physiology" Helps Explain Paul's Obscure Discussion of Enslavement to the Weak Στοιχεῖα τοῦ Κόσμου

Chapter 2 introduced the idea, which this chapter will develop, that Philo prescribed study and practice of the law to liberate the soul from enslavement to the weakness of the elemental body. To that end, Philo's teaching promotes, as a single package, several key ideas which Paul opposes in his letter to the Galatians: the use of the law to attain righteousness and freedom (or life); the effective benefits of circumcision; observance of days, months, seasons, and years; and harmony with the cosmos (see Gal 2.16, 19, 21; 3.21; 4.3, 9–10, 21–30; 5.6; 6.12, 14). While some of these ideas are present in one ancient source or another, I have found no other single writer in which all are present.

6. Conclusion

While the lexical data require us to read Philo, and while scholars point repeatedly to the pertinence of Philo's work, it is reading Philo himself that will confirm his relevance to the quest for the elusive meaning of στοιχεῖα τοῦ κόσμου in Gal 4. This chapter considers Philo's exegetical program, the structural use of στοιχεῖον to mediate harmony within his philosophy, the redemptive benefits of particular nomistic practices, and the allegorical pattern of Abraham and his family. The chapter will show that Philo promotes the law as the παιδεία that leads the human spirit in a spiritual exodus from enslavement to the flesh into freedom, righteousness, and inheritance, ideas that Paul opposes in Galatians. The following sections discuss Philo's scholarly program, his use of στοιχεῖον to structure his philosophy and mediate a κόσμος–νόμος harmony, the redemptive benefits of circumcision and Moses's calendar, and the pattern of redemption in the allegoresis of Abraham, his migration, and his wives.

B. PROGRAM: READING MOSES THROUGH PLATO'S LENS

Philo's position determines his perspective, which in turn sets his program.[14] From his position as a Jewish scholar in first-century Alexandria, Philo sees himself as heir to two masters and their philosophies. First, as a Jew, Philo identifies himself as one of the "scholars and disciples of Moses" (*Spec. Laws* 1.345), the philosophers according to Moses (*Names* 223).[15] Second, as an Alexandrian, Philo is a student of Plato and, sharing much in common with Middle Platonism, joins the scholarly debates of Greek philosophy.[16] At this intersection of Jewish and Greek philosophies, Philo's exegetical project is conceived: reading Moses through Plato's lens.

The complex biculturalism of Philo's work defies simplistic classification within the outdated categories "Jewish" or "Hellenistic." Philo is both. On the one hand, he writes at the high point of "the rich Jewish exegetical tradition that flourished in Alexandria from the end of the third century B.C.E. to the beginning of the second century C.E." (see *Creation* 77; *Good Person* 82; *Contempl. Life* 28).[17] On the other hand, Philo sees himself also as a student of Plato. As in Middle Platonism generally, Philo augments and adapts the foundational ideas of Plato with Peripatetic, Stoic, and Pythagorean concepts.[18] As Runia notes, "The strongest influence was exerted by Platonism, in particular its division between the intelligible realm and the realm which is perceptible to the senses, its idea of the creation of the cosmos by a divine Creator and Plato's view of the life and immortality of the soul."[19] With this, Philo mixes some Stoic ideas, like the Logos and ethics, while rejecting others, like pantheism or the final conflagration of the cosmos.[20] Disagreements between Philo's antecedents create ambiguity within Philo's own thought: consider, for example, how he vacillates between Plato's four elements and Aristotle's proposal of a fifth, the quintessence, ether (*Dreams* 1.21–24).[21]

"As an individual, Philo is faithfully Jewish and thoroughly Hellenized, without any great tension."[22] Indeed, for him the Jewish and Greek worlds are complementary: Philo applies the perspectives and methods of Middle Platonism, together with insights from Stoic and Neopythagorean thought, to the interpretation of the Old Greek of the law of Moses.[23] Runia notes that, in some cases, for example when "Philo perceives a far-reaching parallelism between the Mosaic creation account and Plato's famous mythic cosmogony,"[24] "the result is an intellectual world which reads like a synthesis of Greek and biblical thought."[25] Though scholars have long disputed whether Philo subordinates Moses's law to a universal law (as Erwin Goodenough and Samuel Sandmel suggest[26]) or "compromises" the two (as Hindy Najman asserts[27]), Maren Niehoff sees rightly that Philo is "exploiting" "terms and doctrines," not borrowing them.[28] Indeed, a consensus is emerging among scholars that Philo "sees in the Torah the best formulation of the law of nature."[29] For Philo, as Niehoff discerns, Moses's law "is not based on human convention, but on the very structure of the world which has been shaped at the time of the creation."[30] Philo is thus a "Platonizing expositor of Scripture."[31] As John Barclay claims, in Philo "the whole gamut of Hellenistic culture is subordinated to Moses, pressed into service to endorse *his* original achievement."[32]

As such, Philo stands out among likely sources for the teaching opposed in Galatians. The Jewishness of Galatians' argument against the misuse of the law of Moses does not rule him out as irrelevant. In fact, that letter finds an intelligent interlocutor, and strong critic, in Philo.

C. STRUCTURE: ELEMENTALLY MEDIATED HARMONY

While there is a growing consensus among scholars on the program of Philo's philosophy—considering Moses's God through Plato's lens—and while several scholars have presented select passages from Philo to explain the meaning of στοιχεῖα τοῦ κόσμου,[33] Eduard Schweizer and Geurt van Kooten are among the few who have noted the role of the elements in maintaining harmony.[34] And no scholar that I have found has observed the load-bearing role that στοιχεῖα play in the structure of Philo's philosophy.

Philo uses the στοιχεῖα to mediate harmonies between earth and heaven and between the κόσμος and the νόμος. For Philo, these harmonies converge in the elemental symbolism of the cult and climax in the magnificence of the high priest and his vestments. But Paul's main concern lies with the suggestion that the στοιχεῖα can communicate redemptive benefits to the souls of those who practice the law.

1. Στοιχεῖα Mediate the Harmony of Earth with Heaven

When Philo studies Gen 1 as a map and then looks through Middle Platonism as a telescope, he sees a strikingly similar sky.[35] From this perspective, he sees heaven and the stars ruling over earth, giving light, marking times, showing signs, and setting seasons (*Creation* 55, 58–59; see Gen 1.14–18).[36] Philo explains that the lights are signs because they influence events on earth through a sympathetic affinity mediated by the elements. In keeping with his preference to refer to elements in sublunar regions, Philo rarely uses the term στοιχεῖον when discussing heaven, but, nonetheless, the elements play a crucial role in mediating the harmony of earth with heaven.

Philo explains that the stars fulfill their role as signs by modulating changes in the elements that effect events on earth. "Of all the things that happen upon earth, the signs are graven in the face of heaven" (*Spec. Laws* 1.92), because "things on earth are dependent on the heavenly realm through a natural affinity" (*Creation* 117; see *Spec. Laws* 1.16).[37] This affinity is mediated through elemental sympathy. Moses declares "the universe to be one and to have been made," and since the "interdependence of the parts is a characteristic of bodies which constitute a unity," "it stands to reason that all its completed several parts have the same elementary substances (στοιχειώδεις οὐσίαι) for their substratum" (*Migration* 180). God knows that "the interchanges of the στοιχεῖα out of which the κόσμος was framed and now consists" are "a vital operation," and he "produces them in unimpeded succession" (*Providence* 2.45). These "changes in the στοιχεῖα" are nature's "essential works" and are beneficial, just as rainstorms and breezes cleanse earth and air and sustain life (*Providence* 2.43, 45, 53).

The different heavenly bodies effect a variety of changes on earth. According to Julius Röhr, Philo is the first extant author to explain that the planets, especially the sun and moon, "display a very close affinity with the air and the earth. The air they convert and change into the annual seasons" and all sorts of weather (*Creation* 113).[38] The sun produces the yearly seasons (*Spec. Laws* 1.16). The moon's phases cause changes in the sky and affect water levels in rivers and seas (*Creation* 113; *Spec. Laws* 2.143). Among the fixed stars, the Pleiades set to show the time for sowing and rise to announce the good news (εὐαγγελίζομαι) of harvest (*Creation* 115; see Hesiod, *Op.* 383–384). And each of the twelve signs of the zodiac "produces its own particular colouring in the air and earth and water and their phases, and also in the different kinds of animals and plants" (*Moses* 2.126). For this reason, wise men have studied "the heavenly bodies," "observed (παρατηρέω) and recorded" phenomena, and "marked the signs" of hot and cold, dry and wet seasons and their agricultural effects (*Spec. Laws* 1.92).[39]

As the elements mediate the sympathy and causation of heaven with earth, by which the stars serve as signs, so too the elements mediate Philo's second harmony, that of the κόσμος with the νόμος.

2. Στοιχεῖα Mediate the Harmony of the Cosmos and the Law

For Philo, there is an inherent harmony between the κόσμος and the νόμος, both in their natures and in the behaviors that their natures enjoin. While many ancient societies observed "cosmologically-motivated laws," Philo contends throughout his work that the cosmos God made harmonizes with the laws he gave. This view of Moses's law underpins Philo's redemptive nomism, and it reappears in Josephus.

a. Recent Scholarship on Philo's Harmony of the Cosmos with the Law of Moses

Van Kooten documents a widespread first-century "cosmological rationalization of religious rituals."[40] He notes that Philo regards "some of the regulations of Jewish law"—for example, the feast of trumpets (*Spec. Laws* 2.186–192; see *Spec. Laws* 2.266; *Dreams* 1.21)—as "connected with cosmic phenomena." Van Kooten cites Plutarch to show that some Romans and some Egyptians also appealed to the elements or the physical nature of things

102   *3*

to explain their rituals (*Quaest. rom.* 263d–e; *Is. Os.* 353e–f).[41] Speaking of the material elements of the cosmos, he concludes, "In Graeco-Roman philosophy, these elements were considered to have given rise to religious legislation. People were convinced that some laws which prescribe particular religious festivals, purification rites and other rituals and rules are connected with cosmic phenomena."[42]

Schweizer exposes one set of cosmologically rationalized religious rituals in an overlooked, and previously untranslated, text from Alexander Polyhistor (DK 1.58b1). The text, he claims, "embodies all the characteristics mentioned in Col 2:16–23 except the celebration of sabbath and festivals."[43] There Schweizer shows us earth, water, air, and fire; the effect of their qualities on the seasons and the seasons' relative health; the ascent of pure souls to the ether; and, most significantly, the use of purifications and abstinence from sex, defilement, and various foods to attain purity. Here, clearly set forth in "the thoughts of the Pythagoreans," is a cosmologically motivated religious philosophy.

Niehoff also observes similarities between Philo and his contemporaries, though she notes significant differences as well. Stoics "had already applied the notion of natural law to a written law code," a "moral philosophy" "based . . . on the notion of 'living in agreement with nature'" (Diogenes Laertius 7.88).[44] "'Law,' Cicero insisted, 'is the highest reason implanted in Nature'" (*Leg.* 1.18).[45] Niehoff suggests that Philo "may have had similar objectives in mind when grounding Mosaic law in nature."[46] However, "Philo stresses that, contrary to other legislations, [the Mosaic law] is not based on human convention, but on the very structure of the world. . . . It is thus not an invention of the human mind, but a reflection of unchanging realities."[47] Niehoff exhibits this "intrinsic congruence between Mosaic law and the structure of nature" in Philo's particular teaching on the health of body and soul and on the Jewish holidays.[48] I consider these specifics in section D below.

b. Philo and Josephus

The prominence of a κόσμος:νόμος harmony in the introductions to both Philo's and Josephus's corpora suggests that this view of the law was well known throughout the Jewish diaspora in the first century. Philo writes *Creation* as an introduction to what will become two or three exegetical series on the Law of Moses.[49] He opens straightway with admiration for the "marvellous" way Moses wrote his "exordium" (*Creation* 1–3). Moses begins his laws not with injunctions but with "an account of the making of the κόσμος, the reasoning for this being that the κόσμος is in harmony with the law and the law with the κόσμος" (*Creation* 3). In *Moses*, which is a sort of extended biographical preface to Philo's philosophical program,[50] Philo explains that this harmony exists because "the Father and Maker of the κόσμος was in the truest sense also its Lawgiver" (*Moses* 2.47). On this basis, Moses designed "the particular enactments" of the law to "attain to the harmony of the universe," and they are in fact "in agreement with the principles of eternal nature" (*Moses* 2.52).[51] Thus, "the man who observes the law is at once a citizen of the cosmos, directing his actions in relation to the rational purpose of nature, in accordance with which the entire κόσμος also is administered" (*Creation* 3; see *Moses* 2.48).

Half a century later, as Josephus opens *Antiquities*, he describes Moses and the cosmos in similar terms. Moses "did not begin the arrangement of the laws with contracts and the rights of people with one another in a manner similar to others, but he led their thoughts up to God and the structure of the κόσμος" (1.21). Josephus then sets out to present his own work as congruent "with the majesty and benevolence of God. For all things have their arrangement in harmony with the nature of the universe" (*Ant.* 1.21).

Though Runia says Josephus "is surely dependent on Philo,"[52] Louis Feldman notes that Dieter Georgi acknowledges "the parallel with Philo" but argues that both Josephus and Philo "depend upon a common apologetic tradition."[53] Regardless of its lineage, Elias Bickerman's judgment stands: there was a view, common to many "Jews in the Greek age," that "the Torah was not just another code, but the revealed, fundamental order within which man, all other creatures, and all the elements of the cosmos as well ought to live."[54] This common Jewish view is a cornerstone of Philo's redemptive nomism.

Following Niehoff's example, the following sections will show the details of Philo's κόσμος:νόμος harmony. In most aspects of the harmony, the texts show that it is the στοιχεῖα of the cosmos that mediate the harmony and, thereby, that transfer the impetus of Moses's cosmological principles to the imperative of Moses's distinctive practices: the temple cult, the Sabbath and the festivals, and the food laws.[55]

3. Στοιχεῖα as Medium and Message in the Symbolism of the Cult

Philo's principles of harmony converge when he refracts the glories of the tabernacle and the high priest through the lens of his Middle Platonic hermeneutic. Philo—and, later, Josephus following Philo—presents an ἔκφρασις, or "descriptive exposition," that portrays with "vivid" "clarity" the wonders of Moses's cult.[56] Whereas in others of Philo's harmonies the στοιχεῖα play the significant role of mediating the harmony, in this most detailed expression of the harmony, the elements are both medium and message.

From Philo's perspective, the Mosaic cult is a symbol of "the whole κόσμος," which is God's "truest" temple (*Spec. Laws* 1.66). The στοιχεῖα make the symbolism work (*QE* 2.85). The altar of incense is a symbol of "thanksgiving for the στοιχεῖα": "the altar . . . contains parts of the four," and the four parts of the incense are "a symbol of the στοιχεῖα" (*Moses* 2.101; *Heir* 226; see *J.W.* 5.218). The curtains are woven from materials "symbolical of the four στοιχεῖα"; they frame the holy place and set the three articles in the symbolic space of the cosmos (*Prelim. Studies* 117; *Moses* 2.88; see *J.W.* 5.212–513; *Ant.* 3.183). And the blood "poured upon the altar" represents the mind that is "reduced to a single element (ἀναστοιχειόω)" in its total service of God (*Heir* 182–184).

The cosmic symbolism builds to a crescendo in Philo's depiction of the high priest's vestments. In the Exposition, he identifies the high priest's vesture, as a whole and "in its parts," as "a typical representation of the κόσμος and its particular parts" (*Moses* 2.117, see 143; *Spec. Laws* 1.84).[57] In the Allegory, he reads the high priest as "a Divine Word," for the supreme Word's garments are the cosmos: earth, water, air, fire, "and all that comes forth from these" (*Flight* 108–110). The ephod and the breast-piece are symbols of heaven (*Spec. Laws* 1.86),[58] and the color and design of the high priest's robe represent the three sublunar elemental spaces: earth, water, and air.[59]

The manifold beauty of the sacred vesture suggests three marvelous "philosophical conceptions" to Philo (*Spec. Laws* 1.95–96). First, the vesture shows that the high priest himself becomes a microcosm, "transformed from a man into the nature of the κόσμος" (*Moses* 2.135; see *Heir* 155). Second, the vesture shows that the cosmos joins with the high priest and intercedes for him (*Moses* 2.133–134; see *Heir* 199–200; *Dreams* 1.215). Third, the vesture shows that "the high priest of the Jews makes prayers and gives thanks not only on behalf of the whole human race but also for the parts of nature, earth, water, air, fire" (*Spec. Laws* 1.97; see 2.163, 167). In Josephus's words, the design of the sacred vestments befits the "ceremonies of cosmical significance" performed within the temple (*J.W.* 4.324).[60]

Here on the person of the high priest and in the structure of the sanctuary, Philo's cosmology reaches its zenith. Here, framed by the harmonies of earth with heaven and the cosmos with the law, Philo's use of the term and the concept στοιχεῖα comes to most frequent expression. And here converge the themes dearest to Philo: the worship of the one God, according to the instruction of his servant Moses, in a symbol of the intelligible cosmos, together with and on behalf of the whole cosmos.

But here is not where Paul's concerns lie.

The Argument for Redemptive Nomism in Philo's Philosophy

4. Στοιχεῖα Mediate the Redemptive Benefits of the Law to Its Practitioner

Paul is concerned by an amalgam of early Jewish thought that promotes the redemptive benefit of keeping the law of Moses. It promises that the minds of those who observe the law, its teachings and its practices, will be liberated from enslavement to the body's πάθη, pleasures, and lusts (*Rewards* 121, 124). By keeping the law's calendar—its days, months, seasons, and years—they will cultivate self-control and other virtues (*Spec. Laws* 2.56–175). By circumcising their foreskins, they will suppress superfluous impulses (*QG* 3.47). By doing the law they will live in harmony with the cosmos (*Creation* 3). And by leaving behind body, senses, and speech, as Abraham left land, kinsfolk, and father's house, they will qualify to inherit the reward God promised Abraham and his son (*Heir* 69). These are the δόγματα in the philosophy according to the στοιχεῖα τοῦ κόσμου that concern Paul, and these we find articulated best in Philo, an influential Jewish teacher of Paul's own day.

Sections D and E describe the specifics of Philo's redemptive nomism and the general pattern modelled allegorically in Abraham's migration.

D. SPECIFICS: REDEMPTIVE BENEFITS OF PARTICULAR NOMISTIC PRACTICES

For Philo, the grand significance of the law's symbolism of intellectual things does not obviate "careful attention" to its "literal sense" (*Migration* 89). Both are important.[61]

> We should look on all these outward observances as resembling the body, and their inner meanings as resembling the soul. It follows that, exactly as we have to take thought for the body, because it is the abode of the soul, so we must pay heed to the letter of the laws. If we keep and observe these, we shall gain a clearer conception of those things of which these are the symbols. (*Migration* 93)

The point must not be missed: the practices themselves benefit the soul, both directly—by giving it a clear conception of the "inner meanings"—and indirectly—by attending to the body. To those who "set the holy laws before them to guide them in all they do" God promises "a healthy body," not only free of disease and elemental imbalance, but also "redeemed" from "slavery" to the body's πάθη, pleasures, and lusts (*Rewards* 118–124). This is Philo's redemptive nomism in a nutshell.

In *Migration*, three particular laws come to Philo's mind: circumcision, "the Seventh Day," and "the Feast" (*Migration* 91–92). The practice of these rituals and the regimen of Moses's diet bless the redeemed soul with a healthy body not subject to weaknesses caused by elemental forces.[62]

1. Practicing Circumcision Cuts Off Excessive Desires

Philo promotes both the symbol and the practice of circumcision as effective for cutting off excessive desires. Philo discusses circumcision's benefits for the soul in the Exposition and in Questions and Answers. He opens his four-book Exposition of the *Special Laws* with a defense of circumcision. Philo finds four reasons for circumcision in the "old-time studies of divinely gifted men who made deep research into the writings of Moses": (1) it prevents "the malady of the prepuce"; (2) "it promotes the cleanliness of the whole body"; and (3) it enhances the fertility of intercourse (*Spec. Laws* 1.2–7). However, the third traditional reason, which is similar to Philo's own reasons, stands apart from the other three: circumcision "assimilates the circumcised member to the heart" (*Spec. Laws* 1.6).[63] Philo's own ideas about circumcision hint at what he means by "assimilation to the heart." "For since the intercourse of man with woman wins the victory prize among the love-charms of pleasures," "the legislators thought good to dock the organ which ministers to such intercourse, thus making circumcision the figure of the excision of excessive and superfluous pleasure, not only of one pleasure but of all the other pleasures signified by one, and that the most imperious" (*Spec. Laws* 1.9).[64]

But circumcision is more than just figurative; it is operative. In *QG* Philo suggests that circumcision itself is effective at cutting off desires. Moses "rightly . . . suppresses the superfluous impulses of the male by the sign of circumcision" (*QG* 3.47).[65] He continues: "they say that the circumcision of the skin is a symbol, as if (to show that) it is proper to cut off superfluous and excessive desires by exercising continence and endurance in matters of the Law" (*QG* 3.48).

Finally, the "outward observance" of circumcision's "inner meaning" also has a social benefit.[66] "If we keep and observe these, we shall gain a clearer conception of those things of which these are the symbols; and besides that we shall not incur the censure of the many and the charges they are sure to bring against us" (*Migration* 92–93).[67] For restraining desires and for social acceptance, Philo affirms that circumcision is more effective than having a foreskin.

2. Observing the Sabbath and Festivals Inculcates Self-Control and Other Virtues

In Philo's view, the "particular enactments" of Moses's calendar, like the rest of the laws, "seek to attain to the harmony of the universe and are in agreement with the principles of the eternal nature" (*Moses* 2.52). The stars mark times: "days and months and years," and, "the rhythm of the Jewish year imitates" their "eternal movement."[68] Beyond that, "the halachic provisions for the Jewish holidays create that special framework where *enkrateia* is cultivated."[69] Thus, as Niehoff observes, "by observing the Jewish holidays the soul is attuned to the universe."[70] Moses's νόμος corresponds to the κόσμος, and each of the days and feasts in their respective months and seasons of the year nurtures one virtue or another in the soul.

a. The Sabbath

Since every "section of the cosmos," its structures and times, is "philhebdomadic," the Sabbath confers many benefits on those who practice it (*Creation* 101–116, 128; see *Decalogue* 102–105; *Spec. Laws* 2.40, 57–59).[71] It preserves the balance of body and soul in their cycle of work and rest. While the body rests and is refreshed, "the soul and the dominant mind" (ὁ ἡγεμών νοῦς) study philosophy to gain "good sense, temperance, courage, justice and the other virtues" (*Spec. Laws* 2.60–64; see *Moses* 2.212–216; *Decalogue* 98–101). In this pattern of soul activity after bodily work, Sabbath-keepers imitate the Creator. They also join heaven and earth in celebrating the feast of "the birthday of the world" (*Moses* 2.210; *Decalogue* 100–101).[72] The Sabbath's rest allows the slave a "spark of freedom," a nudge "towards the perfection of virtue," and it compels the master to work with his own body and thereby maintains his courage (*Spec. Laws* 2.66–70).[73] In sum, observing the Sabbath "adjusts the Jew to the rhythm and structure of nature, cultivating in him an orientation towards manliness and sovereignty," the "two virtues . . . necessary to develop *enkrateia* and become an authentic Jew."[74]

For Philo, "the sacred seventh day" is the pattern for the other feasts, and each promotes virtue in its own way (*Spec. Laws* 2.39–222).[75] Philo assures us that "the mere recital" of these laws "is enough to make the naturally gifted perfect in virtue without any effort on their part and to produce some degree of obedience in the rebellious and hard-natured" (*Spec. Laws* 2.39). But the careful observation of Moses's laws for days, months, seasons, and years and for rites of purification achieves even more. The laws "restrict the pleasures of the belly and the parts below it and the horde . . . setting reason to guide the irrational senses, and also check and rein in the wild and extravagant impulses of the soul" (*Spec. Laws* 2.163).[76]

b. The Crossing Feast (Pascha)

Seven sets the day of the Crossing Feast, which falls on the fourteenth day of the month. The ritual preparations purify the people to act as priests, and they dispose them not "to indulge the belly with wine and viands" (*Spec. Laws* 2.145–148). The Crossing Feast's "literal" practices correspond to its allegorical meaning. For as the Israelites "crossed" out of Egypt, "the type of the body," so too "the lover of wisdom is occupied solely in crossing from the body and the πάθη" with the aid of virtue (2.148).[77]

c. The Feast of Unleavened Bread

The timing, the duration, and the food of the Feast of Unleavened Bread are set "according to conformity with nature and to harmony with the whole cosmos" (*Spec. Laws* 2.150).[78] The feast falls "in the spring equinox," a "likeness" of when "this κόσμος was created. The στοιχεῖα were then separated and placed in harmonious order with reference to themselves and each other" (2.151). The timing of the feast follows the number seven. It is celebrated in the seventh month "as judged by the cycle of the sun"; it "begins at the middle of the month, on the fifteenth day, when the moon is full"; and it "is held for seven days" (*Spec. Laws* 2.150, 155–156; see *QE* 1.1). Finally, the feast's fare corresponds with the καιρός of the year. The bread is unleavened not only "because our forefathers . . . were so intensely hurried," but also because unleavened bread "is paralleled by" the imperfection of grain at that καιρός (*Spec. Laws* 2.158). Philo suggests further that unleavened bread corresponds to the food that the "earliest inhabitants" of the newly created cosmos would have eaten, since they "used the gifts of the κόσμος in their unperverted state before pleasure had got the mastery" (2.160). Thus by coordinating timing and food with καιρός, the feast cultivates righteousness.

d. The Fast (Day of Atonement)

The Fast is, ironically, "the greatest of the feasts" (*Spec. Laws* 2.194). While Moses "exhorted" the Jews to control "the tongue and the belly and the organs below the belly" throughout the year, he appointed the Fast as a whole day dedicated to self-restraint (ἐγκράτεια) (2.195). Since the timing and the food of the Fast are coordinated with the καιρός of harvest, they strengthen the soul in at least two ways. First, the timing "teaches the mind not to put trust in what stands ready prepared before us as though it were the source of health and life" (2.197). Second, those who fast receive temporary relief from the waves of food which, according to Plato's medical theory, hinder the reasoning mind (*Spec. Laws* 2.201–202; see *Tim.* 43a–44c, 86e–87a, 88a–b). As Niehoff observes, "The Day of Atonement thus exemplifies the inculcation

The Argument for Redemptive Nomism in Philo's Philosophy 109

of *enkrateia*, the central Jewish value which informs all parts of Mosaic legislation. By demanding extreme abstinence this holiday . . . restores the spiritual dimension of man which enables him to gain a rational control over daily affairs."[79]

e. Conclusion

According to Philo, since Moses's calendar is coordinated with the times—days, months, καιροί, and years—and substances—the στοιχεῖα—of the Creator's cosmos, those who observe the festivals and their particular diets live in harmony with the cosmos. They grow in self-control and other virtues; they restore the control of reason, the leading mind, over the body's appetites caused by its πάθη; and they become more like God. Paul could not disagree more. As chapter 6 and the conclusion will show, observing days, months, καιροί, and years is a sign of a return to enslavement under the στοιχεῖα (Gal 4.9–10). Instead, it is life in the Son and the Spirit that produces righteousness.

3. Abstaining from Succulent Animals Controls Insatiety

As Philo saw Moses's calendar in harmony with the times of the cosmos, so too in *Special Laws*, he shows the benefit of the harmony between Moses's food laws and the organization of creatures within three elemental spaces.[80] As Christina Termini notes, Philo's hermeneutic follows "basic guidelines" on two levels. "At the cosmic level the Mosaic laws reflect the principles that direct the regular harmony of celestial and terrestrial phenomena. At the anthropological level, they lead one to the virtues, [and] they promote health, thus maintaining the appropriate equilibrium in mind and body."[81]

In his Exposition of laws related to the tenth commandment, Philo's hermeneutic helps him explain Moses's emphasis on food laws. Philo connects his discussion of ἐπιθυμία to Plato's doctrine of the tripartite soul (*Spec. Laws* 4.92–94).[82] He then explains that Moses focused on food laws because the desire for food, operative in the belly, represents other forms of ἐπιθυμία as their leader (4.91, 96). As circumcision taught and effected the cutting off of excessive sexual desire, so also the food laws "bridle" the desires for food and drink and "extinguish" desire (4.97, 118).

Similarly, in order to rescue people from enslavement to the sense of taste, Moses designated as unclean those animals "whose flesh is the finest and fattest" (*Spec. Laws* 4.100). Philo's discussion of Moses's proscription of land animals (4.100–109), water creatures (4.110–115), and "the inhabitants of the air" (*Spec. Laws* 4.116–118; see *Providence* 2.69) reflects the elemental structuring of Lev 11.[83] "Thus in each element (μέρη) of the κόσμος, earth, water, air he withdrew from our use various kinds of each sort, land creatures, water creatures, flying fowls, and by this as by the withdrawal of fuel from a fire he creates an extinguisher to desire" (*Spec. Laws* 4.118).

According to Philo, since Moses's laws are in accord with the cosmos, his food laws, like the laws about circumcision and the calendar, both teach and effect self-restraint. The laws acknowledge the vulnerability of the ἐπιθυμία, reflect the elemental structure of the cosmos, and give instruction that will rescue those who heed it and lead them to "a truly moral life."[84]

4. Conclusion

According to Philo's hermeneutic, Moses's special laws teach and effect self-control. They are effective because of their intentional harmony with a philosophical understanding of the cosmos, its times and substances. Circumcision symbolizes and effects cutting off excessive desire. Moses's feasts, new moons, and sabbaths coordinate with the cosmos's days, months, seasons, and years. And Moses's food laws work with an informed understanding of the soul within the body and of the elemental classification of creatures in order to extinguish insatiate desire. Together these particular laws rescue the soul from slavery to the body and its elementally mediated πάθη and ἐπιθυμίαι—whether the moisture that exacerbates desire for sex or the moisture and heat that intensify desire for food. Together, these laws prepare a person to "be well pleasing to God, to the κόσμος, to nature, to laws, to wise men" (*Spec. Laws* 4.131). As Runia argues in his synthesis of Philo's use of the *Timaeus* in his exegesis of the Pentateuch, "Only when the createdness and structure of the cosmos, man's place in that structure and the nature of man himself are taken into consideration, is the exegete in a position to show how the migratory journey of the soul is possible and how the prescriptions of the Law can aid the soul in its quest for a blessed life."[85] With these words, Runia brings us to the center of Philo's thought and, I shall argue, of Paul's concern in his references to the στοιχεῖα τοῦ κόσμου in Galatians.

E. PATTERN: THE MIGRATION OF THE SOUL
AND THE ALLEGORY OF ABRAHAM

In Valentin Nikiprowetzky's judgment, the soul's migration is the "center," the "constant theme," of Philo's thought.[86] Philo sees the soul's migration symbolized in three historical events: Abraham's journey from the Chaldees, Israel's journey from Egypt, and the exiles' future journey from the nations (*Abraham* 62–80; *Spec. Laws* 2.145–161; *Rewards* 163–167; etc.).

The Argument for Redemptive Nomism in Philo's Philosophy   111

La Migration est l'itinéraire spirituel qui conduit l'âme du sage individuel ou le peuple consacré, dans son ensemble, de la chair à la lumière du monde intelligible, de l'esclavage en Egypte à la liberté en Canaan, terre de la vertu ou cité de Dieu. Le Pentateuque est "une école de prêtrise," c'est-à-dire que par l'intermédiaire de symboles divers, par l'intelligence et la pratique des Lois, il enseigne au progressant à suivre les pas de Moïse et à réaliser sous sa conduite l'Exode spirituel.[87]

Similarly, as Adam Kamesar observes, "the historical part of the Pentateuch constitutes an allegorical portrayal of the ethical and spiritual progress of the individual" which "Philo sees . . . represented allegorically in the various personae of the Pentateuchal narrative."[88] Chief among these personae are Moses, whose law is in harmony with the cosmos, and Abraham, who anticipated the law by living virtuously in harmony with the cosmos.[89] Read allegorically, these "biblical personae-as-exempla" are also "biblical personae-as-minds."[90]

Thus the allegory of the soul is primary. According to Philo, it is essential for understanding the Pentateuch, for, as Kamesar states, "the allegory of the soul . . . stands at the core of Philo's understanding of the intent of the Pentateuchal narrative."[91] And, according to Nikiprowetzky, it is essential for understanding Philo: "Tout le 'système' de Philon consiste à reconnaître inlassablement cet enseignement au fond des textes et derrière les symboles de l'Ecriture."[92]

This section of the chapter shows how Philo uses allegory to present Abraham as a pattern of the soul's migration. Chapter 5 will show that Paul denies that the law can do precisely what Philo says it does: redeem the person from slavery. Further, Paul does so with an explicit allegoresis of Abraham, signaling clearly that he is engaging such an early Jewish appropriation of the Abraham story but using the allegory to reach just the opposite conclusions.[93]

1. Philo's Allegorical Method

Building on his presupposition of the harmony of the cosmos with the law of Moses, Philo combines earlier Alexandrian modes of exegesis to frame his own approach: spiritual allegoresis. While Philo can use his approach to dislodge a literal reading of the text, he uses it normally to develop the text's didactic intent. Philo's allegories are occupied mostly with the characters of Genesis, and he follows a standard method to exhibit the spiritual significance of their lives.

Within the context of his philosophy, Philo develops his own exegetical method by combining the literal and allegorical approaches of his predecessors. Demetrius and other Jewish scholars had produced "literal and surprisingly critical scholarship on the biblical text."[94] In another vein, Aristobulus and Aristeas offered allegorical interpretations without discussing the literal meaning of a text.[95] But Philo recognizes that the Pentateuch, "as an inspired and authoritative text," is in harmony with "universal cosmic principles." So, as Peder Borgen explains, Philo proposes to "interpret one and the same biblical text basically on two, sometimes on three levels, . . . the concrete and specific level, the level of the cosmic and general principles, and the level of the divine realm of the beyond."[96] Like Stoic allegorists before him, Philo can use this "spiritual allegory" to "uproot the mythological level of scripture," but that move is rare (*Alleg. Interp.* 2.19; *Planting* 32–36; *Agriculture* 96–97).[97] According to Philo, the law's own words demand to have their spiritual significance revealed, for Moses himself intended it (*Heir* 197). This Philo does, Niehoff observes, while also "providing an in-depth study of the literal meaning of the text."[98] "As many scholars have recognized," this composite hermeneutic sets Philo apart "from Greek allegorical interpretation."[99]

Philo's approach leads him to a "conservative" method that arises from the text itself. "Indeed the sacred oracles most evidently afford us the clues for the use of this method" (*Planting* 36). So, as Niehoff explains, "Philo proceeds verse by verse in the *Allegory of the Law*, quoting a biblical passage, identifying a particular problem or question raised by it, and then discussing and ultimately resolving it on the allegorical level."[100] Philo often signals this last move with explicit reference to another meaning, whether "symbolic,"[101] "allegorical,"[102] "underlying,"[103] "inner,"[104] "hidden,"[105] "not seen,"[106] "scientific,"[107] or simply "special."[108]

Philo's approach draws his attention to the characters of Genesis and the didactic value of their lives.[109] He interprets Abraham, Isaac, and Jacob as "symbols of virtue acquired respectively by teaching, nature and practice" (*Abraham* 52). These "good and blameless men" followed the law before it was written. "They gladly accepted conformity with nature, holding that nature itself was, as indeed it is, the most venerable of statutes, and thus their whole life was one of happy obedience to the law" (*Abraham* 6). Chief among these exemplary men is Abraham.

2. The Allegory of Abraham's Migration

Philo interprets Abraham's migration from the land of the Chaldeans allegorically as the migration of the soul from the body. As God makes himself known to Abraham, and as Abraham seeks God, Abraham comes to live in harmony with nature, and he becomes a living law. Abraham's migration—of body and soul—thus sets the pattern for Israel's migration from Egypt and for any foreigner who would seek God.

When God calls Abraham to "leave his country," Philo explains that he is summoning him to leave both Chaldea and its polytheism (*Abraham* 62). Philo agrees, to some extent, with the "sympathetic affinity" the Chaldean astronomers see between the movements of the stars and events on earth (*Migration* 178; see *Virtues* 212). Indeed, Moses "endorses" this Chaldean "doctrine" (*Migration* 180; see *Moses* 2.52; *Creation* 117; *Spec. Laws* 1.16, 92). But Philo objects when Chaldean cosmology teaches "that the circuits of sun and moon and of the other heavenly bodies determine for every being in existence both good things and their opposites," for that makes "Fate and Necessity divine" (*Migration* 179).[110]

In Philo's Exposition of the story, the literal sense of Abraham's migration leads necessarily to its allegorical significance. When Abraham discerned God as "a charioteer and pilot presiding over the world" (*Abraham* 69), he left his father's house, lest the "delusions" of Chaldean astrology "render it impossible for him to discover the One, . . . the Father of all things, . . . to know the Existent" (*Virtues* 214–215). Since Abraham's body and soul are interconnected, his "literal" departure from Chaldea was necessarily also a spiritual departure (*Virtues* 214). Seen in this light, Philo's allegoresis is essentially a development of the spiritual significance of the accounts of Abraham's migration already present in other early Jewish sources (see Jub. 11.16–12.24). Thus, "the migrations as set forth by the literal text of the scriptures are made by a man of wisdom, but according to the laws of allegory by a virtue-loving soul in its search for the true God" (*Abraham* 68).

Leaving Chaldea and travelling toward Haran, Abraham journeys from astrology to "sense" and the study of the human self. There, after Abraham discovered his mind's rule of his senses and reasoned that the world, too, must have a ruler, "God . . . was seen by Abraham," that is, God revealed himself to Abraham (*Abraham* 72–80).

In the Allegory, Philo associates Abraham's departure from his "land and kindred and his father's house" with his forsaking "body, sense, and speech" (*Worse* 159). The allegory is mediated elementally. "'Land' or 'country' is a symbol of body . . . because the body took its substance out of earth (or land) and is again resolved into earth" (*Migration* 2–3). From this perspective, Abraham could see God because his soul ascended "free from the encumbrance of this body of ours" (*Worse* 159). Abraham's migration is thus a symbol of the mind's escape from the body.

Abraham journeyed from Haran to the promised land, which Philo interprets variously as wisdom, virtue, and life in harmony with nature (*Heir* 98; see *Rewards* 58). Abraham also believed God, that is, he "grasped a firm and unswerving conception of the truth that there is one Cause above all, and that it provides for the world and all that there is therein" (*Virtues* 216; see *Abraham* 262–274).

114   3

Finally, these many blessings manifested themselves in his life. "Abraham journeyed even as the Lord spoke to him" (*Migration* 127, quoting Gen 12.4). Having left behind his body, his mind "walks in the track of right reason and follows God" (*Migration* 128). Thus Abraham both "did the divine law and the divine commands" and lived "agreeably to nature," for "unwritten nature gave him the zeal to follow where wholesome and untainted impulse led him" (*Abraham* 275, 276; *Migration* 128).

Abraham's migration, following God and nature, prefigures Israel's migration as they follow Moses out of Egypt. Throughout Philo's corpus, Egypt stands for "the land of the body."[111] Thus he describes Israel in Egypt as the soul in the body, burdened "under the pressure of the flesh" and bound to "submit to such injunctions as its merciless ἐπιθυμίαι may lay upon it" (*Migration* 14).[112] As Sarah Pearce explains, for Philo,

> Departure from Egypt, the body, is always associated with the moral or spiritual progress of the soul away from the body and the things of the body. Arriving in Egypt represents the soul in danger, subject to assault, imprisonment or enslavement by the bodily passions. To stay in Egypt long term represents the inexorable decline of the soul into slavery to the passions and the material.[113]

Abraham's migration is also paradigmatic for the migration of each soul from its body, the souls of foreigners included (*Migration* 184–195).[114] Philo is explicit in *Virtues*: "he is the standard of nobility for all proselytes, who, abandoning the ignobility of strange laws . . . which assigned divine honours to . . . soulless things in general, have come to settle in a better land" (*Virtues* 219). Philo connects with non-Jewish inquirers in four ways. First, he identifies Abraham as foreign (*Dreams* 1.161).[115] Second, he reports God's dialogue with Abraham in second person, thus appealing simultaneously to the reader (e.g., *Abraham* 70–71; *Migration* 9–12). Third, Philo asserts that Moses sought not only "to refute the Chaldean opinion" but also "to change the way of thinking of those whose judgement still inclines to Chaldeanism" (*Migration* 184). From this perspective, Philo's description of Chaldeans is also apropos Stoics.[116] "These men imagined that this visible universe was the only thing in existence, either being itself God or containing God in itself as the soul of the whole" (*Migration* 179; see *Abraham* 69; *Heir* 97; *Prelim. Studies* 49). Philo's denigration of the Chaldeans' ancient creed thus prompts his contemporaries to abandon Stoicism and seek the Creator.[117] Fourth, in *Virtues*, Philo associates the Chaldeans with "polytheism" generally, noting their worship of "the stars and the whole heaven and κόσμος" as gods (*Virtues* 212, 214, 219).[118]

Philo presents Abraham's migration from Chaldea via Haran to the promised land as the soul's migration from astrology through sense perception and physiology to wisdom and the knowledge of God. His migration stands also for the soul's migration from the encumbrance of the body, a migration acted out on a national scale by Israel in the exodus and celebrated annually in the Crossing Feast. Philo exhibits each of these migrations to encourage non-Jewish readers to migrate from the lusts of the flesh, heed Moses's laws, and live in harmony with nature, perhaps even, like Abraham, with the aid of the divine spirit.

3. The Allegory of Abraham's Two Wives and Two Sons

In a similar way, Philo also presents Abraham's two wives in a sequential scheme, with Abraham maturing from one stage to the next. Abraham's relationship with each woman produces a son that corresponds to his mother.

For Philo, Sarah's handmaid Hagar stands for "preliminary learning," the course of study taught in schools (*Alleg. Interp.* 3.244). As "preliminary studies," "the school subjects" are necessary, but inferior (*Prelim. Studies* 13, 18, 19; *Alleg. Interp.* 3.245). They serve wisdom as Hagar serves Sarah (*Prelim. Studies* 9–10). After all, Hagar is from Egypt, which stands for the "earthly . . . body" and its senses, and the sensible phenomena which the school subjects study are "the staple," but not the fullness, of philosophy (*Prelim. Studies* 20–21).

The mind's intercourse with "lower instruction" and with "virtue" bears children, and the sons correspond to their mothers. Ishmael inherits sophistry, but "wisdom is Isaac's inheritance," for he is self-taught (*Sobriety* 8–9; *Names* 255). "The school subjects" are fit for a "mere infant" like Ishmael, but "the sciences which deal with the virtues" are appropriate for a "full-grown man" like Isaac (*Sobriety* 9).

Since the school subjects are "preliminary learning," when the soul matures, they are no longer necessary. When Hagar runs away the first time, Abram is still studying nature, and Sarai is sovereign only over herself (*Cherubim* 1–5). But years later their names have changed: Abraham has become "the wise, the lover of God," and Sarah is now the general virtue "sovereignty" (*Cherubim* 7). Indeed, Sarah has "ceased from the manner of women"; that is, she has "died to the πάθη" (*Cherubim* 8, alluding to Gen 18.11). Thus, at that time, it is right for the handmaiden Hagar (preliminary studies) and her son Ishmael (the sophist) to be "cast forth" (*Cherubim* 8–9). Isaac will not inherit alongside Ishmael, for the self whom God has blessed to be its own teacher cannot "still live in concubinage with the slavish (δοῦλαι) arts" (*Prelim. Studies* 36). Beyond that, God even restrains Isaac "from going down into Egypt and from meeting with the ensnaring pleasures of the flesh" (*Migration* 29, alluding to Gen 26.2).

116   *3*

Though scattered through several works, Philo's presentation of the allegory of Abraham's wives is fairly consistent. Unable to beget a child with Sarai (virtue), Abram (mind) mates with Sarai's Egyptian (bodily) handmaiden Hagar (preliminary studies) and begets Ishmael (sophistry). This relationship makes Abraham wise and prepares him to beget Isaac (happiness and joy) with Sarah (sovereignty). No longer needed, Hagar is cast forth with her son, and Isaac (self-taught virtue), like his post-menopausal (passionless) mother, lives free from the passions of the flesh and the slavery of bastard thoughts. As chapter 5 will show, Philo's allegoresis is strikingly similar to and markedly different from Paul's allegoresis in Gal 4.

4. Conclusion

For Philo, Abraham's life is an example of the journey of the soul from enslavement to the body to the freedom of wisdom and virtue. Like Israel's later national exodus, Abraham's migration involves departing from the body and removing his soul from the influence of pantheism and polytheism. Abraham's journey leads him through the school subjects to wisdom and virtue. His life, lived in harmony with the cosmos, is the pattern for all foreigners who would seek wisdom and God, and it becomes the norm that Moses codifies when he gives the written law to Israel. With this reasoning, Philo presents Moses's law as the ideal way to live free from the πάθη and lusts of the flesh and in harmony with the cosmos.

F. CONCLUSION

This chapter opened with the assertion that Philo's works are relevant to the study of Gal 4. It showed that Philo uses στοιχεῖον not only to structure his philosophy but also to mediate a harmony between the κόσμος and the νόμος. Within that paradigm, Philo promotes the observance of the law as the way (1) to control the insatiety of the flesh and experience spiritual exodus from slavery to the elemental flesh, (2) to attain righteousness, (3) to qualify to inherit the promises God gave Abraham, and (4) to live in harmony with the cosmos. Philo also shows the redemptive power of cosmic harmony in the allegoresis of Abraham, his migration, and his wives. With these principles, Philo's redemptive nomism stands as the argument that connects the term στοιχεῖα τοῦ κόσμου and the concept of enslavement under the στοιχεῖα that compose the flesh with Paul's concern about the law in Galatians. In that letter, Paul denies to the law every one of the benefits Philo promises, and he does so while indicating with signal after clear signal that he is opposing an amalgam of early Jewish ideas about the law that is remarkably similar

The Argument for Redemptive Nomism in Philo's Philosophy 117

to Philo's redemptive nomism.[119] For Paul, the law served a limited purpose for a limited time, but, now that faith has come, continuing to use the law for that purpose is regressive, and trying to use it to accomplish what God never intended it to do in the first place is disastrous. God's Son and his Spirit are the only solution to the problem of the στοιχεῖα, the only cure for the ultimate human disease, and the only way to live as Abraham's righteous heirs.

NOTES

1. Gregory E. Sterling, "'Philo Has Not Been Used Half Enough': The Significance of Philo of Alexandria for the Study of the New Testament," *Perspectives in Religious Studies* 30.3 (2003): 267–68, quoting an 1818 letter from Samuel Taylor Coleridge (Samuel Taylor Coleridge, *Collected Letters*, ed. E. L. Griggs, 6 vols. (Oxford: Oxford University Press, 1956), 4:800–804, esp. 803 (no. 1095)).

2. Francis Watson, *Paul and the Hermeneutics of Faith*, 2d ed., Cornerstones (London: Bloomsbury T&T Clark, 2016), xiii.

3. Lagercrantz, *Elementum: Eine lexikologische Studie*, 54.

4. Barclay, *Jews in the Mediterranean Diaspora: From Alexander to Trajan (323 BCE – 117 CE)*.

5. Sterling, "Philo Has Not Been Used Half Enough," 252.

6. Josephus's other use of √αλληγορεω refers to ἀλληγορίαι of other material (*Ag. Ap.* 2.255).

7. Zurawski, "Paul's Allegory," following Peder Borgen, "Some Hebrew and Pagan Features in Philo's and Paul's Interpretations of Hagar and Ishmael," in *The New Testament and Hellenistic Judaism*, ed. Peder Borgen and Søren Giversen (Peabody, MA: Aarhus University Press, 1997), 151–64, against C. K. Barrett, "The Allegory of Abraham, Sarah, and Hagar in the Argument of Galatians," in *Rechtfertigung: Festschrift für Ernst Käsemann zum 70. Geburtstag*, ed. Johannes Friedrich, Wolfgang Pöhlmann, and Peter Stuhlmacher (Tübingen: Mohr, 1976), 1–16 and others.

8. Zurawski, "Paul's Allegory."

9. Sterling, "Philo Has Not Been Used Half Enough," 263; see Eleanor Dickey, "Longinus," *The Oxford Encyclopedia of Ancient Greece and Rome*.

10. Feldman, "Josephus Flavius."

11. Sterling, "Philo Has Not Been Used Half Enough," 261. Folker Siegert, "Early Jewish Interpretation in a Hellenistic Style, 4: Philo of Alexandria," in *Hebrew Bible / Old Testament: The History of Its Interpretation*, ed. Magne Sæbø (Göttingen: Vandenhoeck & Ruprecht, 1996), 197 says he "seems to have read" it. However, in Siegert's opinion, "Of the first Christians, few are likely to have engaged in reading anything like Philo's works" ("Early Jewish Interpretation in a Hellensitic Style, 4: Philo of Alexandria," 188 n. 297), and Paul "was surely not a reader of Philo" ("Philo and the New Testament," in *The Cambridge Companion to Philo*, ed. Adam Kamesar (Cambridge: Cambridge University Press, 2009), 183, http://universitypublishingonline .org/cambridge/companions/ebook.jsf?bid=CBO9781139002394).

118   *3*

12. Compare Josephus's *J.W.* 4.324; 5.212–218, 231–237; *Ant.* 3.123, 159–186 with Philo's *Moses* 2.88, 101–124; *Spec. Laws* 1.85–94, 172; *Heir* 196–200, 216–226; *Prelim. Studies* 117; *Flight* 184–185; *Dreams* 1.214. See David T. Runia, *Philo in Early Christian Literature: A Survey*, CRINT 3 (Assen: Van Gorcum, 1993), 13, citing S. Schwartz, *Josephus and Judaean Politics*, Columbia Studies in the Classical Tradition 18 (Leiden, 1990), 40–43, 51–54; Louis H. Feldman, *Josephus and Modern Scholarship 1937–1980* (Berlin: de Gruyter, 1984), 410–18, 936–37; Thomas W. Franxman, *Genesis and the "Jewish Antiquities" of Flavius Josephus*, Biblica et Orientalia 35 (Rome: Biblical Institute, 1979); and opposing Lewy and Heinemann. Even if Georgi is correct that Josephus's "parallel with Philo" depends "upon a common apologetic tradition," Philo remains the best extant source for the fullest articulation of that early Jewish tradition. See the discussion of Dieter Georgi, *The Opponents of Paul in Second Corinthians*, Rev. ed. (Philadelphia: Fortress, 1986), 202 n. 281 in Louis H. Feldman, *Flavius Josephus: Translation and Commentary*, ed. Steve Mason (Leiden: Brill, 2000), 3:9 n. 26.

13. Sterling 2003, 263, citing Numenius, F 13 (des Places; *Worse* 160); Origen, *Cels.* 4.51. See Sterling 1999a, 21–23.

14. Charles A. Anderson, *Philo of Alexandria's Views of the Physical World*, WUNT 2/309 (Tübingen: Mohr Siebeck, 2011), 33–35.

15. See Anderson, *Philo of Alexandria's Views of the Physical World*, 24–27. In the Exposition, see *Moses* 2.212, 216; *Spec. Laws* 2.61–63; *Rewards* 66; in the Allegory *Heir* 213; *Dreams* 2.123–32; and in other treatises *Good Person* 43; *Embassy* 156, 256, etc.

16. John M. Dillon, *The Middle Platonists, 80 B.C. to A.D. 220* (Cornell University Press, 1996), 139–83.

17. Gregory E. Sterling, "Philo," *EDEJ*, 1069. See also Burton L. Mack, "Philo Judaeus and Exegetical Traditions in Alexandria," in *ANRW*, ed. Wolfgang Haase, Part 2, Principat, 21.1 (Berlin: de Gruyter, 1984), 227–71; Gregory E. Sterling, "'The School of Sacred Laws': The Social Setting of Philo's Treatises," *Vigiliae Christianae* 53 (1999): 148–64; David T. Runia, *On the Creation of the Cosmos According to Moses*, Philo of Alexandria Commentary 1 (Leiden: Brill, 2001), 30; Adam Kamesar, "Biblical Interpretation in Philo," in *The Cambridge Companion to Philo*, ed. Adam Kamesar (Cambridge: Cambridge University Press, 2009), 65—following Wilhelm Bousset, *Jüdisch-Christlicher Schulbetrieb in Alexandria Und Rom* (Göttingen: Vandenhoeck & Ruprecht, 1914), 37–40, 152–54—and Peder Borgen, "Philo and the Jews in Alexandria," in *Ethnicity in Hellenistic Egypt*, ed. Per Bilde et al., Studies in Hellenistic Civilization 3 (Århus: Århus University Press, 1992), 122–38; Peder Borgen, *Philo of Alexandria: An Exegete for His Time* (Leiden: Brill, 1997), 38–45.

18. John M. Dillon, "Platonism, Middle," *OCD*; see Dillon, *The Middle Platonists, 80 B.C. to A.D. 220*, especially 139–83. For a review of Philo's relationship to the "Hellenistic schools of his day" (Anderson, *Philo of Alexandria's Views of the Physical World*, 26), see Gregory E. Sterling, "Platonizing Moses: Philo and Middle Platonism," *SPhilo* 5 (1993): 96–111.

19. David T. Runia, "Philo I.12. Ph. of Alexandria (Philo Judaeus)," *Brill's New Pauly*.

The Argument for Redemptive Nomism in Philo's Philosophy 119

20. Runia, "Philo I.12. Ph. of Alexandria (Philo Judaeus)"; David Winston, "Philo's Ethical Theory," in *ANRW*, Part 2, Principat, 21.1, ed. Wolfgang Haase (Berlin: de Gruyter, 1984), 372–416.

21. Sterling, "Philosophy according to the Elements," 365–66, citing John M. Dillon, ed., *Alcinous: The Handbook of Platonism*, Clarendon Later Ancient Philosophers (Oxford: Oxford University Press, 1993), 118–20, 131–36. See also Runia, *Creation*, 204, 230; Runia, *Philo of Alexandria and the Timaeus of Plato*, 44; John M. Dillon, *The Middle Platonists: A Study of Platonism, 80 BC to AD 220* (London: Duckworth, 1977), 171; Delling, "Στοιχέω," 7:673. Compare Plato, *Tim.*, 49b–c; 53a––b; Aristotle, *Cael.* 1.2–3; 3.2, 7; *Gen. an.* 1.2; 3.5; Alcinous, *Didask.* 15.1.

22. Anderson, *Philo of Alexandria's Views of the Physical World*, 24.

23. Sterling, "Philo," 1069; Natalio Fernández Marcos, "Rewritten Bible or Imitatio? The Vestments of the High Priest," in *Studies in the Hebrew Bible, Qumran, and the Septuagint Presented to Eugene Ulrich*, ed. Peter W. Flint, Emanuel Tov, and James C. VanderKam, Supplements to Vetus Testamentum 101 (Leiden: Brill, 2006), 331. See Runia, *Creation*, 106, quoting Diogenes Laertius 7.88 and citing Diogenes Laertius 7.135–36 and A. A. Long and D. N. Sedley, eds., *The Hellenistic Philosophers*, 2 vols. (Cambridge: Cambridge University Press, 1987), 1:323–32.

24. Runia, *Creation*, 32.

25. Runia, "Philo I.12. Ph. of Alexandria (Philo Judaeus)."

26. Ellen Birnbaum, "Two Millennia Later: General Resources and Particular Perspectives on Philo the Jew," *CBR* 4.2 (2006): 250; see Erwin R. Goodenough, *An Introduction to Philo Judaeus*, 2d ed., Brown Classics in Judaica (Oxford: Blackwell, 1962); Samuel Sandmel, *Philo of Alexandria: An Introduction* (Oxford: Oxford University Press, 1979).

27. Hindy Najman, "The Law of Nature and the Authority of Mosaic Law," *Studia Philonica Annual* 11 (1999): 55–73, following Helmut Koester, "ΝΟΜΟΣ ΦΥΣΕΩΣ: The Concept of Natural Law in Greek Thought," in *Religions in Antiquity: Essays in Memory of Erwin Ramsdell Goodenough*, ed. Jacob Neusner, Studies in the History of Religion; Supplements to Numen 14 (Leiden: Brill, 1968), 521–41; see Francesca Calabi, *The Language and the Law of God: Interpretation and Politics in Philo of Alexandria*, South Florida Studies in the History of Judaism (Atlanta: Scholars, 1998).

28. Niehoff, *Jewish Identity*, 137.

29. Cristina Termini, "Philo's Thought within the Context of Middle Judaism," in *The Cambridge Companion to Philo*, ed. and trans. Adam Kamesar (Cambridge: Cambridge University Press, 2009), 113. Birnbaum notes that "in 1988 Runia's statistics led him to observe that '[t]he study of Philo from a Jewish perspective . . . is gaining a position of dominance in Philonic studies'" (Birnbaum, "Two Millennia Later: General Resources and Particular Perspectives on Philo the Jew," 246, quoting Radice and Runia, *Philo of Alexandria: An Annotated Bibliography 1937–1986*, xxix).

30. Niehoff, *Jewish Identity*, 248, citing *Moses* 2.12–15.

31. Anderson, *Philo of Alexandria's Views of the Physical World*, 27. For similarly nuanced conclusions, see Sterling, "Philo," 1068; Runia, *Creation*, 31–32; Barclay, *Jews in the Mediterranean Diaspora: From Alexander to Trajan (323 BCE – 117*

CE), 163–65. John M. Dillon, "A Response to Runia and Sterling," *SPhilo* 5 (1993): 153 concurs.

32. Barclay, *Jews in the Mediterranean Diaspora*, 173, italics his.

33. Most recently Moo, *Galatians*, 257–64; de Boer, *Galatians*, 252–56; Schreiner, *Galatians*, 268–69; Woyke, "Elementen"; van Kooten, *Cosmic Christology*, 60–79; Sterling, "Philosophy according to the Elements."

34. Schweizer, "Slaves of the Elements"; van Kooten, *Cosmic Christology*, 45–46, 62–65.

35. Runia, *Philo of Alexandria and the Timaeus of Plato*, 222–23.

36. I use the one English word *star* to translate Philo's references to ἄστρον (LSJ; *OED*).

37. See Runia, *Creation*, 285; *SVF* 2.475, 532.

38. Runia, *Creation*, 285, citing Julius Röhr, "Beiträge zur antiken Astrometeorologie," *Philologus* 83 (1928): 270.

39. See παρατηρέω in Gal 4.10 and the discussion of Philo's promotion of the calendar for health, redemption, and righteousness in section B.2.b. Days, Months, Seasons, and Years in chapter 4.

40. van Kooten, *Cosmic Christology*, 71.

41. van Kooten, *Cosmic Christology*, 72–73.

42. van Kooten, *Cosmic Christology*, 206.

43. Schweizer, "Slaves of the Elements," 457.

44. Niehoff, *Jewish Identity*, 249 and 249 n. 8.

45. Niehoff, *Jewish Identity*, 249, citing R. A. Horsley, "The Law of Nature in Philo and Cicero," *Harvard Theological Review* 71 (1978): 35–59.

46. Niehoff, *Jewish Identity*, 250.

47. Niehoff, *Jewish Identity*, 248.

48. Niehoff, *Jewish Identity*, 251–66.

49. James R. Royse, "The Works of Philo," in *The Cambridge Companion to Philo*, ed. Adam Kamesar (Cambridge: Cambridge University Press, 2009), 47.

50. Sterling, "Philo," 1068.

51. See Borgen, *Philo of Alexandria*, 146–47.

52. Runia, *Creation*, 103; see Carl Siegfried, *Philo von Alexandria als Ausleger des Alten Testament: An Sich Selbst und nach Seinem Geschichtlichen Einfluss Betrachtet. Nebst Untersuchungen über die Graecotaet Philo's* (Jena: Verlag von Hermann Dufft, 1875), 278–81.

53. Feldman, *Flavius Josephus*, 3:9 n. 26's discussion of Georgi, *Opponents of Paul*, 202 n. 281.

54. Elias J. Bickerman, *The Jews in the Greek Age* (Cambridge, Mass.: Harvard University Press, 1988), 114, quoted in Runia, *Creation*, 106.

55. See Sterling, "Philo," 1064; Barclay, *Jews in the Mediterranean Diaspora*, 94; Alan Mendelson, *Philo's Jewish Identity*, Brown Judaic Studies 161 (Atlanta: Scholars, 1988), 58–74.

56. Fernández Marcos, "Vestments," 323–24, 331.

57. Fernández Marcos, "Vestments," 330.

58. *Moses* 2.122–123; *QE* 2.109; *Heir* 175–176; see *Ant.* 3.165–166, 185.

The Argument for Redemptive Nomism in Philo's Philosophy 121

59. *Moses* 2.117–119; *Spec. Laws* 1.85, 93–94; *QE* 2.120; see *J. W.* 5.231–237; *Ant.* 3.159, 160, 164, 172, 184, 186.

60. H. St. J. Thackeray, *Josephus*, LCL 3.96–97 n. a. Other early Jewish sources also marvel at the cosmic significance of the high priest's robe (*Let. Aris.* 99; Sir 50.5–15; Wis 18.21–24) (see Fernández Marcos, "Vestments").

61. Termini, "Philo's Thought within the Context of Middle Judaism," 113–14.

62. Niehoff, *Jewish Identity*, 254–55; Termini, "Philo's Thought within the Context of Middle Judaism," 115. See *Spec. Laws* 3.10.

63. For circumcision of the heart in Philo see *Spec. Laws* 1.304–305; *QG* 3.46–52, 61, 62.

64. The translation of the first clause is mine; the rest is Colson's (LCL). See Termini, "Philo's Thought within the Context of Middle Judaism," 117.

65. Substituting Marcus's literal alternative in note *a* for the translation given in the text: "undue" (LCL Supp. I.242).

66. See Peder Borgen, "Observations on the Theme 'Paul and Philo': Paul's Preaching of Circumcision in Galatia (Gal. 5:11) and Debates on Circumcision in Philo," in *Die Paulinische Literatur und Theologie: The Pauline Literature and Theology: Anlässlich der 50. Jährigen Gründungs-Feier der Universitat von Aarhus*, ed. Sigfred Pedersen, Scandinavian Contributions; Teologiske Studier 7 (Århus: Aros, 1980), 85–102; Bruce, *Galatians*, 243.

67. It is important to note, though, that Philo, like Josephus, would not have compelled Gentile proselytes to circumcise their sons (Nancy Calvert-Koyzis, *Paul, Monotheism and the People of God: The Significance of Abraham Traditions for Early Judaism and Christianity*, ed. Mark Goodacre, JSNTSup 273 (London: T&T Clark, 2004), 38, quoting *QE* 2.2; see *Life* 113).

68. Philo inserts "months" into Genesis's list and thus strikes a "compromise between Gen 1:14 and *Tim.* 37e1, 39c1–5" (Runia, *Creation*, 206; see *Creation* 56–57, 116; *QE* 1.1).

69. Niehoff, *Jewish Identity*, 107, 258.

70. Niehoff, *Jewish Identity*, 259, citing F. M. Cornford, "Mysticism and Science in the Pythagorean Tradition," *The Classical Quarterly* 16 (1922): 142–50; J. S. Morrison, "Pythagoras of Samos," *The Classical Quarterly (New Series)* 6 (1956): 152–56.

71. Runia, *Creation*, 260; Niehoff, *Jewish Identity*, 260–62; Termini, "Philo's Thought within the Context of Middle Judaism," 118; see similarly Aristobulus in *Praep. ev.* 13.12:13).

72. Niehoff, *Jewish Identity*, 263; Termini, "Philo's Thought within the Context of Middle Judaism," 118–19.

73. Niehoff, *Jewish Identity*, 107–8.

74. Niehoff, *Jewish Identity*, 263–64. The original misspells it "sovereignity."

75. Niehoff, *Jewish Identity*, 260–61.

76. Colson, *Philo*, 7: 406–7 uses an ellipsis to represent an apparent omission in the Greek manuscripts.

77. Colson, *Philo*, 7: 395 n. a.

78. Translation mine. See Niehoff, *Jewish Identity*, 264–65.

79. Niehoff, *Jewish Identity*, 110.

122   *3*

80. In this "correlation" of "specific beings with the basic elements," Sterling finds the key to a doctrine of angels within Philo's "philosophy according to the elements" (Sterling, "Philosophy according to the Elements"; see Valentin Nikiprowetzky, "Sur une Lecture Démonologique de Philon d'Alexandre: *De Gigantibus*, 6–18," in *Études Philoniennes*, Patrimoines Judaïsme (Paris: Cerf, 1996), 223). However, Philo's concept of elemental spaces and creatures seems more significant for Colossians's opposition to Mosaic food laws. See James D. G. Dunn, *The Epistles to the Colossians and to Philemon: A Commentary on the Greek Text*, NIGTC (Grand Rapids: Eerdmans, 1996), 171–74, 188–98, though he connects the mention of food and drink in Col 2.16, 20–23 with Mosaic food laws only, and not with Philo's discussion of those laws.

81. Termini, "Philo's Thought within the Context of Middle Judaism," 115.

82. Runia, *Philo of Alexandria and the Timaeus of Plato*, 304–5, see chapter 1.

83. Harper, "New Diet"; Termini, "Philo's Thought within the Context of Middle Judaism," 119–21.

84. Runia, *Philo of Alexandria and the Timaeus of Plato*, 409.

85. Runia, *Philo of Alexandria and the Timaeus of Plato*, 408.

86. Nikiprowetzky, *Commentaire de l'Écriture*, 239.

87. Nikiprowetzky, *Commentaire de l'Écriture*, 239.

88. Kamesar, "Biblical Interpretation in Philo," 85.

89. Gregory E. Sterling, "'A Law to Themselves': Limited Universalism in Philo and Paul," *ZNW* 107 (2016): 34, https://doi.org/10.1515/znw-2016-0002.

90. Kamesar, "Biblical Interpretation in Philo," 91.

91. Kamesar, "Biblical Interpretation in Philo," 86.

92. Nikiprowetzky, *Commentaire de l'Écriture*, 239.

93. Zurawski, "Paul's Allegory"; Witherington, *Grace in Galatia*, 324–28.

94. Maren R. Niehoff, "Philo, Allegorical Commentary," *EDEJ*, 1070; Borgen, *Philo of Alexandria*, 38. See Eusebius, *Praep. ev.* 9.21.1–9; 9.29.1–3.

95. Niehoff, "Philo, Allegorical Commentary," 1070.

96. Borgen, *Philo of Alexandria*, 144–49, citing *Moses* 2.48–53; Y. Amir, "Authority and Interpretation of Scripture in the Writings of Philo," in *Mikra: Text, Translation, Reading and Interpretation of the Hebrew Bible in Ancient Judaism and Early Christianity*, ed. M. J. Mulder and Harry Sysling, vol. 1 Literature of the Jewish People in the Period of the Second Temple and the Talmud of CRINT 2 (Assen: Van Gorcum, 1988), 421–51; Siegert, "Early Jewish Interpretation in a Hellensitic Style, 4: Philo of Alexandria," 168–72; Irmgard Christiansen, *Die Technik der allegorischen Auslegungswissenschaft bei Philon von Alexandrien*, Beiträge zur Geschichte der biblischen Hermeneutik 7 (Tübingen: Mohr, 1969), 134. See Kamesar, "Biblical Interpretation in Philo," 80.

97. Borgen, *Philo of Alexandria*, 11 (citing Thomas H. Tobin, *The Creation of Man: Philo and the History of Interpretation*, CBQMS 14 (Washington, D.C.: Catholic Biblical Association of America, 1983)); Kamesar, "Biblical Interpretation in Philo," 77–91; Niehoff, "Philo, Allegorical Commentary," 1070–71.

98. Niehoff, "Philo, Allegorical Commentary," 1070–71.

The Argument for Redemptive Nomism in Philo's Philosophy 123

99. Kamesar, "Biblical Interpretation in Philo," 80, citing Tobin, *Creation of Man*; P. Carny, "Dimuyim Merkaziyim Ba-Teoryah Ha-Allegoristit Shel Filon," in *Meḥqarim Be-Sifrut Ha-Talmud, Bi-Leshon Ḥazal Uvefarshanut Ha-Miqra (Studies in Talmudic Literature, in Post-Biblical Hebrew and in Biblical Exegesis)*, ed. Mordechai Akiva Friedman, Avraham Tal, and Gershon Brin, Te'udah 3 (Tel Aviv: Tel Aviv University Press, 1983), 251–59; P. Carny, "Ha-Yesodot He-Hagutiyim Shel Darshanut Filon Ha-Aleksandroni," *Daat* 14 (1985): 5–19. See Niehoff, "Philo, Allegorical Commentary," 1071.

100. Niehoff, "Philo, Allegorical Commentary," 1071. Chapter 5 will show that Paul follows this exact procedure in Gal 4.21–5.1.

101. *Moses* 2.101–105, 120–122, 128; *Spec. Laws* 1.8, 85, 86, 93, 97, 172, 175, 201, 264; 4.112; *Alleg. Interp.* 1.1; *Cherubim* 21, 23; *Drunkenness* 85, 134; *Migration* 1, 89, 93; *Heir* 112, 197–199, 217, 226–227, 239; *Prelim. Studies* 11, 117; *Flight* 100; *Dreams* 1.144, 218; *Good Person* 80; *Contempl. Life* 28, 78.

102. *Abraham* 68, 119; *Joseph* 28, 125, 151; *Decalogue* 1; *Spec. Laws* 1.327; *Cherubim* 21, 25; *Planting* 36; *Confusion* 14; *Prelim. Studies* 172; *Names* 67; *Dreams* 1.14, 102; *Contempl. Life* 28, 78.

103. *Joseph* 28; *Decalogue* 1; *Prelim. Studies* 172; *Contempl. Life* 28.

104. *Migration* 92–93, 103; *Contempl. Life* 78.

105. *Decalogue* 1; *Flight* 108; *Contempl. Life* 78.

106. *Migration* 89.

107. *Flight* 108.

108. *Sacrifices* 14.

109. Kamesar, "Biblical Interpretation in Philo," 79–91; Niehoff, "Philo, Allegorical Commentary," 1071.

110. Paul, on the other hand, rejects a pattern of life governed by either astrological influence or pantheism (Gal 4.8–11). Calvert-Koyzis, *Paul, Monotheism and the People of God*, 25–39 sees that Philo rejects Chaldean pantheism, but not that he recognizes in Moses some sort of sympathetic affinity by which the stars influence events on earth.

111. Sarah J. K. Pearce, *The Land of the Body: Studies in Philo's Representation of Egypt*, WUNT 2/208 (Tübingen: Mohr Siebeck, 2007), 31, 34 follows David Hay in arguing that this theme seems "to have been taken over from other Jewish allegorists" (David M. Hay, "Philo's References to Other Allegorists," *SPhilo* 6 (1979): 55; Ellen Birnbaum, *The Place of Judaism in Philo's Thought: Israel, Jews, and Proselytes*, Brown Judaic Studies 290 (Atlanta: Scholars, 1996), 24).

112. Stanley Kent Stowers, "Paul and Self-Mastery," in *Paul in the Greco-Roman World: A Handbook*, ed. J. Paul Sampley, 2nd ed. (London: Bloomsbury T&T Clark, 2016), 277 notes a similar perspective in early Roman imperial propaganda.

113. Pearce, *The Land of the Body*, 127.

114. Watson, *Paul and the Hermeneutics of Faith*, 224 n. 33.

115. Borgen, *Philo of Alexandria*, 217–23.

116. On Stoic pantheism see Keimpe Algra, "Stoic Theology," in *The Cambridge Companion to the Stoics*, ed. Brad Inwood (Cambridge: Cambridge University Press, 2003), 153–78.

124   *3*

117. Colson, *Philo*, 1:478; Harry A. Wolfson, *Philo: Foundations of Religious Philosophy in Judaism, Christianity, and Islam*, 2 vols. (Cambridge, MA: Harvard University Press, 1947), 1:176–77, 329; 2:78; Williamson, *Jews in the Hellenistic World: Philo*, 30; Peder Borgen, "Jesus Christ, the Reception of the Spirit, and a Cross-National Community," in *Jesus of Nazareth: Lord and Christ: Essays on the Historical Jesus and New Testament Christology*, ed. Joel B. Green and Max Turner (Grand Rapids: Eerdmans, 1994), 220–35; Feldman, *Flavius Josephus*, 3:57 n. 503; Calvert-Koyzis, *Paul, Monotheism and the People of God: The Significance of Abraham Traditions for Early Judaism and Christianity*, 25–39.

118. Though the stars rule through the elements and Philo calls them "divine images" (*Creation* 55), "souls divine" (*Giants* 8), and "visible gods" (*Eternity* 46), he opposes the worship of the lights or of the στοιχεῖα (*Spec. Laws* 2.255; *Contempl. Life* 3–4; see *Decalogue* 53, 54, 58; *Spec. Laws* 1.13–16; *Virtues* 212–216; *Migration* 177–183). "The στοιχεῖα themselves are lifeless matter incapable of movement of itself" (*Contempl. Life* 4).

119. Sterling, "A Law to Themselves," 42, 46.

4

The Flesh and Sin: Enslaved Under the Στοιχεια Του Κοσμου

As Paul considers the Galatians' impending circumcision, he has two related concerns. First, he must assure the Gentile believers that, through the Son and the Spirit, they have already been made God's sons and, thus, Abraham's heirs. In keeping with this heritage, he, second, calls them as faithful sons to live by the Spirit in righteousness and love. The present threat to their full inclusion in Abraham's family is the law, which marked Jews out from all other nations, and the persistent threat to their righteousness is the flesh, which, in the weakness of its nature, succumbs to sin.

This study argues that the believers in Galatia were adopting the law not only to be counted as Abraham's heirs, but also to address the problem of the flesh. Paul describes the problem of the flesh in Gal 2–3. He says that πᾶσα σάρξ (that is all humans in their physical bodies) are unable to be declared righteous and made complete (2.6; 3.3). He then narrates the problem of transgressions for which scripture imposed the law as a sort of παιδαγωγός to restrain Abraham's wayward children (3.19–25). Paul complements these general statements about human weakness and sin, as seen especially in Abraham's heirs, with a more philosophical assertion about the human condition: "so we also, when we were children, were enslaved under the στοιχεῖα τοῦ κόσμου" (4.3). Or, to unpack this dense statement, "We Jews, like Greeks as well, when we were vulnerable children, were enslaved under the cosmic elements that compose our flesh and mediate its stimuli, desires, and actions."

Chapter 4 presents the several concepts that form that explanation. Chapter 1 showed that the term στοιχεῖα τοῦ κόσμου must be read as earth, water, air, and fire. Chapter 2 argued that the concept "element" (in Gal 4 at least) should be read in the context of Greek medicine. In that discourse, the στοιχεῖα are understood to compose the human body and mediate παθήματα and ἐπιθυμίαι that affect, or even enslave, the body and the soul, especially among children. I now delineate the implications of that reading of στοιχεῖα

126   4

τοῦ κόσμου for Paul's argument about the flesh and sin. First, as an answer to the question "What are the στοιχεῖα?," Paul's physiology shows from Gal 4.3, 9–15 that the weak, material στοιχεῖα are the physical components of the weak, material σάρξ. Second, to the question "How can the elements, as weak, insentient things, enslave a person?," Paul's pathology in Gal 3.22–4.5; 5.13–6.2 and Rom 6–7 responds that sin overpowers the weak σάρξ and works through the dynamics of παθήματα and ἐπιθυμίαι—both mediated by the στοιχεῖα—to bring the human body and person under its control. Finally, Paul's epidemiology shows that children (νήπιοι) are those most susceptible to the condition of being σάρκινοι and thus enslaved ὑπὸ ἁμαρτίαν.

A. PHYSIOLOGY: THE WEAK ΣΤΟΙΧΕΙΑ COMPOSE THE WEAK ΣΑΡΞ

What are the στοιχεῖα τοῦ κόσμου? As chapter 2 demonstrated, for half a millennium before Paul, discussions about the four elements of the cosmos led as a matter of course into descriptions of those same elements as the components of the human body. The human body and the cosmos are made of the same stuff: earth, water, air, and fire. The introduction and chapter 2 showed this concept present in, among others, Empedocles (98/98) and Plato (*Tim.* 27a etc.), 2 Maccabees (7.22) and Philo (*Creation* 146 etc.), in Paul himself (1 Cor 15.47), and in the earliest Christian writers (Aristides, *Apol.* 7.3; Justin, *Dial.* 62.2). This section on Paul's physiology confirms that when Paul uses the phrase στοιχεῖα τοῦ κόσμου he is referring to the elements in the human body, and it argues that when Paul writes "σάρξ" he means the material of which the body is composed. The critical issue here is ἀσθένεια. As a term, ἀσθένεια links the στοιχεῖα in 4.9 with Paul's σάρξ in 4.13, and as a concept it accounts for how a σάρξ that is materially weak becomes morally wicked.

1. Both the Στοιχεῖα and Paul's Σάρξ are Ἀσθενῆ (Gal 4.9–11, 12–15)

Paul's description of the στοιχεῖα in Gal 4 is scanty. They are τοῦ κόσμου; they are by nature not gods; and they are weak and beggarly (4.3, 8, 9). However, few commentators note what English translations also obscure: five lines after calling the στοιχεῖα ἀσθενῆ, Paul refers to an ἀσθένεια τῆς σαρκὸς (4.13).[1] This double use of √ἀσθενεω implies that Paul's flesh, like the elements, is weak because Paul's flesh is made of the elements. Paul's other uses of √ἀσθενεω confirm this hypothesis.

Paul frequently uses √ἀσθενεω to describe bodily weakness or sickness.[2] In a final sense, the body is mortal; it dies and is sown in ἀσθένεια (1 Cor 15.43).

The Flesh and Sin: Enslaved Under the Στοιχεια Του Κοσμου   127

But people experience weakness in life as well. For example, Paul's bodily presence is described as ἀσθενής (2 Cor 10.10). And his ἀσθένεια exposes him to and is exacerbated by a thorn in his σάρξ and by various hardships (2 Cor 12.5–10; see 11.30).[3] Yet it is precisely in and through these ἀσθένειαι, the Lord tells Paul, that his power is made perfect.

As many commentators note, there are several points of contact between 2 Cor 12.5–10 and Gal 4.13–15.[4] Paul has an ἀσθένεια of his σάρξ, yet despite his weakness he is able to continue his apostolic ministry among the nations.[5] However, the mysterious allure of Paul's satanic thorn and the suggestive mention of eyes proves too much for most scholars. Absorbed in reconstructing hypothetical diagnoses of Paul's presenting symptoms, they overlook the solid substance of etiology.[6] Paul is ἀσθενής because his σάρξ, like all human σάρξ, is ἀσθενής because it is composed of ἀσθενῆ στοιχεῖα (Rom 6.19).

As chapter 2 showed, OG translators and New Testament writers also present the σάρξ as ἀσθενής. In a striking parallel with Paul, one psalmist confesses that his eyes have been weakened from πτωχεία (Ps 87 [88].10; see Bar 2.18).[7] Along similar lines, Matthew and Mark report Jesus as saying, "the spirit indeed is willing, but the σάρξ is ἀσθενής" (Matt 26.41, NRSV ‖ Mark 14.38). Again, the weakness of the disciples' flesh relates specifically to their eyes and to prayer.

Thus, interpreting ἀσθενής in Gal 4.9, like ἀσθένεια in 4.13, to refer to bodily weakness corresponds meaningfully with the use of √ἀσθενεω in Paul's writings, in other early Christian documents, and in the Old Greek. Further it coheres with Paul's argument in Gal 4. It shows that Paul locates the problem of the στοιχεῖα τοῦ κόσμου in his σάρξ, for the ἀσθενῆ στοιχεῖα compose, and thus compromise, his σάρξ. However, this interpretation promotes a material understanding of σάρξ as the stuff of the human body, a view, as we will see, eschewed by most scholars.[8]

2. The Σάρξ Becomes Morally Wicked through Its Material Weakness (Gal 4.9–11, 12–15)

Scholars have long puzzled over how Paul can imply that the σάρξ, seemingly the physical material of the body, can have a φρόνημα (Rom 8.6–7), ἐπιθυμίαι (Gal 5.16, 24), and ἔργα (Gal 5.19–21), each of which implies some sort of moral activity.[9] As chapter 3showed, the OG offers little precedent for this view (see only Gen 6.12; Ezek 23.20), since it normally presents human σάρξ as materially weak, not morally wicked.[10] The same connotation holds true in at least nine of Paul's eighteen uses of σάρξ in Galatians (1.16; 2.16, 20; 4.13, 14, 23, 29; 6.12, 13).[11] As Lorenzo Scornaienchi argues in *Sarx und Soma bei Paulus*, "Die unmittelbare Bedeutung von σάρξ bezieht sich bei Paulus auf das biologische Leben des Menschen, auf den ganzen Menschen

128   *4*

in seiner Lebendigkeit. . . . Die Universalität des Fleisches beinhaltet die biblische Konnotation des Menschen in seiner Hinfälligkeit und Schwachheit."[12] Other scholars concur that, for Paul, the σάρξ is, at least primarily, the physical substance of the body.[13] So how can Paul assert that the σάρξ of Gal 1.16; 2.16, which stood there for ἄνθρωπος (see 1.11–12), is not only incapable of being declared righteous ἐξ ἔργων νόμου (2.16), but also has sinful ἐπιθυμίαι and ἔργα that are contrary to the Spirit and its fruit (5.13, 16–21, 24)? He can because he has examined the σάρξ and diagnosed an infection of wickedness in its physical weakness (see the discussion of Rom 6.12–7.25 below).

Most scholars explain the moral activity of the flesh in one of two ways. Some do so by identifying the flesh with a force external to the human person, for example, a personified, "apocalyptic" power. Others insist that the flesh is indeed the substance of the body yet is able, from one perspective or another, to act in morally assessable ways. Barclay shows that the development in Paul's physiology of the σάρξ—from materially weak to morally wicked—corresponds to similar developments among Jews both in Alexandria and at Qumran.[14] Engaging Barclay's points, this section argues that, for Paul, it is precisely in the flesh's weak materiality that it is susceptible to sin's evil coercion.

Philo presents σάρξ not only as weak but also as wicked.[15] For Philo, human weakness (ἡ ἀνθρωπίνη ἀσθένεια) makes the person susceptible to pleasure—"which thinks that it can direct the course of human weakness"—and to untamable ἐπιθυμία (*Alleg. Interp.* 1.69). There, in short, is the link between weak flesh and wicked flesh.

Barclay observes this link, but he denies its relevance to Paul, since he sees a marked difference in Philo's and Paul's views of the flesh. Unlike Paul, Philo's perspective is "firmly in the Platonic tradition in which the passions and sense-impressions (αἰσθήσεις) of the body ensnare and impede the soul."[16] However, as the review of Paul's pathology below will show, Paul clearly says the same about the dynamics of the παθήματα and the ἐπιθυμίαι of the σάρξ, that is, the σῶμα τοῦ θανάτου: they enslave the person (Gal 4.3; 5.16–24; see Rom 6.6–7, 12–19; 7.5–24).

In a similar manner, scrolls at Qumran also reveal a perspective of the flesh (בשר) as wicked. Likely working from the description of בשר in Gen 6.5–13, at least three scrolls present flesh as "sinful" (1QH 4.29; 15.12, 21; 18.21; 1QM 4.3; 1QS 4.19–21; 11.9–12).[17] Several scholars go further and contend that Paul's ἐπιθυμία σαρκὸς is a "Greek rendering" of בשר יצר.[18] But, as similar as the concepts may be, de Boer and others provide no evidence that early Jews actually rendered the term יצר with the term ἐπιθυμία. The OG certainly does not.[19] Indeed Barclay suggests that בשר יצר "is better translated as 'fleshly refuge' or 'creature of flesh.'"[20] Thus, de Boer is overly confident to present בשר יצר in 1QH 18.22–23 as "an exact linguistic parallel to the

The Flesh and Sin: Enslaved Under the Στοιχεια Του Κοσμου   129

expression Paul uses."[21] Following Jewett, Martyn and de Boer also assert further that Paul personifies "the Flesh as a powerful and malevolent actor."[22] But for that claim as well the evidence is lacking. From Barclay's perspective, Paul's descriptions of the flesh "as having desires and as being locked in battle with the Spirit . . . do not, however, amount to the full personification of the flesh."[23]

While Jews both at Qumran and in Alexandria thought of the flesh not only as weak but also as wicked, Paul's discussion of ἐπιθυμία σαρκὸς and his use of terms like πάθημα and, most of all, στοιχεῖον suggest that the texts from Philo will be more relevant for elucidating his meaning than those from Qumran. As chapter 2 argued, it is in the terms and concepts of Greek medical discourse that Paul finds tools that enhance the precision of his analysis of the weak flesh as now wicked.[24]

The concepts of that discourse also address another persistent conundrum in the exegesis of Gal 4.3–9. How can things that are both insentient and weak enslave? This anomaly, of course, abetted the scholarly paradigm as it shifted to center upon a reading of the στοιχεῖα τοῦ κόσμου as elemental spirits. But that shift, in turn, left the modifier ἀσθενής as an outlying datum. Again, long attested and widely known concepts from Greek medicine explain not only how ἀσθενῆ στοιχεῖα can enslave people but also how the ἀσθένεια τῆς σαρκὸς can enslave body parts and weaken the law (Rom 6.19; 8.3; Gal 4.3, 9).

B. PATHOLOGY: SIN AND THE ELEMENTAL ΠΑΘΗΜΑΤΑ, ἘΠΙΘΥΜΙΑΙ, AND ἜΡΓΑ ΤΗΣ ΣΑΡΚΟΣ

As Paul contemplates the flesh and the human condition, he sees sin as the prevailing problem. Sin is over τὰ πάντα, including the weak and insentient στοιχεῖα τοῦ κόσμου, through which it has overrun the vulnerable flesh.[25] The στοιχεῖα mediate the barrage of sin's παθήματα against the flesh as well as the ἐπιθυμίαι of the now subjugated body, thus leading inexorably to sinful ἔργα. For Paul, the human condition is one of slavery, enslavement under the elements under sin.

This section on Paul's pathology examines Paul's argument in Gal 3–5 alongside Rom 6–7. It shows that Paul draws the narrative of his argument from Israel's scriptures and that he uses terms and concepts from Greek philosophy to analyze the anthropological crisis within that eschatological plot.[26] I argue (1) that slavery under sin is through the flesh; (2) that sin works through the παθήματα and ἐπιθυμίαι to dominate the human person; (3) that Paul sees the ἐπιθυμίαι (and παθήματα) as elemental; and thus (4) that, for Paul, being ὑπὸ τὰ στοιχεῖα τοῦ κόσμου relates to being ὑπὸ ἁμαρτίαν, not

130   *4*

to being ὑπὸ νόμον. This analysis of the problem leads then to the two-fold solution in chapter 6: the crucifixion, together with the Son, of the σάρξ, its παθήματα and ἐπιθυμίαι, and a life of righteousness by faith and the Spirit.

1. "I am of the Flesh, Sold Under Sin" (Gal 3.22; 4.3; Rom 6–7)

In Galatians and in Romans, Paul presents a compressed and a fuller analysis of the problem of the flesh and sin.[27] In Gal 3.22, Paul states baldly that τὰ πάντα are ὑπὸ ἁμαρτίαν. In Rom 6–7, Paul develops the various ways in which sin works through the weakness of the flesh to enslave the human person. In both letters, sin's subjugation of the flesh is an existential problem common to all humans. Paul locates this anthropological problem as the crisis in the eschatological narrative of Israel, the people of God among the nations awaiting redemption and the promised gift of the Spirit.

In Rom 7, Paul's speech in character presents the problem of sin, the flesh, and the body as the crisis in an eschatological narrative of Israel.[28] Earlier discussions of this passage identified Paul's speech as autobiographical,[29] with the apostle detailing his struggle with the failure of his own moral effort,[30] whether generally as a human[31] or specifically as a Jew under the law.[32] Dispute focused on the decisive event that moves the tense of the narrative from aorist in 7.7–13 to present in 7.14–25, with Cranfield and others identifying it as faith or regeneration.[33] Following Wright,[34] a growing number of scholars see Paul speaking in the character of Israel.[35] In this salvation-historical reading, the decisive event is the giving of the Torah, and Israel's sin recapitulates Adam's. The shape of this narrative thus opens it up to combination with some features of an autobiographical approach,[36] including that of a religious Jew.[37] As such, the crisis of the miserable ἐγώ will be resolved, not by conversion, but rather by the gift of the Spirit promised in the new covenant. By way of illustration, what the author of Ps 119 lacks is not faith (42), love for the law (47, 48, 113, 159, 163, 165, 167), or a will to do it (35, 112), but rather God himself to save (146, 153, 170), to deliver from the dominion of lawlessness (133), and to make alive (17, 154, 156, 159, 175), so that he will not go astray (176).

However, though the structure of the plot is eschatological, the crisis within the plot—that is, the flesh—remains existential: it has anthropological (contra Thompson), even physical (contra Fee), qualities.[38] As Wright remarks, Rom 7.4–6 "has a salvation-historical dimension (the move from old covenant to new), and obvious anthropological content (from the passions of the flesh to the new life in the spirit)."[39] Israel's problem, he notes, is "the Adamic humanity, 'the body of this death'" (7.24).[40] Thus, the problem is essentially physiological: sin works through ἐπιθυμίαι and παθήματα to enslave the body.

The Flesh and Sin: Enslaved Under the Στοιχεῖα Τοῦ Κόσμου   131

Sin uses the body's ἐπιθυμίαι to rule the person through the body and to recruit its parts as weapons of unrighteousness (Rom 6.12–13). The mode of the desires' functioning is often overlooked or misinterpreted.[41] The desires are the body's, not sin's.[42] And they are desires, not passions; they are processes of the body and its parts, not stimuli that happen to the body.[43]

The παθήματα of sins also operate in the body parts to bear fruit for death (Rom 7.5). This verse too is roughly handled. NRSV and ESV follow RSV in translating τὰ παθήματα τῶν ἁμαρτιῶν as "*our* sinful passions."[44] But the ἡμῶν in 7.5 comes later, and it modifies μέλη. Worse, NLT and NET render παθήματα as "desires." But Wilhelm Michaelis is explicit in his analysis of 7.5: the παθήματα are not "identical with the ἐπιθυμίαι"; they do not "have their seat in the members" but rather "work through the members."[45] The παθήματα τῶν ἁμαρτιῶν are, as the AV puts it, the "motions of sin," the factors of sins that affect human persons.

In this way, I both agree and disagree with Emma Wasserman's critique of Rudolf Bultmann's "unified self."[46] Paul's reference to the body's ἐπιθυμίαι is indeed intelligible in the context of Greek philosophical discourse, but in light of that same discourse, the particular nuance of the term πάθημα would distinguish sin from the person, not identify sin "as a representation" of the person's "sinful passions."[47] Paul's use of ἐγώ must be seen as fluid. At first his ἐγώ is ambiguous: it both wills one thing and also does the other, because it is "σάρκινος, sold ὑπὸ τὴν ἁμαρτίαν" (7.14). Then Paul identifies sin itself as the doing agent which lives "ἐν ἐμοί, τοῦτ᾽ἔστιν ἐν τῇ σαρκί μου" (17, 20). Here he begins to distinguish the ἐγώ from the σάρξ and specifies the ἐγώ as ἔσω ἄνθρωπος (22). In the closing words of the speech, Paul emphasizes the physiological nature of the crisis—"who will rescue me from the body of this death?" (24)—and he returns to the earlier ambiguous use of ἐγώ. On the one hand, in his νοῦς the ἐγώ is a slave to God's law; on the other, in his σάρξ he is a slave to sin's use of the law (25).

In its origin, then, Israel's problem is the same as the problem of all Adam's children: they are inclined to evil (Gen 6.12; Deut 31.21).[48] And in its development, Israel's problem is similar to the problem of the nations, as the rising action of Israel's story shows. Driven by the crisis of their uncircumcised heart, Israel is exiled to live in slavery among the nations (Deut 9.6–24; 10.16; 29.4; 31.16–29). The exposition of the story itself forecasts this trajectory (Deut 4.25–28; 28.64–68). And Jeremiah too interprets Israel's scattering among the nations as a just conclusion to Israel's acting like the nations (5.19; 16.10–13; 25.1–11; see Deut 12.29–31; 18.9–12).

For this reason, it is only fitting for Paul, the apostle to the nations, to describe the anthropological crisis that confronts Israel (still scattered among the nations) with terms and concepts that resonate with the nations' reflections on their own struggles with the same problem. In many ways, Israel's slavery

132   4

is similar to the nations': it is the misery of the human person frustrated by the weakness of the fleshy body and its vulnerability to sin's fatal domination (Rom 6.6, 16, 17, 19, 20; 7.24–25).[49] And that domination sin achieves through the distinct but related processes of the παθήματα and ἐπιθυμίαι.

2. Παθήματα and Ἐπιθυμίαι: Elemental Instruments in Sin's Slavery (Gal 5.16, 24)

Section 1 showed that, for Paul, slavery under sin is through the flesh, the substance of the human body. This section argues that, for Paul, sin works through the παθήματα and ἐπιθυμίαι to effect that slavery. As chapter 2 showed, in Greek medical discourse (1) the material elements mediate πάθη (or παθήματα) and ἐπιθυμίαι; (2) the concept πάθος (and especially πάθημα) includes a passive aspect; and (3) authors use the terms πάθος and πάθημα in a variety of ways. Reading Galatians in the context of that discourse, this section proposes that for Paul an ἐπιθυμία is a desire, a process that happens within a person; a πάθημα is a stimulus, a factor that happens to and affects a person; and sin works through both to enslave the human person.

While ancient writers use the terms πάθος, πάθημα, and ἐπιθυμία with some ambiguity, many modern scholars only obfuscate the concepts further. David deSilva distinguishes "desires, emotions, and physical sensations," but then he groups them all together as "passions."[50] Dunn calls παθήματα "a near synonym" with ἐπιθυμίαι.[51] James Thompson says Paul "equates" the two terms and uses them "interchangeably."[52] Further, though English versions normally translate ἐπιθυμία as lust or desire, they sometimes render it as "passion" (e.g., Rom 6.12, NRSV).[53]

However, chapter 2's review of πάθος, πάθημα, and ἐπιθυμία in Plato, Aristotle, the Stoics, and Philo equips us to appreciate Paul's use of πάθημα and ἐπιθυμία as distinct terms in a nuanced discussion of human flesh and its effects on behavior. The use of πάθημα in those authors and Paul's other uses of πάθημα (and of πάσχω in general) suggest that Paul understands a πάθημα as a factor that the body experiences. In Greek generally, a πάθημα is experienced (παθεῖν) not done (ποιεῖν), as ancient texts show when they contrast πάθημα with ποίημα, πρᾶξις, or ἔργον.[54] And in Paul specifically, scholars agree that παθήματα in Rom 8.18; 2 Cor 1.5, 6, 7; Phil 3.10 is passive, referring to "sufferings" that people experience.[55] Similarly, Paul uses πάσχω consistently to refer to someone experiencing something.[56] There are convincing reasons, then, to read παθήματα in Rom 7.5 and Gal 5.24 not as passions (or worse "desires") but as factors that affect the body.[57]

Hence I dispute Hans Dieter Betz's assertion that it would be unlikely that a simple Jew like Paul would know and observe the finer nuances of a term that was "technical in Hellenistic anthropology."[58] And I contest Moo's

The Flesh and Sin: Enslaved Under the Στοιχεια Του Κοσμου   133

assertion that Schlatter "depends overmuch on the etymology of the word" πάθημα when he suggests that Paul selected it "to connote that the 'passions' in question are aroused from without."[59] Greek medical discourse often distinguishes between these related terms, and it normally posits a complex interaction of παθήματα, σῶμα/σάρξ, ψυχή, ἐπιθυμίαι, and ἔργα, in which the body (or flesh) and the soul are sometimes passive and sometimes active. Even the unsophisticated medical notebook *Anon. Lond.* discusses both primary and secondary affects of the soul (1–2). Indeed if the review of these terms (and of Greek medicine generally) suggests anything about simplicity and complexity, it is that the inability to distinguish particular terms and concepts from each other obscures the dull vision of the modern reader more than the clear expression of the ancient writer.

Thus I propose that, for Paul, πάθημα and ἐπιθυμία are related but distinct concepts. An ἐπιθυμία stems from the heart (or perhaps the belly) within the body (Rom 1.24; 6.12; 16.18).[60] Accordingly, Paul says that the σὰρξ ἐπιθυμεῖ (Gal 5.17). The σάρξ desires a desire which it then expresses as an action, an ἔργον σαρκὸς (Rom 7.15–20; Gal 5.17, 19–21). Since sin has occupied the weak σάρξ from the heart out to the other parts, both the ἐπιθυμίαι σαρκὸς and the ἔργα σαρκὸς which they cause are sinful. Παθήματα also work through the σάρξ and cause sinful ἔργα σαρκὸς, but they do so from a different source. As this review has made clear, while an ἐπιθυμία is a process of the flesh generally or of an organ within the body specifically, a πάθημα is a factor that affects the body or one of its parts from *outside* it. An ἐπιθυμία is designated σαρκός because it is a process *of* the flesh or an organ. A πάθημα is associated with the σάρξ because it happens *to* the body or one of its parts.[61] If unimpeded, both an ἐπιθυμία σαρκὸς and a πάθημα will eventuate in an ἔργον σαρκὸς, but one does so from within the σάρξ and the other from without[62]—and neither is an ἔργον, as Martyn and de Boer suggest.[63]

To sum up then, Greek medical discourse clarifies the connection between Paul's view of the στοιχεῖα, the παθήματα and ἐπιθυμίαι σαρκός, and sin. From Plato's foundational *Timaeus* through to Galen's magisterial synthesis, Greek medical philosophy posited the enslavement of the person, specifically the soul or mind, to the mixture of elements in the body. And Philo's works show how a first-century Jewish scholar integrated this concept within a worldview defined by Israel's scriptures. For his part, Dale Martin argues that Philo "appropriates" "popular medical and scientific views," especially Plato's, but he is "fairly sure" that Paul never "read these medical texts."[64] However, when we read Galatians in conversation with Greek medical discourse, Paul's reference to enslavement under the cosmic elements makes natural sense. Elements do not have to be either sentient or strong to enslave; indeed, it is precisely in their weakness, in their changeability, that they incapacitate. As Dunn states, "the *power* of the flesh is the enticement it engenders

134   4

to pander to its *weakness*."[65] For Paul, this is the physiology of every human's ἀσθενὴς σάρξ composed of ἀσθενῆ στοιχεῖα, and this physiology underlies Paul's understanding of how sin infects and corrupts weak σάρξ.

3. The Ἐπιθυμίαι Σαρκὸς (and the Παθήματα) are Indeed Elemental (Gal 5.13–6.2).

As chapter 2 showed, Paul associates sexual desire with fire (πυροῦσθαι) and ἀκρασία (bad mixture) (1 Cor 7.5–9). In his discussion of the σάρξ in Gal 5–6, Paul's choice of terminology and of structure suggests that he does indeed see the στοιχεῖα as mediating the processes of the ἐπιθυμίαι (and of the παθήματα).

a. The Elemental Overtones of Στοιχέω and Στείχω

Immediately after stating that the Christian has crucified the σάρξ with its παθήματα and ἐπιθυμίαι, Paul challenges those who live by the Spirit to στοιχέω with the Spirit (Gal 5.24–25). Ben Witherington, Richard Hays, Geurt van Kooten, Thomas Schreiner, and Martinus de Boer each suggest that Paul chooses the verb στοιχέω in 5.25 (see 6.16), rather than περιπατέω (see 5.16), to allude to his earlier comments about the στοιχεῖα τοῦ κόσμου in 4.3, 9.[66] As de Boer expounds, "Whereas they once 'followed' the *stoicheia*, they are now to 'follow' (*stoicheō*) the Spirit."[67] An unnoticed pattern in Philo's use of the verb στείχω validates their hunch.

Three of Philo's four uses of στείχω emphasize the "elemental" quality of a particular movement.[68] In his Exposition of Exod 14.9–14, Philo describes both the threat from the Egyptians and the power of the elements (μέρη) of nature, that is, the sea, as fatal (*Moses* 2.249). He has Moses say, "In front is a vast expanse of sea; . . . behind, the menace of the enemy's troops, which march along (στείχοντες) in unresting pursuit. . . . Everything has attacked us suddenly from every side—earth, sea, man, the στοιχεῖα of nature" (*Moses* 2.251). By choosing στείχω (rather than one of several other verbs in the OG) to describe the Egyptians, Philo presents the enemies' marching along (στείχοντες) the earth behind the Israelites as a fitting complement to the threat of the στοιχεῖον ahead of them, the sea.

Second, in the Allegory Philo portrays the mind's heat and fieriness compelling it to march (στείχω) rapidly across the boundaries of material earth, sea, air, and ether to the immaterial world of ideas (*Names* 179–180). In contrast, in the Exposition he describes the mind as intelligible and largely passive, and he chooses the verb ἔρχομαι to portray it going through the elemental regions (*Creation* 69–70). In *Creation*, the generic verb ἔρχομαι

The Flesh and Sin: Enslaved Under the Στοιχεια Του Κοσμου   135

suffices; in *Names*, the elemental overtone of στείχω expresses the mind's elemental quality (viz. its fieriness).

Third, in *Eternity*, the choice of a verb with elemental overtones complements Philo's philosophical description of earth, fire, and their natural forces in the formation of mountains. "When the fiery element enclosed in the earth is driven upward by the natural force of fire, it travels (στείχω) towards its proper place, and . . . pulls up with it a large quantity of earthy stuff" (*Eternity* 135).

Though unobserved in the scholarship, this pattern in Philo's use of στείχω validates Witherington's, Hays's, van Kooten's, Schreiner's, and de Boer's intuitive hermeneutic that Paul uses στοιχέω in Gal 5.25; 6.16 to connect with his references to στοιχεῖα in 4.3, 9.[69] Along with Paul's use of συστοιχέω in 4.25, these instances represent five of the New Testament's twelve occurrences of √στοιχεω.[70] Their presence together in one letter suggests that Paul may well be using both the denotative and connotative qualities of √στοιχεω to connect particular parts of his argument in Galatians.[71] As van Kooten explains, Paul "makes a clever use . . . of these cognate words with more than one meaning."[72] Thus, in Gal 5.24–25 Paul's connection with 4.3, 9 implies, "Though sin once enslaved us under the στοιχεῖα τοῦ κόσμου which mediate the ἐπιθυμίαι and παθήματα of our σάρξ, Christians have crucified the σάρξ. Since we now live by the Spirit, let us στοιχέω with the Spirit."

b. The Chiastic Structure of Gal 5.13–6.2

As he was intentional in his choice of the term στοιχέω, Paul is also intentional in his placement of στοιχέω, ἐπιθυμίαι, and σάρξ in the chiasm of Gal 5.13–6.2. Both choices reinforce the idea that Paul sees the στοιχεῖα τοῦ κόσμου as enslaving people by mediating the ἐπιθυμίαι of their σάρξ.

In his carefully argued monograph *Chiasmus in the Pauline Letters*, Ian Thomson identifies and develops the significance of a chiasmus in Gal 5.13–6.2.[73] Though Stanley Porter and Jeffrey Reed dismiss Thomson's judicious criteria—along with all other attempts to establish norms for discerning chiasms[74]—David deSilva approves both of Thomson's criteria and of his application of those criteria to Gal 5.13–6.2.[75] The two halves of Paul's admonitory chiasm (5.13–21a; 5.22–6.2) present "warnings" about the σάρξ and "injunctions" about the πνεῦμα on opposite sides of a central concern: the inheritance of the kingdom of God by the offspring of Abraham the blessed (5.21b).[76] Within that structure, Paul discusses the ἐπιθυμία σαρκὸς in stichs C, D, and D' (5.16, 17, 24), contrasting it with πνεύματι στοιχέω in stich C' (5.25). It is here in the C and D stichs, as he contrasts ἐπιθυμία σαρκὸς with πνεῦμα, that Paul uses στοιχέω to allude to the στοιχεῖα τοῦ κόσμου in 4.3,

136   4

9. This placement suggests that Paul understands the material στοιχεῖα as instrumental in the operation of the ἐπιθυμίαι of the physical σάρξ.

Paul's choice of the term στοιχέω and its placement opposite and beside the ἐπιθυμίαι in the chiasm of 5.13–6.2 suggest that Paul sees ἐπιθυμία issuing from within the person and being communicated by the material στοιχεῖα to expression by the body's parts as the ἔργα τῆς σαρκός. If so, two implications follow. First, if the problem of the ἐπιθυμία σαρκὸς begins within, that too must be the place where the Spirit, as the solution, is sent (hence Gal 4.6). Second, by pairing the παθήματα with the ἐπιθυμίαι and then using στοιχέω in the following sentence, Paul suggests that he sees them, like the ἐπιθυμίαι, as processes related to the physical σάρξ and mediated by the material στοιχεῖα (Gal 5.24–25). This, then, is how he can say, "we were enslaved ὑπὸ τὰ στοιχεῖα τοῦ κόσμου." Jewish believers, like humans from any nation, were enslaved under the cosmic elements that compose the substance of their body, the σάρξ, and mediate its παθήματα, ἐπιθυμίαι, and ἔργα.[77] The elemental physiology of the παθήματα, ἐπιθυμίαι, and ἔργα τῆς σαρκὸς leads then to a significant implication.

4. Under the Elements, Under Sin, and Under the Law (Gal 3.22–4.5)

If people are enslaved under the στοιχεῖα τοῦ κόσμου that compose their bodies and mediate the παθήματα, ἐπιθυμίαι, and ἔργα τῆς σαρκὸς, then the exegetical "truism" that being ὑπὸ τὰ στοιχεῖα τοῦ κόσμου is parallel to or the same as being ὑπὸ νόμον is fundamentally misleading.[78] The paradigm of Paul's physiology and pathology implies that being ὑπὸ τὰ στοιχεῖα τοῦ κόσμου is parallel rather to being ὑπὸ ἁμαρτίαν, under the control of sin through its infection of the flesh made of στοιχεῖα.

In Galatians, seven of Paul's ten uses of ὑπό as "under" fall in 3.19–4.7. When Abraham's offspring transgress and are ὑπὸ ἁμαρτίαν, scripture responds by confining them ὑπὸ νόμον (3.19, 22–23; see 4.4, 5). Paul compares the law's oversight to being ὑπὸ παιδαγωγόν or ὑπὸ ἐπιτρόπους καὶ οἰκονόμους (3.25; 4.2). There are thus, in these verses, two sorts of being ὑπό:[79]

Table 4.1: Two Sorts of Being "Under" in Gal 3.19–4.7

ὑπὸ νόμον *(3.23)*	ὑπὸ ἁμαρτίαν *(3.22)*
ὑπὸ παιδαγωγόν (3.25)	
ὑπὸ ἐπιτρόπους καὶ οἰκονόμους (4.2)	
ὑπὸ νόμον (4.5; cf. 4.4)	

The Flesh and Sin: Enslaved Under the Στοιχεια Του Κοσμου   137

Martyn and de Boer, however, deny the difference: all of these together describe a single enslavement.[80] But Moo explains more clearly: subjection under the law "is related to, but not identical to, subjection to the domination of sin."[81]

In which column then does ὑπὸ τὰ στοιχεῖα τοῦ κόσμου belong? The syntax of Gal 4.1–3 seems to suggest that being ὑπὸ τὰ στοιχεῖα τοῦ κόσμου is parallel to being ὑπὸ νόμον.[82]

Subject + time particle + νήπιος + enslavement + ὑπὸ + object

Λέγω δέ, ἐφ' ὅσον χρόνον ὁ κληρονόμος νήπιός ἐστιν, οὐδὲν διαφέρει δούλου κύριος πάντων ὤν, ἀλλὰ ὑπὸ ἐπιτρόπους ἐστὶ καὶ οἰκονόμους. . . . (4.1–2)

οὕτως καὶ ἡμεῖς, ὅτε ἦμεν νήπιοι, ὑπὸ τὰ στοιχεῖα τοῦ κόσμου ἤμεθα δεδουλωμένοι· (4.3)

The structural parallel suggests that the restrictive experience of the Jews under the law and its commands as παιδαγωγός, stewards, and managers was as negative as their experience as slaves under the στοιχεῖα τοῦ κόσμου.[83] And the parallel leads interpreters to the conclusion that the law of Moses is, actually or effectively, a στοιχεῖον.[84]

However, despite its structural warrant, classing ὑπὸ τὰ στοιχεῖα τοῦ κόσμου in the left column above faces at least three difficulties. First, while the children's enslavement under the elements is clearly negative, we would expect stewards and managers—and the παιδαγωγός too—to work for the child's good. Sin, on the other hand, is a malevolent master. Second, in Paul's pathology of sin and the flesh, the material στοιχεῖα are the media that constitute both the person's vulnerability to the infection of sin and the growth and expression of that infection. Ὑπὸ τὰ στοιχεῖα τοῦ κόσμου then functions much more like ὑπὸ ἁμαρτίαν than like ὑπὸ νόμον. Third, as Rom 6–7 shows, ὑπὸ ἁμαρτίαν and ὑπὸ νόμον, like coughs and cough syrup, can be synchronous (6.14–15; 7.14) without being synonymous. Paul's "I" experiences the law, which is holy and spiritual, in two distinct ways: in his mind he is a slave to the law of God, but in his flesh to the law of sin (7.25). One is enslavement to sin, impurity, and lawlessness (6.6, 16, 17, 19, 20); the other is enslavement to obedience, righteousness, and God (6.18, 19, 22).[85]

Thus, read together, Romans and Galatians clarify (1) that Paul sees Jews under the law and under sin at the same time but in different ways, and (2) that he associates the material στοιχεῖα with the processes of the body through which sin enslaves the person. An understanding of the nature of children in Jewish and Greek discourses and in Paul confirms this reading. I will argue in section C below that the νήπιος of v. 1 and the νήπιοι of v. 3 are innately

138   *4*

enslaved by virtue of their physiological nature as νήπιοι. For this condition they were then placed under supervision, whether that of stewards and managers or of the law as παιδαγωγός.

In this section on pathology, we have seen that Paul's discussion of the σάρξ in Gal 5.13–6.2 helps make sense of his abrupt statement in 4.3 that Jews, like Gentiles, were enslaved under the στοιχεῖα τοῦ κόσμου. For Paul—as for Plato, Aristotle, and Philo—the material elements mediate the παθήματα, ἐπιθυμίαι, and ἔργα of the σάρξ. Paul's careful choice of the term στοιχέω links back to his earlier statement about the στοιχεῖα, and his placement of that term opposite and beside his discussion of the ἐπιθυμίαι σαρκὸς in the chiasm of 5.13–6.2 links the ἐπιθυμίαι and, I argued, παθήματα σαρκὸς to the material στοιχεῖα. Working from without and within, the παθήματα and ἐπιθυμίαι σαρκὸς lead to the ἔργα σαρκὸς. Through these processes of body and soul, all people are enslaved under the στοιχεῖα τοῦ κόσμου, and, in their weakness, they surrender control to the infection of sin (3.22). As we shall now see, this disease is most prevalent in that population that is most naturally σαρκινός, children.

C. EPIDEMIOLOGY: "YOU ARE LIKE THOSE OF THE FLESH, LIKE CHILDREN"

As in Greek medical discourse, Paul sees that the pathology of sin is epidemic among children. For this reason, within his redemptive-historical analogy of Israel as a child (4.1–2), Paul uses the metaphor of a νήπιος to point primarily to the σάρκινος physiology of children and their susceptibility to παθήματα.

Scholars dispute whether Paul's reference to an heir as a child under ἐπίτροποι and οἰκονόμοι should be read as a Greco-Roman legal analogy, a redemptive-historical one, or simply a common one.[86] But Scott Hafemann is the only scholar to consider the rebellious nature of the νήπιος itself. Νήπιοι are no better than slaves because they are enslaved by a rebellious nature. As chapter 2 showed, this theme is present in Greek medical discourse. David Lull summarizes their perspective: "Children were considered no different from slaves, not only socially, but also anthropologically, to the extent that they were characterized by unbridled passions."[87] In his exegesis of Gal 4.1–2, Hafemann affirms that this theme is present in Israel's scriptures and Paul as well.

Hafemann closely associates "Israel's rebellious nature" with their childhood.[88] The scriptures present Israel as a rebellious child not only in Egypt but also "as still a 'youth' during her time of rebellion leading up to the Exile."[89] Hafemann's analysis of the discourse of Gal 4.1–2 reinforces the idea that youth are by nature rebellious. He interprets the ἀλλά in 4.2 as "'rhetorically

The Flesh and Sin: Enslaved Under the Στοιχεῖα Τοῦ Κόσμου 139

ascensive' to the main assertion of verse 1. . . . As a child, not only is the heir in no way different from the slave (οὐδὲν διαφέρει δούλου), but (ἀλλὰ) she is ὑπὸ ἐπιτρόπους καὶ οἰκονόμους ἄχρι τῆς προθεσμίας τοῦ πατρός."[90] Though Hafemann does not infer this, that semantic relationship implies that the heir's "no difference" from a slave is established in verse 1 and amplified in verse 2. In other words, verse 1 presents the heir's slavery as consisting primarily in being a νήπιος. This, to my knowledge, has not been argued before, and the inference will hold only if Paul sees sinful rebellion as a form of slavery. But that, of course, is precisely how he, like the Hebrew scriptures, views sin (Rom 6.12–23).[91]

As in Israel's scriptures and in Greek medical discourse, Paul too sees νήπιοι as by nature prone to sin's infection of the σάρξ. In 1 Cor 3.1, Paul pairs νήπιος with σάρκινος as complementary descriptions of spiritual immaturity: "I could not speak to you as spiritual people, but as σάρκινοι, as νήπιοι in the Anointed One." Fee explains that σάρκινος "emphasizes especially their humanness and the physical side of their existence."[92] Anthony Thiselton observes that it points to *"the self-centered competitive naïveté which characterizes young children who have not yet learned to respect the interests of the Other."*[93] Paul also uses this rare term in the first-person litany in Rom 7: "I am σάρκινός, sold under sin" (14).[94] Joined to each other, these texts form a chain that links Paul's ideas of (1) νήπιοι as δοῦλοι, (2) νήπιοι as σάρκινοι, and (3) σάρκινοι as δοῦλοι. All of these together are subjected to the dominion of sin, whose παθήματα overcome the ἀσθένεια τῆς σαρκὸς and co-opt the body's ἐπιθυμίαι (see Rom 6.12–20; 7.5, and the discussion in section 2 above).[95]

From this perspective then, the Jewish νήπιοι in Gal 4.3 are like the inheriting νήπιος in 4.1 in two ways. First, as Paul states explicitly in verse 3, both groups, as νήπιοι, are enslaved under the στοιχεῖα τοῦ κόσμου, that is the material elements that compose, but weaken, the body and mediate the παθήματα and ἐπιθυμίαι of the flesh. As comparison with 1 Cor 3.1 and Rom 7.14 shows, it is primarily in this sense of being controlled that "the heir, as long as he is a νήπιος, differs in no way from a slave" (Gal 4.1).[96] Secondarily, both the heir and the Jews share the similar experience of being placed under supervision, whether under stewards and managers or under the law as a παιδαγωγός (3.19–24; 4.2–3).

D. CONCLUSION

This review of Paul's perspective on flesh and sin in Galatians reveals the nature of his concern about the στοιχεῖα τοῦ κόσμου in Gal 4.3. The scripture promised Abraham and his offspring that God would bless the nations in both

140   *4*

Abraham and his offspring by justifying the nations by faith (3.6–9, 14–18). This, in Barclay's terms, was the "narrative arc" from promise to blessing.[97] But that eschatological narrative has an anthropological problem, for, as Lull notes, Abraham's descendants were children and, as νήπιοι are by nature, they were enslaved under the passions (3.19; 4.1–3).[98] Sin enslaved them through the material στοιχεῖα, which mediated the παθήματα from without and the ἐπιθυμίαι within their bodies, thereby effecting the ἔργα τῆς σαρκός (5.16–25). Since everything was under sin and sin had infected Abraham's descendants, these stimuli and desires of their flesh led to uniformly sinful actions: "fornication, impurity, licentiousness, idolatry, sorcery, enmities, strife, jealousy, anger, quarrels, dissensions, factions, envy, drunkenness, carousing, and things like these" (5.19–21, NRSV; see 3.22).[99] And, as Paul is at pains to show, "those who do such things will not inherit God's kingdom" (5.21). So, as Lull explains in convincing detail, until πίστις should come, scripture imposed upon Abraham's heirs the stopgap measure of supervision under the law (3.19–24). As Paul retells this narrative to Jews and Greeks in the Galatian assemblies, he will present the law in this role as a παιδαγωγός (3.24).[100]

NOTES

1. The lone exception may be David Alan Black, *Paul, Apostle of Weakness: Astheneia and Its Cognates in the Pauline Literature*, rev. ed. (Eugene, OR: Pickwick, 2012), 31–52, but he reads the term's uses as referring to two distinct ideas, and he does not consider the possibility that the στοιχεῖα may be material, let alone physiological.

2. For Paul's other uses of √ἀσθενεω to refer to bodily weakness, see 1 Cor 2.3; 12.22. See also √ἀσθενεω describing faith or conscience in Rom 4.19; 14.1, 2, 21 (𝔓46vid, א2, B); 1 Cor 8.7, 9, 10, 11, 12. For ambiguous references see Rom 5.6; 8.26; 1 Cor 1.25, 27; 4.10; 9.22; 2 Cor 11.21, 29; 1 Thess 5.14. For major works on weakness in Paul, see David Alan Black, *Paul, Apostle of Weakness: Astheneia and Its Cognates in the Pauline Literature* (New York: Lang, 1984); David Alan Black, "Weakness," in *Dictionary of Paul and His Letters*, ed. Gerald F. Hawthorne, Ralph P. Martin, and Daniel G. Reid (Downers Grove, IL: InterVarsity, 1993), 966–67; Black, *Paul, Apostle of Weakness* (2012); Mark Edwards, Robert, "Weak Enough to Lead: Paul's Response to Criticism and Rivals in 2 Corinthians 10–13: A Rhetorical Reading" (Vanderbilt University, PhD diss., 2002); Justin M. Glessner, "Ethnomedical Anthropology and Paul's 'Thorn' (2 Corinthians 12:7)," *BTB* 47.1 (2017): 15–46, https://doi.org/10.1177/0146107916682197.

3. See the weakness/power contrast in 2 Cor 13.3, 4, 9. See Epaphroditus's weakness in Phil 2.25–30. See also 1 Tim 5.23; 2 Tim 4.20.

The Flesh and Sin: Enslaved Under the Στοιχεια Του Κοσμου   141

4. See Douglas J. Moo, *Galatians*, BECNT (Grand Rapids: Baker, 2013), 282; Martinus C. de Boer, *Galatians: A Commentary*, NTL (Louisville, KY: Westminster John Knox, 2011), 280; Hans Dieter Betz, *Galatians: A Commentary on Paul's Letter to the Churches in Galatia*, Hermeneia (Philadelphia: Fortress, 1979), 224–25.

5. James D. G. Dunn, *The Epistle to the Galatians*, BNTC (London: A & C Black, 1993), 233.

6. See, for example, Ben Witherington III, *Grace in Galatia: A Commentary on St. Paul's Letter to the Galatians* (Grand Rapids: Eerdmans, 1998), 308–10.

7. See also weak σάρξ in Pss 6.3; 72[73].26; 108 [109].24.

8. Thus de Boer, *Galatians*, 337–39; James Louis Martyn, *Galatians: A New Translation with Introduction and Commentary*, AB 33A (New York: Doubleday, 1997), 528–30; Richard Longenecker, *Galatians*, WBC 41 (Dallas: Word, 1990), 165–66.

9. For recent discussion see Moo, *Galatians*, 343–44. See also the θελήματα, διανοίαι, and νοῦς τῆς σαρκὸς (Eph 2.3; Col 2.18).

10. Lorenzo Scornaienchi, *Sarx und Soma bei Paulus: Der Mensch zwischen Destruktivität und Konstruktivität*, NTOA/SUNT 67 (Göttingen: Vandenhoeck & Ruprecht, 2008), 281–85.

11. See Scornaienchi, *Sarx und Soma*, 287–91.

12. Scornaienchi, *Sarx und Soma*, 287.

13. Stanley Kent Stowers, *A Rereading of Romans: Justice, Jews, and Gentiles* (New Haven, CT: Yale University Press, 1994), 279; Karl Olav Sandnes, *Belly and Body in the Pauline Epistles*, SNTSMS 120 (Cambridge: Cambridge University Press, 2002); John M. G. Barclay, *Paul and the Gift* (Grand Rapids: Eerdmans, 2015), 505–6; see Moo, *Galatians*, 343–44, 354.

14. John M. G. Barclay, *Obeying the Truth: A Study of Paul's Ethics in Galatians*, Studies of the New Testament and Its World (Edinburgh: T&T Clark, 1988), 184; Martyn, *Galatians*, 526–27.

15. *Spec. Laws* 4.94–95; *Rewards* 124; *Giants* 29–35; *Unchangeable* 140–144; *Heir* 57, 268. See Emma Wasserman, "The Death of the Soul in Romans 7: Revisiting Paul's Anthropology in Light of Hellenistic Moral Psychology," *JBL* 126 (2007): 809; see also Barclay, *Obeying the Truth*, 185–87; citing Egon Brandenburger, *Fleisch und Geist: Paulus und die Dualitische Weisheit*, WMANT 29 (Neukirchen-Vluyn: Neukirchener, 1968), 114–221; and see Eduard Schweizer, Friedrich Baumgärtel, and Rudolf Meyer, "Σάρξ, Σαρκικός, Σάρκινος," in *TDNT*, 7:121–23.

16. Barclay, *Obeying the Truth*, 186.

17. Alexandria Frisch and Lawrence H. Schiffman, "The Body in Qumran Literature: Flesh and Spirit, Purity and Impurity in the Dead Sea Scrolls," *DSD* 23 (2016): 155–82, https://doi.org/10.1163/15685179-12341386; see de Boer, *Galatians*, 335–39, citing Martyn, *Galatians*, 485, 492–94, 526–29; Joel Marcus, "The Evil Inclination in the Epistle of James," *CBQ* 44.4 (1982): 606–21; Joel Marcus, "The Evil Inclination in the Letters of Paul," *Irish Biblical Studies* 8.1 (1986): 8–21.

18. de Boer, *Galatians*, 337–38; Martyn, *Galatians*, 492, 526–27, citing Marcus, "The Evil Inclination in the Letters of Paul."

19. See יצר in Gen 6.5; 8.21; Deut 31.21; 1 Chron 28.9; 29.18; Ps 103.14; Isa 26.3; 29.16; Hab 2.18, rendered by πλάσμα, διάνοια, ἔγκειμαι, ἐνθύμημα, and πονηρία.

142   *4*

20. Barclay, *Obeying the Truth*, 188 n. 24, citing Géza Vermes, trans., *The Dead Sea Scrolls in English*, 2d ed. (Harmondsworth: Penguin, 1975), 184; R. E. Murphy, "'Yeser' in the Qumran Literature," *Biblica* 39 (1958): 341, respectively.

21. de Boer, *Galatians*, 337.

22. Martyn, *Galatians*, 483–86, 492–93, 528; de Boer, *Galatians*, 337–39; Robert Jewett, *Paul's Anthropological Terms: A Study of Their Use in Conflict Settings*, AGJU 10 (Leiden: Brill, 1971), 100–101.

23. Barclay, *Obeying the Truth*, 213; see Dunn, *Galatians*, 297.

24. Stowers, *A Rereading of Romans*, 45, 257; Wasserman, "Death of the Soul"; Emma Wasserman, "Paul among the Philosophers: The Case of Sin in Romans 6–8," *JSNT* 30 (2008): 387–415, https://doi.org/10.1177/0142064X08091441; Scornaienchi, *Sarx und Soma*, 307–23, 348.

25. Scott J. Hafemann, "Paul and the Exile of Israel in Galatians 3–4," in *Exile: Old Testament, Jewish, and Christian Conceptions*, ed. James M. Scott, JSJSup 56 (Leiden: Brill, 1997), 341, 347–48.

26. Both Barclay, *Obeying the Truth*, 203 and David Charles Aune, "Passions in the Pauline Epistles: The Current State of Research," in *Passions and Moral Progress in Greco-Roman Thought*, ed. John T. Fitzgerald, Routledge Monographs in Classical Studies (London: Routledge, 2008), 222 note that Paul's terms are common in Greek philosophy.

27. Barclay, *Obeying the Truth*, 211.

28. For a recent critical review of interpretations of law and sin in Rom 7, see David Johnston, "The Problem of Romans 7" (University of St Andrews, PhD thesis, 2017).

29. C. H. Dodd, *The Epistle of Paul to the Romans*, MNTC (London: Collins, 1959), 104–5.

30. Rudolpf Bultmann, "Romans 7 and the Anthropology of Paul," in *Existence and Faith: Shorter Writings of Rudolf Bultmann*, trans. Schubert Ogden (London: Collins, 1960), 173–85.

31. Ernst Käsemann, *Commentary on Romans*, trans. Geoffrey W. Bromiley (Grand Rapids: Eerdmans, 1980), 192; Joseph A. Fitzmyer, *Romans: A New Translation with Intorduction and Commentary*, AB (New York: Doubleday, 1993), 462–77; Jean-Noël Aletti, "Rm 7.7–25 Encore Une Fois: Enjeux et Propositions," *NTS* 48.3 (2002): 375.

32. Robert H. Gundry, "The Moral Frustration of Paul Before His Conversion: Sexual Lust in Romans 7:7–25," in *Pauline Studies: Essays Presented to Professor F. F. Bruce on His 70th Birthday*, ed. Donald A. Hagner and Murray J. Harris (Exeter: Paternoster, 1980), 228–45.

33. C. E. B. Cranfield, *A Critical and Exegetical Commentary on the Epistle to the Romans*, 2 vols., ICC (Edinburgh: T&T Clark, 1975), 1:341–47; Alan F. Segal, "Romans 7 and Jewish Dietary Law," *Studies in Religion/Sciences Religieuses* 15.3 (1986): 365, 371; James D. G. Dunn, *Romans*, 2 vols., WBC (Waco, TX: Word, 1988), 1:382–83.

34. N. T. Wright, *The Climax of the Covenant: Christ and the Law in Pauline Theology* (London: T&T Clark, 1991), 196–200.

35. Gordon D. Fee, *God's Empowering Presence: The Holy Spirit in the Letters of Paul* (Peabody, MA: Hendrickson, 1994), 508–15; Walt Russell, "Insights from

The Flesh and Sin: Enslaved Under the Στοιχεια Του Κοσμου   143

Postmodernism's Emphasis on Interpretive Communities in the Interpretation of Romans 7," *JETS* 37.4 (1994): 511–27; Brendan Byrne, *Romans*, SP 6 (Collegeville, MN: Liturgical, 1996), 216–24; Paul Trudinger, "An Autobiographical Digression? A Note on Romans 7:7–25," *ExpTim* 107.6 (1996): 173–74, https://doi.org/10.1177 /001452469610700604. Douglas J. Moo, *The Epistle to the Romans*, NICNT (Grand Rapids: Eerdmans, 1996), 426 n. 8 traces this view to Chrysostom.

36. So Moo, *Romans*, 423–31; Colin G. Kruse, *Paul's Letter to the Romans*, PNTC (Grand Rapids: Eerdmans, 2012), 319–21.

37. Jean-Baptiste Édart, "De la Nécessité d'un Sauveur: Rhétorique et Théologie de Rm 7,7–25," *RB* 105.3 (1998): 359, https://doi.org/10.2307/44089394.

38. James W. Thompson, *Moral Formation According to Paul: The Context and Coherence of Pauline Ethics* (Grand Rapids: Baker Academic, 2011), 143; Fee, *God's Empowering Presence*, 819–22.

39. Wright, *Paul and the Faithfulness of God*, 1010.

40. Wright, *Paul and the Faithfulness of God*, 1018, see 894.

41. Kruse, *Paul's Letter to the Romans*, 267–68 overlooks it.

42. Contra Byrne, *Romans*, 194; Thompson, *Moral Formation*, 149–51. Manuscripts vary on the phrase ταῖς ἐπιθυμίαις αὐτοῦ, but NA28 cites no variant that identifies the desires as sin's (see Scornaienchi, *Sarx und Soma*, 345 n. 235).

43. Contra Moo, *Romans*, 353, 383–84; Thomas R. Schreiner, *Romans*, BECNT (Grand Rapids: Baker, 1998), 322–23. This confusion is worse in Scornaienchi, *Sarx und Soma*, 296–98, 307–9, 319–21, who uses *Affekte* ambiguously to render παθήματα, πάθη, ἐπιθυμίαι, and even ἔργα.

44. So too Stowers, *A Rereading of Romans*, 270. Italics mine.

45. Wilhelm Michaelis, "Πάσχω, Παθητός, Προπάσχω, Συμπάσχω, Πάθος, Πάθημα, Συμπαθής, Συμπαθέω, Κακοπαθέω, Συγκακοπαθέω, Κακοπάθεια, Μετριοπαθέω, Ὁμοιοπαθής, Πραϋπάθεια," in *TDNT*, 5.931.

46. Emma Wasserman, *The Death of the Soul in Romans 7: Sin, Death, and the Law in Light of Hellenistic Moral Psychology*, WUNT 2.256 (Tübingen: Mohr Siebeck, 2008), 795–97.

47. Wasserman, *The Death of the Soul in Romans 7*, 812.

48. See Moo, *Galatians*, 28–29.

49. I read ἀνθρώπινον in Rom 6.19 ("ἀνθρώπινον λέγω διὰ τὴν ἀσθένειαν τῆς σαρκὸς ὑμῶν') as a simple accusative: "I am speaking about the human person, the human condition as caused by the weakness of the flesh" (contra Moo, *Romans*, 403; see Thompson, *Moral Formation*, 147). See a comparable collocation of ἀνθρώπινος and ἀσθένεια in *Alleg. Interp.* 1.69.

50. David Arthur deSilva, *Reading Paul through Asian Eyes: A Sri Lankan Commentary on Galatians* (Kohuwela: CTS, 2014), 211.

51. Dunn, *Galatians*, 314.

52. Thompson, *Moral Formation*, 143, 146.

53. *Passion* stands for ἐπιθυμία in NIV at Tit 2.12 (a change from "desire" in the 1984 edition); 3.3; in NET at 2 Tim 2.22; Tit 3.3; in NRSV there and at Eph 2.3; and in ESV in all those verses and at 2 Tim 3.6; 4.3.

54. LSJ.

144

55. As also in Col 1.24; 2 Tim 3.11.

56. 1 Cor 12.26; 2 Cor 1.6; Gal 3.4; Phil 1.29; 1 Thess 2.14; see 2 Thess 1.5; 2 Tim 1.12.

57. On the other hand, when read carefully in each of its contexts, Paul's use of πάθος seems to refer not to factors that affect or move someone, but to the affections or emotions they cause, which, in turn, prompt particular actions (Rom 1.26; 1 Thess 4.5; see Col 3.5). See chapter 6 below.

58. Betz, *Galatians*, 289 n. 173.

59. Moo, *Romans*, 419 n. 52; see Adolf Schlatter, *Gottes Gerechtigkeit* (Stuttgart: Calwer, 1959).

60. See Sandnes, *Belly and Body in the Pauline Epistles*; Stanley Kent Stowers, "Paul and Self-Mastery," in *Paul in the Greco-Roman World: A Handbook*, ed. J. Paul Sampley, 2d ed. (London: Bloomsbury T&T Clark, 2016), 294. Paul's location of human motivation in both the καρδία and the κοιλία resonates with the two lower portions of Plato's tripartite soul. However, the volitional capacity of the belly is present already in the Hebrew scriptures. For example, see Eliphaz's attribution of deceit to the κοιλία, there translating בטן (Job 15.35; see BDAG). Paul, like Jesus, follows the Hebrew scriptures in identifying the human heart as a fount of evil (Deut 10.16; Isa 29.13; Jer 17.9; Ezek 6.9; Mark 7.21; Rom 1.21, 24; 2.5; etc.). But human hearts and desires can also be made righteous (Rom 2.15; 6.17; 10.1–10; Phil 1.23; 1 Thess 2.17; see Jer 17.10, 14).

61. It is certainly not that the ἐπιθυμίαι "direct" the παθήματα "this way or that," as F. F. Bruce, *The Epistle to the Galatians*, NIGTC (Grand Rapids: Eerdmans, 1982), 256 asserts. If anything, causation flows the other way (see *Anon. Lond.* 1.27–37).

62. See R. James Hankinson, "Actions and Passions: Affection, Emotion, and Moral Self-Management in Galen's Philosophical Psychology," in *Passions & Perceptions: Studies in Hellenistic Philosophy of Mind: Proceedings of the Fifth Symposium Hellenisticum*, ed. Jacques Brunschwig and Martha Craven Nussbaum (Cambridge: Cambridge University Press, 1993), 208 n. 77; Erica Nicole Daigle, "Reconciling Matter and Spirit: The Galenic Brain in Early Modern Literature" (University of Iowa, PhD thesis, 2009), 46, http://citeseerx.ist.psu.edu/viewdoc/download?doi=10.1.1.614.7061.

63. Martyn, *Galatians*, 500; de Boer, *Galatians*, 367.

64. Martin, *The Corinthian Body*, xiii, 12–13. Martin's "medical texts" would seem to include *Timaeus*, as he quotes *Tim.* 86d on p. 12.

65. Dunn, *Galatians*, 297; see Thompson, *Moral Formation*, 147.

66. Witherington, *Grace in Galatia*, 413; Richard B. Hays, "The Letter to the Galatians: Introduction, Commentary, and Reflections," in *The New Interpreter's Bible* (Nashville: Abingdon, 2000), 328–29, 345; Geurt H. van Kooten, *Cosmic Christology in Paul and the Pauline School: Colossians and Ephesians in the Context of Graeco-Roman Cosmology, with a New Synopsis of the Greek Texts*, WUNT 2/171 (Tübingen: Mohr Siebeck, 2003), 78–79; Thomas R. Schreiner, *Galatians*, ZECNT (Grand Rapids: Zondervan, 2010), 356–57; de Boer, *Galatians*, 374.

67. de Boer, *Galatians*, 372, 403–4; see Witherington, *Grace in Galatia*, 285, 413; Hays, "Galatians," 328–29, 345; Peter J. Leithart, *Delivered from the Elements of the*

The Flesh and Sin: Enslaved Under the Στοιχεια Του Κοσμου   145

World: Atonement, Justification, Mission (Downers Grove, IL: IVP Academic, 2016), 225 n. 11.

68. For the fourth use see *Sobriety* 48.

69. Philo also uses the verb ἀναστοιχειόω with elemental overtones in *Heir* 200; *Eternity* 94. See chapter 3, section C.3 above.

70. See Schreiner, *Galatians*, 356–57.

71. Since the elements are virtually absent from Paul's argument in Romans and Philippians (but see Rom 9.17, 27, 28; 10.18; Phil 2.10; 3.19), there is no reason to think he uses στοιχέω in those letters with anything other than its denotative sense: advance in line with something (Rom 4.12; Phil 3.16).

72. van Kooten, *Cosmic Christology*, 78.

73. Ian H. Thomson, *Chiasmus in the Pauline Letters*, JSNTSup 111 (Sheffield: Sheffield Academic, 1995), 116–51. Dunn, *Galatians*, 295 posits a similar "abc-cba pattern" in 5.16–24. Moo, *Galatians*, 351–52 follows Dunn, and Jean-Noël Aletti, "Paul's Exhortations in Gal 5,16–25: From the Apostle's Techniques to His Theology," *Biblica* 94.3 (2013): 399–401 develops him, but neither seems to know Thomson.

74. Stanley E. Porter and Jeffrey T. Reed, "Philippians as a Macro-Chiasm and Its Exegetical Significance," *NTS* 44.2 (1998): 220–21, https://doi.org/10.1017/S0028688500016489, criticizing Thomson, *Chiasmus in the Pauline Letters*, 24–29. However, they offer no positive criteria of their own and, while ignoring the likely influence of rhetorical devices in Israel's ancient literature on early Jews writing in Greek, nonetheless reach totalizing conclusions about "the ancients" and their rhetorical simplicity (Porter and Reed, "Philippians as a Macro-Chiasm and Its Exegetical Significance," 216–17.).

75. David Arthur deSilva, "X Marks the Spot?: A Critique of the Use of Chiasmus in Macro-Structural Analyses of Revelation," *JSNT* 30.3 (2008): 347–48, https://doi.org/10.1177/0142064X07088407. For the "état de la question" of chiasm in biblical and Semitic rhetoric, see R. Meynet, "La Rhétorique Biblique et Sémitique: État de La Question," *Rhetorica* 28.3 (2010): 292–96, and for mature reflections on "ring composition" in diverse ancient and modern contexts, see Mary Douglas, *Thinking in Circles: An Essay on Ring Composition* (New Haven, CT: Yale University Press, 2007).

76. Thomson, *Chiasmus in the Pauline Letters*, 142–44.

77. Here I read ἡμεῖς in 4.3 as referring "primarily to Paul's fellow Jews or, more precisely, Christian Jews" (Dunn, *Galatians*, 212; see Ambrosiaster, *Galatians* 43; Bruce, *Galatians*, 193; Longenecker, *Galatians*, 164; Hafemann, "Exile," 340–41; Wright, *Paul and the Faithfulness of God*, 878). Others read "we" as Christians, or all humans, generally (Jerome, *Galatians* 106; Betz, *Galatians*, 204; Martyn, *Galatians*, 388; de Boer, *Galatians*, 251, 256–58; Moo, *Galatians*, 260). Few follow Augustine in seeing a reference to Gentiles only (*Galatians* 177; see Moo, *Galatians*, 260 n. 2). Paul's οὕτως καί, though, renders the dispute inconsequential, for it implies that the Jews' enslavement under the elements is similar to that of all humans.

78. Leithart, *Delivered from the Elements of the World*, 37 n. 32.

79. David J. Lull, "'The Law Was Our Pedagogue': A Study in Galatians 3:19–25," *JBL* 105 (1986): 496.

80. Martyn, *Galatians*, 370–73; de Boer, *Galatians*, 257–61.

81. Moo, *Galatians*, 242, cf. 239, 246, 261.

82. de Boer, *Galatians*, 258; Hafemann, "Exile," 346–47; citing Linda Belleville, "'Under Law': Structural Analysis and the Pauline Concept of Law in Galatians 3.21–4.11," *JSNT* 26 (1986): 64–69.

83. de Boer, *Galatians*, 260–61.

84. Betz, *Galatians*, 205; Longenecker, *Galatians*, 164–65; Dunn, *Galatians*, 212–13; Robert Ewusie Moses, *Practices of Power: Revisiting the Principalities and Powers in the Pauline Letters* (Minneapolis: Fortress, 2014), 120, 128–33.

85. See Wright, *Paul and the Faithfulness of God*, 893–94, 1017–20.

86. J. B. Lightfoot, *Saint Paul's Epistle to the Galatians: A Revised Text with Introduction, Notes, and Dissertations* (London: Macmillan, 1887), 165–66; Ernest De Witt Burton, *A Critical and Exegetical Commentary on the Epistle to the Galatians*, ICC (Edinburgh: T&T Clark, 1921), 212–15; Betz, *Galatians*, 202–4; Longenecker, *Galatians*, 163–64; James M. Scott, *Adoption as Sons of God: An Exegetical Investigation Into the Background of Yiothesia in the Pauline Corpus*, WUNT 2/48 (Tübingen: Mohr Siebeck, 1992), 123–25; Schreiner, *Galatians*, 265–67; de Boer, *Galatians*, 258–60. Scott, *Adoption as Sons of God*, 149–51, 186 finds the exodus motif here (now developed by Hafemann, "Exile," 331–49; Sylvia C. Keesmaat, "Paul and His Story: Exodus and Tradition in Galatians," *HBT* 18.1 (1996): 133–68, https://doi.org/10.1163/187122096X00077; Sylvia C. Keesmaat, *Paul and His Story: (Re)Interpreting the Exodus Tradition*, LNTS 181 (Sheffield: Sheffield Academic, 1999), 155–214 and followed by Schreiner, *Galatians*, 265–67). Moo, *Galatians*, 260 interprets it as a general analogy (citing Betz, *Galatians*, 203, 204; Longenecker, *Galatians*, 163–64).

87. Lull, "Pedagogue," 494.

88. Hafemann, "Exile," 345–46.

89. Hafemann, "Exile," 338, citing Hos 11.1–5 among other scriptural references.

90. Hafemann, "Exile," 339, citing *BAGD*, 38, meaning 5.

91. See Ps 119.133.

92. Fee, *God's Empowering Presence*, 124; see Archibald Robertson and Alfred Plummer, *A Critical and Exegetical Commentary on the First Epistle of St Paul to the Corinthians*, 2nd ed., ICC (Edinburgh: T&T Clark, 1914), 52.

93. Anthony C. Thiselton, *The First Epistle to the Corinthians: A Commentary on the Greek Text*, NIGTC (Grand Rapids: Eerdmans, 2000), 291.

94. Paul's other use is in 2 Cor 3.3.

95. These ideas converge in Eph 2.3's description of the saints' former life among "the sons of disobedience": "Among them all of us also once engaged in the ἐπιθυμίαι of our σάρξ, performing the will of the σάρξ and of the thoughts, and we were by nature children of wrath, as also are the rest."

96. Lull, "Pedagogue," 493–96.

97. Barclay, *Paul and the Gift*, 401.

98. Lull, "Pedagogue," 493–95.

99. For recent comparison of Paul's lists with virtue and vice lists in other ancient sources, see Thompson, *Moral Formation*, 87–110.

100. Lull, "Pedagogue," 494–95.

5

The Law Against the Στοιχεια and the Flesh

Chapter 4 considered Paul's idea of enslavement under the στοιχεῖα τοῦ κόσμου from the perspective of Greek medical discourse. It found that Paul, like Greek philosophers and like Philo, considers the material στοιχεῖα to be the components of the human body and that he identifies those στοιχεῖα as the cause of the weakness of human flesh and its susceptibility to biological and moral disease. Chapter 5 turns from diagnosis to prescription. In Galatians, Paul reviews two distinct treatments for the flesh. First, he notes that scripture promised Abraham and his heirs the blessing of the Spirit through faith (3.14). Second, he states that, until faith came, scripture interposed the law as a sort of παιδαγωγός to guard and guide Abraham's wayward heirs (3.23–24). Section A shows how Greek medical discourse clarifies the particular responsibilities of a παιδαγωγός for children and their fleshy tendencies. It surveys disputes among modern scholars, and it explicates the argument between Paul and the Galatian agitators. The agitators are urging the believers to practice the law's works, and Paul is warning them not to. Section B reads Paul's polemic in conversation with Philo's redemptive nomism. From the perspective of "discourse," it finds Galatians to be a thoughtful rebuttal to an attested first-century Jewish use of the law. At point after point, in exposition and in allegory, Paul uses terms and concepts in Philo's argument to show from scripture that the law does not offer the life, freedom, righteousness, or inheritance that teachers like Philo attribute to it. Applied to those ends, the law actually produces entirely opposite results.

A. THE LAW WAS A ΠΑΙΔΑΓΩΓΟΣ TO GUARD ABRAHAM'S CHILDREN

As Paul says in Galatians 3, scripture foresaw God's intent and promised to bless the nations in Abraham, but when Abraham's descendants transgressed, it responded by adding the law. Law is also a corrective measure in Greek medical discourse: the Hippocratic corpus prescribes "νόμος" as a regimen to instill traits that people do not have within their souls by nature (*Aër.* 24). But, in Galatians, Paul is telling scripture's story. And when he sees within that narrative that the law is responsible to pen Israel in and guard them until faith is revealed, he recognizes that the law is a sort of παιδαγωγός, a servant appointed to supervise children and foster their development. While a παιδαγωγός had a range of responsibilities, Paul highlights the law's responsibilities to guard and guide Abraham's children. As we saw in chapter 2, these tasks correspond to the reasons for which Greek medical discourse advises employing a παιδαγωγός to supervise a child or a childish soul. From Paul's perspective, the law as guide commanded Abraham's children to walk in righteousness, and, as guard, it restricted Abraham's wayward children, revealed their transgressions, and warned them of a curse. But, Paul states clearly, the law's role as παιδαγωγός has come to an end now that God has sent the Son and his Spirit.[1]

1. As a Παιδαγωγός the Law Guides Children (3.19–4.2; see 5.13–23)

Paul's παιδαγωγός analogy may strike modern readers as abrupt and out of place—few of us have met a παιδαγωγός—but it is entirely at home. As chapter 2 showed, it is not unusual for the term παιδαγωγός to occur in medical contexts alongside νήπιος, ἐπιθυμία, or νόμος, because παιδαγωγός is a role, not a mere concept. It is someone appointed to work for the good (the protection and moral nurture) of a child or some other person vulnerable to being taken over, indeed enslaved, by desire or another malicious agent. Section one shows that scholars dispute whether Paul saw this role as negative or positive, though most now favor the latter. In antiquity, this role had many features. Plato and Aristotle prescribe a παιδαγωγός to guide a παῖς, a νήπιος, or some other childish thing, like the appetitive part of the soul. And Philo compares God's word to a παιδαγωγός and says that God sends it forth into people's minds to correct and heal them. But it is Paul's argument in Galatians and the purposes and functions he attributes to the law in that letter that reveal how, for him, the law is like a παιδαγωγός.

a. One Scholar's Beloved Guide is Another Scholar's Bilious Guard

Research in the 1980s and 1990s moved the scholarly consensus away from an earlier negative evaluation of the law's role as παιδαγωγός. Hans Dieter Betz, for example, associates Paul's "radical devaluation of the Law" with Paul's use of "a grim concept of παιδεία" and "the rather ugly type of the pedagogue."[2] This negativism continues in Louis Martyn and Martinus de Boer, who describe the παιδαγωγός as a "jailer."[3] But Richard Longenecker critiques Betz's data as one-sided: "the depiction of the ancient pedagogue as a grim and ugly character is indeed a caricature."[4]

In the 1980s, David Lull's and Norman Young's thick descriptions of the role of a παιδαγωγός as seen in ancient texts and art combined with new perspectives on the law to foster appreciation for the law's functions of supervising, guarding, and protecting Israel.[5] Their articles are longer and more nuanced than earlier studies and remain the best treatments of the role of a παιδαγωγός. They present the wide range of responsibilities assigned to a παιδαγωγός, the various ways—abusive or nurturing, negligent or diligent— in which παιδαγωγοί fulfilled (or did not fulfill) those responsibilities, and the mixture of feelings that a child or an adult may hold toward a current or former παιδαγωγός. Their solid work has won the support of most interpreters since. Virtually everyone now agrees that the law's role as παιδαγωγός is temporary,[6] as opposed to "something like the classic Lutheran view of the law showing people their need for grace."[7] Most scholars also agree that its role was supervisory.[8]

Opinions differ though on whether the law's temporary, supervisory role was to guard, to protect, or to train. According to Young, "the presence of φρουρέω and συγκλείω in close conjunction makes it clear that Paul's main point—if not his only point—in the metaphor is not a matter of discipline, education, instruction or punishment, but of restriction."[9] Young then identifies the Law's "immature" or "primitive religious customs and restrictions" as the στοιχεῖα τοῦ κόσμου.[10]

Against Young, David Gordon notes the positive uses of φρουρέω that "suggest protection or protective custody" (2 Cor 11.32; Phil 4.7).[11] According to Gordon, "there was indeed a period when circumcision, the dietary code and the Jewish calendar properly functioned to protect the integrity and purity of the covenant community from the defiling influence of the (then-idolatrous) Gentiles."[12] James Dunn, Philip Esler, and Peter Oakes advance similar interpretations.[13] And Esler concludes that this view of a παιδαγωγός is "perfectly compatible" with "the notion that a wayward boy who simply will not accept instruction is likely to bring the full weight of the angry pedagogue down on

152   5

his head." However, this view "rules out of court the notion that the law had the purpose of producing or provoking transgression."[14]

Lull argues further, though more recent scholars overlook the point, that the law was added "to bridle the passions and desires" of Israel's flesh.[15] "As a 'pedagogue,' the Law was limited to the task of curbing 'the desires of the flesh' of those who were kept in its custody. . . . For Paul, 'the desires of the flesh' were restrained by the Law, acting as a 'pedagogue,' during the period before Jesus Christ came as Abraham's 'offspring.'"[16] As Lightfoot states, "the παιδαγωγός had the whole moral direction of the child."[17] Though this aspect of the Law's role as παιδαγωγός has not garnered much support, it has at least three strengths. First, it was the consensus interpretation of Paul's interpreters in the first millennium.[18] Second, it corresponds to the frequent prescription in Greek medical discourse of a παιδαγωγός as a moral guide for people weakened by their elemental flesh. Third, as Lull explains it, the law's guiding role integrates most thoroughly into the concern that scripture and Paul share of addressing sin's rule over Abraham's children through their flesh, its stimuli and desires.

b. The Law's Actions as Παιδαγωγός

Paul uses the νόμος-as-παιδαγωγός motif in his own way. Like many other ancient thinkers, he describes the supervisory role of the παιδαγωγός as both guarding and guiding children. But, unlike Plato, Aristotle, and Philo, Paul sees no ongoing role for the law to discipline the desires of the offspring who are no longer children.

This section develops the law's responsibilities as παιδαγωγός under two main heads: guarding and guiding. It uses explicit (3.23–24) and implicit data to fill out the job description for the law as παιδαγωγός in God's household. It draws inferences about the law by comparing the law with the functions of those agents which have ended the law's role. It then cross-checks them with texts from the law itself. The two sets of data show that the law both guarded and guided Abraham's children, commanding them to love their neighbors, setting them a distinct pattern of life, and offering them blessing when they obeyed.

As παιδαγωγός the law guarded and confined Abraham's children.[19] Paul states this task explicitly in 3.23: "Now before faith came we were guarded under law, confined until the coming faith would be revealed." The combination of the verbs φρουρέω and συγκλείω prompts Paul to describe the law as Israel's παιδαγωγός in the following verse, and, as Young argues, this seems to be the law's primary task.[20] Further, in 5.1 Paul compares the law's role in this capacity to a "yoke of slavery."[21] The reason and purpose of the law's guarding and confining are implicit. Paul's discourse in 3.19–25 shows the reason

The Law Against the Στοιχεια and the Flesh   153

to be Israel's παραβάσεις and the condition of all things as "under sin" (3.19, 22).[22] And, now that the law has been removed, Paul's pre-emptive warning implies that the law's former purpose had been to impede the advance of the flesh (5.13).[23] As guard, then, the law was to restrict the proclivities of Israel's expansive flesh.[24] Israel's confinement also involved separation from the nations and their sinful practices, but that aspect seems more important in Deuteronomy than in the argument of Galatians.[25]

Paul is clear and repetitive: the law's role as guard ended with the coming of πίστις Χριστοῦ (3.19–25). Though the law cursed everyone who did not continue to do everything written in it (Gal 3.10, quoting Deut 27.26), the Anointed One redeemed Israel from the law's curse by becoming a curse for them (Gal 3.13). Through the faithfulness of the Anointed, believers are rescued from their sins (1.4), redeemed from enslavement to sin through the flesh (4.1–7), declared righteous (2.16), and made God's sons (3.26; 4.5). From another perspective, Paul describes these radical changes as death. Paul himself has been crucified with the Anointed, and he states that Christians generally have crucified the flesh with its stimuli and desires (2.19–20; 5.24).[26] Now that the believers' dying flesh is nailed to the cross, they no longer need to be restrained by the law. Instead, faith empowers their hopeful wait for righteousness while it expresses itself in love (5.5–6).

As παιδαγωγός the law also guided Abraham's children. This secondary duty is implicit in the way that the root √αγω links 5.18 to 3.23–25 (see Chrysostom 13.41–42).[27] Abraham's sinful children were confined ὑπὸ νόμον as under a παιδαγωγός until the coming of faith (3.23–25). But now that the Galatian believers are led (ἄγω) by the Spirit, they are not ὑπὸ νόμον (5.18).[28]

Paul shows the law guiding Abraham's children in three main ways. First, as a guide the law commanded each of Abraham's children to love his or her neighbor (Gal 5.14, quoting Lev 19.18; see Gal 5.6). As such, the law did not speak against love and the actions that follow it, but, by implication, it did condemn fleshy behaviors that oppose love (Gal 5.19–23).[29] Though the law guided Israel truly, its role in this capacity, like its role as guard, has come to an end. However fine the distinction may seem, for Paul it is a significant one: scripture as teacher still instructs (Rom 15.4)—indeed, scripture is the basis for much of Paul's argument in Gal 3–5—but law as παιδαγωγός no longer guides God's children (Gal 5.8).[30] Instead, God's Spirit does so, through πίστις, and it bears love as the first of its fruit (2.20; 3.2–5, 25; 4.6; 5.5–6, 17–25; see Ezek 36.27).[31]

Second, as a guide the law set a distinct pattern of life. In Deuteronomy, Moses repeatedly calls the Israelites to walk in God's way (Deut 5.33; 8.6; 10.12; 19.9; 26.17; 28.9; 30.16). Though Paul does not use πορεύομαι or ὁδός in Galatians, περιπατέω and other verbs of forward motion—like τρέχω, ὀρθοποδέω, and στοιχέω—suggest that he sees the law as having directed

154 5

a way of life, a sort of הלכה (Gal 5.16; see 2.2, 14; 5.7; 6.16). For Paul, the distinct features of this way of life were (1) circumcision (2.3, 12; 5.2–6; 6.12–13); (2) days, months, seasons, and years (4.9); and perhaps also (3) separation from other nations (2.11–18).[32] However, again, now that πίστις has come, Paul repudiates this distinct way of life: circumcision is no more effective than having a foreskin (Gal 5.6), Israel's calendar is analogous to the nations' calendars (4.9),[33] and separation from the nations is antithetical to the good news, because scripture promised that blessing to Abraham precisely for the nations (2.11–14).[34]

Third, as a guide the law also offered blessing. This final mode of guidance is implicit in Paul's blessing on those who advance in line with the rule of new creation (6.15–16). His mention of εἰρήνη and ἔλεος evokes the Aaronic blessing (Num 6.22–26), and the collocation of peace with harvesting fruit in season resonates with Lev 26.4–6. But this function too has come to an end, for believers have moved from old κόσμος to new κτίσις (Gal 6.14–16).

Paul's description of the law's responsibilities to guard and guide Abraham's children coheres with ancient medical perspectives on the role of a παιδαγωγός. The law's restriction of the rampant proclivities of the flesh corresponds to the prescription of a παιδαγωγός in Greek medical discourse. The law's command to love, its distinct pattern of life, and its blessing marked it as a reliable guide that worked for the good of its vulnerable charge. Comparison with Greek medical discourse also highlights a difference in Paul's use of the metaphor. For Paul, the law as παιδαγωγός has no further role in guiding the behavior of childish souls. Those who are enslaved by sin's infection of the elemental flesh, its stimuli and desires, find redemption and righteousness in the Son and the Spirit, not under the law. Yet, for a long tradition of scholarship on Galatians, the law as παιδαγωγός served—or perhaps still serves—a role more negative than positive. Section two considers what Paul means when he writes that scripture interposed the law "because of transgressions."

2. Scripture Interposed the Law on Account of Transgressions (3.19)

I have asserted repeatedly that, for Paul, the law was scripture's response to the transgressions of Abraham's descendants. That is a straightforward reading of "the law was added on τῶν παραβάσεων χάριν" (3.19). However, scholars dispute the particular senses of both the postposition χάριν and the noun παράβασις.[35]

Χάριν is ambiguous. It can point backward to a "reason" ("because of") or forward to a "goal" ("for the sake of").[36] Thus the law could have been added for sins in the past: either (a) to give "people a realization of their

The Law Against the Στοιχεια and the Flesh   155

sinfulness";[37] (b) to have transgression "defined, tabulated, and punished";[38] (c) "to provide some sort of remedy for transgressions";[39] or (d), in light of sins in the past, to restrain Israel from further sin. Or the law could have been added for sins in the future: either (e) to provoke or "produce" sins[40] or (f) to "turn sin into transgressions."[41] Options *a*, *b*, *d*, and *f* correlate with the multifaceted role of a παιδαγωγός and the several responsibilities that Paul describes the law performing.[42] From this narrative perspective then, Israel's transgressions showed Israel's need for a law that would (a, b) convict them of and punish past sins, (f) show them the gravity of existing sins, and, especially, (d) restrain them from further sins.

But this reading is called into question by the term παράβασις as well. For Moo, Paul's choice of παράβασις rather than ἁμαρτία is "a crucial factor," because "the former word has a very definite sense in Paul, referring to the violation of a known law."[43] Witherington and others are certainly right to adduce Rom 4.15: "οὗ δὲ οὐκ ἔστιν νόμος, οὐδὲ παράβασις."[44] However, a detailed reading of Israel's story does not bear out the assumption that it was impossible for Israel to commit παραβάσεις before scripture added on what the OG designates precisely as ὁ νόμος.

Texts in the Pentateuch show at least three counterexamples. First, God's laws and commands were known before scripture added what it labels νόμος. Long before Moses, Abraham himself kept God's νόμιμα along with his προστάγματά, ἐντολαί, and δικαιώματα (Gen 26.5).[45] In Israel's history, while there are instances of νόμος and νόμιμον before Sinai (Exod 12.43, 49; 13.9, 10; 16.4, 28; 18.16, 20), neither the words that God spoke directly to the people at Sinai nor the words that God spoke through Moses for the people were designated νόμος; they were termed λόγοι, ῥήματα, and δικαιώματα (Exod 21.1; 24.3). The precise designation νόμος does not appear until God summons Moses up into the mountain to receive the stone tablets (Exod 24.12). Second, a παράβασις can be a transgression of God's ὁδός and not only of his νόμος. It is while Moses is receiving the νόμος, and before he has declared it to Israel, that the people παρέβησαν ἐκ/ἀπὸ the ὁδός that God commanded them (Exod 32.8; see Deut 9.12, 16).[46] The narrative portrays their actions as point for point violations of the λόγοι, ῥήματα, and δικαιώματα that God had spoken to them both directly and through Moses (Exod 20; 21–23). In that sense, God's words have exacerbated a ἁμαρτία and revealed it as a παράβασις. But, speaking technically, it is God's λόγοι, ῥήματα, and δικαιώματα that have revealed this, not his νόμος. Third, the people of Israel do not receive what the scriptures term "νόμος" until after their παράβασις with the golden calf. Then, after God gives Moses his νόμος in Exod 24.12, the term νόμος comes in abundance in Leviticus and Numbers. It is then, after Israel's παράβασις with the golden calf, that God's νόμος comes to his people ἐν χειρὶ Μωυσῆ (Lev 26.25; see Lev 10.11, etc.) or, as

156 5

Paul says, ἐν χειρὶ μεσίτου (Gal 3.19). God speaks to Moses from between the angelic cherubim and gives him his commands for the children of Israel (Num 7.89; see Exod 25.22).[47]

In sum, God adds νόμος *after* the παράβασις to guard and guide Abraham's heirs as a παιδαγωγός until the coming of the Anointed and faith. However, despite its responsibility to guard and guide, the law could not make the heirs either alive or righteous. As a result, those heirs who had no faith (i.e., whose hearts were not circumcised) did not do the works of the law and thus found themselves under the law's curse. In this way, the νόμος—within its larger and primary task of directing the heirs to act in accordance with life and righteousness—also revealed ἁμαρτία as παράβασις.

Since the law was their guide, many early Jews looked to it to lead them forward in moral progress or προκοπή.[48] Paul himself describes his former life as one of exceptional progress in "Judaism" because he was more zealous than his compatriots for the traditions of his ancestors (Gal 1.14).[49] However, others, like Philo, require even more of the παιδαγωγός. Through its supervision, they seek to attain life, righteousness, and the inheritance. But Paul is clear: those duties were never part of the law's job description as παιδαγωγός.[50] Its role is beneficial but limited. It will lead and restrain, but it is powerless to make alive, declare righteous, or confer the inheritance. Pressed to those ends, the law does not redeem; indeed, it leads back to slavery and under a curse. Life, righteousness, and the inheritance come only from πίστις, and when πίστις is revealed the παιδαγωγός bows out.

B. THE LAW IS NOT A MEANS TO REDEMPTION

The quest for the elusive meaning of the curious term στοιχεῖα in Gal 4.3, 9 leads us now to consider how the "agitators" in the Galatian assemblies may have spoken about the elements, the flesh, its stimuli, desires, and actions, and about the law and its works in response to all of these. I turn, as before, to consider the extant writings of Philo, whose works were known beyond the shores of Egypt in the first-century Mediterranean world.

This study has argued for and demonstrated the relevance of Philo's corpus to the interpretation of the Pauline epistles. Chapter 1 showed that Philo's abundant use of the term στοιχεῖον revealed its range of meanings (both material and immaterial) and defined the particular meaning of the phrase στοιχεῖα κόσμου. In chapter 2, Philo's description of the body's composition from material στοιχεῖα and his analysis of the role of the στοιχεῖα in mediating the body's πάθη and ἐπιθυμίαι filled out an early Jewish understanding of a person's enslavement under the elements.

Section B now compares some of Paul's statements against the agitators with the teachings of his contemporary Philo. It shows that many of the agitators' thoughts and practices which caused Paul such concern correspond to actual propositions in Philo's works. To state the point absurdly, I am not suggesting that Philo received a letter from "the rabbis in Palestine" and left to tour and teach in the Galatian assemblies.[51] I am suggesting, however, that the agitators were influenced by an amalgam of early Jewish thought best articulated by Philo (and now most available to us in his extant works). And I am arguing that this paradigm used terms and concepts, seen as significant in Galatians, to promote a way of thinking about and practicing the law of Moses which Paul sets aside as anathema.[52]

1. Checking Barclay in the Mirror

This argument meets both challenge and encouragement in John Barclay's scholarship. In "Mirror-Reading," Barclay deconstructs the "essential and extremely problematic" practice of looking at a polemical text "as a *mirror* in which we can see reflected the people and the arguments under attack."[53] By way of contemporary example, Barclay attempts to use Secretary of State for Energy Peter Walker's letter to *The Times* to reconstruct the sermon, given by Bishop of Durham David Jenkins a few days earlier, to which Walker was replying.[54] Barclay's experiment exposes several "pitfalls" of mirror-reading, including "latching onto particular words and phrases as direct echoes of the opponents' vocabulary and then hanging a whole thesis on those flimsy pegs."[55] In this pit Barclay finds Wegenast's and Schlier's treatments of Galatians, which are overconfident in making extrapolations from Paul's "rather obscure phrase, τὰ στοιχεῖα τοῦ κόσμου."[56] An approach like theirs, Barclay notes, assumes four things: "(a) Paul's knowledge of the exact vocabulary used by his opponents; (b) Paul's willingness to re-use this vocabulary either ironically or in some attempt to redefine it; (c) our ability to discern where Paul is echoing his opponents' language; and (d) our ability to reconstruct the meaning that they originally gave to it."[57]

Barclay's salutary warning demands that I justify my method. This study does not attempt to reconstruct the terms and arguments of Paul's opponents. Rather, it begins with the actual terms and arguments of Paul's Jewish contemporary Philo and evaluates the hypothesis that ideas like his informed and shaped the teachings and practices that Paul opposes. In this way, my method follows the second stage of Barclay's experiment more than the first. I am not, as it were, trying to reconstruct Jenkins's sermon from Walker's letter but am rather comparing Walker's letter against people who think like Jenkins. As Barclay found with Walker and Jenkins, this study finds that many (rather, most) of Paul's insinuations about his opponents' views on the στοιχεῖα and

158   5

related issues are present in Philo. It finds further that there is a great deal in Philo about which Paul says nothing and, indeed, that Paul and Philo would share many points of agreement.[58] For example, both Paul and Philo would say that "salvation is now available to Gentiles, in fulfilment of the promises to Abraham," and that "God's people should abstain from idolatry and the passions of the flesh."[59]

Barclay himself provides much evidence in support of this hypothesis. Several of the results of the application of his "possible methodology" to Galatians are true of Philo or would be true of Christians influenced by Philo's works. As Barclay summarizes:

Certain or Virtually Certain . . .

2. They wanted the Galatians to be circumcised and to observe at least some of the rest of the law, including its calendrical requirements. . . .

Highly Probable

1. They were Jewish Christians.
2. They argued from Scripture using, in particular, the Abraham narratives.
3. They expected the Galatians to become circumcised proselytes and to observe the law, as the hallmark of the people of God. . . .

Probable . . .

2. Their scriptural arguments made reference to Genesis 17 and the Sarah-Hagar narratives. . . .

Conceivable

They . . . used the word στοιχεῖα.[60]

Philo's relevance is seen further in Barclay's exegesis of Galatians. First, Philo is useful for understanding the στοιχεῖα as material elements.[61] Second, though Barclay claims that "it would be dangerous to assume that Philo's allegorical fantasies were an integral part of the agitators' theology," he cites Philo as evidence that "Jewish theology" in the first century connected the themes of circumcision, Abraham, and Gentile proselytes.[62] Third, Philo illustrates how "Jews presented and commended the law in the Diaspora," especially by listing the virtues that the law produces and depicting those virtues in "the lives of Jewish heroes."[63] Fourth, Philo helps clarify what Paul means by "works of the law."[64] Finally, Philo is one of several "strands" in the "rich tapestry of Second Temple Judaism" that identifies "the Torah as the true definition of virtue or righteousness."[65] On that basis, Barclay concludes, "the missionaries in Galatia could draw on the Scriptures and on any number of strands in the Jewish tradition to take pride in the Torah as the center-piece of God's engagement with Israel and the world."[66]

With Barclay's challenge and his example then—and with encouragement from Malherbe, Thompson, and others[67]—this section will read Galatians in the light of corresponding terms and concepts in Philo's corpus. Alert to the Greek medical concept that the person is enslaved by the weakness of the flesh, this section will show that Philo promotes the practice of the law, especially circumcision and the calendar, in order (1) to live in harmony with the cosmos, (2) to gain life, righteousness, and the inheritance, and (3) to be redeemed from slavery. Thus, when read against Philo's terms and concepts and "the broader context in which apparently similar statements occur,"[68] Galatians emerges as a meaningful Christian exposition of the elements, the flesh, and the law in response to a set of ideas that bears the signs of influence by a philosophy like Philo's.

2. Practicing the Law in Harmony with the Cosmos (4.8–11; 5.2–12; 6.12–15; see 2.12)

Some of Paul's strongest language in Galatians would shake Philo's world-view from its very foundations. "Through the law I died to the law, so that I might live to God" (2.19). "May it never fall to me to boast except in the cross of our Lord Jesus the Anointed, through which the world is crucified to me, and I to the world" (6.14). These words would pull the cornerstone out from under a philosophy like Philo's.

As chapter 3 showed, Philo opens his exegetical series by explaining that Moses begins his laws with "an account of the making of the κόσμος," because "the κόσμος is in harmony with the law and the law with the κόσμος" (*Creation* 3). This principle of a κόσμος:νόμος harmony governs Philo's entire philosophical program.[69] It is grounded in God himself—because "the Father and Maker of the κόσμος was in the truest sense also its Lawgiver" (*Moses* 2.47)—and it benefits all who accept it. Indeed, "the man who observes the law is at once a citizen of the cosmos, directing his actions in relation to the rational purpose of nature, in accordance with which the entire κόσμος also is administered" (*Creation* 3; see *Moses* 2.48).

But Philo's κόσμος:νόμος harmony could not differ more from Paul. Read one after the other, their lyrics weave through a steady rhythm in jarring dissonance.

ὡς καὶ τοῦ κόσμου τῷ νόμῳ καὶ τοῦ νόμου τῷ κόσμῳ συνᾴδοντος
(*Creation* 3)

160   5

ἐγὼ γὰρ διὰ νόμου νόμῳ ἀπέθανον (Gal 2.19)
ἐμοὶ κόσμος ἐσταύρωται κἀγὼ κόσμῳ (Gal 6.14)

As Barclay notes, "the cross of Christ shatters every ordered system of norms, however embedded in the seemingly 'natural' order of 'the world' (cf. 4:3). . . . Whereas Philo took 'the world' (ὁ κόσμος) to be the properly ordered gift of God, . . . Paul parades the cross as the standard by which every norm is judged and every value relativized."[70]

In Galatians, Paul's principle of death to the law and the cosmos challenges a κόσμος:νόμος harmony such as Philo's on two fronts: circumcision and Moses's calendar.

a. Circumcision

Paul's alarm at the Galatians' impending practice is dire. "If you get circumcised, the Anointed will benefit you in no way! . . . You are dismissed from the Anointed, those who are 'being justified' in the law! You have fallen out of grace! . . . For in the Anointed Jesus neither circumcision nor a foreskin is effective, but rather faith being activated through love" (Gal 5.2, 4, 6). For first-century readers, the shock of Paul's statement is twofold: first, that circumcision is ineffective, and second, that it is just as ineffective as having a foreskin. Philo would be appalled.

As chapter 3 showed, some early Jewish scholars teach that circumcision "assimilates the circumcised member to the heart" (*Spec. Laws* 1.6). As Philo elaborates, circumcision is not only figurative "of the excision of excessive and superfluous pleasure" (*Spec. Laws* 1.9; *QG* 3.48), but also operative: "the sign of circumcision" "suppresses the superfluous impulses of the male" (*QG* 3.47). Further, together with its spiritual benefit, the physical practice of circumcision also has a social advantage: "we shall not incur the censure of the many and the charges they are sure to bring against us" (*Migration* 92–93).

Read against Philo, Paul's statements stop short of and go way beyond his teaching on circumcision. "In the Anointed One neither circumcision nor a foreskin is effective" (Gal 5.6). Indeed, "neither circumcision nor a foreskin is anything at all, but rather new creation" (6.15). And the way into new creation is not the excision of one extremity of the body but rather the crucifixion of the flesh as a whole (5.24; see 2.19; 6.14). That is how those who belong to the Anointed One deal with the elemental stimuli and desires of the flesh. This crucifixion may bring reproach—and the sign of circumcision might offer social acceptance—but the enactment of crucifixion in baptism joins every believer to the Anointed and to every Jew and Greek, slave and free, male and female in Abraham's family (3.26–29; 6.12). This is the life and practice of faith that Paul sets forth as he opposes the agitation for

The Law Against the Στοιχεῖα and the Flesh   161

circumcision and, with it, the observance of the law's calendar in pursuit of redemption and righteousness.

b. Days, Months, Seasons, and Years (4.8–10)

Paul's principle of death to the law and the cosmos also challenges any κόσμος:νόμος harmony posited of the law's calendar. "How are you turning back again to the weak and miserable στοιχεῖα, whose slaves you want to be all over again? You are observing days and months and times and years!" (4.9–10).

Paul's concern is urgent, for by observing days, months, times, and years, the Galatians are forsaking their new relationship with God and are enslaving themselves all over again to the στοιχεῖα. Paul insists that the Galatians' calendar observance is not a step forward, but rather a step backward, and that into a snare.[71] He emphasizes this relapse by using πάλιν twice—ἐπιστρέφετε πάλιν . . . πάλιν ἄνωθεν—and then by presenting the calendar in ambiguous terms that apply equally to their former enslavement and to their imminent enslavement (4.9).[72] The Galatians' current practice is similar to their former practice because both are enslavement to the στοιχεῖα, "things which, by nature, are not gods" (4.8). They left their former enslavement behind when they came to know God. That was a step forward, a move from slavery to freedom which many early Jews saw paradigmatically in Abraham's migration from the land of the Chaldeans. But now the Galatians are going back to slavery, violating both the example of their father Abraham and the instruction of Moses.[73]

This section proposes that Paul's ambiguous list of days, months, times, and years is a fitting description both of the Galatians' former slavery and of their imminent slavery. It considers two possibilities for how the Galatians were enslaved under the weak, miserable, not-divine elements in the past. Then it narrates Abraham's migration from Chaldea to the knowledge of God. Finally, it presents Philo's commendation of the law's calendar as, from Paul's perspective, a form of enslavement to the elements surprisingly similar to Chaldean and Stoic ways of thinking about the cosmos, its times and materials.

(1) Days, Months, Times, and Years and Any Astronomically Coordinated Calendar. Paul's list of ἡμέρας . . . καὶ μῆνας καὶ καιροὺς καὶ ἐνιαυτούς connects calendar observance to the created cosmos by evoking God's assignment of the stars to be εἰς καιροὺς καὶ εἰς ἡμέρας καὶ εἰς ἐνιαυτοὺς (Gen 1.14).[74] By connecting his list to creation, and not specifically to the law, Paul refers inclusively to all calendars set according to the movement of the stars.[75] Thus, his list applies equally to the Galatians' former enslavement

162   5

to the things that are not gods and to their imminent enslavement under the στοιχεῖα.[76]

(2) Enslaved to Things Which by Nature Are Not Gods. Ancients were devoted to the not-divine things in a variety of ways. While some people serve the elements by worshiping them, others serve them simply by allowing their arrangement to order their lives. De Boer proposes that the Galatians' former enslavement to the elements entailed venerating them as gods.[77] Though, as chapter 1 showed, the term στοιχεῖον was not used to denote a spirit or god until the third century AD, the four elements were associated with gods from at least the fifth century BC (Empedocles 12/6). Philo notes that "some have deified the four elements, earth, water, air and fire, others the sun, moon, planets and fixed stars, others again the heaven by itself, others the whole κόσμος" (*Decalogue* 53; see *Contempl. Life* 3). It is entirely possible, then, that the Galatians used to worship the elements as gods. That practice could correspond to Paul's reference to their former masters as "things which, by nature, are not gods" (4.8).[78] Further, Paul's rejection of their former practice in 4.9 would agree with Philo: "the στοιχεῖα themselves are lifeless matter incapable of movement of itself," and no one should "suppose any of the parts of the universe to be the omnipotent God" (*Contempl. Life* 4; *Decalogue* 58). However, while Paul may have the Galatians' former worship of the στοιχεῖα in mind, he is more urgently concerned by their observance of a calendar (Gal 4.10).

The worship of the elements and the observance of a calendar fit together as complementary practices in a particular way of thinking about the cosmos, its substances, processes, and times.[79] As Philo states, many ancient peoples posit both that the four στοιχεῖα are the "substratum" of the cosmos and all its parts (*Contempl. Life* 5), and also that the elements thereby establish a "sympathetic affinity of its parts" in which the stars influence events on earth (*Migration* 180; see *Creation* 113; *Providence* 2.45–53). A cosmology built on these conceptual bases gives rise to what Moo calls "astronomically governed religious observances."[80] Greeks and Romans, like Egyptians and Babylonians before them, observe the stars in order to understand or anticipate their effects on earth.[81] Beyond setting their calendars according to them, as modern societies still do, the ancients observe the stars to determine auspicious times. As Ambrosiaster explains, "People who observe days are those who say things like: 'We must not travel tomorrow,' 'Nothing should be started the day after tomorrow'" (46). Furthermore, as chapter 2 showed from the Hippocratic corpus, a good physician must be "familiar with the progress of the seasons and the dates of rising and setting of the stars," because "the changes of the seasons produce changes in diseases" (*Aër.* 2). Health of body and soul varies according to the seasons and their elemental qualities: dry, wet, cool, or hot (*Nat. hom.* 7; *Aph.* 3.20–23). Thus, for many ancients, the

The Law Against the Στοιχεῖα and the Flesh   163

stars not only set times, but also, through the στοιχεῖα, cause weather, influence events, and affect human health and behavior.

As chapter 3 showed from Philo, such slavish attention to the stars is most associated with the Chaldeans. They extend astrological determinism so far that they honor the cosmos as God and "put their trust in heaven" (*Migration* 178–180; *Heir* 97–99; see Wis 13.1–3).[82] For Philo, Abraham's migration from Chaldea and its pantheism is the typical pattern for the soul's liberation from a weak, elemental body and for its inheritance of the divine promises.

(3) Following Abraham's Migration to the Knowledge of God. Chaldea and its cosmology appear frequently in early Jewish discussions of Abraham's migration (see Josh 24.2).[83] Jubilees portrays Abram, sitting "up during the night on the first of the seventh month, so that he might observe the stars from evening until daybreak so that he might see what the nature of the year would be with respect to rain" (12.16).[84] Then a word in his heart causes him to see that rainfall and "all of the signs of the stars . . . are all in the hand of the LORD" (Jub. 12.17–18). In Josephus's retelling, Abraham reasoned that since "the sun and the moon and . . . all the happenings in heaven" effect "changes in land and sea," yet do not provide "for their own orderliness," they must act "not by their own authority but in accordance with the power of their commander," God, "the one craftsman of the universe" (*Ant.* 1.155–156). As chapter 3 showed from Philo, once Abraham, in body and soul, left the "delusions" of Chaldean pantheism, God revealed himself to him, and Abraham "saw for the first time" that the "Maker" and not "the world is . . . sovereign" (*Abraham* 78; *Virtues* 214–215). Thus Abraham "gained faith" and the "inheritance of the wisdom which . . . is apprehended by a wholly pure and clear mind," the wisdom that enables the soul to migrate "from the world to its Maker and Father" (*Virtues* 216; *Heir* 98). As Philo looks back at Abraham's migration from ignorant pantheism to the knowledge of God and faith, he sees him as "the standard of nobility for all proselytes" (*Virtues* 219; see *Migration* 184–197).[85]

Paul similarly presents Abraham as the Galatians' father in faith (Gal 3.6–29), and his language in 4.8–9 resonates with both stages in the early Jewish retellings of Abraham's migration.[86] Formerly, the Galatians, like Abraham, did not know God; they had not perceived him. Instead, they were enslaved to (or served) things which, by nature, are not gods. Then, however, they came to know God, as did Abraham, or rather to be known by God.[87] By following Abraham's example in moving from ignorance and slavery to the knowledge of God, the Galatians acted faithfully as Abraham's heirs. But Paul is concerned that the Galatians' journey has continued beyond Abraham, or rather, from Paul's perspective, turned back from him.

Though the Galatians know God and are known by him—and so are free from enslavement to things that are not gods—they are choosing to be

164   5

enslaved all over again to the weak and miserable στοιχεῖα (Gal 4.9). At least, that is how Paul interprets their watching out for days, months, times, and years (4.10). The agitators may well have presented Abraham as a model also for calendar observance, for he not only "made the journey to the knowledge of God by an astrological contemplation of the elements," but, as Martyn notes, was also "the first to observe the holy feasts at the correct times (e.g., *Jubilees* 16)."[88] But, for Paul, the Galatians' new calendar observance is more like their pagan past than like Abraham.

(4) Philo's Promotion of the Calendar for Health, Redemption, and Righteousness. As chapter 3 showed, Philo promotes the observance of the law's calendar—its particular days, months, times, and years—within a general harmony of the κόσμος with the νόμος. The keeping of any calendar begins with determining its days and times according to the position of the stars, that is the fixed stars along with the planets, including the sun and moon. And Jews for centuries discussed which stars to observe more carefully and how to set the calendar's times accurately.[89] But Philo goes beyond setting a calendar to undergirding its practices with an essentially Stoic rationale.[90] For him, the law's "particular enactments . . . seek to attain to the harmony of the universe and are in agreement with the principles of the eternal nature" (*Moses* 2.52).

The terms of Paul's argument in Gal 4.8–10 suggest that he is concerned not only that the Galatians continue to obey the law after the Anointed One has come, but also that they are accepting an early Jewish interpretation of the law, similar to Philo's, which grounds the law's alleged benefits—life, righteousness, and the inheritance—in an imposed cosmological rationale. Paul's concern is clear in his reference to the στοιχεῖα, but it is also implicit in his use of παρατηρέω. The law enjoins Israel to observe or keep the calendar and other commandments. But in those texts the standard verb is φυλάσσω,[91] and here Paul says he is concerned rather by the Galatians' παρατηρέω, their "watching closely," especially for an opportunity.[92] A few decades after Paul, Josephus summarizes the fourth commandment as παρατηρεῖν τὰς ἑβδομάδας (*Ant.* 3.91; see 11.294; 13.234; 14.264; *Ag. Ap.* 2.282).[93] But in Philo's corpus φυλάσσω remains the appropriate verb for keeping the seventh day (*Spec. Laws* 2.260). However, Philo does use παρατηρέω in combination with heaven, the seasons, and the elements. He notes that, since the stars influence events on earth through a sympathetic affinity mediated by the elements, "wise men" have studied the stars, "observed" (παρατηρέω) their "phenomena," and "marked the signs" of hot and cold, dry and wet seasons and their agricultural effects (*Creation* 117; *Spec. Laws* 1.92).[94] This sort of observation is consistent with Philo's harmony of earth with heaven and thus of κόσμος with νόμος. In light, then, of Philo's use of παρατηρέω, while Paul might be using παρατηρέω in Josephus's later sense of keeping the law's calendar, his

The Law Against the Στοιχεῖα and the Flesh   165

reference to the elements suggests that he is concerned about a cosmological rationale for the calendar that promotes careful observation of the stars and the times they set in order to manage their elemental effects.[95] Paul's admonition is clear and pointed: patterning life according to the cosmos, its times and substances, does not liberate one from the enslaving στοιχεῖα, rather it returns one to slavery under the weak and miserable στοιχεῖα.

And Philo says the mirror opposite. Keeping the Sabbath balances body and soul in their work and rest (*Moses* 2.210–216; *Decalogue* 98–101; *Spec. Laws* 2.56–139).[96] The monthly New Moon festival teaches kindness, reason, and propriety (*Spec. Laws* 2.140–144). The Passover rituals represent "the lover of wisdom . . . crossing from the body and the πάθη" with the aid of virtue (*Spec. Laws* 2.145–149). The timing of the Feast of Unleavened Bread—on the fifteenth day of the seventh month of the year—corresponds to the καιρός when God arranged the στοιχεῖα in harmonious order. Keeping this feast cultivates righteousness (*Spec. Laws* 2.150–161; see *QE* 1.1).[97] The Day of Atonement is coordinated with the καιρός of harvest. It teaches trust, inculcates self-control, and frees the reasoning mind (*Spec. Laws* 2.193–203).[98] In these ways, keeping the law's calendar, especially the weekly sabbath, helps a person, as Maren Niehoff says, "to develop *enkrateia* and become an authentic Jew."[99] Thus a philosophy like Philo's calls proselytes to follow Abraham's example and keep Moses's calendar in order to receive life, freedom, righteousness, and the inheritance God promised Abraham and his offspring.

(5) Enslaved All Over Again to the Weak and Beggarly Elements. But Paul, the zealous Pharisee and apostle to the nations, sees something quite different. Scripture did not give the law to confer these alleged benefits (Gal 2.16, 21; 3.18, 21). It imposed the law only as a παιδαγωγός, thus only for a time and only for a limited purpose (3.19–4.7). Indeed, an approach of this sort to the law's calendar, grounding it in harmony with the cosmos and promising redemption from the body, is eerily similar to pantheism, whether the Stoic form of the Galatians' day or the Chaldean form of Abraham's. Niehoff argues that Philo "modelled" his approach to law on "Stoic thought," especially "the Stoic theory of natural law" as "objective, perfect and unchanging."[100] As Cicero deemed a law "proper" only if it conformed to nature, so too Philo grounded "Mosaic law in nature," thereby establishing its permanence (Cicero, *Leg.* 2.13; Philo, *Moses* 2.14–15; *Creation* 3; see *Drunkenness* 142).[101] Thus it is not so much on the issue of astrological influence that Philo differs from the Chaldeans but rather on their view that the universe is god and that the stars are "the primary causes of the things that happen to men" (*Migration* 181).[102] But for Paul, both of these issues seem important. Following the law's calendar in pursuit of redemption from the body's πάθη leads not to life, righteousness, and the inheritance but rather back to

166 5

enslavement, under a curse, and away from the Anointed and the inheritance (Gal 3.10; 4.9–10, 30; 5.4).

This then is Paul's concern with the στοιχεῖα in Gal 4.9: the Galatians are using the law's calendar to manage the ways that the material elements affect them. But this is no cure for the human condition; indeed, it only makes it worse. Philo's writings argue that since the times and substances of the cosmos are in harmony with the law, keeping the law's calendar—its days, months, times, and years—will garner one health, redemption from slavery to the body's πάθη, righteousness, and the inheritance of wisdom. Philo sees this paradigm in Abraham's migration from Chaldea to the knowledge of God. But Paul sees the opposite. Yes, the Galatians, like Abraham, did leave behind enslavement to things that are not gods (i.e., the elements) and have come to know God and to be known by him. But their careful watching out for particular days, months, times, and years in order to manage the realities of life in the material cosmos is effectively a return to the God-ignorance of their past. The ambiguity of Paul's list applies equally to the Galatians' past enslavement and their imminent enslavement. They have turned from relating personally with the God who made the cosmos—who grants them the Spirit and works wonders among them—to, once again, managing mechanically the not-god things of the cosmos (3.5; 4.6, 9). But the στοιχεῖα are weak and miserable. They offer no cure; indeed, they beg.[103] Life, righteousness, and the inheritance come not through the law but from God, who has sent his Son and his Spirit. And believers enter into these blessings through faith, by which they, with the Anointed One, die to the law and the cosmos and live by the Spirit according to the new creation. This is how they are to live life now in the flesh.

For a cosmology like Philo's, Paul's gospel is nothing short of catastrophic. The two things Paul identifies are the twin foci of Philo's entire philosophy—νόμος and κόσμος—but Paul calls the Galatians to die to both of them. This section has shown how the agitators' promotion of these practices (the law's calendar and circumcision) corresponds to Philo's. It showed further that Paul recognizes a link between these nomistic practices and the role that the στοιχεῖα play in the agitators' rationale for the practices, a link that pervades Philo's κόσμος:νόμος harmony. The following section turns from reasons to goals. It shows how Paul opposes the aims that the Galatians seek in observing the calendar and practicing circumcision.

3. Seeking Life, Righteousness, and the Inheritance (2.16–3.21)

Once the ground of the "other gospel" falls away, its hopes of life, righteousness, and the inheritance collapse. Paul not only attacks the cosmological

The Law Against the Στοιχεια and the Flesh   167

rationale behind the agitators' promotion of the law's calendar and circumcision, he also denies the alleged benefits of observing these practices. Paul's three εἰ γὰρ denials focus the Galatians' attention on three of the rewards that the agitators may promise for keeping the law.

> For if righteousness were through the law, then the Anointed One would have died gratuitously. (2.21)

> For if the inheritance were from the law, it would no longer be from a promise. (3.18)

> For if a law had been given that could make alive, then righteousness really would have been from the law. (3.21)

While Philo asserts many benefits for keeping the law, each of Paul's denials finds its mark and counters one of Philo's main claims. The law does not offer life, righteousness, or the inheritance.

a. Life is Not from the Law

The first of the law's alleged benefits is biological in nature. As chapter 3 showed, life and health are two of the primary blessings in Philo's redemptive nomism. In general, Moses "promises that those who take pains to cultivate virtue and set the holy laws before them to guide them . . . will receive as well the gift of complete freedom from disease" (*Rewards* 119). Circumcision, for example, "promotes the cleanliness of the whole body" (*Spec. Laws* 1.2–7).

But, for Philo, the real benefit of the body's health is "quietude" for the soul that it houses (*Rewards* 120). When a soul "resides in a healthy body" that is neither too cold nor too hot, neither too dry nor too damp, it is not subject "to a domination unduly usurped by such πάθη" (*Rewards* 121–122). It lies no longer "under the yoke of many pleasures and many lusts and the innumerable distresses which its vices and lusts entail, but has been redeemed (ἐξαιρέω) into freedom by God, who broke asunder the miseries of its slavery" (*Rewards* 124). In particular, circumcision "suppresses the superfluous impulses of the male," and keeping Moses's calendar sets "reason to guide the irrational senses, and also check and rein in the wild and extravagant impulses of the soul" (*QG* 3.47; *Spec. Laws* 2.163).

Thus, while Philo might accept that circumcision and calendar observance are "boundary markers" or "badges" that mark out the identity of the true people of God, they are for him no peel-and-stick tags at a luncheon.[104] If they are badges, they are the sort of badge that establishes the identity of its wearer as someone who has been granted particular prerogatives and abilities.

For Philo, they are symbols to be practiced, of course,[105] but they are also practices that have consequences—beneficial, life-enhancing consequences.

"Never!" Paul swears. Observing the law's calendar leaves people weak and returns them to slavery to the elements (Gal 4.8–10). Neither circumcision nor a foreskin is anything (6.15). Redemption (ἐξαιρέω) comes not through observing the law but through the death of the Son (1.4; 2.20; 4.4). And life comes not *from* the law but *after* the law, after the believer, along with the Anointed One, dies to the law and the cosmos (2.19–20; 5.24; 6.14). Then, by faith, believers live, as the Anointed lives in them and the Spirit makes them alive, a new creation (2.19–20; 3.21; 5.25; 6.15). This life is a life that is lived now, to God, by faith, even "in the flesh" (2.19–20; see Rom 8.11).[106] Being made alive is not "virtually equivalent" or "tantamount" to being justified, nor is righteousness its cause or "prerequisite" (3.21).[107] Final justification, the gift of righteousness, is future; it is a hope for which believers wait now by the Spirit from faith (2.17; 5.5).[108] Yet believers have already been made alive by the Spirit and "begun by the Spirit" (3.3; 5.25). They live now by the Spirit: they walk with the Spirit, sow into the Spirit, and bear the Spirit's fruit, and they will reap from the Spirit the fulfilment of this present Spirit-life: eternal life (5.16, 22–23; 6.8).[109] Indeed, the order is reversed. As Barclay argues, "the 'life' that counts as 'righteous' before God . . . is given in Christ (2:20), and its presence, marked by faith in Christ, is what God reckons as 'righteousness.'"[110]

b. Righteousness is Not from the Law

The law's alleged biological benefit is, for Philo, the basis of its ethical benefit. Philo extols δικαιοσύνη as the first of "the virtues of universal value" that "each of the ten pronouncements separately and all in common incite and exhort" (*Spec. Laws* 4.134; see 4.226). From Philo's distinctly Hellenistic perspective, δικαιοσύνη is born from equality and relates to harmony (see *Spec. Laws* 2.231–237; *Eternity* 108). "Equality is the mother of justice" (*Planting* 122), and this virtue "appears" in an individual "when the three parts of the soul are in harmony": "when the two, the high-spirited and the lustful, are guided by the reasoning faculty as horses by their driver, then justice emerges" (*Alleg. Interp.* 1.72). Here we see that the life and freedom that Philo promises the soul through the law are, for him, the basis of the righteousness that also comes through the law.

In Philo's redemptive nomism, two festivals are particularly associated with δικαιοσύνη. First, as chapter 3 mentioned, sabbath day schools promote justice, the duty of humans to each other (*Spec. Laws* 2.62–63; see *Moses* 2.215–216; *Rewards* 66). Second, the feast of Tabernacles, which "recurs at the autumn equinox," honors equality, which is the "fountain of justice"

(Spec. Laws 2.204). Those who practice these weekly and annual festivals will develop the virtue of righteousness.

In some of his discussions of Abraham, Philo shares some ground with Paul on the close relationship between righteousness, faith, and the Spirit; yet key differences remain. In his Allegory on Gen 15.6, Philo describes Abraham's faith as an unparalleled "act of justice and conformity with nature" (*Heir* 95). "Having gained faith"—and with faith and piety binding his heart to God (*Migration* 132)—Abraham "gained with it all the other virtues. . . . For the divine spirit which was breathed upon him from on high made its lodging in his soul" (*Virtues* 216–217). In this sort of relationship, "Abraham journeyed even as the Lord spoke to him" (*Migration* 127; see Gen 12.4). In this way, "unwritten nature" led Abraham not only to do "the divine law," but to become "himself a law" (*Abraham* 275–276). Points of overlap with Paul are several: Abraham as the model of righteousness by faith (Gal 3.6; Rom 4.3), faith binding the believer to God (Gal 2.20; 3.26), virtue proceeding from God's Spirit within (Gal 5.22–23), and fulfilling the law by nature rather than by doing laws (Rom 2.14–15; 8.4).

Paul differs from Philo on at least three points. First, while for Paul the possibility of fulfilling the law's righteous requirement obviates calendar observance and circumcision (Gal 4.9–10; 5.2–6), for Philo both remain essential (*Migration* 89–93). Second, though Paul states plainly that faith acts (Gal 5.6), his sharp faith-works contrast sits at odds with a description of faith as something that one does or acquires (Gal 2.16; 3.2–14). But, third, it is Philo's emphasis on justice as something that one attains through effort that Paul would oppose most. Philo interprets the nuts that sprout on Aaron's rod as showing that "practisers" must labor through the bitter and hard layers of "austerity and hardship" to get at the fruit of righteousness (*Moses* 2.182–185). Philo says elsewhere that the person who, like Noah, "attains to justice" is rewarded with "his salvation" (*Rewards* 22).

Paul's letter to the Galatians is a full-faced rebuke to this way of thinking. Just as the law makes no one alive, so too no one is declared righteous by doing the things the law prescribes (2.16).[111] Δικαιοσύνη does not come through the law (2.21; 3.11, 21), and being without a foreskin is no more advantageous in the quest for righteousness than having one (5.5–6). Rather, righteousness comes through faith. Righteousness is a blessing that God gives through the faithful death of the Anointed to those who put their faith in the Anointed (2.16–20; 3.6–9, 24–26).[112] To justify (δικαιόω) is to pronounce righteous or to vindicate.[113] The declaration of righteousness is forensic.[114] But that forensic declaration is a gift that proceeds from a relationship: the believer is placed in the Anointed One, who is God's Son.[115] This relationship also leads to relationships: in the Anointed, the believer is counted both

170   5

among the offspring of Abraham the faithful and among the sons of God (3.7, 16, 18, 26–29; 4.4–7).[116] Thus, at the heart of Paul's concern in Galatians, the confident hope of receiving God's gift of righteousness is expressed or confirmed by affirming those relationships, or, contrariwise, lost by denying those relationships.[117]

Finally, righteousness seems also to be ethical. Paul contrasts δικαιοσύνη with sin, sinners, and trespasses (2.15–17; 3.19–22), and he sets it in close parallel to love (5.5–6).[118] The Spirit and faith by which believers await the hope of righteousness are the Spirit who bears his fruit in their lives (5.5, 22–23; 6.8–9; see 4.19) and the faith that is activated in love which fulfills the law (5.5–6, 13–14).[119] It is true that justification does not entail an ethical transformation,[120] and it is true that, in Galatians, Paul associates ethical behavior with δικαιοσύνη but does not actually label it δίκαιος or δικαιοσύνη. However, restricting the meanings of δικαιοσύνη and δίκαιος to refer only to the status of someone who has been justified, as de Boer and Moo do,[121] disconnects those terms from Paul's descriptions of his conduct as δικαίως (1 Thess 2.10), of the deeds of the wicked as ἀδικία (Rom 1.18, 29; 2.8; see 1 Cor 6.9), and of lives of intentional obedience as in the service of δικαιοσύνη (Rom 6.13, 16, 18, 19).[122] Moo and Wright agree with Fee and deSilva that the life of the Son and the Spirit necessarily effects moral transformation through faith and that this good living is also God's gracious gift to believers—and not achievement through the works of the law—they simply do not attach the label δικαιοσύνη to that transformed life.[123]

Thus, for Paul, neither life (including the medical benefit of health and its consequence, redemption from the flesh) nor righteousness is from the law. Nor, Paul insists in 3.18, is the inheritance.

c. The Inheritance is Not from the Law

While Paul and Philo see life and righteousness in distinct ways, their views of the inheritance that God promised Abraham are almost irreconcilable. Paul associates the inheritance with the Spirit, righteousness, and the kingdom of God (Gal 3.2–9, 14–22, 29; 4.6–7; 5.21–23). And in Romans, he identifies the inheritance promised to Abraham and his offspring as the cosmos (4.13–14).[124] But, in contrast to Paul's vision of the inheritance as God's heirs in transformed bodies ruling over a renewed creation (Rom 8.14–25; 1 Cor 15.12–58), Philo associates the inheritance with the mind's reception of incorporeal, heavenly wisdom.

Philo answers the question "who is the heir of divine things?" in *Heir* 1–129. He quotes God's promise to Isaac that he and his offspring will inherit the land and that "all the nations of the earth shall be blessed" in his offspring (*Heir* 8, quoting Gen 26.3–5).[125] But for Philo, the "treasury

The Law Against the Στοιχεια and the Flesh 171

of divine blessings" is to be found in the heaven that God called Abraham out to see (*Heir* 76, quoting Gen 15.5; Deut 28.12). The "divine things" are heavenly wisdom, and since they are "intellectual" the one who inherits them must be "incorporeal" (*Heir* 64, 66, 98). Thus, in order to become an "heir of divine things," a soul must migrate from its body, the senses, speech, and, indeed, itself (*Heir* 69–70, 98). Moses's law is the one reliable means to such a "wholly purified mind" (*Heir* 64). As Philo says in *Rewards*, God grants "a mind purged clean of every spot" to those who "set the holy laws before them to guide them" (119–120).

Paul objects: the inheritance was promised in the covenant God ratified with Abraham 430 years before the introduction of the law (Gal 3.16–18). The law may have confined Abraham's offspring, and it may instruct them (Rom 15.4; 1 Cor 9.8–10),[126] but nothing about the law impinges on or can alter God's prior covenant with Abraham and the gracious character of his promise of the inheritance. Abraham's heirs, both male and female, are his heirs because they are his sons, and they are his sons because they believe as he did (Gal 3.6–9, 26–29; 4.4–7; see Rom 4.13–14). They receive the Spirit and righteousness ἐκ πίστεως, not ἐξ ἔργων νόμου, and by that Spirit and faith they await righteousness, live in love, and are qualified to inherit God's kingdom (Gal 3.2–9, 14; 5.5–6, 18–23; see 1 Cor 6.9–11). Should some of Abraham's children take on the law as well, they will end up aligning themselves with a different covenant, the Sinai covenant; they will, as it were, accept the pedigree of Abraham's enslaved woman and her son and, no longer counted among Abraham's heirs, be dismissed from the Anointed and his promise of grace (Gal 4.21–5.4). Thus the law does not lead heirs to inherit the blessing and the kingdom; rather it brings slaves under a curse and sends them out into exile (3.10; 4.30).

Paul's three εἰ γὰρ denials stop in its tracks a view of the law similar to Philo's. Paul is clear: the law does not offer the life, the righteousness, or the inheritance that the agitators claim it does. Indeed, for Paul, taking on the law does the very opposite (Rom 7.5–25). It does not create or sustain life; it leaves people weak and enslaved under the elements. It does not declare righteous; it confines things under sin and places lawbreakers under a curse. And it does not confer the inheritance; it dispossesses Abraham's offspring. For Paul, the law is, or rather was, a παιδαγωγός, but now that faith has come in the Son and the Spirit, its role has come to an end. To those who would still heed its counsel, the law says again, as it always did, that Abraham believed God and it was counted to him as righteousness, and that all nations will be blessed in Abraham (Gal 3.6, 8; 4.21, quoting Gen 15.6; 12.3; 18.18). Thus Paul states, explains, and argues from Israel's scripture. And thus he now pleads in a startling analogy.

4. Returning to Slavery (4.1–11; 4.21–5.1)

As shown in sections two and three above, the agitators likely (a) grounded the law—particularly circumcision and calendar observance—in a cosmological rationale and (b) practiced the law in order to gain life, righteousness, and the inheritance. Section four now explains Paul's view of their practice of the law and its unintended consequences: those who take on the law are returning to slavery, not escaping from it. Paul makes this point clearly in his allegoresis of Abraham's family (Gal 4.21–5.21). There, and in two other mini narratives in Gal 4, Paul turns Philo's favorite migration stories around to show the Galatian believers that they are actually walking back into slavery, not out of it.

a. Paul's Allegory of Abraham's Two Wives and Two Sons (4.21–5.1)

At no point in his letters does Paul engage more obviously with an early Jewish philosophy like Philo's than in his allegoresis of Abraham's family.[127] Paul's allegory in Gal 4.21–5.1 is similar to Philo's in its content, plot, and rhetoric, but its distinct hermeneutic sets Paul's point in sharp contrast: the law is not a means to free the person from slavery to the flesh.

Some similarities in content and plot are more obvious than others. First, Paul works with Philo's favorite allegorical character: Abraham. Second, Paul uses two of Philo's schematic pairs—Hagar and Sarah, and Ishmael and Isaac—and both writers use Hagar and Ishmael to "represent a preliminary and preparatory stage."[128] Finally, Paul situates the allegory within an argument that addresses Philo's central aim: the freedom of the person (or the soul) from enslavement by the flesh.

Paul and Philo are also similar in their rhetoric. Paul follows the allegorical method that Philo uses: he cites a scripture, raises an issue, indicates explicitly that he is moving to allegory, and then solves the issue on the level of allegory.[129] As Steven di Mattei asserts, the operation of allegory as a rhetorical trope "in Philo . . . is exactly the same as allegory for Paul."[130] "Paul's allegory is no different" from Philo's; both allegorize by using a pesher-like "this is that" formula.[131] Paul's allegory is what he says it is, an allegory.[132]

Other scholars follow Richard Hanson in denying that Paul's is an allegory like Philo's, because "the invariable function of Alexandrian allegory" is "to emancipate the meaning of the passage from its historical content."[133] But de Boer, quoting Büchsel, argues that this is a misreading of Philo. "Philo does not see his allegorical interpretation as a substitute for a literal understanding of the text, but as a supplement to it: 'On the whole, Philo himself intends to maintain the historicity of what is narrated.'"[134] So too does Paul.

The Law Against the Στοιχεια and the Flesh 173

Paul's differences with Philo, then, lie not in his rhetorical use of allegory or whether he sees Genesis as historical, but rather in his hermeneutic. As Moo argues, Paul's reading of Sarah and Hagar, like "any other contemporizing reading of the OT, . . . is inevitably the product of some set of extratextual hermeneutical axioms."[135] For Paul, those axioms are "eschatological": "his basic convictions about Christ as the fulfillment and culmination of salvation history."[136] The coming of faith in the sending of the Son and the Spirit adds an act to Paul's redemptive-historical framework that is, at most, only a shadow in Philo's metanarrative (*Moses* 1.289–291; *Rewards* 93–97).[137]

So is Paul dependent on Philo? "No," says Richard Longenecker. The two are "certainly not . . . to be equated."[138] But Ben Witherington's response is both more astute and more in keeping with Emma Wasserman's concept of discourse and the presence of "creative elaboration" in "ordinary" language. He asserts, following Richard Hays, that Paul is "stealing another's thunder by taking his best argument and using it to support [his] own case."[139]

Indeed he is. Paul picks up the main characters and basic plot of Philo's allegories, but he makes one simple change that has a dramatic effect. As Table 2 shows, both Philo and Paul present Hagar as a provisional character that serves Sarah, and in both versions, Hagar and her son are cast out, and Isaac becomes Abraham's sole heir. What is shocking though, is Paul's alignment of the Sinai covenant not with Sarah, but with Hagar (see *Prelim. Studies* 81–88). Lined up this way, the adherents of the law find themselves not freed, as Philo promises, but enslaved, indeed cast out of Abraham's family and cut off from the inheritance.

In this paragraph which many scholars recognize as operating with the terms of his opponents' argument,[140] Paul has taken the momentum of an allegorical scheme like Philo's, slipped the law in alongside the lower studies, and thrown both out together, so that the son born by the Spirit according to promise might inherit the blessing.[141] The similarity of the allegories sets their critical difference in even sharper contrast: the law is lower, not higher learning; it brings slavery, not freedom; it leads to dismissal, not inheritance. Abraham's heirs live not according to the flesh, which leads to enslavement, but through the promise according to the Spirit, which leads to freedom and the inheritance.

With this subtle move Paul turns the essence of Philo's allegory on its head. Earlier in Gal 4, two other allusions to exodus or migration achieve a similar effect. As with Paul's allegory, they expose the startling truth that since the Son and the Spirit have come, following the law leads backward into slavery, not forward into freedom.

174   5

Table 5.1: Philo's and Paul's Allegories

Feature	Philo	Paul
Abraham	Wise mind	[No equivalent]
(Abram)	(Mind studying nature)	
Hagar	Preliminary learning	Enslavement
		Covenant from Mt. Sinai
		Gives birth εἰς δουλείαν
		Present Jerusalem
	To be cast out	*To be cast out*
Egypt	Body and its senses	[No equivalent]
Ishmael	Sophistry	Born κατὰ σάρκα
		Enslaved
		Children of present Jerusalem
	To be cast out	*To be cast out*
	Will not inherit	*Will not inherit*
Sarah	Sovereignty	Freedom
(Sarai)	(Virtue)	A second covenant
		Jerusalem above
Postmenopausal	Without πάθη	[No equivalent]
Isaac	Happiness and joy,	Born δι' ἐπαγγελίας
	self-taught virtue	Born κατὰ πνεῦμα
		Free
		Children of Jerusalem above
	Will inherit	*Will inherit*

b. Migration in Reverse (4.1–11)

Earlier sections in this and the previous chapter argued that Paul's reference
to slavery and redemption in Gal 4.3, 5 alludes to Israel's exodus from Egypt,
and his reference to coming to know God in 4.8–9 alludes to Abraham's
migration from Chaldea. These allusions would make ready sense among
first-century Jews: Israel's exodus is the paradigmatic redemption in Israel's
scriptures, and both it and Abraham's migration are common themes in
early Jewish writings. In the flow of Paul's argument, Israel's exodus and
Abraham's migration appear as redemptive-historical types of, on the one
hand, the rescue of God's people from the present evil age (1.4) and, on
the other, the conversion of the nations to God (3.8, 14). However, since, in
4.21–51, Paul engages obviously with an allegory like Philo's, it seems possible that, in 4.3–9, he may also be playing on the symbolic value that early
Jewish allegoresis assigns to Israel's exodus and Abraham's migration.

In Sarah Pearce's analysis, Philo sees Egypt as "the land of the body," a
land of "enslavement by the bodily passions." According to Philo's cartogra-
phy of the soul, Egypt is the place to be "left behind."[142] It is for Paul as well.
As chapter 4 demonstrated, in Gal 4.3 Paul is referring to the Jews' enslavement under the στοιχεῖα τοῦ κόσμου that compose the flesh of the human

The Law Against the Στοιχεῖα and the Flesh 175

body and mediate its stimuli and desires. Further, Paul sees humans as most susceptible to domination by the flesh when they are νήπιοι.[143] It seems probable then, that Paul's reference to childhood, enslavement, and redemption is an allusion not only to the redemptive-historical type of Israel's exodus from Egypt but also to the allegory of the person's redemption from the flesh, which Israel's exodus symbolizes. On this reading, both Philo and Paul would admonish people not to return to Egypt, the land of enslavement to the flesh and its desires.[144] However, Philo presents the law as the means to redemption, and Paul argues strongly that using the law to deal with the flesh only leads one back under the dominion of the flesh. Redemption comes instead by the Son, and it leads to life in the Spirit by faith.

Similarly, in Philo's writings, Abraham's migrations are, "according to the laws of allegory," the journeys of "a virtue-loving soul" which leaves the body behind and seeks to know and follow God directly (*Abraham* 68; *Worse* 159; *Migration* 127–128; *Heir* 98). While Paul too would have people renounce their flesh and know and follow God personally (Gal 4.9; 5.16, 18, 24), he denies that the law, especially its calendar, is an aid to those ends. As shown above in section two, people who now follow the calendar in order to suppress the flesh are actually returning to a fixation on the body and the senses. Using the law for this purpose does not lead the soul to freedom, rather it bundles Abraham back to Chaldea and its pantheism. For Paul, real freedom from the flesh comes apart from the law to those who walk by the Spirit (Gal 5.16).

Thus, both in the mini narratives of Israel's exodus and Abraham's migration and in the allegory of Abraham's two wives and two sons, Paul has taken three of Philo's favorite stories and turned them right around. The effect is alarming. The law appears in all the wrong roles, doing the wrong thing. It sells the Israelites back to the Egyptians, misdirects Abraham back to Chaldea, and takes up company with Hagar and Ishmael, at best as slaves, at worst as exiled vagrants. But for Paul the alarm is entirely appropriate. The law was a reliable παιδαγωγός for Abraham's children, but now that faith has come, now that God has sent the Son and the Spirit, it serves no more as guide or guard. And it is ill-suited now—as ever—to fill the role of liberator. On that quest it fails, and its loyal companions fall again under the tyranny of sin's rule over the domain of the flesh. From that slavery, the rescuer is the Son, and, following redemption, the guide is the Spirit.

C. CONCLUSION

Following Barclay's example, this chapter has shown how Paul's arguments against the law correspond point for point with some of the principles in

176 5

Philo's writings. Again, this comparison demonstrates not that Philo toured Galatia and taught in the assemblies, but that his philosophy, which we know to have influenced writers outside of Egypt in the first century,[145] corresponds at most points with the principles that Paul's letter implies the agitators were imposing on the believers.[146] This discursive approach to reading Paul in mediated conversation with Philo has demonstrated its validity, and it offers at least four advantages when reading Galatians.

1. It clarifies that when Paul says the Galatians are returning to enslavement under the weak and miserable στοιχεῖα, he is referring to their attempt to practice the law's calendar in harmony with the cosmos in order to manage (or indeed be redeemed from) the way that the material στοιχεῖα provoke the stimuli and desires of their flesh;
2. It shows more fully how, and not just that, Paul and the agitators disagree on the practice of the law and three of its alleged benefits: life (i.e., health and redemption from slavery to the flesh), righteousness, and the inheritance (however differently Paul and Philo may conceive of δικαιοσύνη);
3. It elucidates Paul's hermeneutic in his allegoresis of Abraham's family; and
4. It reveals one tenuous point of agreement between Paul and Philo: each writer says that God's Spirit, apart from any doing of the law, lodges itself within a person when that person believes God (*Virtues* 216–217; Gal 3.2, 5).

However, Philo, of course, would say that the divine spirit then aids one in practicing the law and gaining redemption, and Paul, as chapter 6 sets forth, argues that death with the Son and life by the Spirit redeem believers from the στοιχεῖα and the flesh and do for them what the law never could.

NOTES

1. John M. G. Barclay, *Paul and the Gift* (Grand Rapids: Eerdmans, 2015), 401–2.
2. Hans Dieter Betz, *Galatians: A Commentary on Paul's Letter to the Churches in Galatia*, Hermeneia (Philadelphia: Fortress, 1979), 178.
3. James Louis Martyn, *Galatians: A New Translation with Introduction and Commentary*, AB 33A (New York: Doubleday, 1997), 360–61; Martinus C. de Boer, *Galatians: A Commentary*, NTL (Louisville, KY: Westminster John Knox, 2011), 240–41.
4. Richard Longenecker, "The Pedagogical Nature of the Law in Galatians 3:19–4:7," *JETS* 25.1 (1982): 55; Richard Longenecker, *Galatians*, WBC 41 (Dallas: Word,

The Law Against the Στοιχεῖα and the Flesh   177

1990), 148; see James D. G. Dunn, *The Epistle to the Galatians*, BNTC (London: A & C Black, 1993), 263.

5. David J. Lull, "'The Law Was Our Pedagogue': A Study in Galatians 3:19–25," *JBL* 105 (1986): 481–98; Norman H. Young, "Paidagogos: The Social Setting of a Pauline Metaphor," *NovT* 29 (1987): 150–76; Norman H. Young, "The Figure of the Paidagōgos in Art and Literature," *BA* 53.2 (1990): 80–86. E. P. Sanders, though, holds a negative view of the law as παιδαγωγός (E. P. Sanders, *Paul, the Law, and the Jewish People* (Minneapolis: Fortress, 1983), 66–67; see Lull, "Pedagogue," 495–96.).

6. Frank J. Matera, *Galatians* (Collegeville, MN: Liturgical, 1992), 139–40; Thomas R. Schreiner, *Galatians*, ZECNT (Grand Rapids: Zondervan, 2010), 248–49; Barclay, *Paul and the Gift*, 402–3.

7. Peter Oakes, *Galatians*, Paideia (Grand Rapids: Baker Academic, 2015), 127.

8. Longenecker, *Galatians*, 148; Bruce Longenecker, *The Triumph of Abraham's God: The Transformation of Identity in Galatians* (Edinburgh: T&T Clark, 1998), 54, 127–28; Douglas J. Moo, *Galatians*, BECNT (Grand Rapids: Baker, 2013), 243–44.

9. Young, "Paidagogos," 171. Ben Witherington III, *Grace in Galatia: A Commentary on St. Paul's Letter to the Galatians* (Grand Rapids: Eerdmans, 1998), 266 agrees; Schreiner, *Galatians*, 248–49 disagrees.

10. Young, "Paidagogos," 172.

11. T. David Gordon, "A Note on Παιδαγωγος in Galatians 3.24–25," *NTS* 35 (1989): 153–54, https://doi.org/10.1017/S0028688500024553; see 1 Pet 1.5.

12. Gordon, "Παιδαγωγος," 154.

13. Dunn, *Galatians*, 198–99; Philip F. Esler, *Galatians*, New Testament Readings (London: Routledge, 1998), 200–202; Oakes, *Galatians*, 127; see Witherington, *Grace in Galatia*, 266 n. 52.

14. Esler, *Galatians*, 201–2.

15. Lull, "Pedagogue," 495. Witherington, *Grace in Galatia*, 264–65 shows from Plato, *Leg.* 7.808e that a παιδαγωγός was a "moral guide" to a child "driven by passions," but he seems not to find this role in Paul's use of the metaphor.

16. Lull, "Pedagogue," 497.

17. J. B. Lightfoot, *Saint Paul's Epistle to the Galatians: A Revised Text with Introduction, Notes, and Dissertations* (London: Macmillan, 1887), 149.

18. John Riches, *Galatians Through the Centuries*, Wiley-Blackwell Bible Commentaries (Oxford: Wiley-Blackwell, 2013), 192, citing Chrysostom (*NPNF*1 13.28–29), Augustine (Eric Plumer, ed., *Augustine's Commentary on Galatians*, Oxford Early Christian Studies (Oxford: Oxford University Press, 2003), 171, http://www.oxfordscholarship.com/view/10.1093/0199244391.001.0001/acprof -9780199244393), and Aquinas (Fabian R. Larcher, trans., *Thomas Aquinas: Super Epistolam B. Pauli Ad Galatas Lectura: Commentary on Saint Paul's Epistle to the Galatians*, Online., Aquinas Scripture Series 1 (Albany: Magi, 1966), 95, http:// dhspriory.org/thomas/SSGalatians.htm).

19. Young, "Paidagogos," 170–71.

20. Young, "Paidagogos," 171.

21. de Boer, *Galatians*, 309; N. T. Wright, *Paul and the Faithfulness of God*, Christian Origins and the Question of God 4 (London: SPCK, 2013), 1139–40.

22. Lull, "Pedagogue," 488–89, 494–97.

23. Betz, *Galatians*, 273; Longenecker, *Galatians*, 246; Gordon D. Fee, *God's Empowering Presence: The Holy Spirit in the Letters of Paul* (Peabody, MA: Hendrickson, 1994), 422, 427; Martyn, *Galatians*, 485; Moo, *Galatians*, 340–41. In Rom 7.8, Paul notes that sin (not the flesh) was devious enough to use the law itself as an ἀφορμή.

24. Dunn, *Galatians*, 301.

25. See Gordon, "Παιδαγωγος," 154; Dunn, *Galatians*, 198–99; Esler, *Galatians*, 200–202; Oakes, *Galatians*, 127.

26. Wright, *Paul and the Faithfulness of God*, 1142.

27. Lull, "Pedagogue," 495 n. 95. Similarly, Aristotle prescribes a παιδαγωγός for someone who "is led (ἄγω) by his ἐπιθυμία" (*Eth. nic.* 3.11–12).

28. John M. G. Barclay, *Obeying the Truth: A Study of Paul's Ethics in Galatians*, Studies of the New Testament and Its World (Edinburgh: T&T Clark, 1988), 116; Longenecker, *Galatians*, 246; Matera, *Galatians*, 207.

29. In support of love and its related actions, see Exod 34.6; Lev 26.6; Num 6.26; 10.32; 12.3; 14.18; Deut 9.23; 30.15; 32.20. Against fleshy acts, see Exod 20.4–5, 14; 22.18 (17); 23.4–5; Lev 16.16–19; 19.4; 20.21; Num 14.33; 25.1–2; Deut 5.8–9; 18.9–14; 23.18.

30. See 2 Tim 3.16. Douglas J. Moo, *The Epistle to the Romans*, NICNT (Grand Rapids: Eerdmans, 1996), 869; see Richard B. Hays, "The Letter to the Galatians: Introduction, Commentary, and Reflections," in *The New Interpreter's Bible* (Nashville: Abingdon, 2000), 322–24.

31. Lull, "Pedagogue," 495–98; Moo, *Galatians*, 357.

32. Young, "Paidagogos," 172–73. See Deut 4.5–8; 26.16–19.

33. Moo, *Galatians*, 277–78.

34. Barclay, *Paul and the Gift*, 426.

35. For recent reviews of the disputes, see Moo, *Galatians*, 233; Barclay, *Paul and the Gift*, 403 n. 34.

36. BDAG, s.v. "χάριν."

37. Moo, *Galatians*, 233, summarizing Calvin.

38. Frank Thielman, *From Plight to Solution: A Jewish Framework for Understanding Paul's View of the Law in Galatians and Romans*, SupNovT 61 (Leiden: Brill, 1989), 74–75.

39. Dunn, *Galatians*, 189–90.

40. Betz, *Galatians*, 164–65; Thomas R. Schreiner, *The Law and Its Fulfillment: A Pauline Theology of Law* (Grand Rapids: Baker, 1993), 74.

41. Moo, *Galatians*, 234, quoting Franz Mussner, *Der Galaterbrief*, 5th ed., HTKNT 9 (Freiburg: Herder, 1988), 245–46, and citing Heinrich Schlier, *Der Brief an die Galater*, 15th ed., KEK 7 (Göttingen: Vandenhoeck & Ruprecht, 1989), 152–53; Witherington, *Grace in Galatia*, 255–56; Herman Ridderbos, *Paul: An Outline of His Theology*, trans. John R. de Witt (Grand Rapids: Eerdmans, 1975), 150–51; see also Calvin. This is Moo's interpretation.

The Law Against the Στοιχεῖα and the Flesh 179

42. Longenecker, *Galatians*, 138–39. In line with sense *c*, see χάριν in Plato's prescription of παιδαγωγοί (*Leg.* 7.808d–e).

43. Moo, *Galatians*, 234.

44. Witherington, *Grace in Galatia*, 254. See Rom 5.14.

45. There accurately translating תורות and מצות, משמרת, and חקות.

46. See Thielman, *Plight to Solution*, 75.

47. I have found this explanation for Paul's reference to διαταγεὶς δι᾽ ἀγγέλων nowhere else (Gal 3.19; see Acts 7.38, 53). For χερουβιμ as ἄγγελοι see 1 En. 61.10.

48. John T. Fitzgerald, "The Passions and Moral Progress: An Introduction," in *Passions and Moral Progress in Greco-Roman Thought*, ed. John T. Fitzgerald, Routledge Monographs in Classical Studies (London: Routledge, 2008), 1–25.

49. Gustav Stählin, "Προκοπή, Προκόπτω," *TDNT* 6:703–19; Betz, *Galatians*, 68.

50. Lull, "Pedagogue," 497; Barclay, *Paul and the Gift*, 406–7.

51. Samuel Sandmel, "Parallelomania," *JBL* 81.1 (1962): 5.

52. James W. Thompson, *Moral Formation According to Paul: The Context and Coherence of Pauline Ethics* (Grand Rapids: Baker Academic, 2011), 142; David Arthur deSilva, *Reading Paul through Asian Eyes: A Sri Lankan Commentary on Galatians* (Kohuwela: CTS, 2014), 211.

53. John M. G. Barclay, "Mirror-Reading a Polemical Letter: Galatians as a Test Case," *JSNT* 31 (1987): 73–74.

54. Barclay, "Mirror-Reading," 77–78.

55. Barclay, "Mirror-Reading," 79–82.

56. Barclay, "Mirror-Reading," 82, 92 n. 30; citing Klaus Wegenast, *Das Verständnis der Tradition bei Paulus und in den Deuteropaulinen* (Neukirchen: Neukirchener, 1962), 36–40; Heinrich Schlier, *Der Brief an die Galater*, KEK 7 (Göttingen: Vandenhoeck & Ruprecht, 1971), 202–7.

57. Barclay, "Mirror-Reading," 82.

58. Barclay, "Mirror-Reading," 77–78.

59. Barclay, "Mirror-Reading," 89; Barclay, *Paul and the Gift*, 324.

60. Barclay, "Mirror-Reading," 88–89.

61. Barclay, *Paul and the Gift*, 409 n. 45, citing *Eternity* 107.

62. Barclay, *Obeying the Truth*, 50–55, citing *Virtues* 212ff; *QG* 3.46–52.

63. Barclay, *Obeying the Truth*, 66–68, 124–25, citing *Moses*; *Creation* 73; *Abraham*; *Virtues* 181–182; *Sacrifices* 27; *Drunkenness* 23.

64. Barclay, *Paul and the Gift*, 373 n. 58, citing *Embassy* 159, 170, 256; 374 n. 59, citing *Rewards* 126.

65. Barclay, *Paul and the Gift*, 400–401, citing *Abraham* 1–6, 276; *Rewards* 126.

66. Barclay, *Paul and the Gift*, 401.

67. Abraham J. Malherbe, "Hellenistic Moralists and the New Testament," *ANRW* 26.1, 332; Thompson, *Moral Formation*, 16.

68. Barclay, *Obeying the Truth*, 175.

69. Barclay, *Obeying the Truth*, 67–68; Elias J. Bickerman, *The Jews in the Greek Age* (Cambridge, Mass.: Harvard University Press, 1988), 114; Peder Borgen, *Philo of Alexandria: An Exegete for His Time* (Leiden: Brill, 1997), 146–47; Maren R. Niehoff, *Philo on Jewish Identity and Culture*, TSAJ 86 (Tübingen: Mohr Siebeck, 2001),

180

247–66; David T. Runia, *On the Creation of the Cosmos According to Moses*, Philo of Alexandria Commentary 1 (Leiden: Brill, 2001), 106; Geurt H. van Kooten, *Cosmic Christology in Paul and the Pauline School: Colossians and Ephesians in the Context of Graeco-Roman Cosmology, with a New Synopsis of the Greek Texts*, WUNT 2/171 (Tübingen: Mohr Siebeck, 2003), 77; Barclay, *Paul and the Gift*, 400–401.

70. Barclay, *Paul and the Gift*, 394–95; citing Edward Adams, *Constructing the World: A Study in Paul's Cosmological Language*, Studies of the New Testament and Its World (Edinburgh: T&T Clark, 2000).

71. For the metaphor of stepping forward and backward, see de Boer, *Galatians*, 276–77.

72. Contrast "days, months, times, and years" with "a festival, a new moon, or sabbaths" (Col 2.16).

73. For the metaphor of stepping forward and backward, see de Boer, *Galatians*, 276–77.

74. F. F. Bruce, *The Epistle to the Galatians*, NIGTC (Grand Rapids: Eerdmans, 1982), 205–6; Dunn, *Galatians*, 229; Martyn, *Galatians*, 416–17; Hays, "Galatians," 288; Schreiner, *Galatians*, 279; Moo, *Galatians*, 279. Philo too inserts months when he alludes to Gen 1.14 and the stars' purposes as of "καιρῶν, . . . καὶ ἐπὶ πᾶσιν ἡμερῶν, μηνῶν, ἐνιαυτῶν" (*Creation* 55). See Runia, *Creation*, 206; and see Martyn, *Galatians*, 417 n. 80, citing D. Lührmann, "Tage, Monate, Jahreszeiten, Jahre (Gal 4,10)," in *Werden und Wirken des Alten Testaments: Festschrift für Claus Westermann zum 70. Geburtstag*, ed. Rainer Albertz (Göttingen: Vandenhoeck & Ruprecht, 1980), 428–45.

75. Martyn, *Galatians*, 416–18.

76. Oakes, *Galatians*, 140–41, citing de Boer, *Galatians*, 276, who in turn cites Betz, *Galatians*, 218; Barclay, *Obeying the Truth*, 63–64.

77. de Boer, *Galatians*, 255–56.

78. Against most scholars, I follow Matera, *Galatians*, 152; Martyn, *Galatians*, 410; and Nancy Calvert-Koyzis, *Paul, Monotheism and the People of God: The Significance of Abraham Traditions for Early Judaism and Christianity*, JSNTSup 273 (London: T&T Clark, 2004), 106 in reading τοῖς in 4.8 as neuter.

79. de Boer, *Galatians*, 253–56.

80. Moo, *Galatians*, 277; citing Longenecker, *Galatians*, 181; Dunn, *Galatians*, 228–29; Witherington, *Grace in Galatia*, 297; Martinus C. de Boer, "The Meaning of the Phrase τα Στοιχεια του Κοσμου in Galatians," *NTS* 53 (2007): 216–22; Walter Wink, *Naming the Powers* (Philadelphia: Fortress, 1984), 67–77.

81. Clinton Arnold, *The Colossian Syncretism: The Interface Between Christianity and Folk Belief at Colossae*, WUNT 2/77 (Tübingen: Mohr Siebeck, 1995), 162–66; Andrew Pyle, *Atomism and Its Critics: Problem Areas Associated with the Development of the Atomic Theory of Matter from Democritus to Newton* (Bristol: Thoemmes, 1995), 149–50; Jonathan T. Pennington and Sean M. McDonough, eds., *Cosmology and New Testament Theology*, LNTS 355, ed. Mark Goodacre (London: T&T Clark, 2008), 1; Gad Freudenthal, "The Astrologization of the Aristotelian Cosmos: Celestial Influences on the Sublunary World in Aristotle, Alexander of Aphrodisias, and Averroes," in *New Perspectives on Aristotle's De Caelo*, ed. Alan C. Bowen and Christian

The Law Against the Στοιχεῖα and the Flesh 181

Wildberg, Philosophia Antiqua 117 (Leiden: Brill, 2009), 239–82; Juan Antonio Belmonte, "In Search of Cosmic Order: Astronomy and Culture in Ancient Egypt," in *The Role of Astronomy in Society and Culture: Proceedings of the 260th Symposium of the International Astronomical Union Held at the UNESCO Headquarters, Paris, France, January 19–23, 2009*, ed. David Valls-Gabaud and Alexander Boksenberg, IAU Symposium Proceedings 260 (Cambridge: Cambridge University Press, 2011), 74–86; Hermann Hunger, "The Relation of Babylonian Astronomy to Its Culture and Society," in *The Role of Astronomy in Society and Culture: Proceedings of the 260th Symposium of the International Astronomical Union Held at the UNESCO Headquarters, Paris, France, January 19–23, 2009*, ed. David Valls-Gabaud and Alexander Boksenberg, IAU Symposium Proceedings 260 (Cambridge: Cambridge University Press, 2011), 62–73.

82. F. H. Colson, trans., *Philo*, LCL, 1:478; Harry A. Wolfson, *Philo: Foundations of Religious Philosophy in Judaism, Christianity, and Islam*, 2 vols. (Cambridge, MA: Harvard University Press, 1947), 1:176–77, 329; 2:78; Ronald Williamson, *Jews in the Hellenistic World: Philo*, Cambridge Commentaries on Writings of the Jewish and Christian World, 200 BC to AD 200 I.2 (Cambridge: Cambridge University Press, 1989), 30; Louis H. Feldman, *Flavius Josephus: Translation and Commentary*, ed. Steve Mason (Leiden: Brill, 2000), 3:57 n. 503; Calvert-Koyzis, *Paul, Monotheism and the People of God*, 25–39.

83. Francis Watson, *Paul and the Hermeneutics of Faith*, 2d ed., Cornerstones (London: Bloomsbury T&T Clark, 2016), 217 notes similarity in Jubilees' and Philo's interpretations of the scriptures written about Abraham. See also Borgen, *Philo of Alexandria*, 1–13. Feldman, *Flavius Josephus*, 3:57 nn. 502; 59 509, citing Carl R. Holladay, ed., *Fragments from Hellenistic Jewish Authors*, 4 vols., *Texts and Translations* 20, 30, 39–40 (Missoula, MT; Atlanta: Scholars, 1996), 4:181–85, points to Eusebius, *Praep. ev.* 9.17.3; 9.18.1; 13.13.50. See also Josephus, *Ant.* 1.158.

84. For a similar practice see Treat. Shem and the discussion in Lester J. Ness, "Astrology and Judaism in Late Antiquity" (Miami University, PhD dissertation, 1990), http://www.smoe.org/arcana/diss.html.

85. Calvert-Koyzis, *Paul, Monotheism and the People of God*, 27–39; Watson, *Paul and the Hermeneutics of Faith*, 245–47.

86. Martyn, *Galatians*, 400; Calvert-Koyzis, *Paul, Monotheism and the People of God*, 109–10.

87. Paul's restatement reflects the tension between theocentric and anthropocentric emphases in early Jewish writings (see Watson, *Paul and the Hermeneutics of Faith*, 223–28).

88. Martyn, *Galatians*, 400. See Gen 26.5; *Abraham* 6, 275; Hindy Najman, "The Law of Nature and the Authority of Mosaic Law," *SPhilo* 11 (1999): 61–62.

89. See Exod 12.1–20; the Book of the Luminaries (1 En. 82.7, 9); Jub 2.9; and several scrolls in Qumran cave 4: 317 Phases of the Moon, 318 Brontologion, and 320–321 Calendrical Documents A and B. Dunn, *Galatians*, 228 summarizes a sectarian dispute among early Jews over a solar vs. lunar calendar. See 1 En. 82.4–7; Jub. 6.32–35; 1QS 1.14–15; CD 3.14–15.

90. Niehoff, *Jewish Identity*, 249–52.

182   5

91. Gen 26.5; Exod 12.17, 24, 25; 15.26; 19.5; 20.6, etc.; see also Rom 2.26; Gal 6.13.

92. This is the sense in all of the OG's and NT's other uses: Ps 36 (37).12; 129 (130).3; Mark 3.2; Luke 6.7; 14.1; 20.20; Acts 9.24. OG uses τηρέω once of observing a command (1 Sam 15.11).

93. See Longenecker, *Galatians*, 182. Josephus's five other uses of παρατηρέω have the normal sense "watch closely" (*Ant.* 2.206; 15.154; 16.312; *J.W.* 2.468; 4.268).

94. See the discussion of the elements mediating the harmony of earth with heaven in chapter 3, section C.1 above.

95. Martyn, *Galatians*, 415 and Longenecker, *Abraham's God*, 49 think Paul is referring to "watching the movements of the stars" in order to "practise the law and maintain the covenant properly." See de Boer, *Galatians*, 276.

96. Niehoff, *Jewish Identity*, 107–8, 263–64; Cristina Termini, "Philo's Thought within the Context of Middle Judaism," in *The Cambridge Companion to Philo*, ed. and trans. Adam Kamesar (Cambridge: Cambridge University Press, 2009), 118–19.

97. Niehoff, *Jewish Identity*, 264–65.

98. Niehoff, *Jewish Identity*, 110.

99. Niehoff, *Jewish Identity*, 263–64.

100. Niehoff, *Jewish Identity*, 249.

101. Niehoff, *Jewish Identity*, 248–51.

102. Calvert-Koyzis, *Paul, Monotheism and the People of God*, 26–30 seems to overlook this distinction.

103. Victorinus 145–46.

104. See Dunn, *Galatians*, 227–29.

105. So Wright, *Paul and the Faithfulness of God*, 90–95.

106. de Boer, *Galatians*, 370; David Arthur deSilva, *Galatians: A Handbook on the Greek Text*, BHGNT (Waco, TX: Baylor University Press, 2014), 145; Barclay, *Paul and the Gift*, 386.

107. Thus I agree with Fee, *God's Empowering Presence*, 398 n. 111 and disagree with Ernest De Witt Burton, *A Critical and Exegetical Commentary on the Epistle to the Galatians*, ICC (Edinburgh: T&T Clark, 1921), 195; E. P. Sanders, *Paul and Palestinian Judaism* (Philadelphia: Fortress, 1977), 503; Bruce, *Galatians*, 180; Longenecker, *Galatians*, 143–44; Douglas A. Campbell, *The Deliverance of God: An Apocalyptic Rereading of Justification in Paul* (Grand Rapids: Eerdmans, 2009), 866–67; de Boer, *Galatians*, 233; Moo, *Galatians*, 238; deSilva, *Reading Paul through Asian Eyes*, 144.

108. Moo, *Galatians*, 60; Wright, *Paul and the Faithfulness of God*, 941 n. 469; deSilva, *Reading Paul through Asian Eyes*, 25.

109. deSilva, *Reading Paul through Asian Eyes*, 111; Barclay, *Paul and the Gift*, 441.

110. Barclay, *Paul and the Gift*, 377 n. 71; see Dunn, *Galatians*, 193.

111. I interpret "ἔργα νόμου" as referring generally to the practices "done in obedience to the law" of Moses (Moo, *Galatians*, 158 (citing James D. G. Dunn, *Christianity in the Making* (Grand Rapids: Eerdmans, 2009), 2:2:475 in agreement), 173–76;

The Law Against the Στοιχεῖα and the Flesh 183

see de Boer, *Galatians*, 145–48; deSilva, *Reading Paul through Asian Eyes*, 97–99; Barclay, *Paul and the Gift*, 371–75). I appreciate that Paul's particular concern in Galatians is with practices that separate Jewish believers from non-Jewish believers, especially circumcision and the law's calendar (Moo, *Galatians*, 158; see James D. G. Dunn, *The New Perspective on Paul: Collected Essays* (Tübingen: Mohr Siebeck, 2005), 23–28, 213–15, cited and opposed by Barclay, *Paul and the Gift*, 374 n. 61). And I recognize that, for early Jews, the distinct features of the law were circumcision, the sabbath, food laws, and the temple (Wright, *Paul and the Faithfulness of God*, 184–87.).

112. I follow Richard B. Hays, *The Faith of Jesus Christ: The Narrative Substructure of Galatians 3:1–4:11*, 2nd edn. (Grand Rapids: Eerdmans, 2002); de Boer, *Galatians*, 148–50; Wright, *Paul and the Faithfulness of God*, 835–51 in reading πίστις Ἰησοῦ Χριστοῦ as the "faithfulness of Jesus the Anointed" (contra Dunn, *Galatians*, 138–39; Moo, *Galatians*, 38–48, 160–61; deSilva, *Reading Paul through Asian Eyes*, 99–106; Barclay, *Paul and the Gift*, 378–81).

113. See LSJ.

114. de Boer, *Galatians*, 152–56; Moo, *Galatians*, 53–57; see Wright, *Paul and the Faithfulness of God*, 898–902, 934–49.

115. That is, participation in the Anointed is the ground of justification (Moo, *Galatians*, 56–57; Wright, *Paul and the Faithfulness of God*, 858–59, 891–902, 949–52; Barclay, *Paul and the Gift*, 374–78).

116. Wright, *Paul and the Faithfulness of God*, 851–79, 966–76.

117. Moo, *Galatians*, 161–62; Wright, *Paul and the Faithfulness of God*, 852–60, 968–71; Barclay, *Paul and the Gift*, 387.

118. Longenecker, *Galatians*, 95; Fee, *God's Empowering Presence*, 419–20 (which, curiously, Moo, *Galatians*, 331 n. 18 cites in agreement); deSilva, *Reading Paul through Asian Eyes*, 95.

119. Moo, *Galatians*, 328–31.

120. Moo, *Galatians*, 56–57; Wright, *Paul and the Faithfulness of God*, 954–59; contra Ernst Käsemann, "The Righteousness of God in Paul," in *New Testament Questions of Today*, ed. Ernst Käsemann (Philadelphia: Fortress, 1969), 168–82; Michael J. Gorman, *Inhabiting the Cruciform God: Kenosis, Justification, and Theosis in Paul's Narrative Soteriology* (Grand Rapids: Eerdmans, 2009); Campbell, *The Deliverance of God*.

121. de Boer, *Galatians*, 163–65; Moo, *Galatians*, 53–57, 173, 327–28; see Wright, *Paul and the Faithfulness of God*, 945–46.

122. Moo recognizes δικαιοσύνη in Rom 6.13, 16, 18, 19 as "moral" or "ethical" (Moo, *Romans*, 386–87, 399–400, 403–5). See δίκαιος behavior in Eph 6.1; Col 4.1; Titus 1.8, and "training in δικαιοσύνη" in 2 Tim 3.16.

123. Moo, *Galatians*, 327–31; Wright, *Paul and the Faithfulness of God*, 954–59; Fee, *God's Empowering Presence*, 416–71; deSilva, *Reading Paul through Asian Eyes*, 95–97, 111, 201–2; see Barclay, *Paul and the Gift*, 439–45.

124. McCaulley (2017) demonstrates that when Paul refers to the inheritance in Galatians, he has the land promise in view there as well. Esau McCaulley, *Sharing in*

184   5

the Sons Inheritance: Davidic Messianism and Pauls Worldwide Interpretation of the Abrahamic Land Promise in Galatians, LNTS (London: T&T Clark, 2019).

125. Philo does hope that Israel will return from exile, but that return, like Abraham's migration from Chaldea and Israel's exodus from Egypt, applies as much to the movement of Jews from distant islands and continents to Jerusalem as to the bringing of the mind from ἐπιθυμία to "salvation" (*Rewards* 117, 162–165). And in the end, for Philo, the soul's salvation is not the body's resurrection, but the dissolution of the body's elements (*Alleg. Interp.* 2.54–59; *Giants* 31) (Barclay, *Obeying the Truth*, 186).

126. See Rom 2.17–24; 2 Tim 3.15–17.

127. Witherington, *Grace in Galatia*, 324 is "frankly surprised" that Barrett could "dismiss" Philo's relevance to Paul's allegory with "a mere wave of the hand," for, in early Jewish literature, "only Philo and Paul . . . really engage in a contemporizing of the text by means of allegorizing" (see C. K. Barrett, "The Allegory of Abraham, Sarah, and Hagar in the Argument of Galatians," in *Rechtfertigung: Festschrift für Ernst Käsemann zum 70. Geburtstag*, ed. Johannes Friedrich, Wolfgang Pöhlmann, and Peter Stuhlmacher (Tübingen: Mohr, 1976), 11 n. 24). I analyze Paul's allegory further in "Listening with Philo to Our Mother Sarah: Assessing the Validity and Value of Allegoresis Implicit in Paul's Use of It," in *Scripture, Texts and Tracings in Galatians*, ed. A. Andrew Das and B. J. Oropeza (Lanham, MD: Lexington/Fortress Academic, forthcoming).

128. Longenecker, *Galatians*, 205; see Witherington, *Grace in Galatia*, 325–26; Jason Zurawski, "Mosaic Torah as Encyclical Paideia: Reading Paul's Allegory of Hagar and Sarah in Light of Philo of Alexandria's," in *Wisdom & Apocalypticism* (presented at the SBL Chicago, 2012).

129. Maren R. Niehoff, "Philo, Allegorical Commentary," *EDEJ*, 1071.

130. Steven Di Mattei, "Paul's Allegory of the Two Covenants (Gal 4.21–31) in Light of First-Century Hellenistic Rhetoric and Jewish Hermeneutics," *NTS* 52 (2006): 108, https://doi.org/10.1017/S0028688506000063.

131. Di Mattei, "Paul's Allegory," 109, citing Richard Longenecker, *Biblical Exegesis in the Apostolic Period* (Grand Rapids: Eerdmans, 1974), 28, 39, 54.

132. Witherington, *Grace in Galatia*, 326; Di Mattei, "Paul's Allegory," 102–9; de Boer, *Galatians*, 296.

133. Richard P. C. Hanson, *Allegory and Event: A Study of the Sources and Significance of Origen's Interpretation of Scripture* (London: SCM, 1959), 82–83; see Longenecker, *Galatians*, 209–10; Moisés Silva, "Galatians," in *Commentary on the New Testament Use of the Old Testament* (Grand Rapids: Baker Academic, 2007), 808; Moo, *Galatians*, 300.

134. de Boer, *Galatians*, 295–96, quoting Friederich Büchsel, "Ἀλληγορέω," *TDNT* 1:262. See Niehoff, "Philo, Allegorical Commentary," 1070–71; Adam Kamesar, "Biblical Interpretation in Philo," in *The Cambridge Companion to Philo*, ed. Adam Kamesar (Cambridge: Cambridge University Press, 2009), 80; Di Mattei, "Paul's Allegory," 109; Borgen, *Philo of Alexandria*, 144–49.

135. Moo, *Galatians*, 296.

136. Moo, *Galatians*, 294. See the criterion "eschatology" in de Boer, *Galatians*, 296; Witherington, *Grace in Galatia*, 334–36; Dunn, *Galatians*, 248; Longenecker, *Galatians*, 209–10; and see Martyn, *Galatians*, 436.

137. Borgen, *Philo of Alexandria*, 269–76.

138. Longenecker, *Galatians*, 209.

139. Witherington, *Grace in Galatia*, 328. See Richard B. Hays, *Echoes of Scripture in the Letters of Paul* (New Haven, CT: Yale University Press, 1989), 111–17; de Boer, *Galatians*, 287.

140. Moo, *Galatians*, 292, citing Barrett, "The Allegory of Abraham, Sarah, and Hagar in the Argument of Galatians"; de Boer, *Galatians*, 286; Calvert-Koyzis, *Paul, Monotheism and the People of God*, 88; Hays, "Galatians," 300; G. Walter Hansen, *Galatians*, IVP New Testament Commentary 9 (Downers Grove, IL: InterVarsity, 1994), 140–41; Dunn, *Galatians*, 243; Longenecker, *Galatians*, 207–8; Bruce, *Galatians*, 218.

141. Zurawski, "Paul's Allegory." See Witherington, *Grace in Galatia*, 324–28.

142. Sarah J. K. Pearce, *The Land of the Body: Studies in Philo's Representation of Egypt*, WUNT 2/208 (Tübingen: Mohr Siebeck, 2007), 127.

143. Gal 4.1–2; see Rom 7.14; 1 Cor 3.1. See Scott J. Hafemann, "Paul and the Exile of Israel in Galatians 3–4," in *Exile: Old Testament, Jewish, and Christian Conceptions*, ed. James M. Scott, JSJSup 56 (Leiden: Brill, 1997), 338–39.

144. For the scriptural association of Egypt with the indulgence of the flesh see Exod 16.3.

145. See chapter 3, section A.4 above.

146. See Peder Borgen, "Observations on the Theme 'Paul and Philo': Paul's Preaching of Circumcision in Galatia (Gal. 5:11) and Debates on Circumcision in Philo," in *Die Paulinische Literatur und Theologie: The Pauline Literature and Theology: Anlässlich der 50. Jährigen Gründungs-Feier der Universitat von Aarhus*, ed. Sigfred Pedersen, Scandinavian Contributions; Teologiske Studier 7 (Århus: Aros, 1980), 85–102.

6

The Son and the Spirit Against the Στοιχεια and the Flesh

To this point in this study, Greek medical discourse and the corpus of Philo's extant writings have shed light on the terms and concepts of Paul's arguments in Galatians. Chapter 4 argued that Greek medicine gave Paul the tools and perspective to analyze the etiology of sin, to see how composition from the weak στοιχεῖα weakens human physiology, and to discern in the pathology of the flesh its corruption from weakness into wickedness. Chapter 5 showed that Greek medicine gave Paul the perspective to recognize the law's role in the lives of Abraham's children as something like a παιδαγωγός. In these ways, Greek medicine and an amalgam of early Jewish thought like Philo's have been useful to us—as they seem also to have been to Paul—for the crucial task of diagnosing the problem.

But when Paul turns from problem to prescription, he finds little help from either source. Having located the human problem in the weakness of the στοιχεῖα, both Greek medical theory and Philo use some sort of νόμος or regimen to manage the balance of elemental qualities in the flesh and so bring the soul to ordered harmony with the cosmos. As chapter 5 made clear, Paul rejects this approach completely. His answer is simple, and it emerges in two extreme phrases that would shock a first-time reader: crucifixion of the flesh and death to the cosmos. That is how the Anointed's people receive life, righteousness, and the inheritance and thus align with the new creation while still living in their bodies.[1]

As a treatment for the problem of the flesh, the procedure of crucifixion and new life is a radical one. It was carried out first in the case of God's Son, who was "born of a woman," thus taking on human flesh composed of weak elements (Gal 4.4; see Rom 8.3). He lived "under law," and, in "faith functioning through love," he "gave himself," according to Paul, "for our sins," becoming a curse to redeem "us from the law's curse" (Gal 1.4; 2.16, 20; 3.13; 4.4; see 5.6). The Father raised his Son "from among the dead," and he now not only redeems Abraham's children "who are under the law," but also rescues "us from the present evil age" (1.1, 4; 4.5). Correspondingly, "those who are of the Anointed Jesus" then participate in this procedure through faith; they die with him, and he lives in their flesh (2.19–20; 5.24). Thus they too "have crucified the flesh with its stimuli and desires" and now "live by the Spirit" (5.24–25).

Chapter 6 now presents believers' death with the Anointed One and their life with the Spirit. As it does so it gives renewed attention to motifs often slighted in Galatians studies: the Spirit's life alongside the Son's death, believers' death to the cosmos alongside their death to the law, and believers' lived righteousness alongside their declared righteousness.[2] Considered together, these conceptual pairs reveal that Paul would find it inadequate to set believers free from the law as guard and guide without then directing them to the Son's Spirit within them as guard and guide. After all, the law was not the original problem; sin's corruption of the weak flesh was. The law was scripture's stopgap measure to restrain the expansive desires of Abraham's offspring's flesh. And Paul's instructions address the same problem, though in surprising ways. Unlike Greek doctors or Philo, he calls not for altering the *medium* by adjusting the flesh and the στοιχεῖα that compose it; nor, as he will in Romans, for enhancing the *means* by reformulating the heart or renewing the mind; but rather for adopting the same *mode*—desire—and simply introducing an agent with counter-desires directly into the system of human attitude and action. The profoundly physiological quality of Paul's double prescription—crucifixion of the flesh on the Son's cross and following the Spirit's desires against the flesh—reaffirms the physiological emphasis that this study has exhibited in Paul's diagnosis of the problem of enslavement under the στοιχεῖα τοῦ κόσμου.

I consider in turn, then, believers' death with the Son and life by the Spirit. This is not to suggest, however, that Paul sees the two as independent nor even that the Son has no role in the believer's ongoing life (2.20).

A. CRUCIFIXION WITH THE ANOINTED: FAITHFUL DEATH TO THE ΚΟΣΜΟΣ AND THE ΝΟΜΟΣ

As the means of rescue from enslavement under the στοιχεῖα τοῦ κόσμου, Paul points the Galatians to the death of the Anointed One and to their death with him. Paul remarks that he himself has been crucified with the Anointed. The statement is obviously metaphorical—for Paul describes himself as living even while participating in the Anointed's death—yet it attaches to a very physical, even fleshy, reality. Paul also calls the Galatians to live as though they have died with the Anointed. This death frees believers from sin's

The Son and the Spirit Against the Στοιχεῖα and the Flesh   189

dominion exercised through the weak στοιχεῖα that compose and compromise the body, and it leads them into the life of faith, a life that gives itself in love apart from the law's supervision.

1. Paul has been Crucified with the Anointed and is Dead to the Law and the Cosmos

Paul's prescription for enslavement under the στοιχεῖα τοῦ κόσμου begins not with a course of treatment, but with an event: Χριστῷ συνεσταύρωμαι (Gal 2.19). From this radical experience he draws two significant implications: (1) he is dead to the law, and (2) he is dead to the cosmos.

First, as a crucified person, Paul is dead to the law, for the law has no jurisdiction over the dead (Gal 2.19; see Rom 7.1–6).[3] Curiously, the law itself was the instrument of Paul's death to the law: διὰ νόμου νόμῳ ἀπέθανον. Two complementary perspectives from Rom 6–8 clarify this obscure statement. First, Paul says he died because sin and its παθήματα worked through the law to kill him. As he narrates in Rom 7, the law was the instrument by which sin was killing him (Rom 7.5, 11, 13, 24, 25; 8.2).[4] Second, Paul tells the Romans that the body is crucified with the Anointed, and it is "through the Anointed's body" that they "have died to the law" (6.2, 6, 11; 7.4). Together, these two perspectives help make sense of Paul's juxtaposed statements in Gal 2.19–20: (1) that he died "through the law to the law" and (2) that he has been crucified with the Anointed. And these perspectives emphasize again that Paul's concern lies not only with the law but also with sin's dominion through the flesh. Weakened as it was by the flesh, the law was (and is) not able to make people alive and guide them to live for God (Rom 8.3). That is what death and life with the Anointed do (6.11; 7.4).

Second, through the Lord's cross, the cosmos has been crucified to Paul and Paul to the cosmos (Gal 6.14). Since Paul uses the term κόσμος in Galatians only in 4.3 and 6.14, his double use here makes a clear point:[5] his crucifixion with Jesus the Anointed was the end of his enslavement under the στοιχεῖα τοῦ κόσμου which compose and compromise his flesh. Indeed, that flesh has now been hung upon a cross (5.24).[6] As chapter 5 showed, the answer to the problem of enslavement under the στοιχεῖα τοῦ κόσμου is neither seeking to live in harmony with the κόσμος, whether according to Moses's law or some other regimen or calendar, nor cutting off an extremity of the flesh made of στοιχεῖα.[7] The answer to the problem of enslavement under the στοιχεῖα τοῦ κόσμου is the crucifixion of the whole flesh, that is, death to the κόσμος, and then advancing in line with new creation (6.14–16). As such, it is not Paul's *worldview* that has been crucified to him[8]—"This language of the world's crucifixion should not be understood merely as an event within the psyche

190   6

of the individual believer"[9]—but *the world itself,* the stuff that makes up the cosmos and his flesh. As Victorinus comments,

> Our Lord Jesus Christ . . . hung his flesh upon the cross for a moment, and triumphed on it over the power of this world, and the whole world was crucified through him. And because he had a body consisting of the universal nature of all humankind, everything that he suffered he made universal—that is, so that all flesh would be crucified in him. (171)

Yes, Paul's death with the Anointed to the law and the cosmos is metaphorical or symbolic, but, as Wright notes, symbols are things that people practice.[10] Thus, as the following sections will show, beginning with the enacted symbolism of baptism, when Paul and the Galatians participate in the death of the Anointed, they do so with their physical bodies in actual practice (2.20).

2. Paul's Participation by Faith in the Anointed's Death is Bodily

As in Gal 2.19; 6.14, Paul's careful phrasing in 2.20 presents a grand principle in a few slight words: ζῶ ἐν σαρκί, ἐν πίστει ζῶ. Paul's present life is an anomaly.[11] On the one hand, he lives ἐν σαρκί, breathing and eating and moving in a body still made of weak στοιχεῖα. On the other hand, he lives ἐν πίστει, by the πίστις of God's Son.[12] For Paul, faith creates a new reality by which believers transcend the problem of the weak flesh even while living within it.

For Paul, faith is the means by which the Anointed lives in him (Gal 2.20). This is the starting point of Paul's identity and ministry as an apostle. Since God was pleased to reveal his Son in Paul, as Paul travels and speaks, his body made of flesh is itself an announcement of the crucified Jesus, written out and tacked up before the general public (1.15–16; 2.20; 3.1).[13] Indeed, the Galatians' first encounter with the good news was despite—rather, as Scott Hafemann argues, on the basis of—the weakness of Paul's flesh (Gal 4.13; see 1 Cor 2.3).[14] And, as Paul recalls, they responded appropriately, receiving him not just "as God's messenger," but "as the Anointed Jesus," for God was pleased to reveal his Son in Paul (Gal 4.14).

In other letters, Paul writes that the weak quality of his flesh does not determine his attitudes and actions. He is no longer enslaved under the στοιχεῖα τοῦ κόσμου that compose and compromise his body. Instead, he has attained the ideal of αὐτάρκεια, yet not through a philosopher's regimen, but rather as, by faith, the Anointed lives in him and he experiences the Anointed's παθήματα and death (Phil 3.10; 4.13). For Greek medical philosophers and Philo, hunger, thirst, and cold are classic examples of elemental disproportion

The Son and the Spirit Against the Στοιχεῖα and the Flesh   191

in the body impinging on the soul, but Paul says he is content whether well-fed or hungry, having little or plenty (2 Cor 6.5; 11.27; Phil 4.11–12).[15] All this he is able to do through the one who strengthens him (Phil 4.13). Paul still lives in his flesh (2 Cor 1.5–7; 4.7–12; see Col 1.24), and the elements that compose it are still weak, but the features in his body that define him now are not τὰ στοιχεῖα τοῦ κόσμου but rather τὰ στίγματα τοῦ Ἰησοῦ (Gal 6.17).

3. Paul Calls the Weak Galatians to Be Like Him: To Live by Faith Apart from Law

In turn, Paul calls the Galatians to be like him: to respond to the weakness of their flesh and the threat of enslavement under the στοιχεῖα by dying and living with the Anointed by faith, not by taking on the law (Gal 4.9, 12).[16] In his extended discourse on the flesh, sin, the limitations of the law, and the effectiveness of faith, Paul builds on his scriptural argument (3.1–4.7) with a personal argument, grounding his call for the Galatians to become like him in their experience of his being like them (4.8–20).[17] Most scholars agree that Paul's "γίνεσθε ὡς ἐγώ" refers to his life apart from the law,[18] initiated by dying to the law through the law and living by faith, that is, by the Anointed in him (Gal 2.19–21).[19] But they struggle to connect Gal 4.12–20 with its preceding context. Attention to Paul's "ὅτι κἀγὼ ὡς ὑμεῖς" clarifies why Paul argues from experience at this point. His appeal is effective not only because the Galatians loved him, but also because their common experience proved Paul's point: they had seen in Paul that living by faith apart from law was indeed an effective solution to the problem of enslavement under the στοιχεῖα τοῦ κόσμου.[20]

Paul was like the Galatians in at least three ways. Scholars recognize the third way, but I have found none that notes the first two.[21] First, as himself a creature of flesh made from weak στοιχεῖα, Paul—like all humans, whether Jew or Gentile—had been enslaved ὑπὸ τὰ στοιχεῖα τοῦ κόσμου (4.3). Second, in keeping with his apostolic practice, Paul was weak like the weak Galatians when he proclaimed the good news among them (Gal 4.12–13; see 1 Cor 9.22). And this proclamation in weakness Paul achieved apart from the law's restraint on his flesh, for, third, he had become like the lawless Galatians by living apart from God's law (Gal 2.14–18; see 1 Cor 9.21).[22] In this way, Paul's personal example among the Galatians confirms his conceptual argument: the answer to the human problem of enslavement under the weak στοιχεῖα is not the law but rather dying and living with the Anointed by faith (Gal 2.19–20; 4.14). For this reason Paul says, "Become like me" (4.12).

From Paul's comments, it seems that, earlier on, the new Galatian believers too had been living by faith. All of them—Jew and Greek, slave and free, male and female—were immersed into the Anointed and so were clothed with

192   6

the Anointed (Gal 3.26–28).[23] And, as the Anointed's, they had "crucified the flesh with its παθήματα and ἐπιθυμίαι" (5.24).[24] This principle bore itself out in practice as the Galatians' faith showed itself effective apart from the law. Through faithful hearing, the Galatians received the Spirit and experienced God's miracles among them (Gal 3.2–5). They came to be known by God, to know him, and to be freed from enslavement under the στοιχεῖα (4.3, 8–10). They did not act unrighteously toward Paul but welcomed him as God's messenger, indeed as the Anointed Jesus who lives in Paul (4.12–14). Like the Anointed, who gives himself in self-sacrificing love, they too would, if possible, have dug out their eyes and given them to Paul (4.15; see 1.4; 2.20).[25] In principle, this is what faith does: apart from the law's oversight, it functions through love that fulfills the whole law (5.6, 14). And in practice, this is what faith did, for the Galatians were "running well" (5.7). Thus they should need no further evidence that faith is an—indeed the only—effective medium to overcome the weak στοιχεῖα that compromise the flesh and to live in righteousness and love (3.1–5; 5.5–6).

For Paul, crucifixion with the Anointed One is no mere concept; it is concrete practice.[26] By faith he, like all Christians, participates bodily in the Anointed's death, having died to the cosmos and its elements that compose their flesh. As the Galatians' own experience with Paul proves, believers need no law to guard them from the expansive desires of their flesh. Rather they receive God's righteousness as a gift as, by faith, the Anointed, who loved them, lives in them (Gal 2.19–21).

While Paul focuses in Gal 2 on God's Son, in chapter 3 it is "the Spirit of God's Son" that God has sent "into our hearts" (4.6). Similarly, in chapter 4 Paul associates life πνεύματι with life ἐν Χριστῷ Ἰησοῦ (5.5–6). Then, for most of the rest of the letter, his attention is on the Spirit as the personal agent of transformation in the Galatians' lives. Paul's prescription for redemption from enslavement under the στοιχεῖα τοῦ κόσμου is not only crucifixion with the Anointed but life and στοιχεῖν with the Spirit.

B. LIFE WITH THE SPIRIT: FRUITFUL ALIGNMENT WITH HIS DESIRES

Now that Paul has nailed the whole flesh to a cross, he has no more need of the law to confine sin's metastasis within weak elemental flesh (3.19–22; 5.24). The Anointed's faithful death has brought an end to the law's responsibility as παιδαγωγός to confine Abraham's children (3.23–25). But, of course, Abraham's offspring must not only be guarded from transgressions, they must also be guided to conduct themselves as befits Abraham's heirs, that is, in righteousness. So, as Paul recounts, God has not only sent his Son to live in

The Son and the Spirit Against the Στοιχεῖα and the Flesh   193

human flesh and redeem those whom the law confined, but, now that they—
and believers from the nations with them—are God's sons, he has also sent
his Son's Spirit into their hearts (4.4–6). From within (unlike the παιδαγωγός
from without), the Spirit guides believers, not by decrees, but through desires
(5.16–18). And, according to Paul, the παιδαγωγός, now retired, is satisfied,
for none of the Spirit's fruit transgress its instruction. Indeed, they fulfill its
governing concern: "love your neighbor as yourself" (5.14, 22–23).

This closing section, then, presents the Spirit's work within believers'
hearts, his use of desire, and his production of love and other fruit in the
καιροί of the new creation.

1. The Spirit in the Heart

The Spirit enters the twin narrative of Israel's and the nations' redemption from sin at the beginning of Galatians' dénouement. In the narrative,
Paul's Jewish "we" have received adoption as sons (4.5), as did his Gentile
"you" along with them in baptism (3.26–28; 4.6), and now God has sent his
Son's Spirit into the hearts of this newly unified "us" (4.6).[27] In each of the
thought-worlds represented by these narratives, the heart appears frequently
at the center, as it does in Paul's letters to other assemblies. But here in
Galatians Paul will not mention it again. His prescription for the problem of
the elemental flesh and its expansive desires is focused elsewhere.

The heart is a central motif in Israel's narrative of redemption and in the
Greek medical tradition. The law instructs the heart but despairs of it (Deut
6.4–6; 29.3; 30.1–6). And the prophets promise its renewal (Jer 17.9; 31
(38).33; 32 (39).40; Ezek 11.19; 36.26).[28] Similarly, the heart is a central
motif for Empedocles (96/105) and Plato (*Tim.* 70a; see *Resp.* 4.442b).

The heart is also central in Romans. Following Israel's scriptures, Paul
locates the human problem both in the καρδία and its ἐπιθυμίαι, and in the
νοῦς and its διαλογισμοί and ἐπίγνωσις (1.20–21, 24, 28).[29] His solution
also centers on the heart: the συνείδησις and λογισμοί interact with the law
inscribed on the καρδία (2.15), the Spirit circumcises the καρδία (2.29), God
pours out his love through the Holy Spirit into καρδίαι (5.5), and obedience
proceeds from the καρδία (6.17). Then, through the rest of Rom 6–8, Paul's
argument is meaningfully conversant with Plato's perspective. His focus
shifts from the heart to the body's own sinful ἐπιθυμίαι (6.12), the corruption
of the σάρξ by the παθήματα of sins (7.5), and the struggle of the νοῦς with
the flesh, the body, and its parts (7.14–25).[30] Throughout Rom 1–8, then,
human volition and action are the expressions of a complex interaction of
organs and parts in body and soul. Not so in Galatians.

In contrast with Israel's prophetic tradition, Greek medical discourse, and
even Romans, the heart is not central in Galatians.[31] While Romans addresses

194   6

καρδία, νοῦς, σῶμα, and σάρξ as the locations of the human problem, Galatians focuses on the σάρξ alone. While in Romans every human is ψυχή and σάρξ (2.9; 3.20; 13.1), in Galatians every human is simply σάρξ (1.16; 2.16). If the human condition is to be analyzed in finer detail, one must consider not a volitional organ within the human person but the weak στοιχεῖα τοῦ κόσμου that compose and compromise the flesh of the body.[32] It is the στοιχεῖα that explain the etiology of human corruption. While the Galatians' ignorance (ἀνόητος) is an issue (3.1), Paul addresses the corrupt ἐπιθυμίαι not of the καρδία or νοῦς, but of the σάρξ (5.16, 17, 24). Similarly, sinful attitudes and actions are not expressions of a volitional organ, but functions of the σάρξ seen as a whole (5.19–21). The heart is missing too from Paul's fuller discussion of the Spirit in Gal 5. And any reference to the new exodus motif that the Spirit, who dwells in the heart, will act upon the heart (as for example in 2 Cor 1.20–22; see 3.1–4.6) is conspicuously absent.[33]

Paul's focus falls elsewhere. In his argument, the Spirit is effective at opposing the flesh not because it removes believers from the flesh—Paul himself continues to live ἐν σαρκί (2.20)—nor because it alters the material of the flesh (i.e., the στοιχεῖα), nor because it enhances a human volitional organ, such as the heart or mind, to oppose the flesh.[34] For Paul the Spirit is effective because it adopts the *mode* of the flesh—desire—and operates in direct opposition to it.

2. The Spirit's Counter-Desiring

If Paul's marginalization of the heart was surprising, his prescription of ἐπιθυμεῖν as a treatment for ἐπιθυμία is even more so. This move may find some antecedent in Greek philosophical traditions (though certainly none in Philo) and some legitimacy in Israel's scriptures. But Paul's ideas about ἐπιθυμία remain groundbreaking; they are the fruit of his theological reflection on the promise of the Spirit in the new covenant. Whatever he may mean in Gal 5.17d, Paul can assert confidently that those who follow the Spirit's desiring will not fulfill the desire of the flesh and so are no longer under the law.

As ethical advice within the complex of Greek physiology and psychology, Paul's prescription of ἐπιθυμεῖν to curtail ἐπιθυμία is largely unprecedented, and it is directly contrary to Philo and some other early Jews. Plato acknowledges the possibility of positive ἐπιθυμία within humans. But when the mind's "desire of wisdom" confronts the body's "desire of food," "the motions of the stronger part prevail" and make the soul dull (*Tim.* 88b). So Plato prescribes balanced exercise of body and soul to save the mind's desire from suppression by the body's (88b). Epicurus too acknowledges that there are some ἐπιθυμίαι that are both natural and necessary: the desires for happiness, the

The Son and the Spirit Against the Στοιχεῖα and the Flesh   195

removal of "uneasiness," and life (*Ep. Men.* 127–128).[35] But for Plato and Epicurus, it is people, not their desires, who should direct their lives.

In contrast with his master Plato, Philo finds no positive ἐπιθυμία within humans. Ἐπιθυμία is "a battery of destruction to the soul" that must be either "done away with or brought into obedience to the governance of reason" (*Spec. Laws* 4.95). Moses's food laws are effective in the first regard, for they are "an extinguisher to ἐπιθυμία" (4.118). And the rational mind is generally effective in the second, working, in Philo's appropriation of Plato's imagery, like a charioteer who reins in and directs the restless power of θύμος and ἐπιθυμία (see *Alleg. Interp.* 1.72–73; 3.118; *Agriculture* 73–78; *Migration* 67). This consistently negative appraisal of desire will appear again in 4 Macc 1–3.[36] Thus Greek philosophical discourse, and especially Jewish contributions to it, offer little precedent for Paul's use of ἐπιθυμία to oppose ἐπιθυμία.

In contrast, Israel's scriptures open the door to a more positive view of ἐπιθυμία.[37] Although the tenth commandment forbids ἐπιθυμεῖν for one's neighbor's property (Exod 20.17; Deut 5.21), and though the law records that a rabble ἐπεθύμησαν ἐπιθυμίαν for meat at Kibroth-hattaavah (Num 11.4, 34; Deut 9.22), scripture still displays a surprising openness to ἐπιθυμία. Moses permits the Israelites to eat meat "ἐὰν ἐπιθυμήσῃ ἡ ψυχή σου" (Deut 12.15, 20, 21) and to select as fare for the tithe feast "ἐὰν ἐπιθυμῇ ἡ ψυχή σου" (14.26). The Greek Psalter similarly knows not only of the ἐπιθυμία of the wicked (9.24; 111.10; 139.9)—including Israel's for meat in the wilderness (77.29–30; 105.14)—but also of the righteous, especially for God's words (118.20, 40; see Wis 6.11; Sir 1.26; 6.37). Indeed, the psalmists bless the Lord for hearing and satisfying their ἐπιθυμία with good things (9.38; 20.3; 37.10; 102.5; see Prov 10.24). In Isaiah, the Lord rebukes his people because their ἐπιθυμία to approach him and know his ways is incongruent with their violence and oppression (Isa 58.2–4). Yet he promises that when they free the oppressed and aid the poor, he will lead them, satisfy them as their soul ἐπιθυμεῖ, and feed them with Jacob's inheritance (58.11, 14). Yet while these texts validate and fulfill the ἐπιθυμία of the righteous, none of them presents the ἐπιθυμία of God within the faithful as a guard against the flesh or a guide into righteousness.

Paul's ethics—the ἐπιθυμία of the flesh opposes that of the Spirit—and the confidence with which he affirms it—"Walk with the Spirit, and you will certainly not fulfill the ἐπιθυμία of the flesh"[38]—seem to follow from his theological reflections on prophetic promises of the Spirit more than from earlier concepts of ἐπιθυμία (5.16–17).[39] In Ezekiel, when the Lord promises to restore Israel and give them a new heart, he says he will put his Spirit within them and make them walk in his δικαιώματα and keep and do his judgments (Ezek 36.24–27; see 11.19–20). The one-sidedness of agency in this promise—"I will make you"—underlies Paul's confident tone. And Paul's statements reveal the logic of his reflection. God sends his Son's Spirit into believers' hearts. From there, the urge of the Spirit's ἐπιθυμεῖν within believers leads them;[40] it compels them along a path, much as the Spirit led the Lord's people in the exodus (Gal 5.16–18).[41] The believers' response is correspondingly acquiescent: walk, be led, advance in line with (5.16, 18, 25).[42] And those who walk with the Spirit will certainly not fulfill the desire of the flesh, because the Spirit's desire is opposite the desire of the flesh (5.16–17).

Those premises lead to Paul's bewildering conclusion: ἵνα μὴ ἃ ἐὰν θέλητε ταῦτα ποιῆτε. Scholars have proposed four ways of reading 5.17d:[43]

1. the believers want to do right things but the flesh's desire results in them not being able to do them;[44]
2. the believers want to do fleshy things but the Spirit purposes to keep them from doing them;[45]
3. the expression of the believers' attitude in action is always contested, if not determined, whether by the flesh or by the Spirit;[46] and
4. as a result of the opposing desires, believers are not free to do as they want.[47]

Choosing one of these readings over the others is difficult, as each reading has its weakness.[48] But none of the readings alters Paul's basic insistence that the effective way to enable righteous conduct is the Spirit's desiring.

From any perspective then, the Spirit is the answer to the fundamental problem that has plagued Paul since 2.15: the problem of sin and the flesh. Those who live and walk by the Spirit will not fulfill the desire of the flesh (5.16–25).[49] Related to that problem is the secondary, but more urgent, problem of the law. Scripture appointed the law as a παιδαγωγός to guard and guide Abraham's offspring, but the agitators are misusing it as a means to life, righteousness, and the inheritance.[50] The law is contingent on—it is a response to—the behavior of Abraham's offspring: it was imposed to restrain their transgressions, and it is removed now that the Spirit leads them (3.19–25; 5.18). Paul's statement "οὐκ ἐστὲ ὑπὸ νόμον" is thus not a condemnation of "Judaism" or of religion more broadly.[51] It is rather the apodosis attached directly to a clearly stated protasis: "εἰ δὲ πνεύματι ἄγεσθε . . ." (5.18). Paul is motivated to remove the law not by his disapprobation of the concept of religion but by his attention to the concrete reality of human action.[52] As Fee concludes, "'It is all right to be done with Torah,' [Paul] says, 'because the Spirit can handle the flesh; indeed, to be led by the Spirit eliminates the need to be under Law.'"[53] The proof of Paul's bold assertion and the warrant for its epoch-changing implication is in its fruit.[54]

3. The Spirit's Fruit

With his daring claim still drying on the scribe's page, Paul moves quickly to present his evidence. For him, the fruit of the Spirit's life within believers is not seen primarily in miraculous healing of their physical weaknesses—again, his solution to the problem of the flesh is not its change but its death (Gal 2.19–20; 3.5; 5.24). Rather, the Spirit's life and desiring are evident in the astonishing liberty and righteousness that characterize believers' lives even though they live in weak flesh. Paul has summarized this principle already. "We, with the Spirit, from faith, are waiting for the hope of righteousness. For in the Anointed Jesus neither circumcision nor a foreskin is effective, but rather faith functioning through love" (5.5–6).

The first fruit of the Spirit's living and desiring within believers is love (Gal 5.22). In the context of the problem of the flesh and his related concern about the law, Paul privileges the internal attitude and interpersonal action of love because it is both the opposite of the functions of the flesh and the fulfilment of the aims of the law (5.14).[55]

While early Christians would emphasize the Spirit's first fruit, love, as the fulfilment of the law, Aristotle, Philo, and others might focus on the last, self-control, as essential to any ethical system (Gal 5.23).[56] For Aristotle, "the self-restrained man (ὁ ἐγκρατής) stands firm against πάθος and ἐπιθυμία' (*Eth. nic.* 7.9.2). He "has bad ἐπιθυμίαι" and "does feel pleasure in such things, but he is not led" (ἄγω) by them (7.9.6).[57] Philo is ever alert to the threat that ἐπιθυμία poses to souls resident in weak bodies, and he finds a prophylactic in its opposite, ἐγκράτεια, "the greatest and most perfect of blessings promoting personal and public welfare alike" (*Spec. Laws* 1.149, see 173). In Niehoff's analysis, ἐγκράτεια is "the central Jewish value which informs all parts of Mosaic legislation."[58] Together, Moses's calendar, particularly the Day of Atonement, and his food laws develop this essential virtue.[59] Looking out for these days, months, and seasons each year and complying with the law's general and particular diets will help the devout to restore the control of reason over the body's elementally-mediated ἐπιθυμίαι and other πάθη.

For Paul, on the other hand, ἐγκράτεια is a fruit. In keeping with his horticultural metaphor, believers may (should) sow its seed, foster its growth, and preserve it by weeding away the flesh and its stimuli and desires, but self-control remains a fruit, the expression of the Spirit's life within them (Gal 5.18, 23–24; 6.8). As Fee argues, Paul's focus here is on the Spirit's opposition to the individual's flesh and its desires.[60] Within the discourse of ancient ethics, self-control restrains one from the actions of the flesh that Paul mentions in 5.19–21, especially sexual immorality, impurity, licentiousness, and the excesses of drinking binges and carousals (see Plato, *Resp.* 390b, 430e).[61] The Spirit desires against these indulgences and in this way leads

198   *6*

believers to live in self-control and thus realize the ethical ideal propounded by Greek philosophy and promoted by the Augustan imperial government.[62] But this virtue, rigorous as it may seem, is attained not by the imposition of the law nor, fundamentally, by the resurgence of reason over passion, but rather through faith, as the Spirit lives within believers.[63]

For Paul, the first and the last of the Spirit's fruit, and the seven in between, are fitting for those who will inherit God's kingdom (Gal 5.21).[64] As the Spirit's expression, they are qualitatively righteous (5.5). From Paul's perspective, believers bear out this principle in practice. They need no law to restrict them from sin, since the Spirit within them desires in the opposite direction (5.18). Nor do they need the law to guide them, for there is no law against the fruit that the Spirit produces (5.23; see Aristotle, *Pol.* 3.13).[65] The Spirit both restrains and guides believers as he desires within their hearts (see Rom 6.17).

4. Aligning with the Spirit in Καιρός and New Creation

In the center of his paraenesis, Paul emphasizes the Spirit's activity as primary: the Spirit desires against the flesh (5.17), the Spirit leads (5.18), the Spirit bears fruit (5.22–23), and, moving outward, the Spirit makes alive (5.25).[66] In the B stichs of the chiasm, Paul focuses on the believers' activity: "πνεύματι περιπατεῖτε" and "πνεύματι καὶ στοιχῶμεν" (5.16, 25). Paul's choice of the verb στοιχέω in 5.25 links back to the στοιχεῖα in 4.3, 9. This connection presents the Spirit as the response to the problem of the στοιχεῖα τοῦ κόσμου. For Paul, life with the Spirit effects such significant change in the way believers relate to the cosmos, both to its substance and to its times, that he calls the new existence "καινὴ κτίσις" (5.25; 6.9–10, 15–16). This final section discusses aligning with the Spirit, doing good and harvesting in καιρός, and aligning with new creation. Together these sections show how Abraham's heirs should live righteously now that the Spirit has freed them from the control of the στοιχεῖα τοῦ κόσμου.

a. Στοιχεῖν with the Spirit

In response to the Spirit's life, leading, and fruitfulness, Paul instructs the Galatian believers to walk with the Spirit and to align with the Spirit (5.16, 25). As Dunn contends, Paul's use of περιπατεῖν to allude to הלך is "deliberate."[67] By choosing this verb, he charges the Galatians in effect not to heed Moses's "statutes and instructions," but rather to walk with the Spirit so they will know "the way they are to walk" (cf. Exod 18.20). While in Gal 5.16–18 the Spirit replaces the law as guide, here in 5.22–23 he appears as

The Son and the Spirit Against the Στοιχεῖα and the Flesh   199

an unprecedented gift of life, a vital force that bears fruit. As Moo notes, the Spirit "both directs and empowers Christian living."[68]

This dual role shapes Paul's charge in the B' stich: "Since we live by the Spirit, let us also στοιχεῖν with the Spirit" (Gal 5.25). At the conceptual level, πνεύματι στοιχεῖν is similar to "ὀρθοποδεῖν with the truth of the good news" and to "the Anointed lives in me" (2.14, 20).[69] On the practical level, πνεύματι στοιχεῖν connects with earlier comments in the letter as well. As Dunn states, "the difference from a life ordered in accord with the elemental forces (4:3) or nature is clear."[70] Witherington, Hays, van Kooten, Schreiner, and de Boer make Dunn's implicit suggestion explicit: στοιχεῖν in 5.25 alludes in some way to στοιχεῖα in 4.3, 9.[71] Though Moo finds these verses "rather distant" from each other, chapter 4 showed that Philo also uses στοιχεῖα's verbal cognates to connect a present statement with an earlier discussion of the elements (see *Eternity* 135).[72] By using στοιχεῖν rather than περιπατεῖν in 5.25, Paul is saying in essence, "Since the Spirit has made us alive, we are no longer enslaved under the miserable στοιχεῖα τοῦ κόσμου that weaken our flesh. So, since we are no longer constrained by the στοιχεῖα, let us στοιχεῖν with the Spirit." In this way believers will live out the Spirit's love and self-control, that is, the righteousness that the law prescribes but that its calendar and circumcision could never produce.[73]

b. Harvesting and Doing Good in Καιρός

In the new life effected by the Spirit, believers relate differently not only to the substance of the cosmos, its στοιχεῖα, but also to its time. In Gal 4.10, Paul responded in alarm to the Galatians' watching out for days, months, καιροί, and years. Chapter 3 showed how Philo promoted Moses's calendar—its days, months, καιροί, and years—to inculcate virtue, and chapter 5 reviewed Paul's vehement opposition to such claims.[74] In Gal 6.6–10, Paul returns to the theme of καιρός and charts out a positive perspective on καιροί and the practices that are appropriate for believers who live and bear fruit by the Spirit.

Concerned perhaps that the Galatians might not acknowledge teaching as a "load," Paul charges them to "make a habit of sharing" with their instructors (6.5–6).[75] He recognizes that both the law and the Lord arrange for teachers to live from their work (1 Cor 9.9, quoting Deut 25.4; Luke 10.7; 1 Cor 9.11–14; Phil 1.5; 4.15).[76] So, on the basis of Moses's instruction to the Israelites that they include the Levites when they offer first fruits and celebrate ἐν πᾶσιν τοῖς ἀγαθοῖς that the Lord has given them, Paul directs the Galatian believers to share with their instructors ἐν πᾶσιν ἀγαθοῖς (Deut 26.11; Gal 6.6).[77]

Paul next encourages the household of faith in the hard work of sowing and laboring on till harvest.[78] He warns them first about sowing "into one's own flesh," representing the flesh as a field (Gal 6.8).[79] "Flesh" points both to the flesh and its actions in 5.13–24[80] and to the pursuit of righteousness by a bodily effort to keep the law (2.16; 3.3; 4.23, 29), especially circumcision (6.12–13).[81] From Paul's perspective, those who misuse the law to restrain the flesh and gain life and righteousness (as in Gal 4.9) find themselves eventually alongside the dissolute (as in Gal 4.3, 8) as the woeful objects of destruction (Gal 5.21; 6.8).[82]

To sow into the Spirit, on the other hand, is to walk with the Spirit, to follow the leading of the Spirit's desire, to advance in line with the Spirit, to plant the seed of the fruit he bears (Gal 5.16–25; 6.8). At reaping time, the fruit that began with the Spirit's life endures in a harvest of "'the life of the age [to come],' . . . resurrection within the renewed creation."[83] In the present life, sowing into the Spirit involves τὸ καλὸν ποιέω, bearing the Spirit's fruit, "faithfulness to the good life of the Pauline gospel," and toiling steadily at one's own work (Gal 5.7; 6.9; see 2 Thess 3.11–13).[84] Such labor requires not allowing oneself to become slack (ἐκλύω), for, as chapter 2 showed, Chrysippus warns that a weak (ἀσθένεια) soul whose "former impetus has gone slack (ἐκλύω)" will be enslaved (δουλόω) by πάθη and ἐπιθυμία (Galen, *PHP* 4.6.8, 10).[85] But, for God's covenant people in the land, it is normal to toil tirelessly ahead of harvest in καιρός. And the promise of patience and fruit καιρῷ encourages the Spirit-laborer (Gal 5.16, 22–23; 6.9; see Lev 26.3–4).

Finally, Paul charges the believers to ἐργάζεσθαι τὸ ἀγαθὸν as they have καιρός (Gal 6.10). Deuteronomy notes that the celebration ἐν πᾶσιν τοῖς ἀγαθοῖς is of the Lord's gifts to you and to your οἰκία, and it instructs the Israelites to include male and female, slave and free, Levite and alien in the rejoicing (16.9–15; 26.11; see Gal 3.28; 6.6, 10). Within Paul's new creation paradigm then, to perform ἀγαθός toward all as one has καιρός is to share with them in the bounty God bestows on the καλός that one did ahead of καιρός (see 2 Cor 9.8).[86]

In Gal 6.6–10 then, Paul presents a program for the community life of the household of faith: how they are to help carry their instructors' load, how they are to live and work, and how they are to do good to others at particular times. This is his vision for στοιχεῖν with the Spirit, for overcoming the στοιχεῖα, and for coordinating faithfully with καιροί. With this program, Paul transforms the law's former calendar and brings it into harmony with the impinging reality of new creation.

c. Στοιχεῖν with the Rule of New Creation

Paul says as much in Gal 6.15–16: "Peace upon those who will στοιχεῖν with this rule, that is, with new creation." In context, καινὴ κτίσις stands in stark contrast to the crucified κόσμος (6.14). As section A.1. above argued, κόσμος

The Son and the Spirit Against the Στοιχεῖα and the Flesh   201

here refers back to 4.3, its only other occurrence in the letter. The κόσμος with its στοιχεῖα (the weak elements that compose and compromise his flesh) has been crucified to Paul, and Paul to it (see 2.19–20; 5.24).

As such, both circumcision and foreskin are defunct; neither category of enslavement under the flesh and the world is operative; and the distinction between their adherents is immaterial (see Gal 3.26–4.11). "Foreskin" labels "sinners from the nations," those enslaved to the weak στοιχεῖα through their dissipation (2.15; 4.8). "Circumcision" labels Jews, particularly those who use the law to curtail the expansive desires of the flesh, but, ironically, who have thus enslaved themselves to the στοιχεῖα once again (4.9). As Paul implies in 6.8, both sorts of people are "sowing into the flesh," and both will reap destruction from the flesh. But this distinction disappears in the one family of those who have been baptized into the Anointed, who have been crucified with him to the old world of the flesh and the law. The change is so radical that Paul calls it "new creation."

Στοιχεῖν with the rule of new creation then is to live by and στοιχεῖν with the Spirit who brings it about (Gal 5.25): to be baptized into the Anointed; to be crucified with him and to live by the Spirit; to have the Anointed formed within; to walk with the Spirit, sensitive to the leading of the Spirit's desire; and by faith to bear love, the essence of righteousness, and the Spirit's other fruit (2.19–20; 3.27; 4.19; 5.5–6, 14–18, 22–24; 6.14). In short, it is to advance in line with the ability and freedom the Spirit gives believers to walk righteously despite (1) continuing to live in fleshy bodies made of weak στοιχεῖα and (2) being unrestrained by the law.

"And as many as will στοιχεῖν with this rule, peace upon them and mercy, that is upon God's Israel" (6.16). Here is Paul's final term, one that comes only at the end of painstaking argumentation: people from any nation who are "of faith"—who are "Abraham's sons," "God's sons," "Abraham's offspring," "heirs according to promise" of "God's kingdom," and "promised children" of the free woman, that is of mother Jerusalem Above; and who, as "one in the Anointed Jesus," are "God's assembly" and "the household of faith" (1.13; 3.7–8, 26, 28–29; 4.7, 26, 28, 31; 5.21; 6.10)—are, in truth, "God's Israel." As the overwhelming majority of scholars agree, it is "unthinkable" that Paul could use this term to label any other group.[87] As Aaron Sherwood argues, the terms καινὴ κτίσις and Ἰσραήλ stand together in the "Jewish tradition" "that the inauguration of the New Creation also comprises the restoration of Israel and—in the 'Israelification' of the ἔθνη—of humanity" (see Isa 66.18–23).[88] The openness of Paul's blessing comes thus not from invoking mercy upon those who might oppose him—he has already devoted to destruction any who proclaim a contrary "gospel" (1.8–9)—but rather by making peace and mercy contingent on a future condition: στοιχήσουσιν. There is yet time for

202

6

those who oppose Paul, whether ethnically Jewish or Greek, to believe like Abraham and be counted among his heirs as "God's Israel" (3.7–9, 29).

C. CONCLUSION

Here in the closing verses of Galatians the themes of the letter—and Paul's thoughts on the problem of the στοιχεῖα τοῦ κόσμου—converge. The way to life begins with death, crucifixion together with the Son, crucifixion to the κόσμος and its στοιχεῖα, crucifixion of the flesh, and death to the law. The law could never grant life or righteousness. As παιδαγωγός, it was only ever a guard for one and a guide to the other. But the dead have no need of either. Life and righteousness come with πίστις, the sending of the Son, who bears his mother's elemental flesh, and the Spirit, who dwells within and desires from the fleshy organ of the heart. Redeemed from enslavement to sin under the στοιχεῖα τοῦ κόσμου and made alive by the Spirit, believers στοιχεῖν with the Spirit and bear his fruit of love, the essence of righteousness and the fulfillment of the law. Now as members of the household of faith, they are diligent in virtuous labor and heed the καιροί for generous deeds. Thus through the Son and the Spirit, believers from every nation live free of the miserable στοιχεῖα and στοιχεῖν with the new creation as the heirs of the kingdom of God.

NOTES

1. None of this is to suggest that Paul thinks of the resurrection body as immaterial (see chapter 4, section A.2 above) or that he would not use both spiritual and material means to treat the weakness of the body itself (Phil 2.26–27; see further Ps 104.15; Acts 27.21–36; 1 Tim 5.23).

2. See Gordon D. Fee, *God's Empowering Presence: The Holy Spirit in the Letters of Paul* (Peabody, MA: Hendrickson, 1994), 404. John M. G. Barclay, *Paul and the Gift* (Grand Rapids: Eerdmans, 2015), 444–45 appreciates similar tensions in Luther's legacy.

3. Douglas J. Moo, *Galatians*, BECNT (Grand Rapids: Baker, 2013), 168–69.

4. Applied to Gal 2.19, this perspective differs from Moo's that the law was the agent, not the instrument, of Paul's death (see Moo, *Galatians*, 169–70). Peter Oakes, *Galatians*, Paideia (Grand Rapids: Baker Academic, 2015), 92–93 reviews other interpretations.

5. Richard B. Hays, "The Letter to the Galatians: Introduction, Commentary, and Reflections," in *The New Interpreter's Bible* (Nashville: Abingdon, 2000), 344 notes the link between κόσμος and στοιχεῖα τοῦ κόσμου and refers correctly to Col 2.13–15 (see Frank J. Matera, *Galatians* (Collegeville, MN: Liturgical, 1992), 226).

The Son and the Spirit Against the Στοιχεῖα and the Flesh   203

6. Hays, "Galatians," 344; Moo, *Galatians*, 396.

7. See chapter 5, section B.2.a above.

8. For Martyn and de Boer, κόσμος refers to the "nomistic cosmos," that is "Judaism," or, more fully, "the world of *all* religious differentiation" (James Louis Martyn, *Galatians: A New Translation with Introduction and Commentary*, AB 33A (New York: Doubleday, 1997), 564–65, italics his; Martinus C. de Boer, *Galatians: A Commentary*, NTL (Louisville, KY: Westminster John Knox, 2011), 401–2.).

9. Hays, "Galatians," 344.

10. N. T. Wright, *Paul and the Faithfulness of God*, Christian Origins and the Question of God 4 (London: SPCK, 2013), 90–95.

11. See Targoff 2008, 115, commenting on "the single most consistent principle in [Donne's] metaphysics: that no aspect of our devotional experience belongs exclusively to body or soul."

12. Hays, "Galatians," 153–55.

13. S. Kraftchick, "Death in Us, Life in You: The Apostolic Medium," in *Pauline Theology*, ed. David M. Hay (Minneapolis: Fortress, 1993), 156–81; Basil S. Davis, "The Meaning of ΠΡΟΕΓΡΑΦΗ in the Context of Galatians 3.1," *NTS* 45 (1999): 194–212; Dieter Mitternacht, *Forum für Sprachlose: Eine Kommunikationspsychologische und Epistolär-Rhetorische Untersuchung des Galaterbriefs*, Coniectanea Biblica New Testament Series 30 (Stockholm: Almqvist & Wiksell, 1999); Hays, "Galatians," 346; de Boer, *Galatians*, 280–81; see John Anthony Dunne, "Persecution in Galatians: Identity, Destiny, and the Use of Isaiah" (University of St Andrews, PhD thesis, 2016), 21–22, https://research-repository.st-andrews.ac.uk/handle/10023/8569.

14. Scott J. Hafemann, "The Role of Suffering in the Mission of Paul," in *The Mission of the Early Church to Jews and Gentiles*, ed. Jostein Ådna and Hans Kvalbein, WUNT 127 (Tübingen: Mohr Siebeck, 2000), 171; see Dunne, "Persecution in Galatians," 23.

15. In similar terms, Xenophon presents Socrates as "the great model for self-mastery" (Stanley Kent Stowers, "Paul and Self-Mastery," in *Paul in the Greco-Roman World: A Handbook*, ed. J. Paul Sampley, 2nd ed. (London: T&T Clark, 2016), 271; see *Mem.* 1.2.1).

16. Paul's previous use of ἐγώ in Galatians is in 2.20.

17. Moo, *Galatians*, 280; citing Ben Witherington III, *Grace in Galatia: A Commentary on St. Paul's Letter to the Galatians* (Grand Rapids: Eerdmans, 1998), 295–96, 305–7.

18. Oakes, *Galatians*, 145–46; Moo, *Galatians*, 281; citing Beverly R. Gaventa, "Galatians 1 and 2: Autobiography as Paradigm," *NovT* 28 (1986): 309–26; and de Boer, *Galatians*, 278; citing J. B. Lightfoot, *Saint Paul's Epistle to the Galatians: A Revised Text with Introduction, Notes, and Dissertations* (London: Macmillan, 1887), 174; Ernest De Witt Burton, *A Critical and Exegetical Commentary on the Epistle to the Galatians*, ICC (Edinburgh: T&T Clark, 1921), 237; Hans Dieter Betz, *Galatians: A Commentary on Paul's Letter to the Churches in Galatia*, Hermeneia (Philadelphia: Fortress, 1979), 222; Richard Longenecker, *Galatians*, WBC 41 (Dallas: Word, 1990), 189; Matera, *Galatians*, 159; James D. G. Dunn, *The Epistle to the Galatians*,

BNTC (London: A & C Black, 1993), 232; Martyn, *Galatians*, 420. Since in the present context Paul is concerned with the flesh, sin, the law, and faith, it is less likely that his "γίνεσθε ὡς ἐγώ" refers to suffering and persecution as normal features in believers' lives. See Ernst Baasland, "Persecution: A Neglected Feature in the Letter to the Galatians," *Studia Theologica: Nordic Journal of Theology* 38 (1984): 135–50; A. J. Goddard and S. A. Cummins, "Ill or Ill-Treated? Conflict and Persecution as the Context of Paul's Original Ministry in Galatia (Galatians 4.12–20)," *JSNT* 52 (1993): 93–126; Susan Grove Eastman, *Recovering Paul's Mother Tongue: Language and Theology in Galatians* (Grand Rapids: Eerdmans, 2007); Justin K. Hardin, *Galatians and the Imperial Cult: A Critical Analysis of the First-Century Social Context of Paul's Letter*, WUNT 2/237 (Tübingen: Mohr Siebeck, 2008), 101–2; and a summary on Oakes, *Galatians*, 145–46.

19. Oakes, *Galatians*, 145–46.

20. See Oakes, *Galatians*, 146.

21. The similarity of Paul's weakness and the Galatians' is overlooked in, among others, Betz, *Galatians*, 221–23; Longenecker, *Galatians*, 189–91; Dunn, *Galatians*, 231–33; Martyn, *Galatians*, 419–20; Witherington, *Grace in Galatia*, 307–10; de Boer, *Galatians*, 278–81; Moo, *Galatians*, 281–82; Oakes, *Galatians*, 144–47.

22. As recognized by the scholars cited in the previous note.

23. Oakes, *Galatians*, 130–31. The connection between circumcision, burial with the Anointed in baptism, the stripping off of the elemental body of flesh, and the cross is more explicit in Col 2.11–15.

24. Rom 6.1–14 connects the ritual of baptism with the crucifixion of the flesh. See Hays, "Galatians," 238–29; de Boer, *Galatians*, 366–68; Oakes, *Galatians*, 177–78.

25. In Galatians, ὀφθαλμός occurs only in 4.15 and 3.1, where the Galatians' eyes saw Jesus the Anointed portrayed as crucified in Paul's weak flesh.

26. See Stowers, "Paul and Self-Mastery," (ed. Sampley), 282.

27. My reading of the persons in 4.5–6 follows Longenecker, *Galatians*, 172–74; see similarly Witherington, *Grace in Galatia*, 288–89, though he follows D, E, K, and L in reading εἰς τὰς καρδίας ὑμῶν. Matera, *Galatians*, 156 and Hays, "Galatians," 284 read the first ἵνα clause as Jews and the second as Gentile Christians. Betz, *Galatians*, 208 and Dunn, *Galatians*, 216–17 read the first as Jews and the second as all Christians. The majority of scholars read "those under the law," ἀπολάβωμεν, ἐστε, and ἡμῶν as referring to all Christians: Burton, *Galatians*, 219–20; F. F. Bruce, *The Epistle to the Galatians*, NIGTC (Grand Rapids: Eerdmans, 1982), 197–98; Martyn, *Galatians*, 390; de Boer, *Galatians*, 238, 242, 264–65; Moo, *Galatians*, 267, 270.

28. Martyn, *Galatians*, 391–92; Fee, *God's Empowering Presence*, 408–9; de Boer, *Galatians*, 265; Moo, *Galatians*, 269 cite Jeremiah and Ezekiel.

29. Douglas J. Moo, *The Epistle to the Romans*, NICNT (Grand Rapids: Eerdmans, 1996), 107.

30. See the earlier discussion in chapter 4, section B.2. The body and its parts are implicated in sin in 1.24; 3.13–15, 18; 6.6, and the σάρξ is weak in 6.19.

31. I have encountered this observation in none of the sources I have read.

32. The only other volitional agent in Galatians may perhaps be the Galatians' πνεῦμα (Gal 6.18).

The Son and the Spirit Against the Στοιχεῖα and the Flesh   205

33. Contra Dunn, *Galatians*, 301; Moo, *Galatians*, 371, though see Moo's more nuanced comparison of Gal 5.17 with Rom 8.5–6 on 354.

34. Michael Hill, "Paul's Concept of 'Enkrateia,'" *The Reformed Theological Review* 36.3 (1977): 70–78, as discussed by David Charles Aune, "Passions in the Pauline Epistles: The Current State of Research," in *Passions and Moral Progress in Greco-Roman Thought*, ed. John T. Fitzgerald, Routledge Monographs in Classical Studies (London: Routledge, 2008), 232.

35. Friedrich Büchsel, "Θυμός, Ἐπιθυμία, Ἐπιθυμέω, Ἐπιθυμητής, Ἐνθυμέομαι, Ἐνθύμησις," *TDNT* 3:169.

36. Büchsel, "Θυμός," 3:170; David Arthur deSilva, *Reading Paul through Asian Eyes: A Sri Lankan Commentary on Galatians* (Kohuwela: CTS, 2014), 211.

37. Büchsel, "Θυμός," 3:169–70.

38. With Fee, *God's Empowering Presence*, 432–33 and "almost all commentators" (Barclay, *Paul and the Gift*, 446 n. 17), I read τελέσητε as indicative, not imperative as in NRSV.

39. Spirit and flesh are, of course, an established antithetical pair in both Jewish and Greek writings (see Betz, *Galatians*, 277–80; Martyn, *Galatians*, 492–94; Geurt H. van Kooten, *Paul's Anthropology in Context: The Image of God, Assimilation to God, and Tripartite Man in Ancient Judaism, Ancient Philosophy and Early Christianity*, WUNT 232 (Tübingen: Mohr Siebeck, 2008), 384; Oakes, *Galatians*, 174). DeSilva, *Reading Paul through Asian Eyes*, 210–13 notes that Philo contrasts humans "who live by the divine Spirit and reason" with "those who exist according to blood and the pleasure of the flesh" (see *Heir* 57).

40. Dunn, *Galatians*, 300; Gregory K. Beale, "The Old Testament Background of Paul's Reference to 'the Fruit of the Spirit' in Galatians 5:22," *BBR* 15.1 (2005): 20 n. 58. Dunn cites BAGD, *agō* 3 and notes that "the idea of being 'led' by feelings (desire, anger, pleasures), as in 2 Tim. 3:6, was familiar in Greek thought" (see Euripides, *Med.* 310; Plato, *Prot.* 355a; Aristotle, *Eth. nic.* 7.3 1147a).

41. Several scholars note resonance with Luke 4.1, where Jesus ἤγετο ἐν τῷ πνεύματι ἐν τῇ ἐρήμῳ (Dunn, *Galatians*, 300; Moo, *Galatians*, 357 n. 6; Oakes, *Galatians*, 175.). Oakes follows N. T. Wright, "The Letter to the Galatians: Exegesis and Theology," in *Between Two Horizons: Spanning New Testament Studies and Systematic Theology*, ed. Joel B. Green and Max Turner (Grand Rapids: Eerdmans, 2000), 205–36 in "seeing the Jesus movement as a new people being led through the wilderness, with the Spirit as the pillar of cloud going ahead of them." Beale, "Fruit of the Spirit," 13–14 argues that the themes of Spirit, leading, and fruit in Isa 48.16–17; 57.16–18; 63.11–14 are the source for much of Paul's thought in Gal 5.16–23 (see Matthew S. Harmon, *She Must and Shall Go Free: Paul's Isaianic Gospel in Galatians*, BZNW 168 (Berlin: De Gruyter, 2010), 222–25; Moo, *Galatians*, 357 n. 6.).

42. Dunne, "Persecution in Galatians," 297; Oakes, *Galatians*, 172. Witherington, *Grace in Galatia*, 396 follows John Bligh, *Galatians: A Discussion of St Paul's Epistle*, Householder Commentaries 1 (London: St Paul, 1969), 203 in reading ἄγεσθε in 5.18 as a reflexive middle (see Longenecker, *Galatians*, 246.).

43. See John Riches, *Galatians Through the Centuries*, Wiley-Blackwell Bible Commentaries (Oxford: Wiley-Blackwell, 2013), 264–83; Moo, *Galatians*, 354–56.

44. Martyn, *Galatians*, 494–95, 536–40; Jan Lambrecht, "The Right Things You Want to Do: A Note on Galatians 5,17d," *Biblica* 79.4 (1998): 515–24; Oakes, *Galatians*, 174–75. Moo, *Galatians*, 355 also cites Augustine; Calvin; Herman Ridderbos, *The Epistle of Paul to the Churches of Galatia: The English Text with Introduction, Exposition and Notes*, NICNT (Grand Rapids: Eerdmans, 1953), 203–4; Timothy George, *Galatians: An Exegetical and Theological Exposition of Holy Scripture*, NAC (Nashville: Broadman & Holman, 1994), 387–88; Leon L. Morris, *Galatians: Paul's Charter of Christian Freedom* (Downers Grove, IL: InterVarsity Press, 1996), 169; see NLT. While ἐὰν θέλητε can refer to righteous willing (see Isa 1.19), the dejected tone of this reading does not harmonize with the confident hope of the promise in 5.16 (John M. G. Barclay, *Obeying the Truth: A Study of Paul's Ethics in Galatians*, Studies of the New Testament and Its World (Edinburgh: T&T Clark, 1988), 112; Witherington, *Grace in Galatia*, 394; Barclay, *Paul and the Gift*, 428 n. 18).

45. Witherington, *Grace in Galatia*, 395. However, throughout this letter, Paul consistently depicts the Galatian believers as wanting to do right, typically by taking on the law. Only as an ironic consequence of this righteous, but misdirected, desire does he say they "want to be enslaved" to the elements.

46. Longenecker, *Galatians*, 246; Dunn, *Galatians*, 299. Moo, *Galatians*, 356 also cites Franz Mussner, *Der Galaterbrief*, 5th ed., HTKNT 9 (Freiburg: Herder, 1988), 377–78; Troels Engberg-Pedersen, *Paul and the Stoics* (Edinburgh: T&T Clark, 2000), 162–63.

47. So Barclay, *Obeying the Truth*, 110–16; Barclay, *Paul and the Gift*, 428 n. 18; Fee, *God's Empowering Presence*, 436; Hays, "Galatians," 326; see NIV.

48. Moo, *Galatians*, 356.

49. Betz, *Galatians*, 277.

50. deSilva, *Reading Paul through Asian Eyes*, 210–11.

51. Contra Betz, *Galatians*, 178–80; Martyn, *Galatians*, 369; see Barclay, *Paul and the Gift*, 445. Nor does ὑπὸ νόμον refer only to the curse of the law (see Moo, *Galatians*, 357; Barclay, *Paul and the Gift*, 446 n. 22; contra Herman Ridderbos, *Paul: An Outline of His Theology*, trans. John R. de Witt (Grand Rapids: Eerdmans, 1975), 282–83; Todd A. Wilson, *The Curse of the Law and the Crisis in Galatia: Reassessing the Purpose of Galatians*, WUNT 2/225 (Tübingen: Mohr Siebeck, 2007), 117–20).

52. See Barclay, *Obeying the Truth*, 116; *Paul and the Gift*, 428, 438–45. As Moo, *Galatians*, 357 explains, "Christians, *precisely because they are under the influence of the Spirit*, are members of the new-covenant era in which the law of Moses no longer has binding authority" (emphasis mine). Moo cites Longenecker, *Galatians*, 246; Thomas R. Schreiner, *Galatians*, ZECNT (Grand Rapids: Zondervan, 2010), 345.

53. Fee, *God's Empowering Presence*, 438. See Longenecker, *Galatians*, 246–48; Hays, "Galatians," 327; Oakes, *Galatians*, 175.

54. Barclay, *Paul and the Gift*, 429–30.

55. Stephen Westerholm, "On Fulfilling the Whole Law (Gal 5:14)," *SEÅ* 51–52 (1986): 229–37; Barclay, *Obeying the Truth*, 135–42; Fee, *God's Empowering Presence*, 426; Wright, *Paul and the Faithfulness of God*, 1037; Barclay, *Paul and the Gift*, 431.

The Son and the Spirit Against the Στοιχεῖα and the Flesh   207

56. See Walter Grundmann, "Ἐγκράτεια (Ἀκρασία), Ἐγκρατής (Ἀκρατής), Ἐγκρατεύομαι," *TDNT* 2:340–41; Betz, *Galatians*, 288; James W. Thompson, *Moral Formation According to Paul: The Context and Coherence of Pauline Ethics* (Grand Rapids: Baker Academic, 2011), 138, 141; deSilva, *Reading Paul through Asian Eyes*, 218–19; Stowers, "Paul and Self-Mastery" (2016).

57. See Longenecker, *Galatians*, 263.

58. Maren R. Niehoff, *Philo on Jewish Identity and Culture*, TSAJ 86, ed. Martin Hengel and Peter Schäfer (Tübingen: Mohr Siebeck, 2001), 110.

59. Niehoff, *Jewish Identity*, 107, 258; Stowers, "Paul and Self-Mastery" (2016), 278–80; see *Spec. Laws* 1.193; 2.56–214; 4.91–131.

60. Fee, *God's Empowering Presence*, 452; contra Dunn, *Galatians*, 313; Martyn, *Galatians*, 499; see Stanley Kent Stowers, "Paul and Self-Mastery," in *Paul in the Greco-Roman World: A Handbook*, ed. J. Paul Sampley (London: Continuum, 2003), 544; "Paul and Self-Mastery," (2016), 276.

61. Burton, *Galatians*, 318; Longenecker, *Galatians*, 263; Fee, *God's Empowering Presence*, 452; Witherington, *Grace in Galatia*, 410–12; Moo, *Galatians*, 366; Stowers, "Paul and Self-Mastery" (2016).

62. Betz, *Galatians*, 488; Dunn, *Galatians*, 313; Stowers, "Paul and Self-Mastery" (2016), 277.

63. See Betz, *Galatians*, 489; Stowers, "Paul and Self-Mastery" (2016), 280; cf. *Eth. nic.* 7.7.8.

64. Moo, *Galatians*, 366–67, citing Ridderbos, *The Epistle of Paul to the Churches of Galatia*, 208; R. Y. Fung, *The Epistle to the Galatians*, NICNT (Grand Rapids: Eerdmans, 1988), 273; R. Alastair Campbell, "'Against Such Things There Is No Law'? Galatians 5:23b Again," *ExpTim* 107.9 (1996): 271–72; Don Garlington, *An Exposition of Galatians: A New Perspective/Reformational Reading* (Eugene, OR: Wipf and Stock, 2003), 259.

65. Bruce, *Galatians*, 255; Longenecker, *Galatians*, 264; Oakes, *Galatians*, 177.

66. Similarly in 4.6, the Son's Spirit arrives in "our hearts" and cries "Abba, Father."

67. Dunn, *Galatians*, 295; see Moo, *Galatians*, 353–54.

68. Moo, *Galatians*, 353.

69. Longenecker, *Galatians*, 265; Barclay, *Paul and the Gift*, 367 n. 44.

70. Dunn, *Galatians*, 318.

71. Witherington, *Grace in Galatia*, 413; Hays, "Galatians," 328–29; Geurt H. van Kooten, *Cosmic Christology in Paul and the Pauline School: Colossians and Ephesians in the Context of Graeco-Roman Cosmology, with a New Synopsis of the Greek Texts*, WUNT 2/171 (Tübingen: Mohr Siebeck, 2003), 78; Schreiner, *Galatians*, 356–57; de Boer, *Galatians*, 372.

72. Moo, *Galatians*, 372 n. 4. See chapter 4, section B.3.a.

73. See Dunn, *Galatians*, 313; Hays, "Galatians," 329; de Boer, *Galatians*, 372; deSilva, *Reading Paul through Asian Eyes*, 220; Barclay, *Paul and the Gift*, 446 n. 20.

74. See section B.2.b above.

75. Barclay, *Obeying the Truth*, 162–63; Dunn, *Galatians*, 326; Moo, *Galatians*, 382; see de Boer, *Galatians*, 384.

76. See Longenecker, *Galatians*, 278; Dunn, *Galatians*, 327; Moo, *Galatians*, 382; contra Betz, *Galatians*, 304–6; Martyn, *Galatians*, 551. The collocation of σπείρω, √σαρξ, and √πνευμα in Gal 6.8 and 1 Cor 9.11 is unobserved in the literature. See also Rom 15.26–27; 1 Tim. 5.18.

77. Ἐν πᾶσιν . . . ἀγαθοῖς occurs only here and in 3 Kgdms 8.56 (OG).

78. Dunn, *Galatians*, 331–32; Moo, *Galatians*, 387.

79. de Boer, *Galatians*, 386–88; see σπείρω with εἰς in Matt 13.22||Mark 4.18. For the warning, see cultic infidelity as μυκτηρίζω in 2 Chron 36.16; Ezek 8.17.

80. Longenecker, *Galatians*, 281; deSilva, *Reading Paul through Asian Eyes*, 236; see Dunn, *Galatians*, 330.

81. Witherington, *Grace in Galatia*, 431–32; Hays, "Galatians," 336–37; Oakes, *Galatians*, 182–83; see Schreiner, *Galatians*, 369.

82. Dunn, *Galatians*, 330; Fee, *God's Empowering Presence*, 467; Roji T. George, *Paul's Identity in Galatians: A Postcolonial Appraisal* (New Delhi: Christian World Imprints, 2016), 227; see Betz, *Galatians*, 308–9.

83. Wright, *Paul and the Faithfulness of God*, 1069; deSilva, *Reading Paul through Asian Eyes*, 236.

84. Moo, *Galatians*, 388; de Boer, *Galatians*, 389–90; Oakes, *Galatians*, 182–83; see Barclay, *Paul and the Gift*, 430.

85. See chapter 2, section B.3.

86. Contra Moo, *Galatians*, 388. Further, contra Witherington, *Grace in Galatia*, 431, supporting instructors is thus an example, in this particular context, of ἀγαθός, not καλός (Gal 6.6, 9–10; but see Eph 4.28). See also Barclay, *Paul and the Gift*, 438–39.

87. See the thorough defense in Wright, *Paul and the Faithfulness of God*, 1142–51, citing in agreement scholars as varied as Betz, *Galatians*, 322–23; E. P. Sanders, *Paul, the Law, and the Jewish People* (Fortress Press, 1983), 174; Longenecker, *Galatians*, 298–99; Martyn, *Galatians*, 574–77; Witherington, *Grace in Galatia*, 453; Hays, "Galatians," 346; Schreiner, *Galatians*, 381–83; S. J. D. Cohen, "The Letter of Paul to the Galatians," in *The Jewish Annotated New Testament: New Revised Standard Version*, ed. Amy-Jill Levine and Marc Z. Brettler (New York: Oxford University Press, 2011), 344, and others. For "God's Israel" as referring to ethnic Israel, whether all Jews generally or specifically Jews who follow Jesus the Anointed, see Burton, *Galatians*, 357–58; G. Peter Richardson, *Israel in the Apostolic Church* (Cambridge: Cambridge University Press, 1969); Mussner, *Galaterbrief*; Michael Bachmann, *Anti-Judaism in Galatians?: Exegetical Studies on a Polemical Letter and on Paul's Theology*, trans. Robert L. Brawley (Grand Rapids: Eerdmans, 2008), 101–23; Susan Grove Eastman, "Israel and the Mercy of God: A Re-Reading of Galatians 6.16 and Romans 9–11," *NTS* 56 (2010): 369; de Boer, *Galatians*, 404–8. Dunn, *Galatians*, 344–46 reads "God's Israel" as "ethnic Israel and the new movement among Gentiles." More recently see Moo, *Galatians*, 400–403; deSilva, *Reading Paul through Asian Eyes*, 242, agreeing with the majority, and Oakes, *Galatians*, 192; Barclay, *Paul and the Gift*, 420–21; A. Andrew Das, "Galatians 6:16's Riddles and Isaiah 54:10's Contribution: Gentiles Joining the Israel of God?" in *Scripture, Texts, and Tracings*

in Galatians and 1 Thessalonians, ed. by A. Andrew Das and B. J. Oropeza (Lanham, MD: Lexington Books/Fortress Academic, 2023), 133–51, following Eastman et al.

88. Aaron Sherwood, *Paul and the Restoration of Humanity in Light of Ancient Jewish Traditions*, AGJU 82 (Leiden: Brill, 2012), 231; see Moo, *Galatians*, 403 n. 10; Wright, *Paul and the Faithfulness of God*, 1057, 1506–7.

Conclusion

On careful re-examination, Victorinus's commentary proves to be as informed as Donne's poetry is insightful. Applying Emma Wasserman's concept of "discourse" to Paul's mention of enslavement under στοιχεῖα τοῦ κόσμου confirms both of their perspectives.[1] It reveals Paul's phrase as a distinct part of an intelligible contribution to ancient medical discourse on the στοιχεῖα, the weakness of the body, and the regulation of human behavior.

The study applied the method of "discourse" by moving from terms to concepts to arguments. The method not only made meaningful sense of Paul's concerns about enslavement under the στοιχεῖα τοῦ κόσμου but also recorded several original observations.

In chapter 1, the study observed for the first time that the phrase στοιχεῖα κόσμου appears in extant sources as an early Jewish innovation to refer unambiguously to the material elements of which the cosmos and its bodies, including human bodies, are made (Sib. Or. 3.80–81; *Heir* 134, 140; *Eternity* 109; see Col 2.8, 20).[2] It showed further that, for centuries before Paul, Greek philosophers recognized that, by virtue of their interchangeability, the material στοιχεῖα are inherently unstable and weaken the bodies they compose.

In order to explain how weak στοιχεῖα can enslave, chapter 2 connected Gal 4.3, 9 for the first time with the next extant use of στοιχεῖον as the active subject of a δουλ- verb. As Galen writes, whether the soul is "mixed with the substances of the body" or "(merely) takes up residence in bodies, it is subservient (δουλεύει) to their natures, which are, as I have said, derived from some mixture of the four στοιχεῖα" (*Prop. plac.* 15).

Following Galen's prompt, the study showed that, beginning centuries before Paul, Greek and then Jewish sources posited that the weakness of the elemental flesh impedes, or even enslaves, the person, that is, the soul or the spirit. This, according to James Hankinson, is "one of the few genuine commonplaces in ancient moral thought,"[3] and this is what concerns Paul when he says, "We too . . . were enslaved under τὰ στοιχεῖα τοῦ κόσμου."

212   *Conclusion*

Having established that Paul's physiology is elemental, the study analyzed the role of the στοιχεῖα in the pathology of sin, that is, in the παθήματα, ἐπιθυμίαι, and ἔργα τῆς σαρκός. It argued that παθήματα and ἐπιθυμίαι are distinct but complementary processes. While a πάθημα σαρκὸς is a factor that affects a body or person from outside it, an ἐπιθυμία σαρκὸς is an expression of an internal organ. However, each of these is corrupted by sin and, if unhindered, precipitates a sinful ἔργον σαρκός. Finally, all three processes—παθήματα, ἐπιθυμίαι, and ἔργα—are mediated by the στοιχεῖα that compose, and compromise, the σάρξ (Gal 3.22–4.5; 5.13–6.2; see Rom 6–7).

Greek medical discourse recognizes that children and childish people are most susceptible to being corrupted by their weak, elemental flesh, and it recommends a variety of remedies (*Tim.* 44a–b; *Eth. nic.* 2.3; 3.12). The Hippocratic corpus, for example, advises the use of νόμος, and, following Plato, Aristotle prescribes reason as a παιδαγωγός to guide the person and guard against ἐπιθυμία and πάθη (*Aër.* 24 (see *QAM* 801); *Tim.* 87b–89d; *Eth. nic.* 3.10–12). Consonant with the discourse, Paul too describes the law as a sort of παιδαγωγός that scripture imposed to guard and guide Abraham's wayward offspring who, when they were children, were enslaved under τὰ στοιχεῖα τοῦ κόσμου (Gal 3.19–4.3; 5.17–23; see 1 Cor 3.1).[4]

While enslavement under the στοιχεῖα τοῦ κόσμου (which compromise the flesh and allow its corruption by sin) is a persistent concern for Greek medical texts and for Paul, Paul's present concern is the agitators' misuse of the law to address that concern. Using Wasserman's concept of "discourse," the study compared Paul's argument against the agitators with Philo's writings. Chapter 3 showed that Philo advocates observing the law as the effective way (1) to be redeemed from slavery to the flesh, (2) to achieve righteousness, and (3) to live in harmony with the cosmos (see *Moses* 2.48; *Spec. Laws* 4.134). For Philo, these last two ethical benefits depend on the first medical benefit: those who "set the holy laws before them to guide them in all they do or say," are no longer plagued by the body's necessities and the elemental πάθη of cold, heat, dryness, or moisture. Instead, their mind is "redeemed" from "slavery" to the body's "many pleasures and many lusts" (*Rewards* 119, 121, 124; see Deut 7.15; 28.1–14).

This last text is key, though it is rarely cited in studies of Galatians. Corresponding to Deuteronomy's own description of the law's blessings (28.1–14; see 7.15), it stands at the climax of Philo's exegesis of the law's *Rewards* and states plainly one of several reasons he thinks people should take on the law. In light of this significant statement, this study posits the label "redemptive nomism" for Philo's approach to Moses's law.

As chapters 4, 5, and 6 argue, Paul says the mirror opposite of Philo. Life, righteousness, and the inheritance do not come through the law, but from the Son and the Spirit through faith (Gal 2.21; 3.18, 21).

Though Philo claims that circumcision helps a man "supress the superfluous impulses" of his flesh, Paul asserts that being without a foreskin is no more effective than having one (*QG* 3.47; Gal 5.6). The answer to the problem of enslavement under the στοιχεῖα τοῦ κόσμου is not cutting off one extremity of the flesh but rather crucifying the whole thing (Gal 5.24). With the flesh and its stimuli and desires nailed to a cross, believers need no law to guard against sin's metastasis within their weak flesh made of στοιχεῖα (3.19–22; 5.24). Rather, as they align (στοιχέω) with the Spirit, his desiring guides them into righteousness, love, patience, and self-control (Gal 5.5–6, 22–25).

Similarly, watching out carefully for particular days, months, καιροί, and years in order to manage the effects of the material στοιχεῖα τοῦ κόσμου does not lead onward to freedom and harmony with the κόσμος but rather backward to slavery to those "weak and miserable στοιχεῖα" (4.9–10). As this study observed for the first time, adopting Philo's κόσμος:νόμος harmony would be analogous to Abraham, who now knows and is known by God, returning to the astrological determinism of the Chaldeans, to serving things that are not gods (4.8–9). Paul's ideal is not harmony with the cosmos, its στοιχεῖα and its times (καιροί), but crucifixion to the cosmos and alignment (στοιχεῖν) with new creation (Gal 5.14–16). And in that new creation, God promises a harvest in time (καιρός) to those who sow to the Spirit and are diligent in virtuous labor; they will receive many good things to share with instructors, with the family of faith, and with all (Gal 6.6–10).

Thus for Paul, the sending of the Son (who bears his mother's flesh made of στοιχεῖα) and of the Son's Spirit brings the new creation forward into the present evil age (1.4; 4.4–6). In the overlap of the ages, believers are at once dead and alive, crucified with the Anointed, yet living because the Anointed lives in them (2.19–20). But this life is not a concept in their heads. From Paul's perspective, it emanates from the fleshy organ of their heart and activates a very bodily, indeed fleshy, participation in new creation: believers live "ἐν σαρκί" by living "ἐν πίστει . . . τῇ τοῦ υἱοῦ τοῦ θεοῦ" (2.20; 4.6).

With the Son and his Spirit living within believers and producing the sort of loving righteousness appropriate to Abraham's heirs, they have no need of the law as a παιδαγωγός without (3.19–4.7; 4.19; 5.5–6, 16–25). Thus Paul addresses his present concern—reliance on the law for life, righteousness, and the inheritance—by resolving his underlying, persistent concern: enslavement to sin through the flesh composed and compromised by weak στοιχεῖα. Indeed, the Galatians have seen in Paul's life, and experienced in their own, that faith produces loving self-giving apart from the law's guidance (1.4; 2.20–3.1; 4.12–15; 5.6–7, 14). Through the Son and the Spirit, then, and apart from the law, believers from every nation live free of the miserable στοιχεῖα, and they στοιχεῖν with the new creation as the righteous heirs of God's kingdom.

214   *Conclusion*

IMPLICATIONS

This study entails one general and two specific implications. First, it has produced a body of research that demonstrates the validity and profitability of Wasserman's concept of "discourse" as a hermeneutical approach. The study showed that Wasserman's "discourse" can incorporate N. T. Wright's "engagement" and Dean Fleming's "contextualization" as variant forms of "creative elaboration," and that it can assess the mutual intelligibility of texts while avoiding Samuel Sandmel's "parallelomania" and John Barclay's pitfalls of mirror-reading.[5] It is thus a credible method to be tested and developed through further application.

Second, the study has demonstrated the relevance of Greek medical discourse to the study of Pauline and other first-century Jewish writings. While Troels Engberg-Pedersen and Wasserman have argued for the relevance of Stoic and Platonic psychology respectively, this study has introduced the related discipline of physiology to the discussion.[6] The fruitfulness of its contribution as seen in this study suggests that the previously unexplored field of Greek medical discourse has much to offer scholars who investigate the motifs of flesh, body, soul, mind, heart, and, above all, στοιχεῖα and παθήματα in early Jewish writers. The method of "discourse" should bring to light some formerly unappreciated senses within such texts, but it must not be used to prize a predetermined meaning out of a text—or worse, pound one into it. "Discourse" recognizes "creative elaboration" as an "ordinary feature of language," and for texts written across or among cultures—like Philo's, Paul's, the Gospels, and Josephus's—scholars should expect such adaptation as normal. For example, read side by side, Paul uses the common term ψυχή much less frequently than Philo, perhaps because Paul's concept of ψυχή is grounded in the scriptural concept of נפש, and Philo's is attuned to the perspectives dominant in Greek philosophy, especially medical discourse. Most significant among other terms and concepts is the use of σάρξ, especially in Paul, where its identity and influence is legendary. More broadly, there is a need for a sensitive re-examination of the physicality of physiological and psychological terms and concepts in early Jewish writings. Ideally, such a study should compare early Jewish writers not only with Greek medical discourse but also with Jewish traditions beginning in the Hebrew scriptures and running through their old Greek translations.[7]

Third, the study has demonstrated the relevance of Philo to the study of Paul. Some scholars have maintained this for years, but Philo is usually ignored or, at best, raided for a proof text. In contrast, this study has demonstrated a sustained mutual intelligibility between Galatians and Philo's corpus, especially his Exposition of the Law, but also parts of his Allegory

Conclusion   215

of the Law. Quotations from Philo in this study reveal not only similar terms with Galatians, but also similar concepts, corresponding arguments, and, in at least one place, the same peculiar hermeneutical method (Gal 4.21–5.1).[8] With this evidence, the study posits that the agitators in the Galatian assemblies were heavily influenced by an amalgam of early Jewish thought—which I label "redemptive nomism"—most fully articulated by Philo and now most accessible to us in his extensive corpus.

Philo's relevance for the study of Pauline letters is obviously most pertinent to the other "Pauline" use of the phrase this study has studied: τὰ στοιχεῖα τοῦ κόσμου (Col 2.8, 20). Stepping around the significant—but, for purposes of this study, ancillary—question of authorship, the method of "discourse" will likely show that Colossians and Galatians not only use the same term, but do so in the same argument. Colossians uses the phrase "τὰ στοιχεῖα τοῦ κόσμου" to frame a more detailed theology of the physiology of circumcision and baptism, an explicit repudiation of food laws and calendrical events, and a denial of the commandments' ability to restrain the insatiety of the flesh (Col 2.8–23). Indeed, preliminary readings suggest that comparison with Philo may prove even more relevant for Colossians than for Galatians.[9]

Applying the method of "discourse" to Philo and Greek medical discourse has illuminated the hidden meaning of "τὰ στοιχεῖα τοῦ κόσμου" in Galatians and sharpened the contours of its frequently studied motifs of flesh and law. Along with Donne, the study appreciates the real physicality of the human problem of enslavement under the material elements that compose and compromise our "little worlds." And, with Victorinus, it discerns both the agitators' misapplication of the law to remedy that problem and the life-altering hope that Galatians attributes to the Son and the Spirit. There, in "serving Christ," Victorinus says, believers have attained "liberty in their actions under the Spirit's ruling" (139). And there, Paul concludes, God's Israel assembles under the blessing of his peace and mercy (Gal 6.16).

NOTES

1. Wasserman, "Paul among the Philosophers," 393–95.

2. In none of these texts can στοιχεῖα κόσμου refer to immaterial elements—that is, to elementary principles—and in no source before Origen in about AD 240 has στοιχεῖον been shown to denote an elemental spirit (*Hom. Jer.* 10.6).

3. Hankinson, "Actions and Passions," 206; see Tieleman, *Chrysippus' On Affections*, 197.

4. Lull, "Pedagogue."

5. Sandmel, "Parallelomania"; Barclay, "Mirror-Reading"; Fleming, *Contextualization in the New Testament: Patterns for Theology and Mission*; Wright, *Paul and the Faithfulness of God*, 44–45.

6. Engberg-Pedersen, *Paul and the Stoics*; Troels Engberg-Pedersen, *Cosmology and Self in the Apostle Paul: The Material Spirit* (Oxford: Oxford University Press, 2010); Wasserman, "Death of the Soul"; Wasserman, "Paul among the Philosophers"; Wasserman, *The Death of the Soul in Romans 7*.

7. For a step in this direction, see Belinda E. Samari, "Conceptualizations of the Human: The First Domino in Medicine?," in *Medicine in Bible and Talmud* (presented at the European Asociation of Biblical Studies Annual Meeting, Leuven, 2016).

8. See Zurawski, "Paul's Allegory"; Barclay, *Paul and the Gift*, 373–74, 400–401, 409; Ernest Clark, "Listening with Philo to Our Mother Sarah: Assessing the Validity and Value of Allegoresis Implicit in Paul's Use of It," in *Scripture, Texts and Tracings in Galatians*, ed. A. Andrew Das and B. J. Oropeza (Lanham, MD: Lexington/Fortress Academic, 2023), 113–31.

9. See Ernest Clark, "Countering a 'Philosophy According to the Elements of the Cosmos': Reading Colossians in Conversation with Philo of Alexandria," in *Disputed Pauline Consultation* (Society of Biblical Literature Annual Meeting, 2022).

Bibliography

1 En. = 1 Enoch. In *1 Enoch 1: A Commentary on the Book of 1 Enoch, Chapters 1–36; 81–108*, edited by George W. E. Nickelsburg. Hermeneia. Minneapolis: Fortress, 2001.

——. In *1 Enoch 2: A Commentary on the Book of 1 Enoch Chapters 37–82*, edited by George W. E. Nickelsburg and James C. VanderKam. Hermeneia. Minneapolis: Fortress, 2012.

Alcinous. *Didask.* = *Didaskalikos*. In *Alcinoos, Enseignement des doctrines de Platon*, translated by Pierre Louis, edited by J. Whittaker. Collection des universités de France Série grecque 336. Paris: Les Belles Lettres, 1990.

Adams, Edward. *Constructing the World: A Study in Paul's Cosmological Language.* Studies of the New Testament and Its World. Edinburgh: T&T Clark, 2000.

——. "Graeco-Roman and Ancient Jewish Cosmology." In *Graeco-Roman and Ancient Jewish Cosmology*, edited by Jonathan T. Pennington and Sean M. McDonough, 5–27. LNTS 355. London: T&T Clark, 2008.

——. *The Stars Will Fall from Heaven: Cosmic Catastrophe in the New Testament and Its World.* LNTS 347. London: T&T Clark, 2007.

Aletti, Jean-Noël. "Paul's Exhortations in Gal 5,16-25: From the Apostle's Techniques to His Theology." *Biblica* 94, no. 3 (2013): 395–414.

——. "Rm 7.7–25 encore une fois: Enjeux et propositions." *NTS* 48, no. 3 (2002): 358–76.

Alexander of Aphrodisias. *Comm. Metaph.* = *In Aristotelis Metaphysica commentaria.*

——. *Comm. Mete.* = *In Aristotelis Meteorologicorum libros commentaria.*

——. *Fat.* = *De fato.*

Alexander Polyhistor. In DK.

Algra, Keimpe. "Stoic Theology." In *The Cambridge Companion to the Stoics*, edited by Brad Inwood, 153–78. Cambridge: Cambridge University Press, 2003.

Amand de Medieta, David. *Fatalisme et liberté dans l'antiquité grecque.* Amsterdam: Hakkert, 1973.

Ambrosiaster. *Ambrosiastri qui dicitur commentarius in epistulas Paulinas pars III: in epistulas ad Galatas, ad Efesios, ad Filippenses, ad Colosenses, ad Thesalonicenses, ad Timotheum, ad Titum, ad Filemonem.* Edited by Henrich Joseph Vogels. CSEL 81/3. Vienna: Hoelder-Pichler-Tempsky, 1969.

218   *Bibliography*

———. *Commentaries on Galatians–Philemon*. Translated and edited by Gerald L. Bray. ACT. Downers Grove, IL: IVP Academic, 2009.

———. *Commentaries on Romans and 1–2 Corinthians*. Translated and edited by Gerald L. Bray. ACT. Downers Grove, IL: IVP Academic, 2009.

Amir, Y. "Authority and Interpretation of Scripture in the Writings of Philo." In *Mikra: Text, Translation, Reading and Interpretation of the Hebrew Bible in Ancient Judaism and Early Christianity*, edited by M. J. Mulder and Harry Sysling, 1 Literature of the Jewish People in the Period of the Second Temple and the Talmud:421–51. CRINT 2. Assen: Van Gorcum, 1988.

Andersen, F. I. "2 (Slavonic Apocalypse of) Enoch." In *OTP* 1:91–221. 1983.

Anderson, Charles A. *Philo of Alexandria's Views of the Physical World*. WUNT 2/309. Tübingen: Mohr Siebeck, 2011.

Anderson, Hugh. "Maccabees, Books of: Fourth Maccabees." In *ABD*, 4:452–54, 1992.

Anon. Lond. = *The Medical Writings of Anonymus Londinensis*. Edited by W. H. S. Jones. Cambridge Classical Studies. Cambridge: Cambridge University Press, 1947.

Ansari, Asloob Ahmad. "Two Modes of Utterance in Donne's Divine Poems." In *Essays on John Donne: A Quarter Centenary Tribute*, edited by Asloob Ahmad Ansari, 139–56. Aligarh: Aligarh Muslim University, 1974.

Aquinas, Thomas. *Summa theologica*. Translated by the Fathers of the English Dominican Province. 1947. sacred-texts.com/chr/aquinas/summa/index.htm.

———. *Super epistolam b. Pauli ad Galatas lectura: Commentary on Saint Paul's Epistle to the Galatians*. Edited by Joseph Kenny. Translated by Fabian R. Larcher. Aquinas Scripture Series 1. Albany: Magi, 1966. dhspriory.org/thomas/SSGalatia ns.htm.

Aristides. *Apol.* = *Apology*. In *L'apologia di Aristide*, edited by C. Vona. Rome: Facultas Theologica Pontificii Athenaei Lateranensis, 1950.

Aristotelean Corpus. *Div. Arist.* = *Divisiones quae vulgo dicuntur Aristoteleae*. Edited by H. Mutschmann, 1–66. Leipzig: Teubner, 1906.

Aristotle. *Cael.* = *Heavens*. Edited by W. K. C. Guthrie. LCL, 1939.

———. *De an.* = *Soul*. Edited by W. S. Hett. LCL, 1957.

———. *Eth. eud.* = *Eudemian Ethics*. Edited by H. Rackham. LCL, 1935.

———. *Eth. nic.* = *Nicomachean Ethics*. Edited by H. Rackham. LCL, 1926.

———. *Gen. corr.* = *Generation and Corruption*. Edited by Harold H. Joachim. Oxford: Clarendon, 1922.

———. *Metaph.* = *Metaphysics*. Edited by Hugh Treddenick. LCL, 1933.

———. *Part. an.* = *Parts of Animals*. Edited by A. L. Peck. LCL, 1961.

———. *Poet.* = *Poetics*. Edited by Stephen Halliwell. LCL, 1995.

———. *Pol.* = *Politica*. Edited by H. Rackham. LCL, 1932.

———. *Rhet.* = *Rhetoric*. Edited by J. H. Freese. LCL, 1926.

Arnold, Clinton. *The Colossian Syncretism: The Interface Between Christianity and Folk Belief at Colossae*. WUNT 2/77. Tübingen: Mohr Siebeck, 1995.

———. "Returning to the Domain of the Powers: 'Stoicheia' as Evil Spirits in Galatians 4:3,9." *NovT* 38 (1996): 55–76.

Athenagoras, *Leg.* = *Plea* in *Athenagoras: Legatio and De Resurrectione*, edited by William Richard. OECT. Oxford: Clarendon, 1972.

Attridge, Harold W. *The Epistle to the Hebrews: A Commentary on the Epistle to the Hebrews*. Hermeneia. Philadelphia: Fortress, 1989.

Augustine, *Commentary on Galatians*, edited by Eric Plumer. OECS, 2003.

Aune, David Charles. "Passions in the Pauline Epistles: The Current State of Research." In *Passions and Moral Progress in Greco-Roman Thought*, edited by John T. Fitzgerald, 221–37. Routledge Monographs in Classical Studies. London: Routledge, 2008.

Baasland, Ernst. "Persecution: A Neglected Feature in the Letter to the Galatians." *ST* 38 (1984): 135–50.

Bachmann, Michael. *Anti-Judaism in Galatians? Exegetical Studies on a Polemical Letter and on Paul's Theology*. Translated by Robert L. Brawley. Grand Rapids: Eerdmans, 2008.

Bakhtin, Mikhail M. *The Dialogic Imagination: Four Essays*. Edited by Michael Holquist. Translated by Caryl Emerson and Michael Holquist. Austin: University of Texas Press, 1981.

———. *Speech Genres and Other Late Essays*. Austin: University of Texas Press, 1986.

Bandstra, Andrew J. *The Law and the Elements of the World: An Exegetical Study in Aspects of Paul's Teaching*. Kampen: Kok, 1964.

Barclay, John M. G. *Jews in the Mediterranean Diaspora: From Alexander to Trajan (323 BCE – 117 CE)*. Edinburgh: T&T Clark, 1996.

———. "Mirror-Reading a Polemical Letter: Galatians as a Test Case." *JSNT* 31 (1987): 73–93.

———. *Obeying the Truth: A Study of Paul's Ethics in Galatians*. Studies of the New Testament and Its World. Edinburgh: T&T Clark, 1988.

———. *Paul and the Gift*. Grand Rapids: Eerdmans, 2015.

Barnes, Jonathan. "Aristotle." In *The Oxford Companion to the Mind*, 2nd ed. Oxford: Oxford University Press, 2004. oxfordreference.com/10.1093/acref/978019866224 2.001.0001/acref-9780198662242-e-61.

Barrett, C. K. "The Allegory of Abraham, Sarah, and Hagar in the Argument of Galatians." In *Rechtfertigung: Festschrift für Ernst Käsemann zum 70. Geburtstag*, edited by Johannes Friedrich, Wolfgang Pöhlmann, and Peter Stuhlmacher, 1–16. Tübingen: Mohr, 1976.

Bauckham, Richard. "Humans, Animals and the Environment in Genesis 1–3." In *Genesis and Christian Theology*, edited by Nathan MacDonald, Mark W. Elliott, and Grant Macaskill, 175–89. Grand Rapids: Eerdmans, 2012.

———. *Jude, 2 Peter*. WBC 50. Waco, TX: Word, 1983.

Beale, Gregory K. "The Old Testament Background of Paul's Reference to 'the Fruit of the Spirit' in Galatians 5:22." *BBR* 15, no. 1 (2005): 1–38.

———. "Other Religions in New Testament Theology." In *Biblical Faith and Other Religions: An Evangelical Assessment*, edited by David W. Baker, 79–105. Grand Rapids: Kregel, 2004.

220   Bibliography

Becker, J. *Paul: Apostle to Gentiles*. Translated by O. C. Dean, Jr. Louisville, KY: Westminster/John Knox, 1993.

Belleville, Linda. "'Under Law': Structural Analysis and the Pauline Concept of Law in Galatians 3.21–4.11." *JSNT* 26: (1986) 53–78.

Belmonte, Juan Antonio. "In Search of Cosmic Order: Astronomy and Culture in Ancient Egypt." In *The Role of Astronomy in Society and Culture: Proceedings of the 260th Symposium of the International Astronomical Union Held at the UNESCO Headquarters, Paris, France, January 19–23, 2009*, edited by David Valls-Gabaud and Alexander Boksenberg, 74–86. IAU Symposium Proceedings 260. Cambridge: Cambridge University Press, 2011.

Bertram, Georg. "Νήπιος, Νηπιάζω." In *TDNT*, 4:912–23. 1967.

Betz, Hans Dieter. *Galatians: A Commentary on Paul's Letter to the Churches in Galatia*. Hermeneia. Philadelphia: Fortress, 1979.

Bhabha, Homi K. "Culture's In-Between." In *Questions of Cultural Identity*, edited by Stuart Hall and Paul du Gay, 53–60. London: Sage, 1996.

———. *The Location of Culture*. London: Routledge, 1994.

Bickerman, Elias J. *The Jews in the Greek Age*. Cambridge, MA: Harvard University Press, 1988.

Birnbaum, Ellen. *The Place of Judaism in Philo's Thought: Israel, Jews, and Proselytes*. BJS 290. Atlanta: Scholars, 1996.

———. "Two Millennia Later: General Resources and Particular Perspectives on Philo the Jew." *Currents in Biblical Research* 4, no. 2 (2006): 241–76.

Black, David Alan. *Paul, Apostle of Weakness: Astheneia and Its Cognates in the Pauline Literature*. New York: Lang, 1984.

———. *Paul, Apostle of Weakness: Astheneia and Its Cognates in the Pauline Literature*. Rev. ed. Eugene, OR: Pickwick, 2012.

———. "Weakness." In *Dictionary of Paul and His Letters*, edited by Gerald F. Hawthorne, Ralph P. Martin, and Daniel G. Reid, 966–67. Downers Grove, IL: InterVarsity, 1993.

Bligh, John. *Galatians: A Discussion of St Paul's Epistle*. Householder Commentaries 1. London: St Paul, 1969.

Blinzler, Josef. "Lexikalisches zu dem Terminus τὰ στοιχεῖα τοῦ κόσμου bei Paulus." In *Studiorum Paulinorum Congressus Internationalis Catholicus 1961: simul Secundus Congressus Internationalis Catholicus de Re Biblica: completo undevicesimo saeculo post S. Pauli in urbem adventum*, 2:429–43. AnBib 17–18. Rome: Pontifical Biblical Institute, 1963.

Block, Daniel I. "Other Religions in Old Testament Theology." In *Biblical Faith and Other Religions: An Evangelical Assessment*, edited by David W. Baker, 43–78. Grand Rapids: Kregel, 2004.

Böck, Barbara, and Vivian Nutton. "Medicine." In *Brill's New Pauly*, Antiquity volumes edited by Hubert Cancik and Helmuth Schneider. Leiden: Brill, 2006, dx.doi.org/10.1163/1574-9347_bnp_e728380.

Borgen, Peder. "Jesus Christ, the Reception of the Spirit, and a Cross-National Community." In *Jesus of Nazareth: Lord and Christ; Essays on the Historical Jesus*

Bibliography 221

and New Testament Christology, edited by Joel B. Green and Max Turner, 220–35. Grand Rapids: Eerdmans, 1994.

———. "Observations on the Theme 'Paul and Philo': Paul's Preaching of Circumcision in Galatia (Gal. 5:11) and Debates on Circumcision in Philo." In *Die paulinische Literatur und Theologie: The Pauline Literature and Theology: Anlässlich der 50. Jährigen Gründungs-Feier der Universitat von Aarhus*, edited by Sigfred Pedersen, 85–102. Scandinavian Contributions; Teologiske Studier 7. Århus: Aros, 1980.

———. "Philo and the Jews in Alexandria." In *Ethnicity in Hellenistic Egypt*, edited by Per Bilde, Troels Engberg-Pedersen, Lise Hannestad, and Jan Zahle, 122–38. Studies in Hellenistic Civilization 3. Århus: Århus University Press, 1992.

———. *Philo of Alexandria: An Exegete for His Time*. Leiden: Brill, 1997.

———. "Some Hebrew and Pagan Features in Philo's and Paul's Interpretations of Hagar and Ishmael." In *The New Testament and Hellenistic Judaism*, edited by Peder Borgen and Søren Giversen, 151–64. Peabody, MA: Aarhus University Press, 1997.

Böttrich, C. *Weltweisheit, Menschheitsethik, Urkult: Studien zum slavischen Henochbuch*. WUNT 2/50. Tübingen: Mohr, 1992.

Bourdieu, Pierre. *The Field of Cultural Production: Essays on Art and Literature*. Edited by Randal Johnson. New York: Columbia University Press, 1993.

Bourdieu, Pierre, and J. D. Wacquant. *An Invitation to Reflexive Sociology*. Chicago: University of Chicago Press, 1992.

Bousset, Wilhelm. *Jüdisch-Christlicher Schulbetrieb in Alexandria und Rom*. Göttingen: Vandenhoeck & Ruprecht, 1914.

Bousset, Wilhelm, and H. Gressmann. *Die Religion des Judentums im späthellenistischen Zeitalter*. 3rd ed. HNT 21. Tübingen: Mohr, 1966.

Brandenburger, Egon. *Fleisch und Geist: Paulus und die dualistische Weisheit*. WMANT 29. Neukirchen-Vluyn: Neukirchener, 1968.

Brayford, Susan. *Genesis*. Septuagint Commentary. Leiden: Brill, 2007.

Brown, William P. *Structure, Role, and Ideology in the Hebrew and Greek Texts of Genesis 1:1–2:3*. SBLDS. Atlanta: Scholars, 1993.

Bruce, F. F. *The Epistle to the Galatians*. NIGTC. Grand Rapids: Eerdmans, 1982.

———. *Epistles to the Colossians, to Philemon and to the Ephesians*. NICNT. Grand Rapids: Eerdmans, 1995.

Büchsel, Friederich. "Ἀλληγορέω." In *TDNT*, 1:260–63. 1964.

———. "Θυμός, Ἐπιθυμία, Ἐπιθυμέω, Ἐπιθυμητής, Ἐνθυμέομαι, Ἐνθύμησις." In *TDNT*, 3:167–72. 1965.

Buitenwerf, Rieuwerd. *Book III of the Sibylline Oracles and Its Social Setting: With an Introduction, Translation, and Commentary*. SVTP 17. Leiden: Brill, 2003.

Bultmann, Rudolf. "Romans 7 and the Anthropology of Paul." In *Existence and Faith: Shorter Writings of Rudolf Bultmann*, translated by Schubert Ogden, 173–85. London: Collins, 1960.

Bundrick, D. R. "Ta Stoicheia tou Kosmou (Gal. 4:3)." *JETS* 34 (1991): 353–64.

Burkert, Walter. "Στοιχεῖον. Eine semasiologische Studie." *Phil* 103 (1959): 167–197.

222 Bibliography

Burton, Ernest De Witt. *A Critical and Exegetical Commentary on the Epistle to the Galatians*. ICC. Edinburgh: T&T Clark, 1921.

Busch, Peter. *Das Testament Salomos. Die älteste christliche Dämonologie, kommentiert und in deutscher Erstübersetzung.* TUGAL 153. Berlin: de Gruyter, 2006.

Byrne, Brendan. *Romans*. SP 6. Collegeville, MN: Liturgical, 1996.

Cain, Andrew, trans. *St. Jerome: Commentary on Galatians*. FC 121. Washington, D.C.: Catholic University of America Press, 2010.

Calabi, Francesca. *The Language and the Law of God: Interpretation and Politics in Philo of Alexandria*. South Florida Studies in the History of Judaism. Atlanta: Scholars, 1998.

Calvert-Koyzis, Nancy. *Paul, Monotheism and the People of God: The Significance of Abraham Traditions for Early Judaism and Christianity*. Edited by Mark Goodacre. JSNTSup 273. London: T&T Clark, 2004.

Calvin, John. *Commentaries on the Epistles of Paul to the Galatians and Ephesians*. Translated by William Pringle. Edinburgh: Calvin Translation Society, 1854.

———. *Commentarii in quatuor Pauli epistolas: Ad Galatas, ad Ephesios, ad Philippenses, ad Colossenses*. Geneva: Jean Gérard, 1548.

Campbell, Douglas A. *The Deliverance of God: An Apocalyptic Rereading of Justification in Paul*. Grand Rapids: Eerdmans, 2009.

Campbell, R. Alastair. "'Against Such Things There Is No Law'? Galatians 5:23b Again." *Expository Times* 107, no. 9 (1996): 271–72.

Carny, P. "Dimuyim Merkaziyim Ba-Teoryah Ha-Allegoristit Shel Filon." In *Meḥqarim Be-Sifrut Ha-Talmud, Bi-Leshon Ḥazal Uvefarshanut Ha-Miqra (Studies in Talmudic Literature, in Post-Biblical Hebrew and in Biblical Exegesis)*, edited by Mordechai Akiva Friedman, Avraham Tal, and Gershon Brin, 251–59. Te'udah 3. Tel Aviv: Tel Aviv University Press, 1983.

———. "Ha-Yesodot He-Hagutiyim Shel Darshanut Filon Ha-Aleksandroni." *Daat* 14 (1985): 5–19.

Carr, W. *Angels and Principalities*. SNTSMS 42. Cambridge: Cambridge University Press, 1981.

Chesnutt, Randall D. "Solomon, Wisdom of." In *EDEJ*, 1242–44. 2010.

Christiansen, Irmgard. *Die Technik der allegorischen Auslegungswissenschaft bei Philon von Alexandrien*. Beiträge zur Geschichte der biblischen Hermeneutik 7. Tübingen: Mohr, 1969.

Chrysostom, John. "The Commentary and Homilies of St. John Chrysostom Archbishop of Constantinople, on the Epistles of St. Paul the Apostle to the Galatians and Ephesians." Translated by Gross Alexander. In *NPNF* 13:ix–172, 1889.

———. "The Commentary and Homilies of St. John Chrysostom Archbishop of Constantinople, on the Epistles of St. Paul the Apostle to the Philippians, Colossians, and Thessalonians." Translated by John Broadus. In *NPNF* 13:173–398, 1889.

Ciampa, Roy E. and Brian S. Rosner. *The First Letter to the Corinthians*. PNTC. Grand Rapids: Eerdmans, 2010.

Cicero. *Leg. = De legibus*. Translated by Clinton W. Keyes. LCL, 1928.

———. *Tusc.* = *Tusculanae disputationes*. Translated by J. E. King. LCL, 1927.

Clark, Ernest P. "Countering a 'Philosophy According to the Elements of the Cosmos': Reading Colossians in Conversation with Philo of Alexandria." Paper presented to the Disputed Paulines Consultation at the SBL Annual Meeting, Denver, 2022.

———. "Listening with Philo to Our Mother Sarah: Assessing the Validity and Value of Allegoresis Implicit in Paul's Use of It." In *Scripture, Texts and Tracings in Galatians*. Edited by A. Andrew Das and B. J. Oropeza, 113–31. Lanham, MD: Lexington Books/Fortress Academic, 2023.

———. "'What Sort of Persons Ought You to Be?' Early Christian Identity and the Dissolution of the Elements in 2 Peter." Paper presented at Muted Voices Conference, Durham, April 2015.

Clement, T. Flavius, of Alexandria. Translated by William Wilson. *ANF* 2:171–587, 1885.

———. *The Exhortation to the Greeks. The Rich Man's Salvation. To the Newly Baptized*. Translated by G. W. Butterworth. LCL, 1919.

———. *Ecl.* = *Extracts from the Prophets*. In *Clemens Alexandrinus*, edited by L. Früchtel, O. Stählin, and U. Treu, 137–55. Vol. 3. 2nd ed. GCS 17. 1970.

———. *Paed.* = *Christ the Educator*. In *Clément d'Alexandrie. Le pedagogue*, edited by M. Harl, H.-I. Marrou, C. Matray, and C. Mondésert. 3 vols. SC 70, 108, 158. 1960, 1956, 1970.

———. *Protr.* = *Exhortation to the Greeks*. In *Clément d'Alexandrie. Le protreptique*, edited by C. Mondésert. 2nd ed. SC 2, 1949.

———. *Strom.* = *Miscellanies*. In *Clemens Alexandrinus*, edited by L. Früchtel, O. Stählin, and U. Treu. Vol. 2, 3rd ed. and vol. 3, 2nd ed. GCS 52 (15), 17. 1960, 1970.

Cockerill, Gareth Lee. *The Epistle to the Hebrews*. NICNT. Grand Rapids: Eerdmans, 2012.

Cohen, S. J. D. "The Letter of Paul to the Galatians." In *The Jewish Annotated New Testament: New Revised Standard Version*, edited by Amy-Jill Levine and Marc Z. Brettler, 332–44. New York: Oxford University Press, 2011.

Coleridge, Samuel Taylor. *Collected Letters*. Edited by E. L. Griggs. 6 vols. Oxford: Oxford University Press, 1956.

Coles, Kimberly Anne. "The Matter of Belief in John Donne's Holy Sonnets." *Renaissance Quarterly* 68 (2015): 899–931.

Collins, Billie Jean, Bob Buller, and John F. Kutsko, eds. *The SBL Handbook of Style*. 2nd ed. Atlanta: SBL, 2014.

Collins, John J. "Sibylline Oracles." In *OTP*, 1:317–472. 1983.

———. "Sibylline Oracles." In *ABD*, 6:2–6, 1992.

Colson, F. H. et al., trans. *Philo*. 10 vols. LCL. Cambridge, MA: Harvard University Press, 1929–62.

Cooper, Stephen Andrew. *Marius Victorinus' Commentary on Galatians*. OECS. Oxford University Press, 2005. oxfordscholarship.com/view/10.1093/0198270275 .001.0001/acprof-9780198270270.

Cornford, F. M. "Mysticism and Science in the Pythagorean Tradition." *CQ* 16 (1922): 142–50.

Bibliography

Cosgrove, Charles H. *The Cross and the Spirit: A Study in the Argument and Theology of Galatians*. Macon, GA: Mercer University Press, 1988.

Cousar, C. B. *Galatians*. Interpretation. Louisville, KY: John Knox, 1982.

Cranfield, C. E. B. *A Critical and Exegetical Commentary on the Epistle to the Romans*. 2 vols. ICC. Edinburgh: T&T Clark, 1975.

Crowley, Timothy J. "Aristotle's 'So-Called Elements.'" *Phronesis* 53 (2008): 223–42, doi:10.1163/156852808X307061.

Daigle, Erica Nicole. "Reconciling Matter and Spirit: The Galenic Brain in Early Modern Literature." PhD thesis, University of Iowa, 2009.

Daniel, Robert W. "The Testament of Solomon XVIII 27–28, 33–40." In *Festschrift zum 100-Jährigen Bestehen der Papyrussammlung der Österreichische Nationalbibliothek: Papyrus Erzeherzog Rainer*, 1:294–304. Vienna: Brüder Holinek, 1983.

Das, A. Andrew. "Galatians 6:16's Riddles and Isaiah 54:10's Contribution: Gentiles Joining the Israel of God?" In *Scripture, Texts, and Tracings in Galatians and 1 Thessalonians*, edited by A. Andrew Das and B. J. Oropeza, 133–51. Lanham, MD: Lexington Books/Fortress Academic, 2023.

Davids, Peter H. *The Letters of 2 Peter and Jude*. PNTC. Grand Rapids: Eerdmans, 2006.

Davies, J. P. *Paul Among the Apocalypses? An Evaluation of the "Apocalyptic Paul" in the Context of Jewish and Christian Apocalyptic Literature*. LNTS 562. London: T&T Clark, 2016.

Davies-Browne, Bankole P. "The Significance of Parallels between the Testament of Solomon and Jewish Literature of Late Antiquity (between the Closing Centuries BCE and the Talmudic Era) and the New Testament." Ph.D. thesis, University of St Andrews, 2004.

Davila, James R. *The Provenance of the Pseudepigrapha: Jewish, Christian, or Other?* JSJS 105. Leiden: Brill, 2005.

Davis, Basil S. "The Meaning of ΠΡΟΕΓΡΑΦΗ in the Context of Galatians 3.1." *NTS* 45 (1999): 194–212.

de Boer, Martinus C. *Galatians: A Commentary*. NTL. Louisville, KY: Westminster John Knox, 2011.

———. "The Meaning of the Phrase τα στοιχεια του κοσμου in Galatians." *NTS* 53 (2007): 204–24.

Delling, Gerhard. "Στοιχέω, Συστοιχέω, Στοιχεῖον." In *TDNT*, 7:666–87. 1971.

deSilva, David Arthur. *4 Maccabees: Introduction and Commentary on the Greek Text in Codex Sinaiticus*. Septuagint Commentary Series. Leiden: Brill, 2006.

———. *Galatians: A Handbook on the Greek Text*. Baylor Handbook on the Greek New Testament. Waco, TX: Baylor University Press, 2014.

———. *Reading Paul through Asian Eyes: A Sri Lankan Commentary on Galatians*. Kohuwela: CTS, 2014.

———. "X Marks the Spot?: A Critique of the Use of Chiasmus in Macro-Structural Analyses of Revelation." *JSNT* 30, no. 3 (2008): 343–71. doi:10.1177/01420 64X07088407.

Di Mattei, Steven. "Paul's Allegory of the Two Covenants (Gal 4.21-31) in Light of First-Century Hellenistic Rhetoric and Jewish Hermeneutics." *NTS* 52 (2006): 102–122. doi:10.1017/S0028688506000063.

Dibelius, Martin. *Die Geisterwelt im Glauben des Paulus*. Göttingen: Vandenhoeck & Ruprecht, 1909.

Dickey, Eleanor. "Longinus." In *The Oxford Encyclopedia of Ancient Greece and Rome*, edited by Michael Gagarin. Oxford: Oxford University Press, 2010. oxfordreference.com/view/10.1093/acref/9780195170726.001.0001/acref-9780195170726-e-727.

Diels, Hermann. *Elementum: Eine Vorarbeit zum griechischen und lateinischen Thesaurus*. Leipzig: Teubner, 1899.

Dillmann, August. *Das Buch Henoch*. Leipzig: Vogel, 1853.

Dillon, John M., ed. *Alcinous: The Handbook of Platonism*. Clarendon Later Ancient Philosophers. Oxford: Oxford University Press, 1993.

———. *The Middle Platonists, 80 B.C. to A.D. 220*. Ithaca, NY: Cornell University Press, 1996.

———. *The Middle Platonists: A Study of Platonism, 80 BC to AD 220*. London: Duckworth, 1977.

———. "Platonism, Middle." In *Oxford Classical Dictionary*, edited by Simon Hornblower and Antony Spawforth. 3rd rev. ed. Oxford: Oxford University Press, 2005. oxfordreference.com/view/10.1093/acref/9780198606413.001.0001/acref-9780198606413-e-5117.

———. "A Response to Runia and Sterling." *SPhilo* 5 (1993): 151–55.

Diogenes Laertius. *Vit. philos.* = *Lives of Eminent Philosophers*, translated by R. D. Hicks. 2 vols. LCL, 1925.

DiTommaso, Lorenzo. "Sibylline Oracles." In *EDEJ*, 1226–28. 2010.

Dodd, C. H. *The Epistle of Paul to the Romans*. MNTC. London: Collins, 1959.

Donini, Pierluigi. "Psychology." In *The Cambridge Companion to Galen*, edited by R. J. Hankinson, 184–209. Cambridge: Cambridge University Press, 2008.

Donne, John. *Complete English Poems*. Edited by C. A. Patrides. 2nd ed. Everyman Library. London: J. M. Dent, 1994.

———. *The Sermons of John Donne*. Edited by Evelyn Mary Simpson and George Reuben Potter. 10 vols. Berkeley: University of California Press, 1953.

Douglas, Mary. *Thinking in Circles: An Essay on Ring Composition*. New Haven, CT: Yale University Press, 2007.

Duling, Dennis C. "Testament of Solomon." In *OTP*, 1:935–87. 1983.

Dunn, James D. G. *Christianity in the Making*. Vol. 2, *Beginning from Jerusalem*. Grand Rapids: Eerdmans, 2009.

———. *The Epistle to the Galatians*. BNTC. London: A & C Black, 1993.

———. *The Epistles to the Colossians and to Philemon: A Commentary on the Greek Text*. NIGTC. Grand Rapids: Eerdmans, 1996.

———. *The New Perspective on Paul: Collected Essays*. Tübingen: Mohr Siebeck, 2005.

———. *Romans*. 2 vols. WBC. Waco, TX: Word, 1988.

226 Bibliography

Dunne, John Anthony. "Persecution in Galatians: Identity, Destiny, and the Use of Isaiah." Ph.D. thesis, University of St Andrews, 2016. research-repository.st-andrews.ac.uk/handle/10023/8569.

Eastman, Susan Grove. "Israel and the Mercy of God: A Re-Reading of Galatians 6.16 and Romans 9–11." *NTS* 56 (2010): 367–95.

———. *Recovering Paul's Mother Tongue: Language and Theology in Galatians.* Grand Rapids: Eerdmans, 2007.

Édart, Jean-Baptiste. "De la nécessité d'un Sauveur: Rhétorique et théologie de Rm 7,7–25." *RB* 105, no. 3 (1998): 359–96. doi:10.2307/44089394.

Ellis, E. Earle. *History and Interpretation in New Testament Perspective.* Biblical Interpretation 54. Leiden: Brill, 2001.

Empedocles. *The Poem of Empedocles.* Edited by Brad Inwood, rev. ed. Phoenix Pre-Socratics 3. Toronto: University of Toronto Press, 2001.

Engberg-Pedersen, Troels. *Cosmology and Self in the Apostle Paul: The Material Spirit.* Oxford: Oxford University Press, 2010.

———. *Paul and the Stoics.* Edinburgh: T&T Clark, 2000.

Epicurus. *Ep. Men. = Epistula ad Menoeceum.* In Diogenes Laertius, *Lives* 2:528–678.

Esler, Philip F. *Galatians.* New Testament Readings. London: Routledge, 1998.

Euripides. *Andr. = Andromache.* In *Euripidis fabulae,* edited by J. Diggle, 1:277–332. Oxford: Clarendon, 1984.

———. *Med. = Medea.*

Eusebius. *Praep. ev. = Praeparatio evangelica.*

Everling, Otto. *Die paulinische Angelologie und Dämonologie: ein biblisch-theologischer Versuch.* Göttingen: Vandenhoeck & Ruprecht, 1888.

Fee, Gordon D. *The First Epistle to the Corinthians.* NICNT. Grand Rapids: Eerdmans, 1987.

———. *God's Empowering Presence: The Holy Spirit in the Letters of Paul.* Peabody, MA: Hendrickson, 1994.

Feldman, Louis H. *Flavius Josephus: Translation and Commentary.* Vol. 3. Leiden: Brill, 2000.

———. *Josephus and Modern Scholarship 1937–1980.* Berlin: de Gruyter, 1984.

———. "Josephus Flavius." In *Encyclopedia of the Dead Sea Scrolls,* edited by Lawrence H. Schiffman and James C. VanderKam, 1:427–31. Oxford: Oxford University Press, 2000.

Fernández Marcos, Natalio. "Rewritten Bible or Imitatio? The Vestments of the High Priest." In *Studies in the Hebrew Bible, Qumran, and the Septuagint Presented to Eugene Ulrich,* edited by Peter W. Flint, Emanuel Tov, and James C. VanderKam, 321–36. VTSup 101. Leiden: Brill, 2006.

Fetzer, Margret. *John Donne's Performances: Sermons, Poems, Letters and Devotions.* Manchester: Manchester University Press, 2010.

Fitzgerald, John T. "The Passions and Moral Progress: An Introduction." In *Passions and Moral Progress in Greco-Roman Thought,* edited by John T. Fitzgerald, 1–25. Routledge Monographs in Classical Studies. London: Routledge, 2008.

Fitzmyer, Joseph A. *Romans: A New Translation with Introduction and Commentary.* AB. New York: Doubleday, 1993.

Fleming, Dean. *Contextualization in the New Testament: Patterns for Theology and Mission.* Downers Grove, IL: InterVarsity, 2005.

Franxman, Thomas W. *Genesis and the "Jewish Antiquities" of Flavius Josephus.* BibOr 35. Rome: Biblical Institute, 1979.

Freudenthal, Gad. "The Astrologization of the Aristotelian Cosmos: Celestial Influences on the Sublunary World in Aristotle, Alexander of Aphrodisias, and Averroes." In *New Perspectives on Aristotle's De Caelo,* edited by Alan C. Bowen and Christian Wildberg, 239–82. PHA 117. Leiden: Brill, 2009.

Frisch, Alexandria, and Lawrence H. Schiffman. "The Body in Qumran Literature: Flesh and Spirit, Purity and Impurity in the Dead Sea Scrolls." *DSD* 23: 155–82, 2016. doi:10.1163/15685179-12341386.

Fung, R. Y. *The Epistle to the Galatians.* NICNT. Grand Rapids: Eerdmans, 1988.

Galen. *CC = On Containing Causes.* Arabic, edited and translated by Malcolm Lyons, 51–73; Latin, edited by J. Kollesch, D. Nickel, G. Strohmaier, 131–41. CMG Suppl. Or. 2, 1969.

————. *Hipp. Elem. = The Elements According to Hippocrates.* Edited and translated by Phillip De Lacy. CMG 5.1.2, 1996.

————. *HNH = Galeni in Hippocratis de natura hominis commentaria tria.* Edited by J. Mewaldt, 3–88. CMG 5.9.1, 1914.

————. *HNH = Commentary on Hippocrates' "Nature of Man."* Translated by W. J. Lewis and J. A. Beach. Medicina Antiqua. 1998. ucl.ac.uk/~ucgajpd/medicina%20antiqua/tr_GNatHom.html.

————. *Opt. med. = The Best Doctor is also a Philosopher.* Edited by E. Wenkebach. In "Der hippokratische Arzt als das Ideal Galens," *Quellen und Studien zur Geschichte der Naturwissenschaften und Medizin* 3, no. 4 (1933): 170–75.

————. *Opt. med. = The Best Doctor is also a Philosopher.* In *Galen: Selected Works,* translated by Peter N. Singer. Oxford: Oxford University Press, 1997.

————. *PHP = The Doctrines of Hippocrates and Plato.* Edited and translated by Phillip De Lacy. CMG 5.4.1.2, 1978.

————. *Prop. plac. = My Own Doctrines.* In *On My Own Opinions,* edited and translated by Vivian Nutton. CMG 5.3.2, 1999.

————. *QAM = The Capacities of the Soul.* In *Galen: Psychological Writings,* edited and translated by Peter N. Singer, 333–424. Cambridge Galen Translations. Cambridge: Cambridge University Press, 2013.

————. *Temp. = Mixtures.* In *Galeni de temperamentis libri iii,* edited by G. Helmreich, 1–115. Leipzig: Teubner, 1904.

————. *Temp. = Mixtures.* In *Galen: Selected Works,* translated by Peter N. Singer. Oxford: Oxford University Press, 1997.

Gallavotti, Carlo. *Empedocle: poema fisico e lustrale.* Milan: Mondadori, 1975.

García Martínez, Florentino, ed. *The Dead Sea Scrolls Translated: The Qumran Texts in English.* Translated by Wilfred G. E. Watson. 2nd ed. Leiden: Brill, 1996.

García Martínez, Florentino and Eibert J. C. Tigchelaar, eds. *The Dead Sea Scrolls: Study Edition.* Leiden: Brill, 1997.

Garlington, Don. *An Exposition of Galatians: A New Perspective/Reformational Reading.* Eugene, OR: Wipf and Stock, 2003.

Gaventa, Beverly R. "Galatians 1 and 2: Autobiography as Paradigm." *NovT* 28 (1986): 309–26.

George, Roji T. *Paul's Identity in Galatians: A Postcolonial Appraisal.* New Delhi: Christian World Imprints, 2016.

George, Timothy. *Galatians: An Exegetical and Theological Exposition of Holy Scripture.* NAC. Nashville: Broadman & Holman, 1994.

Georgi, Dieter. *The Opponents of Paul in Second Corinthians.* Rev. ed. Philadelphia: Fortress, 1986.

Gerdmar, Anders. *Rethinking the Judaism-Hellenism Dichotomy: A Historiographical Study of Second Peter and Jude.* ConBNT 36. Stockholm: Almqvist & Wiksell International, 2001.

Gill, Christopher. "Did Galen Understand Platonic and Stoic Thought on the Emotions?" In *The Emotions in Hellenistic Philosophy*, edited by Juha Sihvola and Troels Engberg-Pedersen, 113–48. The New Synthese Historical Library 46. Dordrecht: Kluwer, 1998.

———. "Galen and the Stoics: Mortal Enemies or Blood Brothers?" *Phronesis: A Journal of Ancient Philosophy* 52, no. 1 (2007): 88–120.

———. "Galen versus Chrysippus on the Tripartite Psyche in Timaeus 69–72." In *Interpreting the Timaeus–Critias: Proceedings of the IV Symposium Platonicum; Selected Papers*, edited by Tomás Calvo Martínez and Luc Brisson, 267–73. International Plato Studies 9. Saint Augustin: Academia, 1997.

———. *Naturalistic Psychology in Galen and Stoicism.* Oxford: Oxford University Press, 2010.

———. "The School in the Roman Imperial Period." In *The Cambridge Companion to the Stoics*, edited by Brad Inwood, 33–58. Cambridge: Cambridge University Press, 2003.

Glessner, Justin M. "Ethnomedical Anthropology and Paul's 'Thorn' (2 Corinthians 12:7)." *BTB* 47, no. 1 (2017): 15–46. doi:10.1177/0146107916682197.

Goddard, A. J., and S. A. Cummins. "Ill or Ill-Treated? Conflict and Persecution as the Context of Paul's Original Ministry in Galatia (Galatians 4.12–20)." *JSNT* 52 (1993): 93–126.

Goodenough, Erwin R. *An Introduction to Philo Judaeus.* 2nd ed. Brown Classics in Judaica. Oxford: Blackwell, 1962.

Gordon, T. David. "A Note on Παιδαγωγος in Galatians 3.24–25." *NTS* 35 (1989): 150–154. doi:10.1017/S0028688500024553.

Gorman, Michael J. *Inhabiting the Cruciform God: Kenosis, Justification, and Theosis in Paul's Narrative Soteriology.* Grand Rapids: Eerdmans, 2009.

Green, Barbara. *Mikhail Bakhtin and Biblical Scholarship: An Introduction.* SBL Semeia Studies. Atlanta: SBL, 2000.

Green, Gene L. *Jude and 2 Peter.* BECNT. Grand Rapids: Baker, 2008.

Grundmann, Walter. "Ἐγκράτεια (Ἀκρασία), Ἐγκρατής (Ἀκρατής), Ἐγκρατεύομαι." In *TDNT*, 2:339–42. 1964.

Gundel, Wilhelm. *Dekane und Dekansternbilder: Ein Beitrag zur Geschichte der Sternbilder der Kultervölker.* 1st ed. Studien der Bibliothek Warburg 19. Glückstadt und Hamburg: J. J. Augustin, 1969.

Bibliography

Gundry, Robert H. "The Moral Frustration of Paul Before His Conversion: Sexual Lust in Romans 7:7–25." In *Pauline Studies: Essays Presented to Professor F. F. Bruce on His 70th Birthday*, edited by Donald A. Hagner and Murray J. Harris, 228–45. Exeter: Paternoster, 1980.

Hafemann, Scott J. "Paul and the Exile of Israel in Galatians 3–4." In *Exile: Old Testament, Jewish, and Christian Conceptions*, edited by James M. Scott, 329–71. JSJS 56. Leiden: Brill, 1997.

———. "The Role of Suffering in the Mission of Paul." In *The Mission of the Early Church to Jews and Gentiles*, edited by Jostein Ådna and Hans Kvalbein, 165–84. WUNT 127. Tübingen: Mohr Siebeck, 2000.

Hankinson, R. James. "Actions and Passions: Affection, Emotion, and Moral Self-Management in Galen's Philosophical Psychology." In *Passions & Perceptions: Studies in Hellenistic Philosophy of Mind; Proceedings of the Fifth Symposium Hellenisticum*, edited by Jacques Brunschwig and Martha Craven Nussbaum, 184–222. Cambridge: Cambridge University Press, 1993.

———. "Galen's Anatomy of the Soul." *Phronesis*, 36, no. 2 (1991): 197–233.

Hansen, G. Walter. *Galatians*. IVP New Testament Commentary 9. Downers Grove, IL: InterVarsity, 1994.

Hanson, Richard P. C. *Allegory and Event: A Study of the Sources and Significance of Origen's Interpretation of Scripture*. London: SCM, 1959.

———. *The Search for the Christian Doctrine of God: The Arian Controversy 318–381*. London: T&T Clark, 2005.

Hardin, Justin K. *Galatians and the Imperial Cult: A Critical Analysis of the First-Century Social Context of Paul's Letter*. WUNT 2/237. Tübingen: Mohr Siebeck, 2008.

Harmon, Matthew S. *She Must and Shall Go Free: Paul's Isaianic Gospel in Galatians*. BZNW 168. Berlin: de Gruyter, 2010.

Harper, G. Geoffrey. "Time for a New Diet? Allusions to Genesis 1–3 as Rhetorical Device in Leviticus 11." Paper presented at the International Meeting of the Society of Biblical Literature, St Andrews, 2013.

Hay, David M. "Philo's References to Other Allegorists." *SPhilo* 6 (1979): 41–76.

Hays, Richard B. *Echoes of Scripture in the Letters of Paul*. New Haven, CT: Yale University Press, 1989.

———. *The Faith of Jesus Christ: The Narrative Substructure of Galatians 3:1–4:11*. 2nd ed. Grand Rapids: Eerdmans, 2002.

———. "The Letter to the Galatians: Introduction, Commentary, and Reflections." In *The New Interpreter's Bible*, 11:181–348. Nashville: Abingdon, 2000.

Heiser, Michael S. "Deuteronomy 32:8 and the Sons of God." *BSac* 158 (2001): 52–74.

Hermas, Shepherd of. *Vis.* = *Vision*. In *Die apostolischen Väter I. Der Hirt des Hermas*, edited by M. Whittaker. GCS 48, 2nd ed. 1967.

Hesiod. *Op.* = *Opera et Dies*.

Hill, Michael. "Paul's Concept of 'Enkrateia.'" *RTR* 36, no. 3 (1977): 70–78.

230   *Bibliography*

Hippocrates and the Hippocratic Corpus. *Œuvres complètes d'Hippocrate*. Edited by Émile Littré. 9 vols. Paris: Baillière, 1839–61. (Reprint Amsterdam: Hakkert, 1961–73.)

   Aër. = *Airs, Waters, Places*
   Aph. = *Aphorisms*
   Nat. hom. = *Nature of Man*

———. "The Letter to the Galatians: Introduction, Commentary, and Reflections." In *The New Interpreter's Bible*, 11:181–348. Nashville: Abingdon, 2000.

Heiser, Michael S. "Deuteronomy 32:8 and the Sons of God." *BSac* 158 (2001): 52–74.

Hermas, Shepherd of. *Vis.* = *Vision*. In *Die apostolischen Väter I. Der Hirt des Hermas*, edited by M. Whittaker. GCS 48, 2nd ed. 1967.

Hesiod. *Op.* = *Opera et Dies*.

Hill, Michael. "Paul's Concept of 'Enkrateia.'" *RTR* 36, no. 3 (1977): 70–78.

Hippocrates and the Hippocratic Corpus. *Œuvres complètes d'Hippoc*

———. *Hippocratic Writings*. Translated by J. Chadwick and W. N. Mann. Edited by G. E. R. Lloyd. 2nd ed. Harmondsworth: Penguin, 1978.

Holladay, Carl R., ed. *Fragments from Hellenistic Jewish Authors*. 4 vols. Texts and Translations 20, 30, 39–40. Atlanta: Scholars, 1983–96.

Holquist, Michael. *Dialogism: Bakhtin and His World*. London: New Accents, 1990.

Homer. *Iliad*. Translated by A. T. Murray. Revised by William F. Wyatt. 2 vols. LCL, 1924–25.

Hong, In-Gyu. *The Law in Galatians*. JSNTSup 81. Sheffield: JSOT, 1993.

Horsley, R. A. "The Law of Nature in Philo and Cicero." *HTR* 71 (1978): 35–59.

Hübner, Hans. "Paulusforshung seit 1945: Ein kritischer Literaturbericht." *ANRW* 25.4:2691–94. Part 2, *Principat*, 25.4, edited by H. Temporini and W. Haase. Berlin: de Gruyter, 1987.

Hunger, Hermann. "The Relation of Babylonian Astronomy to Its Culture and Society." In *The Role of Astronomy in Society and Culture: Proceedings of the 260th Symposium of the International Astronomical Union Held at the UNESCO Headquarters, Paris, France, January 19–23, 2009*, edited by David Valls-Gabaud and Alexander Boksenberg, 62–73. IAU Symposium Proceedings 260. Cambridge: Cambridge University Press, 2011.

Hymn. Orph. = *Hymni Ophici*. In *Orphei hymni*, edited by W. Quandt. 3rd ed. Berlin: Weidmann, 1962.

Inwood, Brad, ed. *The Poem of Empedocles*. Rev. ed. Phoenix Pre-Socratics 3. Toronto: University of Toronto Press, 2001.

Irenaeus. *Haer.* = "Against Heresies: On the Detection and Refutation of the Knowledge Falsely So Called." In *Irenaeus of Lyons*, translated by Robert McQueen Grant. The Early Church Fathers. London: Routledge, 1997.

———. *Haer.* = *Against the Heresies, Book 3*. Edited by M. C. Steenberg. Translated by Dominic J. Unger. Ancient Christian Writers 64. New York: Newman, 2012.

———. *Haer.* In *Irénée de Lyon: Contre les hérésies, Livre 3*, edited by François Sagnard, Adelin Rousseau, and Louis Doutreleau. 2 vols. SC 210–211, 1974.

———. *Haer.* In *Sancti Irenaei episcopi Lugdunensis libri quinque adversus haereses*, edited by W. W. Harvey. Cambridge: Cambridge University Press, 1857.

Bibliography 231

Jerome. *Comm. Gal.* = *S. Hieronymi Presbyteri Opera, Pars I, Opera exegetica 6: Commentarii in Epistulam Pauli Apostoli ad Galatas.* Edited by Giacomo Raspanti. CCSL 77a. 2006.

———. *Comm. Gal.* = *Commentary on Galatians.* Translated by Andrew Cain. FC 121. 2010.

———. *Vir. ill.* = *De viris illustribus.*

Jewett, Robert. *Paul's Anthropological Terms: A Study of Their Use in Conflict Settings.* AGJU 10. Leiden: Brill, 1971.

Johnston, David. "The Problem of Romans 7." Ph.D. thesis, University of St Andrews, 2017.

Josephus, Flavius. *Flavius Josephus: Translation and Commentary.* Edited by Steve Mason. 10 vols. Leiden: Brill, 2000–2017.

———. *Works.* Edited by Ralph Marcus, H. St J. Thackeray, and Allen Wikgren. 9 vols. LCL, 1927–1965.

Ag. Ap. = *Against Apion* (*C. Ap.*)

Ant. = *Jewish Antiquities* (*A. J.*)

J. W. = *Jewish War* (*B. J.*)

Life = *The Life* (*Vita*)

Jubilees. "Jubilees." Edited by O. S. Wintermute. *OTP* 2:35–142. 1983.

———. In "Liber Jubilaeorum," in *Fragmenta Pseudepigraphorum Quae Supersunt Graeca*, edited by Albert-Marie Denis, 70–101. PVTG 3. 1970.

Justin Martyr. *2 Apol.* = *Second Apology.* In *Justin, Philosopher and Martyr, Apologies*, edited by D. Minns and P. Parvis, 270–322. OECT. 2009.

———. *Dial.* = *Dialogue with Trypho.* In *Die ältesten Apologeten*, edited by E. J. Goodspeed, 90–265. Göttingen: Vandenhoeck & Ruprecht, 1915.

Juza, Ryan P. "Echoes of Sodom and Gomorrah on the Day of the Lord: Intertextuality and Tradition in 2 Peter 3:7–13." Paper presented at the Annual Meeting of the Institute for Biblical Research, Chicago, 16 November 2012.

Kamesar, Adam. "Biblical Interpretation in Philo." In *The Cambridge Companion to Philo*, edited by Adam Kamesar, 65–92. Cambridge: Cambridge University Press, 2009.

Käsemann, Ernst. *Commentary on Romans.* Translated by Geoffrey W. Bromiley. Grand Rapids: Eerdmans, 1980.

———. "The Righteousness of God in Paul." In *New Testament Questions for Today*, edited by Ernst Käsemann, 168–82. Philadelphia: Fortress, 1969.

Keesmaat, Sylvia C. "Paul and His Story: Exodus and Tradition in Galatians." *Horizons in Biblical Theology* 18, no. 1 (1996): 133–68. doi:10.1163/187122096X00077.

———. *Paul and His Story: (Re)Interpreting the Exodus Tradition.* LNTS 181. Sheffield: Sheffield Academic, 1999.

Kerns, Loren. "Platonic and Stoic Passions in Philo of Alexandria." Ph.D. diss., London: Kings College London, 2013. digitalcommons.georgefox.edu/gfes/6.

Klöpper, Albert. *Der Brief an die Colosser: Kritisch untersucht und in seinem Verhältnisse zum paulinischen Lehrbegriff exegetisch und biblisch-theologisch erörtert.* Berlin: Reimer, 1882.

232 *Bibliography*

Klutz, Todd. *Rewriting the Testament of Solomon: Tradition, Conflict, and Identity in a Late Antique Pseudepigraphon.* LSTS 53. London: T&T Clark, 2006.

Koester, Craig R. *Hebrews: A New Translation with Introduction and Commentary.* AB 36. New York: Doubleday, 2001.

Koester, Helmut. "ΝΟΜΟΣ ΦΥΣΕΩΣ: The Concept of Natural Law in Greek Thought." In *Religions in Antiquity: Essays in Memory of Erwin Ramsdell Goodenough,* edited by Jacob Neusner, 521–41. SHR14. Leiden: Brill, 1968.

Kolarcik, Michael. "The Book of Wisdom: Introduction, Commentary, and Reflections." In *The New Interpreter's Bible,* 5:435–600. Nashville: Abingdon, 2000.

Kraftchick, S. "Death in Us, Life in You: The Apostolic Medium." In *Pauline Theology,* edited by David M. Hay, 2: 1 & 2 Corinthians:156–81. Minneapolis: Fortress, 1993.

Krentz, E. *Galatians, Philippians, Philemon, 1 Thessalonians.* ACNT. Minneapolis: Augsburg, 1985.

Kruse, Colin G. *Paul's Letter to the Romans.* PNTC. Grand Rapids: Eerdmans, 2012.

Kuhn, Thomas S. *The Structure of Scientific Revolutions.* Chicago: University of Chicago Press, 1962.

Lagercrantz, Otto. *Elementum: Eine lexikologische Studie.* Skrifter utgifna af K. Humanistiska Vetenskaps-Samfundet i Uppsala XI.1. Uppsala: Akademiska Bokhandeln, 1911.

Lambrecht, Jan. "The Right Things You Want to Do: A Note on Galatians 5,17d." *Biblica* 79, no. 4 (1998): 515–24.

Lane, William L. *Hebrews 1–8.* WBC 47A. Dallas: Word, 1991.

Larcher, Fabian R., trans. *Thomas Aquinas: Super epistolam b. Pauli ad Galatas lectura: Commentary on Saint Paul's Epistle to the Galatians.* Aquinas Scripture Series 1. Albany: Magi, 1966. dhspriory.org/thomas/SSGalatians.htm.

Leithart, Peter J. *Delivered from the Elements of the World: Atonement, Justification, Mission.* Downers Grove, IL: IVP Academic, 2016.

Lightfoot, J. B. *Saint Paul's Epistle to the Galatians: A Revised Text with Introduction, Notes, and Dissertations.* London: Macmillan, 1887.

Lightfoot, Jane L., ed. *The Sibylline Oracles: With Introduction, Translation, and Commentary on the First and Second Books.* Oxford: Oxford University Press, 2007.

Lloyd, D. R. "Symmetry and Asymmetry in the Construction of 'Elements' in the Timaeus." *CQ* 56 (2006): 459–74.

Lloyd, G. E. R. "Scholarship, Authority and Argument in Galen's *Quod Animi Mores.*" In *Le opere psicologiche di Galeno: Atti del terzo colloquio Galenico Internazionale, Pavia, 10–12 settembre 1986,* edited by Paola Manuli and Mario Vegetti, 11–22. Elenchos 13. Naples: Bibliopolis, 1988.

Long, A. A., and D. N. Sedley, eds. *The Hellenistic Philosophers.* 2 vols. Cambridge: Cambridge University Press, 1987.

Longenecker, Bruce. *The Triumph of Abraham's God: The Transformation of Identity in Galatians.* Edinburgh: T&T Clark, 1998.

Longenecker, Richard. *Biblical Exegesis in the Apostolic Period.* Grand Rapids: Eerdmans, 1974.

Bibliography 233

———. *Galatians*. WBC 41. Dallas: Word, 1990.

———. "The Pedagogical Nature of the Law in Galatians 3:19–4:7." *JETS* 25, no. 1 (1982): 53–61.

Longrigg, James. "Elements and After: A Study in Presocratic Physics of the Second Half of the Fifth Century." *Apeiron: A Journal for Ancient Philosophy and Science* 19, no. 2 (1985): 93–115.

———. *Greek Medicine: From the Heroic to the Hellenistic Age: A Source Book*. London: Duckworth, 1998.

———. *Greek Rational Medicine: Philosophy and Medicine from Alcmaeon to the Alexandrians*. London: Routledge, 1993.

Lührmann, D. "Tage, Monate, Jahreszeiten, Jahre (Gal 4,10)." In *Werden und Wirken des alten Testaments: Festschrift für Claus Westermann zum 70. Geburtstag*, edited by Rainer Albertz, 428–45. Göttingen: Vandenhoeck & Ruprecht, 1980.

Lull, David J. "'The Law Was Our Pedagogue': A Study in Galatians 3:19–25." *JBL* 105 (1986): 481–98.

Luther, Martin. *A Commentary on Saint Paul's Epistle to the Galatians*. Philadelphia: John Highland, 1891.

———. *Die Epistel S. Paul an die Galater*. Wittenberg: Steiner, 1525.

Mack, Burton L. "Philo Judaeus and Exegetical Traditions in Alexandria." *ANRW* 227–71. Part 2, *Principat*, 21.1, edited by Wolfgang Haase. Berlin: de Gruyter, 1984.

Malherbe, Abraham J. "Hellenistic Moralists and the New Testament." *ANRW* 267–333. Part 2, *Principat*, 26.1, edited by Hildegard Temporini and Wolfgang Haase. Berlin: de Gruyter, 1992.

Marcus Aurelius, *Med.* = *Meditations*, in *The Meditations of the Emperor Marcus Aurelius*, edited by A.S.L. Farquharson, 4–250. Oxford: Clarendon, 1944.

Marcus, Joel. "The Evil Inclination in the Epistle of James." *CBQ* 44, no. 4 (1982): 606–21.

———. "The Evil Inclination in the Letters of Paul." *IBS* 8, no. 1 (1986): 8–21.

Marcus, Ralph, ed. *Philo: Supplements*. LCL. 2 vols. London: Heinemann, 1953.

Martin, Dale B. *The Corinthian Body*. New Haven, CT: Yale University Press, 1995.

———. "Paul and the Judaism/Hellenism Dichotomy: Toward a Social History of the Question." In *Paul Beyond the Judaism/Hellenism Divide*, edited by Troels Engberg-Pedersen, 29–62. Louisville, KY: Westminster John Knox, 2001.

Martin, Troy W. "Pagan and Judeo-Christian Time-Keeping Schemes in Gal 4.10 and Col 2.16." *NTS* 42 (1996): 105–19. doi:dx.doi.org/10.1017/S0028688500017100.

———. "Paul's Pneumatological Statements and Ancient Medical Texts." In *The New Testament and Early Christian Literature in Greco-Roman Context: Studies in Honor of David E. Aune*, edited by John Fotopoulos. NovTSup 122. Leiden: Brill, 2006.

Martyn, James Louis. *Galatians: A New Translation with Introduction and Commentary*. AB 33A. New York: Doubleday, 1997.

Matera, Frank J. *Galatians*. Collegeville, MN: Liturgical, 1992.

Mazzeo, Joseph A. "Notes on John Donne's Alchemical Imagery." *Isis* 48 (1957): 103–23.

234 Bibliography

McCaulley, Esau. *Sharing in the Son's Inheritance: Davidic Messianism and Paul's Worldwide Interpretation of the Abrahamic Land Promise in Galatians.* LNTS London: T&T Clark, 2019.

McCown, C. C. *The Testament of Solomon.* Leipzig: Hinrichs, 1922.

McCruden, Kevin B. "2 Peter and Jude." In *The Blackwell Companion to the New Testament*, edited by David Edward Aune, 596–612. Blackwell Companions to Religion. Chichester: Wiley-Blackwell, 2010.

McFarland, Orrey. "The God Who Gives: Philo and Paul in Conversation." Ph.D. thesis, Durham University, 2013. etheses.dur.ac.uk/9409/.

Meeks, Wayne A. "Judaism, Hellenism, and the Birth of Christianity." In *Paul Beyond the Judaism/Hellenism Divide*, edited by Troels Engberg-Pedersen, 17–28. Louisville, KY: Westminster John Knox, 2001.

Meiser, Martin. *Galater.* NTP 9. Göttingen: Vandenhoeck & Ruprecht, 2007.

Mendelson, Alan. *Philo's Jewish Identity.* BJS 161. Atlanta: Scholars, 1988.

Meynet, R. "La rhétorique biblique et sémitique: État de la question." *Rhetorica* 28, no. 3 (2010): 290–312.

Michaelis, Wilhelm. "Πάσχω, Παθητός, Προπάσχω, Συμπάσχω, Πάθος, Πάθημα, Συμπαθής, Συμπαθέω, Κακοπαθέω, Συγκακοπαθέω, Κακοπάθεια, Μετριοπαθέω, Ὁμοιοπαθής, Πραϋπάθεια." In *TDNT*, 5:904–39. 1967.

Mitternacht, Dieter. *Forum für Sprachlose: Eine kommunikationspsychologische und epistolär-rhetorische Untersuchung des Galaterbriefs.* ConBNT 30. Stockholm: Almqvist & Wiksell, 1999.

Montanari, Franco. *The Brill Dictionary of Ancient Greek.* Edited by Madeleine Goh and Chad Schroeder. Leiden: Brill, 2015.

Moo, Douglas J. *2 Peter, and Jude.* NIVAC. Grand Rapids: Zondervan, 1996.

———. *The Epistle to the Romans.* NICNT. Grand Rapids: Eerdmans, 1996.

———. *Galatians.* BECNT. Grand Rapids: Baker, 2013.

———. *The Letters to the Colossians and to Philemon.* PNTC. Grand Rapids: Eerdmans, 2008.

Moore-Crispin, D. R. "Galatians 4:1–9: The Use and Abuse of Parallels." *EvQ* 60 (1989): 203–23.

Morris, Leon L. *Galatians: Paul's Charter of Christian Freedom.* Downers Grove, IL: InterVarsity, 1996.

Morrison, J. S. "Pythagoras of Samos." *CQ* 6 (1956): 152–56.

Moses, Robert Ewusie. *Practices of Power: Revisiting the Principalities and Powers in the Pauline Letters.* Minneapolis: Fortress, 2014.

Murphy, Roland E. "*Yēṣer* in the Qumran Literature." *Biblica* 39 (1958): 334–44.

Mussner, Franz. *Der Galaterbrief.* 5th ed. HTKNT 9. Freiburg: Herder, 1988.

Najman, Hindy. "The Law of Nature and the Authority of Mosaic Law." *SPhilo* 11 (1999): 55–73.

Nanos, Mark D. *The Irony of Galatians: Paul's Letter in First-Century Context.* Minneapolis: Fortress, 2002.

Ness, Lester J. "Astrology and Judaism in Late Antiquity." Ph.D. diss., University of Miami (Ohio), 1990. smoe.org/arcana/diss.html.

Bibliography

Neyrey, Jerome H., ed. *2 Peter, Jude: A New Translation with Introduction and Commentary*. AB 37C. New York: Doubleday, 1993.

Nickelsburg, George W. E., and James C. VanderKam. *1 Enoch 2: A Commentary on the Book of 1 Enoch Chapters 37–82*. Edited by Klaus Baltzer. Hermeneia. Minneapolis: Fortress, 2012.

Niehoff, Maren R. "Philo, Allegorical Commentary." In *EDEJ*, 1070–72. 2010.

———. "Philo, Exposition of the Law." In *EDEJ*, 1074–76. 2010.

———. *Philo on Jewish Identity and Culture*. TSAJ 86. Tübingen: Mohr Siebeck, 2001.

Nikiprowetzky, Valentin. *Le commentaire de l'Écriture chez Philon d'Alexandrie: son caractère et sa portée, observations philologiques*. ALGHJ 11. Leiden: Brill, 1977.

———. "Sur une lecture démonologique de Philon d'Alexandre: *De Gigantibus*, 6–18." In *Études Philoniennes*, 217–42. Patrimoines Judaïsme. Paris: Cerf, 1996.

Nutton, Vivian. "Mental Illness." In *Brill's New Pauly*, Antiquity volumes edited by Hubert Cancik and Helmuth Schneider. Leiden: Brill, 2006. dx.doi.org/10.1163/1574-9347_bnp_e420640.

Oakes, Peter. *Galatians*. Paideia: Commentaries on the New Testament. Grand Rapids: Baker Academic, 2015.

O'Brien, Peter T. *Colossians*. WBC 44. Waco, TX: Word, 1982.

———. *The Letter to the Hebrews*. PNTC. Grand Rapids: Eerdmans, 2010.

Oepke, Albrecht. *Der Brief des Paulus an die Galater*. Edited by Joachim Rohde. 3rd ed. THKNT 9. Berlin: Evangelische Verlagsanstalt, 1973.

Origen Adamantinus, *Cels.* = *Against Celsus*, in *Origen: Contra Celsum*. Edited by Henry Chadwick. Cambridge: Cambridge University Press, 1965.

———. *Comm. Jo.* = *Commentary on the Gospel according to John. Books 13–32*. Translated by Ronald E. Heine. FC 89, 1993.

———. *Comm. Rom.* = *Commentary on Romans*. Edited by A. Ramsbotham in "Documents: The Commentary of Origen on the Epistle to the Romans." *JTS* 13 (1912): 210–24, 357–68; 14 (1912): 10–22.

———. *Comm. Rom.* = *Commentary on Romans*. Edited by O. Bauernfeind, 91–119, in *Der Römerbrieftext des Origenes nach dem codex von der Goltz*. TU 44.3, 1923.

———. *Comm. Rom.* = *Commentary on Romans*. Edited by K. Staab in "Neue Fragmente aus dem Kommentar des Origenes zum Römerbrief." *BZ* 18 (1928): 74–82.

———. *Comm. Rom.* = *Commentary on Romans*. Edited by J. Scherer, 124–232, in *Le commentaire d'Origène sur Rom. III.5–V.7*. Cairo: L'Institut Français d'Archéologie Orientale, 1957.

———. *Hom. Jer.* = *Homilies on Jeremiah* in *Origen: Homilies on Jeremiah; Homily on 1 Kings 28*. Translated by John Clark Smith. FC 97. 2010.

———. *Hom. Num.* = *Homilies on Numbers*

Pearce, Sarah J. K. *The Land of the Body: Studies in Philo's Representation of Egypt*. WUNT 2/208. Tübingen: Mohr Siebeck, 2007.

Pennington, Jonathan T., and Sean M. McDonough, eds. *Cosmology and New Testament Theology*. LNTS 355. London: T&T Clark, 2008.

Philo. *Animals* = *Whether Animals Have Reason*, in *Philonis Alexandrini de Animalibus: The Armenian Text with an Introduction, Translation, and Commentary*.

Translated by Abraham Terian. Studies in Hellenistic Judaism: Supplements to *Studia Philonica* 1. Chico, CA: Scholars, 1981.

———. *On the Creation of the Cosmos according to Moses*. Translated by David T. Runia. Philo of Alexandria Commentary 1. Leiden: Brill. 2001.

———. *Works*. Edited by F. H. Colson, G. H. Whitaker, J. W. Earp, and Ralph Marcus. 12 vols. LCL, 1929–53.

Abraham = *On the Life of Abraham* (*Abr.*). Vol. 6, 1935.

Agriculture = *On Agriculture* (*Agr.*). Vol. 3, 1930.

Alleg. Interp. = *Allegorical Interpretation* (*Leg.*). Vol. 1, 1929.

Cherubim = *On the Cherubim* (*Cher.*). Vol. 2, 1929.

Confusion = *On the Confusion of Tongues* (*Conf.*). Vol. 4, 1932.

Contempl. Life = *On the Contemplative Life* (*Contempl.*). Vol. 9, 1941.

Creation = *On the Creation of the World* (*Opif.*). Vol. 1, 1929.

Decalogue = *On the Decalogue* (*Decal.*). Vol. 7, 1937.

Dreams = *On Dreams* (*Somn.*). Vol. 5, 1934.

Drunkenness = *On Drunkenness* (*Ebr.*). Vol. 3, 1930.

Embassy = *On the Embassy to Gaius* (*Legat.*). Vol. 10, 1962.

Eternity = *On the Eternity of the World* (*Aet.*). Vol. 9, 1941.

Flaccus = *Against Flaccus* (*Flacc.*). Vol. 9, 1941.

Flight = *On Flight and Finding* (*Flug.*). Vol. 5, 1934.

Giants = *On Giants* (*Gig.*). Vol. 2, 1929.

God = *On God* (*Deo*). Vol. 5, 1934.

Good Person = *That Every Good Person is Free* (*Prob.*). Vol. 9, 1941.

Heir = *Who is the Heir?* (*Her.*). Vol. 4, 1932.

Hypothetica (*Hypoth.*). Vol. 9, 1941.

Joseph = *On the Life of Joseph* (*Ios.*). Vol. 6, 1935.

Migration = *On the Migration of Abraham* (*Migr.*). Vol. 4, 1932.

Moses = *On the Life of Moses* (*Mos.*). Vol. 6, 1935.

Names = *On the Change of Names* (*Mut.*). Vol. 5, 1934.

Planting = *On Planting* (*Plant.*). Vol. 3, 1930.

Posterity = *On the Posterity of Cain* (*Post.*). Vol. 2, 1929.

Prelim. Studies = *On the Preliminary Studies* (*Congr.*). Vol. 4, 1932.

Providence = *On Providence* (*Prov.*). Vol. 9, 1941.

QE = *Questions and Answers on Exodus* (*QE*). Suppl. 2, 1953.

QG = *Questions and Answers on Genesis* (*QG*). Suppl. 1, 1953.

Rewards = *On Rewards and Punishments* (*Praem.*). Vol. 8, 1939.

Sacrifices = *On the Sacrifices of Cain and Abel* (*Sacr.*). Vol. 2, 1929.

Sobriety = *On Sobriety* (*Sobr.*). Vol. 3, 1930.

Spec. Laws = *On the Special Laws* (*Spec.*). Vols. 7–8, 1937, 1939.

Unchangeable = *That God is Unchangeable* (*Deus*). Vol. 3, 1930.

Virtues = *On the Virtues* (*Virt.*). Vol. 8, 1939.

Worse = *That the Worse Attacks the Better* (*Det.*). Vol. 2, 1929.

Plato. *Leg.* = *Laws*. Edited by Robert G. Bury. LCL, 1926.

———. *Prot.* = *Protagoras*. Edited by W. R. M. Lamb. LCL, 1924.

Bibliography 237

————. *Resp.* = *Republic.* Edited by Christopher Emlyn-Jones and William Preddy. LCL, 2013.

————. *Tim.* = *Timaeus.* Edited by Robert G. Bury. LCL, 1929.

Plumer, Eric, ed. *Augustine's Commentary on Galatians.* OECS. Oxford: Oxford University Press, 2003. oxfordscholarship.com/view/10.1093/0199244391.001.00 01/acprof-9780199244393.

Plutarch. *Is. Os.* = *De Iside et Osiride.*

————. *Quaest. rom.* = *Quaestiones romanae et graecae (Aetia romana et graeca)*

Porter, Stanley E., and Jeffrey T. Reed. "Philippians as a Macro-Chiasm and Its Exegetical Significance." *NTS* 44, no. 2 (1998): 213–31. doi:10.1017/S0028688500016489.

Posidonius, *Poseidonios. Die Fragmente.* Edited by Willy Theiler. 2 vols. TC 10. Berlin: de Gruyter, 1982.

Preisendanz, K. "Ein Wiener Papyrusfragment zum Testamentum Salomonis." *Eos* 48 (1956): 161–67.

Pyle, Andrew. *Atomism and Its Critics: Problem Areas Associated with the Development of the Atomic Theory of Matter from Democritus to Newton.* Bristol: Thoemmes, 1995.

Radice, Roberto. "Philo's Theology and Theory of Creation." Translated by Adam Kamesar. In *The Cambridge Companion to Philo,* edited by Adam Kamesar, 124–45. Cambridge: Cambridge University Press, 2009.

Radice, Roberto, and David T. Runia. *Philo of Alexandria: An Annotated Bibliography 1937–1986.* Leiden: Brill, 1988.

Reicke, Bo. "The Law and This World According to Paul: Some Thoughts Concerning Gal 4:1–11." *JBL* 70 (1951): 259–76.

Resurrection in *Athenagoras: Legatio and De Resurrectione.* Edited by William Richard. Oxford Early Christian Texts. Oxford: Clarendon, 1972.

Reydams-Schils, Gretchen J. *Demiurge and Providence: Stoic and Platonist Readings of Plato's "Timaeus."* Monothéismes et Philosophie 2. Turnhout: Brepols, 1999.

Richardson, G. Peter. *Israel in the Apostolic Church.* Cambridge: Cambridge University Press, 1969.

Riches, John. *Galatians Through the Centuries.* Wiley-Blackwell Bible Commentaries. Oxford: Wiley-Blackwell, 2013.

Ridderbos, Herman. *The Epistle of Paul to the Churches of Galatia: The English Text with Introduction, Exposition and Notes.* NICNT. Grand Rapids: Eerdmans, 1953.

————. *Paul: An Outline of His Theology.* Translated by John R. de Witt. Grand Rapids: Eerdmans, 1975.

Ritschl, Albrecht. *Die christliche Lehre von der Rechtfertigung und Versöhnung.* Bonn: Adolph Marcus, 1874.

————. *Die christliche Lehre von der Rechtfertigung und Versöhnung.* Vol. 2, *Der biblische Stoff der Lehre.* Bonn: Adolph Marcus, 1882.

Robert, Mark Edwards. "Weak Enough to Lead: Paul's Response to Criticism and Rivals in 2 Corinthians 10–13: A Rhetorical Reading." Ph.D. diss., Vanderbilt University, 2002.

238   *Bibliography*

Robertson, Archibald, and Alfred Plummer. *A Critical and Exegetical Commentary on the First Epistle of St Paul to the Corinthians.* 2nd ed. ICC. Edinburgh: T&T Clark, 1914.

Rohde, J. *Der Brief Des Paulus an Die Galater.* THKNT 9. Berlin: Evangelische Verlagsanstalt, 1989.

Röhr, Julius. "Beiträge zur antiken Astrometeorologie." *Phil* 83 (1928): 259–305.

Royse, James R. "The Works of Philo." In *The Cambridge Companion to Philo,* edited by Adam Kamesar, 32–64. Cambridge: Cambridge University Press, 2009.

Runia, David T. *On the Creation of the Cosmos according to Moses.* Philo of Alexandria Commentary 1. Leiden: Brill, 2001.

———. "Philo I 12. Ph. of Alexandria (Philo Judaeus)." In *Brill's New Pauly,* Antiquity volumes edited by Hubert Cancik and Helmuth Schneider. Leiden: Brill, 2006. dx.doi.org/10.1163/1574-9347_bnp_brill110010.

———. *Philo in Early Christian Literature: A Survey.* CRINT 3. Assen: Van Gorcum, 1993.

———. *Philo of Alexandria and the "Timaeus" of Plato.* PHA 44. Leiden: Brill, 1986.

Rusam, Dietrich. "Neue Belege zu den στοιχεῖα τοῦ κόσμου (Gal 4,3.9; Kol 2,8.20)." *ZNW* 83 (1992): 119–25.

Russell, Walt. "Insights from Postmodernism's Emphasis on Interpretive Communities in the Interpretation of Romans 7." *JETS* 37, no. 4 (1994): 511–27.

Sagnard, François, Adelin Rousseau, and Louis Doutreleau, eds. *Irénée de Lyon: Contre les hérésies, Livre 3.* 2 vols. SC 210–211. Paris: Cerf, 1974.

Samari, Belinda E. "Conceptualizations of the Human: The First Domino in Medicine?" Paper presented at the Annual Meeting of the European Association of Biblical Studies. Leuven, 17–20 July 2016.

Sanders, E. P. *Paul and Palestinian Judaism.* Philadelphia: Fortress, 1977.

———. *Paul, the Law, and the Jewish People.* Philadelphia: Fortress, 1983.

Sandmel, Samuel. "Parallelomania." *JBL* 81, no. 1 (1962): 1–13.

———. *Philo of Alexandria: An Introduction.* Oxford: Oxford University Press, 1979.

Sandnes, Karl Olav. *Belly and Body in the Pauline Epistles.* SNTSMS 120. Cambridge: Cambridge University Press, 2002.

Schatzki, Theodore R. "Practiced Bodies: Subjects, Genders, and Minds." In *The Social and Political Body,* edited by Theodore R. Schatzki and Wolfgang Natter, 49–77. New York: Guilford, 1996.

———. *The Site of the Social: A Philosophical Account of the Constitution of Social Life and Change.* University Park, PA: Penn State University Press, 2002.

———. *Social Practices: A Wittgensteinian Approach to Human Activity and the Social.* Cambridge: Cambridge University Press, 1996.

Scheu, Lawrence E. *Die "Weltelemente" beim Apostel Paulus (Gal. 4,3.9 und Kol. 2,8.20).* Universitas Catholica Americae 37. Washington: Catholic University of America, 1933.

Schlatter, Adolf. *Gottes Gerechtigkeit.* Stuttgart: Calwer, 1959.

Schlier, Heinrich. *Der Brief an die Galater.* KEK 7. Göttingen: Vandenhoeck & Ruprecht, 1971.

Bibliography

———. *Der Brief an die Galater*. 15th ed. KEK 7. Göttingen: Vandenhoeck & Ruprecht, 1989.

Schoenfeldt, Michael Carl. *Bodies and Selves in Early Modern England: Physiology and Inwardness in Spenser, Shakespeare, Herbert, and Milton*. Cambridge Studies in Renaissance Literature and Culture 34. Cambridge: Cambridge University Press, 1999.

Schreiner, Thomas R. *Galatians*. ZECNT. Grand Rapids: Zondervan, 2010.

———. *The Law and Its Fulfillment: A Pauline Theology of Law*. Grand Rapids: Baker, 1993.

———. *Romans*. BECNT. Grand Rapids: Baker, 1998.

Schwartz, Daniel R. *2 Maccabees*. Berlin: de Gruyter, 2008.

———. "Maccabees, Second Book of." In *EDEJ*, 905–7. 2010.

Schwartz, S. *Josephus and Judaean Politics*. Columbia Studies in the Classical Tradition 18. Leiden: Brill, 1990.

Schwarz, Sarah L. "Demons and Douglas: Applying Grid and Group to the Demonologies of the *Testament of Solomon*." *JAAR*, 80, no. 4 (2012): 1–23. doi:10.1093/jaarel/lfs072.

———. "Reconsidering the *Testament of Solomon*." *JSP* 16 (May 2007): 203–37. doi:10.1177/0951820707077166.

Schweizer, Eduard. "Die 'Elemente Der Welt' Gal. 4, 3.9; Kol. 3, 8.20." In *Verborum Veritas: Festschrift für Gustav Stählin zum 70. Geburtstag*, edited by Otto Böcher and Klaus Haacker, 245–59. Wuppertal: Brockhaus, 1970.

———. "Slaves of the Elements and Worshipers of Angels: Gal 4:3, 9; Col 2:8, 18, 20." *JBL* 107 (1988): 455–68.

Schweizer, Eduard, Friedrich Baumgärtel, and Rudolf Meyer. "Σάρξ, Σαρκικός, Σάρκινος." In *TDNT*, 7:98–151. 1971.

Scornaienchi, Lorenzo. *Sarx und Soma bei Paulus: Der Mensch zwischen Destruktivität und Konstruktivität*. NTOA/SUNT 67. Göttingen: Vandenhoeck & Ruprecht, 2008.

Scott, James M. *Adoption as Sons of God: An Exegetical Investigation into the Background of ΥΙΟΘΕΣΙΑ in the Pauline Corpus*. WUNT 2/48. Tübingen: Mohr Siebeck, 1992.

Segal, Alan F. "Romans 7 and Jewish Dietary Law." *SR* 15, no. 3 (1986): 361–74.

Segal, Michael. "Jubilees, Book of." In *EDEJ*, 843–46. 2010.

Selleck, Nancy. "Donne's Body." *SEL* 41 (2001): 149–74.

Sextus Empiricus, *Pyr.* = *Πυρρώνειοι ὑποτυπώσεις*. In *Sexti Empirici opera*, vol. 1, edited by H. Mutschmann. Leipzig: Teubner, 1912.

Shami, Jeanne. "John Donne: Geography as Metaphor." In *Geography and Literature: A Meeting of the Disciplines*, edited by William E. Mallory and Paul Simpson-Housley, 161–67. Syracuse: Syracuse University Press, 1987.

Sherwood, Aaron. *Paul and the Restoration of Humanity in Light of Ancient Jewish Traditions*. AGJU 82. Leiden: Brill, 2012.

Sib. Or. = *Sibylline Oracles*. In *Die Oracula Sibyllina*, J. Geffcken. GCS 8. Leipzig: Hinrichs, 1902.

———. "Sibylline Oracles." Edited by John J. Collins. *OTP* 1:317–472. 1983.

240 *Bibliography*

————. *The Sibylline Oracles: With Introduction, Translation and Commentary on the First and Second Books*. Edited by Jane L. Lightfoot. Oxford: Oxford University Press, 2007.

Siegert, Folker. "Early Jewish Interpretation in a Hellenistic Style, 4: Philo of Alexandria." In *Hebrew Bible / Old Testament: The History of Its Interpretation*, edited by Magne Sæbø, 1.1 Antiquity:162–89. Göttingen: Vandenhoeck & Ruprecht, 1996.

————. "Philo and the New Testament." In *The Cambridge Companion to Philo*, edited by Adam Kamesar, 175–209. Cambridge: Cambridge University Press, 2009.

Siegfried, Carl. *Philo von Alexandria als Ausleger des Alten Testament: An sich selbst und nach seinem geschichtlichen Einfluss Betrachtet; Nebst Untersuchungen über die Graecotaet Philo's*. Jena: Verlag von Hermann Dufft, 1875.

Silva, Moisés. "Galatians." In *Commentary on the New Testament Use of the Old Testament*, edited by Gregory K. Beale and Donald A. Carson, 785–810. Grand Rapids: Baker Academic, 2007.

Simplicius. In *Die Schule des Aristoteles: Texte und Kommentare*, edited by Fritz Wehrli. Basel: Schwabe, 1944.

in Cael. = *in Aristotelis de Caelo Commentarii*

in Phys. = *in Aristotelis de Physica Commentarii*

Singer, Peter N. "The Capacities of the Soul Depend on the Mixtures of the Body." In *Galen: Psychological Writings*, edited by Peter N. Singer, 333–424. Cambridge Galen Translations. Cambridge: Cambridge University Press, 2013.

————. "General Introduction." In *Galen: Psychological Writings*, 1–41. Cambridge Galen Translations. Cambridge: Cambridge University Press, 2013.

Sorabji, Richard. "Chrysippus – Posidonius – Seneca: A High-Level Debate on Emotion." In *The Emotions in Hellenistic Philosophy*, edited by Juha Sihvola and Troels Engberg-Pedersen, 149–70. The New Synthese Historical Library 46. Dordrecht: Kluwer, 1998.

————. *Emotion and Peace of Mind: From Stoic Agitation to Christian Temptation*. Gifford Lectures. Oxford: Oxford University Press, 2000.

Souter, Alexander. *The Earliest Latin Commentaries on the Epistles of St. Paul: A Study*. Oxford: Clarendon, 1927.

Stählin, Gustav. "Προκοπή, Προκόπτω." In *TDNT*, 6:703–19. 1968.

Stählin, Otto, ed. *Clemens Alexandrinus*. GCS 39. Leipzig: Hinrichs, 1936.

Sterling, Gregory E. "'A Law to Themselves': Limited Universalism in Philo and Paul." *ZNW* 107 (2016): 30–47. doi:10.1515/znw-2016-0002.

————. "Philo." In *EDEJ*, 1063–70. 2010.

————. "'Philo Has Not Been Used Half Enough': The Significance of Philo of Alexandria for the Study of the New Testament." *PRSt* 30, no. 3 (2003): 251–69.

————. "A Philosophy according to the Elements of the Cosmos: Colossian Christianity and Philo of Alexandria." In *Philon d'Alexandrie et le langage de la philosophie: actes du colloque international organisé par le Centre d'études sur la philosophie hellénistique et romaine de l'Université de Paris XII-Val de Marne (Créteil, Fontenay, Paris, 26-28 octobre 1995)*, edited by Carlos Lévy, 349–73. Monothéismes et philosophie. Turnhout: Brepols, 1998.

Bibliography

———. "Platonizing Moses: Philo and Middle Platonism." *SPhilo* 5 (1993): 96–111.

———. "Recherché or Representative? What is the Relationship between Philo's Treatises and Greek-Speaking Judaism?" *SPhilo* 11 (1999a): 1–30.

———. "'The School of Sacred Laws': The Social Setting of Philo's Treatises." *VC* 53 (1999b): 148–64.

Stowers, Stanley Kent. "Paul and Self-Mastery." In *Paul in the Greco-Roman World: A Handbook*, edited by J. Paul Sampley, 524–50. London: Continuum, 2003.

———. "Paul and Self-Mastery." In *Paul in the Greco-Roman World: A Handbook*, 2nd ed., edited by J. Paul Sampley, 2:270–300. London: Bloomsbury T&T Clark, 2016.

———. *A Rereading of Romans: Justice, Jews, and Gentiles*. New Haven, CT: Yale University Press, 1994.

Sugg, Richard. *The Smoke of the Soul: Medicine, Physiology and Religion in Early Modern England*. Houndmills: Palgrave Macmillan, 2013.

Svebakken, Hans. *Philo of Alexandria's Exposition of the Tenth Commandment*. Studia Philonica Monographs 6. Atlanta: Society of Biblical Literature, 2012.

T. Sol. = *The Testament of Solomon*. Edited by C. C. McCown. Leipzig: Hinrichs, 1922.

———. "Testament of Solomon." Edited by D. C. Duling. *OTP* 1:935–87. 1983.

Targoff, Ramie. *John Donne, Body and Soul*. Chicago: University of Chicago Press, 2008.

Tatian. *Ad Graec.* = *Oratio ad Graecos*. In *Die ältesten Apologeten*, edited by E. J. Goodspeed, 268–305. Göttingen: Vandenhoeck & Ruprecht, 1915.

Termini, Cristina. "Philo's Thought within the Context of Middle Judaism." Translated by Adam Kamesar. In *The Cambridge Companion to Philo*, edited by Adam Kamesar, 95–123. Cambridge: Cambridge University Press, 2009.

Thackeray, H. St. J., ed. *Josephus*. 6 vols. LCL. Cambridge, MA: Harvard University Press, 1926–30.

Theodotus. *Exc.* = *Exc.* = *The Excerpta ex Theodoto of Clement of Alexandria*. Translated by Robert Pierce Casey. Studies and Documents 1. London: Christophers, 1934.

———. "Excerpts of Theodotus; or, Selections from the Prophetic Scriptures." Translated by William Wilson. LCL, 1885.

Theophrastus. *Sens.* = *Senses*. In *Theophrastus and the Greek Physiological Psychology Before Aristotle*, edited by George Malcolm Stratton. London: George Allen & Unwin, 1917.

Thielman, Frank. *From Plight to Solution: A Jewish Framework for Understanding Paul's View of the Law in Galatians and Romans*. NovTSup 61. Leiden: Brill, 1989.

Thiselton, Anthony C. *The First Epistle to the Corinthians: A Commentary on the Greek Text*. NIGTC. Grand Rapids: Eerdmans, 2000.

Thompson, James W. *Moral Formation According to Paul: The Context and Coherence of Pauline Ethics*. Grand Rapids: Baker Academic, 2011.

Thompson, Marianne Meye. *Colossians and Philemon*. THNTC. Grand Rapids: Eerdmans, 2005.

Thomson, Ian H. *Chiasmus in the Pauline Letters*. JSNTSup 111. Sheffield: Sheffield Academic, 1995.

242   *Bibliography*

Tieleman, Teun. *Chrysippus' "On Affections": Reconstruction and Interpretation.* PHA 94. Leiden: Brill, 2003.

Tobin, Thomas H. *The Creation of Man: Philo and the History of Interpretation.* CBQMS 14. Washington, D.C.: Catholic Biblical Association of America, 1983.

Todorov, Tzvetan. *Mikhail Bakhtin: The Dialogical Principle.* Minneapolis: University of Minnesota Press, 1984.

Treat. Shem = Treatise of Shem. Edited by James H. Charlesworth. *OTP* 1:473–86. 1983.

Trudinger, Paul. "An Autobiographical Digression? A Note on Romans 7:7–25." *ExpTim* 107, no. 6 (1996): 173–74. doi:10.1177/001452469610700604.

van der Horst, Pieter W. "'The Elements Will Be Dissolved with Fire': The Idea of Cosmic Conflagration in Hellenism, Ancient Judaism, and Early Christianity." In *Hellenism, Judaism, Christianity: Essays on Their Interaction,* 2nd enlarged ed, 271–92. CBET 8. Leuven: Peeters, 1998.

van Henten, Jan Willem. *The Maccabean Martyrs as Saviours of the Jewish People: A Study of 2 and 4 Maccabees.* JSJS 57. Leiden: Brill, 1997.

———. "Maccabees, Fourth Book of." In *EDEJ,* 909–10. 2010.

van Kooten, Geurt H. *Cosmic Christology in Paul and the Pauline School: Colossians and Ephesians in the Context of Graeco-Roman Cosmology, with a New Synopsis of the Greek Texts.* WUNT 2/171. Tübingen: Mohr Siebeck, 2003.

———. *Paul's Anthropology in Context: The Image of God, Assimilation to God, and Tripartite Man in Ancient Judaism, Ancient Philosophy and Early Christianity.* WUNT 232. Tübingen: Mohr Siebeck, 2008.

Vermes, Geza, ed. *The Dead Sea Scrolls in English.* 4th ed. Sheffield: Sheffield Academic, 1995 [1962].

Victorinus, Gaius Marius. *Commentary on Galatians.* Translated by Stephen Andrew Cooper. In *Marius Victorinus' Commentary on Galatians.* OECS. Oxford: Oxford University Press, 2005.

———. *In epistulam Pauli ad Ephesios, In epistulam Pauli ad Galatas, In epistulam Pauli ad Philippenses.* Edited by Franco Gori. CSEL 83/2. Vienna: Hoelder-Pichler-Tempsky, 1986.

Vielhauer, P. "Gesetzesdienst und Stoicheiadienst im Galaterbrief." In *Rechtfertigung. Festschrift für Ernst Käsemann zum 70. Geburtstag,* edited by Johannes Friedrich, Wolfgang Pöhlmann, and Peter Stuhlmacher, 543–55. Tübingen: Mohr, 1976.

Vollgraff, W. "Elementum." *Mnemosyne* 2 (1949): 89–115.

Wasserman, Emma. "The Death of the Soul in Romans 7: Revisiting Paul's Anthropology in Light of Hellenistic Moral Psychology." *JBL* 126 (2007): 793–816.

———. *The Death of the Soul in Romans 7: Sin, Death, and the Law in Light of Hellenistic Moral Psychology.* WUNT 2/256. Tübingen: Mohr Siebeck, 2008.

———. "Paul among the Philosophers: The Case of Sin in Romans 6–8." *JSNT* 30 (2008): 387–415. doi:10.1177/0142064X08091441.

Watson, Duane F. "Comparing Two Related Methods: Rhetorical Criticism and Socio-Rhetorical Interpretation Applied to Second Peter." In *Reading Second Peter*

Bibliography 243

with New Eyes: Methodological Reassessments of the Letter of Second Peter, edited by Robert L. Webb and Duane F. Watson. LNTS 382. London: T&T Clark, 2010.

Watson, Francis. *Paul and the Hermeneutics of Faith*. 2nd ed. Cornerstones. London: Bloomsbury T&T Clark, 2016.

Wegenast, Klaus. *Das Verständnis der Tradition bei Paulus und in den Deuteropaulinen*. Neukirchen: Neukirchener, 1962.

Westerholm, Stephen. "On Fulfilling the Whole Law (Gal 5:14)." *SEÅ* 51–52 (1986): 229–37.

White, Michael J. "Stoic Natural Philosophy (Physics and Cosmology)." In *The Cambridge Companion to the Stoics*, edited by Brad Inwood, 124–52. Cambridge: Cambridge University Press, 2003.

Wigodsky, Michael. "*Homoiotetes, Stoicheia* and *Homoiomereiai* in Epicurus." *CQ* 57 (2007): 521–42.

Williamson, Ronald. *Jews in the Hellenistic World: Philo*. Cambridge Commentaries on Writings of the Jewish and Christian World, 200 BC to AD 200, I.2. Cambridge: Cambridge University Press, 1989.

Wilson, Todd A. *The Curse of the Law and the Crisis in Galatia: Reassessing the Purpose of Galatians*. WUNT 2/225. Tübingen: Mohr Siebeck, 2007.

Wink, Walter. "The 'Elements of the Universe' in Biblical and Scientific Perspective." *Zygon* 13, no. 3 (1978): 225–48.

———. *Naming the Powers*. Philadelphia: Fortress, 1984.

Winston, David. "Philo of Alexandria on the Rational and Irrational Emotions." In *Passions and Moral Progress in Greco-Roman Thought*, edited by John T. Fitzgerald, 201–20. Routledge Monographs in Classical Studies. London: Routledge, 2008.

———. "Philo's Ethical Theory." *ANRW* 372–416. Part 2, *Principat*, 21.1, edited by H. Temporini and W. Haase. Berlin: de Gruyter, 1984.

———. "Solomon, Wisdom of." In *ABD*, 6:120–27, 1992.

———. *The Wisdom of Solomon: A New Translation with Introduction and Commentary*. AB 43. Garden City, NY: Doubleday, 1979.

Witherington, Ben, III. *Grace in Galatia: A Commentary on St. Paul's Letter to the Galatians*. Grand Rapids: Eerdmans, 1998.

———. *The Letters to Philemon, the Colossians, and the Ephesians: A Socio-Rhetorical Commentary on the Captivity Epistles*. Grand Rapids: Eerdmans, 2007.

Wolfson, Harry A. *Philo: Foundations of Religious Philosophy in Judaism, Christianity, and Islam*. 2 vols. Cambridge, MA: Harvard University Press, 1947.

Woyke, Johannes. "Nochmals zu den 'schwachen und unfähigen Elementen' (Gal 4.9): Paulus, Philo und die Στοιχεῖα τοῦ Κόσμου." *NTS* 54 (2008): 221–34. doi:10.1017/S002868850800012X.

Wright, N. T. *The Climax of the Covenant: Christ and the Law in Pauline Theology*. London: T&T Clark, 1991.

———. *Galatians. Commentaries for Christian Formation*. Grand Rapids: Eerdmans, 2021.

———. "The Letter to the Galatians: Exegesis and Theology." In *Between Two Horizons: Spanning New Testament Studies and Systematic Theology*, edited by Joel B. Green and Max Turner, 205–36. Grand Rapids: Eerdmans, 2000.

———. *The New Testament and the People of God*. Christian Origins and the Question of God 1. London: SPCK, 1992.

———. *Paul and His Recent Interpreters: Some Contemporary Debates*. London: SPCK, 2015.

———. *Paul and the Faithfulness of God*. Christian Origins and the Question of God 4. London: SPCK, 2013.

———. *The Resurrection of the Son of God*. Christian Origins and the Question of God 3. London: SPCK, 2003.

Young, Norman H. "The Figure of the *Paidagōgos* in Art and Literature." *BA* 53, no. 2 (1990): 80–86.

———. "*Paidagogos*: The Social Setting of a Pauline Metaphor." *NovT* 29 (1987): 150–76.

Zurawski, Jason. "Mosaic Torah as Encyclical Paideia: Reading Paul's Allegory of Hagar and Sarah in Light of Philo of Alexandria's." Paper presented at the Annual Meeting of the Society of Biblical Literature. Chicago, November 2012.

Subject Index

Aaron, 154, 169, 201, 209
Abraham, xiii, 6, 21, 34–37, 57, 77, 83, 90–91, 97–98, 105, 110–17, 125, 135–36, 139–40, 149–66, 169–88, 192, 196, 198, 201–2, 212–13
action, 4–5, 13, 15, 38, 62, 68, 72–73, 76, 81, 89, 92, 103, 107, 125–28, 131, 133, 140, 144, 152–56, 159, 178, 188, 190, 193–200, 215. *See also ergon* (ἔργον)
affect, affections, 13, 16, 59, 61, 67–77, 88–93, 101, 125, 131–33, 143–44, 163, 166, 212, 215. *See also pathos, pathēma, paschō* (πάθος, πάθημα, πάσχω)
air, xii, 3–4, 8–9, 12–14, 17–18, 21, 32–33, 39–46, 50–52, 55, 59–69, 74–75, 81, 85, 87, 101–4, 109–10, 125–26, 134, 162. *See also* cool, cold
aisthēsis (αἴσθησις), 46, 62, 128
alignment, 14–15, 80, 171, 173, 187, 192, 198, 213
allegory, 3, 29, 37, 41, 54, 64, 76, 96–98, 104–5, 108–18, 122–23, 134, 149, 158, 169, 172–76, 184–85, 214, 216
angels, 1, 4, 7, 10–11, 26, 41, 47–51, 55–58, 122, 156, 179. *See also*

demons; gods; *pneuma* (πνεῦμα); spirits
anger, 71, 75, 92, 140, 151, 205
Anointed, xiii, 19, 21, 29, 79–80, 85–86, 95, 124, 127, 139, 144, 152–53, 156, 159–60, 164, 166–71, 183, 187–92, 197, 199, 201, 204–5, 208, 213. *See also* Son
apocalyptic, 13, 27, 47–51, 96, 128, 182, 184
archē (ἀρχή), 32, 37, 52
arid. *See* dry
astheneia (ἀσθένεια), 3, 64–65, 75, 78, 80, 83–84, 92, 126–29, 134, 139–40, 143, 200. *See also* weakness
astral, astrological, 5, 11, 13, 48–50, 61, 82, 93, 113–14, 120, 123, 161–65, 180–81, 213. *See also* planets, stars
autumn, 69–70, 168

baptism, 160, 190, 193, 201, 204, 215
beggarly, 3, 5, 9, 15, 126–27, 165
behavior, xiii, 2, 5, 20–21, 38, 60, 78, 86, 89, 101, 132, 153–54, 163, 170, 183, 196, 211. *See also ergon* (ἔργον)
belief. *See* faith
belly, 77, 88, 91, 107–9, 133, 141, 144
bile, 61, 69, 72, 75, 151

246 *Subject Index*

blame, 76–77, 112
blood, 8, 61, 69, 72–73, 78, 84, 89, 104, 205. *See also* circulation
body, xiii, 1–6, 9–24, 27–28, 31–32, 40–51, 59–92, 96–102, 105–16, 125–33, 136–41, 144, 149, 156, 160–67, 170–71, 174–75, 184–94, 197, 200–204, 211–14
bone, 61, 72, 79
breath, 63–64, 74, 79, 169, 190

calendar, 5–6, 14–15, 84, 86, 95, 98, 105–10, 120, 151, 154, 158–69, 172, 175–76, 181, 183, 189, 197, 199–200, 215
capacity, 66–69, 72–73, 78, 92, 144, 152–53
Chaldeans, 21, 26, 110, 112–14, 123, 161–66, 174–75, 184, 213
chiasm, 63, 135–36, 138, 145, 198
child, 3, 16, 21, 71–83, 92, 115–16, 125–26, 131, 137–40, 146, 149–56, 171, 174–77, 187–88, 192, 201, 212. *See also* nēpios (νήπιος); *pais* (παῖς)
circulation, 50, 64. *See also* blood
circumcision, xiii, 5, 8, 13, 27, 84–86, 95, 98, 105–6, 109–10, 121, 125, 131, 151, 154–61, 166–69, 172, 183, 185, 193, 197–201, 204, 213, 215
component, compose, xii, 1–6, 9–21, 26, 31–34, 37–41, 44, 46, 52–55, 59–72, 78–85, 112, 116, 125–27, 134, 136, 139, 145, 149, 156, 174, 187–94, 201, 211–15
compromise, 1, 4, 6, 12, 18–21, 31, 46, 59–60, 66, 82, 99, 121, 127, 189–94, 201, 212–15
conflagration, 42, 55–56, 99
cool, cold, 53, 61–62, 67–70, 73–74, 82, 93, 101, 162, 164, 167, 190, 212. *See also* air
corporal. *See* body
corruption, 1–2, 11, 13, 16, 62, 80, 134, 187–88, 193–94, 212

cosmos, cosmology, 1–11, 14–16, 19–20, 28, 31–32, 36–47, 51–55, 58–66, 68, 82–88, 95–113, 116, 121, 125–26, 133, 136, 144–45, 159–72, 176, 180–81, 187–92, 198–99, 203, 207, 211–13, 216
courage, 70–73, 107
covenant, 79, 96–97, 130, 142, 151, 171–74, 182, 184, 194, 200, 206
cross, crucifixion, 2, 21, 58, 65, 91, 124, 130, 134–35, 152–53, 159–60, 183, 187–92, 200–204, 213
curse, 150, 153, 156, 166, 171, 187, 206

death, xi, 1, 10, 12, 15–16, 22, 43, 46, 54, 64–67, 83, 87, 91, 93, 97, 115, 126, 128, 130–31, 141–43, 153, 159–61, 166–69, 176–79, 187–92, 197, 202–3, 213, 216
demons, 4, 11, 39, 49, 58. *See also* angels; gods; *pneuma* (πνεῦμα); spirits
desire, desiderative, 5, 17, 41, 71–73, 77–81, 84–85, 89, 106, 109–10, 125, 129, 131–34, 140, 143–44, 150–56, 160, 175–76, 188, 192–202, 205–6, 213. *See also* epithumeō, epithumia (ἐπιθυμέω, ἐπιθυμία); lust
dianoia (διάνοια), 74, 141. *See also* mind
diet, 8, 55, 86, 92, 106, 109, 122, 142, 151, 197. *See also* drink, drunkenness; food; nourishment, nutrition
digestion, 67
dikaios, dikaiosynē (δίκαιος, δικαιοσύνη), 155, 168–70, 176, 183, 195. *See also* justification; righteousness
discourse, 2, 18–21, 31, 42, 59–60, 64, 68, 75, 78, 85–86, 125, 129, 131–33, 137–39, 149–54, 173, 187, 191–97, 211–15

Subject Index

disease, xii, 1, 11, 21–22, 60–63, 69–73, 77, 80–88, 93, 105–6, 117, 126, 138, 149, 162, 167, 175, 204

douleō, doulos (δουλέω, δοῦλος), 67–68, 75, 77–78, 80, 84, 88, 115, 137, 139, 174, 200, 211. *See also* enslavement

drink, drunkenness, 5, 9, 68, 71, 77, 88–89, 93, 109, 122, 140, 197

drugs, 67–68

dry, 42, 53, 61, 67, 69, 73, 92–93, 101, 162, 164, 167, 197, 212. *See also* earth

dynamis (δύναμις), 37, 40, 53, 61–62, 67, 73. *See also* qualities

ear, 48

earth, xi–xii, 2–5, 8–9, 12–14, 17–18, 21, 32–33, 37–44, 46, 48, 50–52, 54, 59, 61–67, 69, 72, 79, 81, 85, 100–104, 107, 109, 113, 115, 123, 125–26, 134–35, 162, 164, 170, 182. *See also* dry; *gē* (γῆ)

east, 70

Egypt, 36, 53, 101, 108–16, 134, 138, 156, 162, 174–76, 181, 184–85

elements, *passim*: elemental spaces, 37, 40–44, 96, 104, 109, 122; elemental spirits, 2, 5–6, 9–10, 13–15, 20, 22, 35, 38–47, 51–52, 56, 60–85, 92, 98, 100, 104–6, 109–10, 113, 116, 122, 129, 132–36, 145, 152, 154, 160–65, 187, 190–93, 197, 199, 202, 204, 211–12, 215; immaterial elements, elementary principles, 3, 8–10, 18, 20–21, 18, 31–46, 50–53, 56, 62–63, 73, 83–84, 88, 95–96, 100, 103, 107, 109, 112, 116, 134, 156, 159–61, 164, 175–76, 190, 192, 197–98, 201–3, 215; material elements, 2–12, 17–22, 31–47, 50–52, 56, 59–60, 63–66, 70–75, 78–81, 86, 96–97, 102, 104, 114, 117, 126–28, 132, 134–40, 149, 156, 158, 161, 166, 176, 194, 202, 211, 213–16. *See*

also air; angels; demons; earth; fire; gods; heaven; *pneuma* (πνεῦμα); sea; spirits; water

emotion, 70, 73, 77, 89–93, 132, 144. *See also pathos, pathēma, paschō* (πάθος, πάθημα, πάσχω)

enkrateia (ἐγκράτεια), 80, 108, 197, 207

enslavement, xii–xiv, 1, 6, 9–21, 26–27, 31, 57–60, 66–68, 71–72, 75–85, 88, 95, 98, 105–11, 114–16, 120, 125–56, 159–68, 171–76, 188–92, 199–202, 206, 211–15. *See also douleō, doulos* (δουλέω, δοῦλος)

epidemiology, 21, 126, 138

epilepsy, 70

epithumeō, epithumia (ἐπιθυμέω, ἐπιθυμία), 13–14, 20–21, 59–60, 70–78, 81–85, 92, 109–10, 114, 125–40, 143–46, 150, 156, 178, 184, 192–97, 200, 205, 212. *See also* desire, desiderative; lust

equinox, 108, 168

ergon (ἔργον), 13–14, 21, 59–60, 70, 73, 78, 81, 127–29, 132–33, 136, 138, 140, 143, 171, 182, 212. *See also* action; behavior; motion

eschatology, 39–42, 129–30, 140, 173, 184

evil, 11, 13, 57, 72, 79, 82, 89, 128, 131, 141, 144, 174, 188, 213

exodus, 38, 83, 85, 95, 98, 115–16, 146, 173–75, 184, 194, 196

eye, xi, 1–2, 55, 80, 127, 143, 179, 182–83, 192, 204–8

faith, xii, 2, 5, 8, 11, 14, 20–22, 52, 56–57, 74, 86–91, 99, 117, 125, 130, 140–46, 149–53, 156, 160, 163, 166, 168–83, 187–92, 195–209, 212–13, 216. *See also pistis* (πίστις)

feast, festival, 8–9, 84, 101–10, 115, 164–65, 168–69, 180, 195

fire, xii, 1–5, 8–9, 12–14, 17–18, 21, 32–33, 38–47, 51–56, 59–69, 74, 77,

248 *Subject Index*

80–81, 85–88, 92–93, 102, 104, 110, 125–26, 134–35, 162. *See also* hot

flesh, 1–2, 5–6, 8–13, 15–18, 20–21, 26–27, 46, 59–60, 65–69, 76–86, 92, 95, 98, 109, 114–16, 125–215. *See also sarx* (σάρξ)

food, 1, 5, 41, 68, 71, 77, 82, 84, 88–89, 93, 102–3, 108–10, 122, 183, 190, 194–97, 215. *See also* diet

foreskin. *See* circumcision

fronēma (φρόνημα), 15, 127. *See also* mind

gē (γῆ), 42, 64. *See also* earth

gods, 3–4, 14, 44–45, 48–49, 62, 71, 83, 114, 124, 126, 161–66, 213. *See also* angels; demons; *pneuma* (πνεῦμα); spirits

guard, guardian, xi, 13, 21, 41, 149–56, 175, 188, 192, 195–96, 202, 212–13

guide, 17, 20, 68, 77–78, 81–84, 105, 107, 149–56, 167–68, 171, 175, 177, 188–89, 192–98, 202, 212–13

Hagar, 29, 97, 115–17, 158, 172–75, 184–85

hand, 6, 19, 68, 74–75, 84, 99, 123, 131, 137, 144, 163, 174, 184, 190, 197, 200

harmony, 8, 12–13, 20, 37, 39, 54, 61, 66, 82–85, 95, 98, 100–116, 159–61, 164–68, 176, 182, 187, 189, 200, 206, 212–13

head, 38, 60, 71, 97, 152, 173, 213

health, healing, xii–xiii, 1, 17, 61, 69–70, 74, 82, 84, 102, 105–9, 120, 150, 162–67, 170, 176, 197

heart, 2, 16–17, 69, 71, 78–79, 106, 121, 131, 133, 144, 156, 160, 163, 169–70, 188, 192–98, 202, 204, 207, 213–14

heaven, 1, 12, 14, 37, 40–45, 48, 54–55, 100–101, 104, 107, 113–14, 162–64, 170–71, 182

heir. *See* inheritance

holiday, 102, 107, 109. *See also* feast, festival

hot, 53, 61–62, 67–74, 77, 80, 82, 93, 101, 110, 134, 162, 164, 167, 212. *See also* fire

humors, 61, 68–69, 72

idol, 4, 9, 14, 140, 151, 158

illness. *See* disease

inheritance, 10, 97–98, 105, 115–17, 125, 135, 138–40, 149, 156, 159, 163–67, 170–76, 183, 187, 192, 195–98, 201–2, 212–13

Jesus. *See* Anointed; Son

justification, 8–10, 16, 78, 140, 145, 157, 160, 168–70, 182–83. *See also dikaios, dikaiosynē* (δίκαιος, δικαιοσύνη); righteousness

kairos (καιρός), 21, 84, 108–9, 161, 165, 180, 193, 198–202, 213. *See also* season

law, xii, 1, 6–25, 37, 41, 49, 56–60, 77–88, 93–125, 129–31, 136–43, 146, 149–208, 212–15. *See also nomos* (νόμος); Torah

life, xiii, 2, 4–5, 9, 15–17, 20–23, 27, 38, 63–66, 70–73, 77, 81–85, 98–99, 101, 103, 105, 108–17, 123, 125, 127, 130–31, 134–35, 146, 149, 152–76, 187–205, 212–15

love, 2, 16, 80, 106, 108, 113, 115, 125, 130, 152–54, 160, 165, 170–71, 175, 178, 187, 189–93, 197–202, 213

luminaries. *See* stars

lunar. *See* moon

lungs, 71

lust, 1, 5, 15, 17, 79, 105, 115–16, 132, 142, 167–68, 212. *See also* desire, desiderative; *epithumeō, epithumia* (ἐπιθυμέω, ἐπιθυμία)

madness, 70, 72, 82

Subject Index

magic, 49–50. *See also* sorcery
malady. *See* disease
marrow, 72
medicine, xi–xiii, 2, 13–14, 20–21, 29,
  59–63, 67–68, 75–80, 85–90, 93, 95,
  108, 125, 129, 132–33, 138–39, 144,
  149–54, 159, 170, 187, 190, 193,
  211–16
menopause, 116
meros (μέρος), 37, 40–41, 44, 54, 71,
  109, 134
metaphor, xiii, 18, 22, 32, 93, 138, 151,
  154, 177, 180, 188, 190, 197
meteorology, 10, 61. *See also* stars;
  weather
migration, 83, 98, 105, 110–16, 161,
  163, 166, 171–75, 184
mind, 7, 15, 17, 28, 45, 68, 71, 74–85,
  89, 92–93, 102, 104–16, 133–37,
  144, 150, 162–65, 170–71, 174,
  184, 188, 194–95, 212, 214. *See
  also dianoia* (διάνοια); *fronēma*
  (φρόνημα); *nous* (νοῦς)
mirror, 21, 37, 157, 165, 212, 214
mixture, 5, 19, 61–62, 67–68, 78,
  80, 133–34, 151, 211. *See also*
  proportion
moist. *See* wet
month, 6, 8, 48, 84, 98, 105, 107–10,
  120–21, 154, 161–66, 180, 197,
  199, 213
moon, 4, 6–9, 14, 48, 61, 101, 108, 110,
  113, 162–65, 180–81
Moses, xiii, 1, 6–10, 19, 25, 29, 33–35,
  39–41, 48, 57–60, 64, 76–77, 83–86,
  90, 93, 97–119, 122–23, 134, 137,
  146, 153–61, 164–73, 179–84, 189,
  195–99, 206, 212
motion, 4–5, 15, 18, 62, 68, 73, 82,
  93, 131, 153, 194. *See also ergon*
  (ἔργον)
mouth, 65

nature, natural, 1–5, 8, 13–16, 21, 28,
  34–39, 44, 54, 61–62, 65–78, 81–82,

87, 89, 93, 99–104, 107–15, 119–20,
  125–26, 131–40, 146, 150, 159–69,
  174, 176, 181, 190, 194, 199, 211
necessity, 4–5, 15, 17, 77, 91, 113, 212
nēpios (νήπιος), 73, 77–84, 92, 126,
  137–40, 150, 175. *See also* child
nomism, 13–14, 16, 19–21, 95, 98,
  101, 103, 105, 116–17, 149, 166–68,
  203, 212, 215. *See also* law; *nomos*
  (νόμος)
nomos (νόμος), xii, 10, 20, 60, 78,
  81–86, 98–103, 107, 116, 119, 128,
  130, 136–37, 150–56, 159–61, 164,
  166, 171, 182, 187–89, 196, 206,
  212–13. *See also* law; nomism
north, 70
nourishment, nutrition, 60, 62, 67, 71,
  81. *See also* diet; food
nous (νοῦς), 76–77, 107, 131, 141,
  193–94. *See also* mind

paidagōgos (παιδαγωγός), 8, 13, 19–21,
  53, 60, 81–93, 125, 136–40, 146–56,
  165, 171, 175–79, 187, 192–93, 196,
  202, 212–15
paideia (παιδεία), 82, 84, 95, 98, 151
pais (παῖς), 82, 150. *See also* child
pantheism, 21, 99, 116, 123, 163,
  165, 175
parabasis (παράβασις), 153–56
parallels, parallelomania, 16, 18–19, 24,
  28–29, 48, 56, 58, 99, 103, 108, 118,
  127–28, 136–37, 170, 179, 214, 216
passion, 3–4, 70–71, 74–78, 88–92, 114,
  116, 128–33, 138–44, 152, 158, 174,
  177, 179, 198, 205, 215. *See also
  pathos, pathēma, paschō* (πάθος,
  πάθημα, πάσχω)
Passover, 108, 165
pathology, 21, 126–29, 136–38,
  187, 212
pathos, pathēma, paschō (πάθος,
  πάθημα, πάσχω), 13–15, 20–21, 39,
  59–60, 62, 70–78, 81–83, 85, 88–90,
  105, 108–10, 115–16, 125–26,

250   *Subject Index*

128–36, 138–40, 143–44, 156, 165–
67, 174, 189–90, 192–93, 197, 200,
212, 214. *See also* affect, affections;
emotion; passion; stimulus
pedagogue. *See paidagōgos*
(παιδαγωγός)
perception, 5, 68, 76, 89, 114, 144
Philo, xi–xii, 13–16, 19–21, 26, 29,
36–60, 63–67, 70–71, 74–87,
90–129, 132–35, 138, 145, 149–52,
156–76, 179–90, 194–99, 205, 207,
212–16
philosophy, 3–4, 13–16, 19–20, 28, 31,
38–39, 43, 52, 56–68, 77, 82–90,
95–107, 110–11, 115–16, 119–22,
125, 129, 131, 133, 135, 142, 144,
159, 165–66, 172, 176, 181, 194–95,
198, 205, 214, 216
phlegm, 61, 69, 72
physiology, 1–2, 5–7, 11–17, 21, 23,
62, 64, 69, 73, 98, 115, 126–31, 134,
136, 138, 140, 187–88, 194, 212–15
pistis (πίστις), 140, 153–56, 171, 183,
190, 202, 213. *See also* faith
planets, 14, 47, 101, 162, 164. *See also*
moon; stars; sun
pleasure, 71–73, 77, 83, 105–10, 115,
128, 160, 167, 190, 197, 205, 212
pneuma (πνεῦμα), 49, 63, 74, 86, 135,
174, 192, 196, 198–99, 204–5,
208. *See also* Spirit; spirits
polytheism, 21, 113–16
prescription, xii–xiii, 16, 20, 60, 68,
81–85, 98, 102, 110, 149–54, 169,
178–79, 187–89, 192–94, 199,
212. *See also* treatment
promise, 17, 78, 84, 105, 113–16, 130,
139–40, 149–50, 154, 158, 163–73,
183, 193–96, 200–201, 206, 213
prophylactic, 83, 197
proportion, 11, 61, 68–69, 74. *See also*
mixture
proselytes, 114, 121, 158, 163, 165
psyche (ψυχή), psychology, 16, 60,
64, 65, 68–70, 76, 79, 87–92, 133,

141–44, 189, 194–95, 214. *See
also* soul

qualities, 4, 8, 17, 46, 53, 61, 69–74, 77,
83, 85, 102, 130, 134–35, 162, 187–
90. *See also* cool, cold; dry; *dynamis*
(δύναμις); hot; wet

rain, 61, 69, 101, 163
redeem, redemption, 13–21, 27, 60,
77–78, 84, 95, 98–106, 111, 116–17,
120, 130, 138, 149, 153–56, 159,
161, 164–70, 173–76, 187–88, 192–
93, 202, 212, 215
regimen, xii–xiii, 20, 60, 81–86, 92,
106, 150, 187–90
resurrection, 16, 65, 87, 184, 200, 202
righteousness, 16, 20–21, 86, 95, 98,
108–9, 116–17, 120, 125, 128, 130,
137, 144, 149–50, 153–61, 164–72,
176, 183, 187–88, 192, 195–202,
206, 212–13. *See also dikaios,
dikaiosynē* (δίκαιος, δικαιοσύνη);
justification
ritual, 10–11, 101–2, 106–8, 165, 204
rudiments. *See* elementary principles

sabbath, 6–8, 84, 102–3, 107, 110, 165,
168, 180, 183
sacrifice, 8–9, 65, 192
sanctuary. *See* temple
Sarah, 29, 58, 97, 114–17, 123, 158,
172–74, 184–85, 216
sarx (σάρξ), 9, 13–15, 21, 26, 59–60,
69, 77–83, 86, 92, 125–43, 146, 174,
190, 193–94, 204, 208, 212–14. *See
also* flesh
Satan, 80, 127
sea, 1–2, 39–41, 43, 50, 54, 61, 64, 101,
134, 163
season, 13, 47–48, 61, 69–70, 84,
98–102, 105, 107, 110, 120, 154,
161–62, 164, 197. *See also kairos*
(καιρός)

Subject Index

sex, 71–72, 76, 79–80, 88, 102, 109–10, 134, 142, 197
sickness. *See* disease
sign, 36, 38, 63, 100–101, 106, 109, 159–60, 163–64
sin, 1–2, 11–18, 21, 28, 60, 79–81, 84–87, 125–47, 152–55, 170–71, 175, 178, 187–98, 201–4, 212–13
sky, 40, 43, 100–101
slave, slavery. *See* enslavement
solar. *See* sun
Son, 2, 15–16, 20, 60, 85–87, 109, 117, 125, 130, 150, 154, 166–76, 187–209, 212–15. *See also* Anointed
son, xiii, 48, 63, 66, 74, 84, 93, 105, 111, 115–16, 121, 125, 146, 153, 170–75, 193, 201
sorcery, 140. *See also* magic
soul, 1, 5, 8, 12–15, 20–22, 44, 48, 60–78, 81–93, 97–102, 105–16, 124–25, 128, 133, 138, 141–44, 150, 154, 162–75, 184, 187, 191–97, 200, 203, 211, 214, 216. *See also psyche* (ψυχή), psychology
speech, 9, 19, 37, 105, 113, 130–31, 171
Spirit, xiii, 1–2, 5, 13–16, 20–22, 47, 50, 58–60, 79–80, 85–86, 91, 95, 109, 117, 124–25, 128–30, 134–36, 141–44, 149–50, 153–54, 166–78, 187–209, 212–16. *See also pneuma* (πνεῦμα)
spirits, spiritual, xi, 3, 5–6, 10–11, 17, 20, 22, 31–32, 37, 41, 44–51, 56–57, 67, 71–72, 79–85, 95, 98, 109–16, 127–30, 137, 139, 160, 162, 168–69, 176, 202, 211, 215. *See also* angels; demons; elemental spirits; gods; *pneuma* (πνεῦμα)
spring, 69–70, 84, 108
stars, 4, 7, 14–15, 24, 31, 42–51, 55–56, 63, 65, 70, 93, 100–101, 107, 113–14, 123–24, 161–65, 180, 182. *See also* moon; planets; sun
stimulus, 62, 70, 81, 125, 131–32, 140, 152–56, 160, 175–76, 188, 197,

213. *See also pathos, pathēma, paschō* (πάθος, πάθημα, πάσχω)
stoicheō, (στοιχέω), 22, 24, 26, 33–36, 47, 51–53, 56–58, 63–66, 86, 119, 134–38, 145, 153, 192, 198–202, 213
Stoics, 28, 39, 42, 62, 66–67, 72–76, 88–91, 99, 102, 112, 114, 123, 132, 161, 164–65, 206, 214, 216
stone, 79, 155
summer, 69–70
sun, 4, 6–9, 14, 48, 61, 70, 72, 101, 108, 113, 162–64, 181. *See also* stars
symbol, symbolism, 7, 39, 85, 100, 103–6, 110–13, 168, 174–75, 190

tabernacle. *See* temple
temper, temperament, 67, 70, 72–73
temple, 2, 9, 39, 57, 103–4, 122, 158, 168, 183
thymos (θύμος), 195, 205
Torah, xi–xiii, 14–16, 29, 65, 99, 103, 130, 158–59, 184, 196. *See also* law; *nomos* (νόμος)
treatment, xii, 11, 16, 44, 65, 67–68, 82–83, 85, 149, 151, 157, 187, 189, 194, 202. *See also* prescription

unleavened, 84, 108, 165

vapor, 72
vein, 112
vestments, 100, 104, 119–21
virtue, 8, 13, 34, 40, 68, 73, 84, 105–16, 138, 147, 158, 163–69, 174–76, 179, 197–99, 202, 211, 213

warm. *See* hot
water, xii, 3–5, 8–9, 12–14, 17–18, 21, 32–33, 39–46, 50–52, 59, 61–73, 81–82, 85–88, 101–4, 109–10, 125–26, 162. *See also* wet
weakness, 2, 8–11, 15–21, 26–27, 59–60, 64–68, 74–75, 79–81, 83–86, 92, 98, 106, 125–34, 138–43, 149, 152, 159–68, 171, 176, 187–204,

252 Subject Index

211–13. *See also astheneia*
(ἀσθένεια)
weather, 13, 47, 101, 163
wet, 47, 53, 61, 67, 69, 72–74, 77, 101,
110, 162, 164, 212. *See also* water
wine, 67, 93, 108
winter, 69–70
woman, 75–76, 79, 106, 115, 171,
187, 201

worship, xiii, 3, 5–10, 13–14, 26, 38,
84, 104, 114, 124, 162

year, 6–9, 12, 17, 32–33, 45, 47, 51, 61,
66, 69, 74, 84, 97–98, 101, 105–10,
115, 120, 154, 161–66, 171, 180,
197, 199, 213–14

Scriptures Index

Page references for figures are italicized.

HEBREW SCRIPTURES

Genesis, 1–2, 38, 65
    1.6–10, 42
    1.14–18, 100, 161, 180n74
    2.1, 38, 54n24
    2.7, 63–65, 79
    2.21–24, 79
    6.3–13, 79, 127, 128, 131, 141n19
    7.11–12, 42
    8.21, 79, 141n19
    12.3–4, 114, 169, 171
    15.5–6, 171
    17, 158
    18.11–27, 64, 115, 171
    26.2–5, 116, 155, 170, 181n88,
        182n91

Exodus, 7–9, 38
    12.1–25, 181n89, 182n91
    12.43–49, 155
    13.9–10, 155
    14.9–14, 134
    15.26, 182n91
    16.3–28, 155, 185n144

    18.16–20, 155, 198
    19.5, 182n91
    20, 10, 155, 178n29, 182n91, 195
    21.1, 155
    22.17–18, 178n29
    23.4–5, 178n29
    24.3–12, 155
    25.22, 156
    28.17–20, *35*
    32.8, 155
    34.6, 178n29
    36.17–20, *35*

Leviticus
    10.11, 155
    11, 55n36, 109
    16.16–19, 178n29
    19.4, 178n29
    19.18, 153
    20.21, 178n29
    26.3–13, 93n121, 154,
        178n29, 200
    26.25, 155

Numbers
    6.22–26, 154, 178n29

254   *Scriptures Index*

7.89, 156
10.32, 178n29
11.4–34, 195
12.3, 178n29
14.18–33, 178n29
25.1–2, 178n29

Deuteronomy
4.19–28, 48, 54n24, 131
5.8–21, 178n29, 195
5.33, 153
6.4–6, 193
7.15, 212
8.6, 153
9.6–24, 131, 155, 178n29, 195
10.12–16, 131, 144n60, 153
12.15–21, 195
12.29–31, 131
14.4–26, 55n36, 195
16.9–15, 200
17.3, 54n24
18.9–14, 131, 178n29
19.9, 153
23.18, 178n29
25.4, 199
26.11, 199, 200
26.17, 153
27.26, 153
28.1–14, 153, 171, 212
28.64–68, 131
29.3–4, 131, 193
30.1–6, 193
30.15–16, 153, 178n29
31.16–29, 131, 141n19
32.8–20, 48, 57n71, 178n29

Joshua
24.2, 163

Judges
5.20, 48

1 Samuel
15.11, 182n92

1 Kings
6.36, *35*
7.6–49, *35*
8.56, 208n77

1 Chronicles
28.9–18, 141n19

2 Chronicles
36.16, 208n79

Esther
5.1d, 92n101

Job
13.26, 92n97
15.35, 144n60
38.7, 48

Psalms
6.3, 141n7
10.3–17, 195
16.9, 79
19.8, 79
21.2, 195
25.7, 79
28.7, 79
37.12, 182n92
38.3–9, 2, 195
58, 48
63.2, 79
73.26, 79, 141n7
78.29–30, 195
82.1, 48
84.3, 79
88.10, 127
97.3–6, 42
103.5–14, 141n19, 195
104.4–15, 10, 47, 202n1
105.29–32, 38
106.14, 195
109.24, 141n7
112.10, 195
116.6, 79
119, 2, 79, 130, 146n91, 195

121.5–6, 48
130.3, 182n92
140.8, 195
148.2–8, 47

Proverbs
1.7, 7
1.22–32, 79–80
10.24, 195

Ecclesiastes
11.6, *34*

Isaiah
1.19, 206n44
6.1–6, 47
13.10, 54n24
24.21–23, 42, 54n24
26.3, 141n19
29.13–16, 141n19, 144n60
34.4, 40, 42
40.26, 54n24
48.16–17, 205n41
57.16–18, 205n41
58.2–14, 195
63.11–14, 205n41
63.19–64.1, 42
66.18–23, 201

Jeremiah
3.25, 79, 92n97
5.19, 131
12.4, 4
16.10–13, 131
17.9–14, 144n60, 193
25.1–11, 131
31.33, 193
32.40, 193

Ezekiel
6.9, 144n60
8.17, 208n79
11.19–20, 79, 193, 195
16.22–60, 92n96
23.3–21, 79, 127

36.24–27, 79, 153, 193, 195
42.3, *34*

Hosea
11.1–5, 146n89

Micah
1.3–4, 42

Nahum
1.5–6, 42

Habakkuk
2.18, 141n19
3.6, 42

NEW TESTAMENT

Matthew
4.24, 48
13.22, 208n79
17.15, 48
26.35–43, 80, 92n100, 127

Mark
3.2, 182n92
4.18, 208n79
7.21, 144n60
14.31–40, 80, 92n100, 127

Luke
4.1, 205n41
6.7, 182n92
14.1, 182n92
10.7, 199
20.20, 182n92

Acts
7.38–53, 179n47
9.24, 182n92
21.24, *34*
27.21–36, 202n1

256   *Scriptures Index*

Romans
    1.18, 170
    1.20–24, 133, 144n60, 193,
       204n30
    1.26, 144n57
    1.28–29, 170, 193
    2.5, 144n60
    2.8, 170
    2.9, 194
    2.14–15, 144n60, 169, 193
    2.17–24, 184n125
    2.26, 182n91
    2.29, 193
    3.13–18, 204n30
    3.20, 194
    4.3, 169
    4.12, *34*, 145n71
    4.13–15, 155, 170–71
    4.19, 140n2
    5.5, 193
    5.6–8, 80, 140n2
    5.14, 179n44
    6–7, 126–30, 137, 212
    6.1–14, 204n24
    6.2, 189
    6.6–7, 128, 132, 137, 189, 204n30
    6.11, 189
    6.12–23, 128, 139
    6.12–13, 131–33, 170,
       183n122, 193
    6.14–16, 132, 137, 170, 183n122
    6.17, 80, 132, 137, 144n60,
       193, 198
    6.18, 80, 137, 170, 183n122
    6.19, 80, 92n100, 127, 129, 132,
       137, 143n49, 170, 183n122,
       204n30
    6.20–23, 92n106, 132, 137
    7.1–6, 130–32, 139, 189, 193
    7.5–25, 128, 171
    7.7–13, 130, 178n23, 189
    7.14–25, 60, 80, 130–31, 133, 193
    7.14, 131, 137, 139, 185n143
    7.23–25, 15, 80–81, 130–32,
       137, 189

    8.2–3, 80, 92n100, 129, 187, 189
    8.4–7, 127, 169, 205n33
    8.11–13, 80, 168
    8.14–26, 132, 140n2, 170
    9.17–28, 145n71
    10.1–10, 144n60
    10.18, 145n71
    13.1, 194
    14.1–21, 140n2
    15.4, 153, 171
    15.26–27, 208n76
    16.18, 133

1 Corinthians
    1.25–27, 140n2
    2.3, 140n2, 190
    3.1, 139, 185n143, 212
    4.10, 140n2
    6.9–11, 170–71
    7.5–37, 80, 134
    8.7–12, 140n2
    9.8–14, 171, 199, 208n76
    9.21–22, 140n2, 191
    12.22–26, 140n2, 144n56
    15.12–58, 19, 65, 126, 170

2 Corinthians
    1.5–7, 132, 144n56, 191
    1.20–22, 194
    3.1–4.6, 194
    3.3, 146n94
    4.7–12, 191
    6.5, 191
    9.8, 200
    10.5–10, 19, 127
    11.21–32, 92n101, 127, 140n2,
       151, 191
    12.5–10, 127
    13.3–9, 140n3

Galatians
    1.1, 43, 168, 187–88
    1.4, 49, 153, 174, 187–88,
       192, 213
    1.8–9, 49, 201

Scriptures Index

1.11–12, 128
1.13–14, 156, 201
1.15–16, 127–28, 190, 194
2.2–3, 154
2.11–18, 154, 159, 170, 191, 199
2.15, 196, 201
2.16, 98, 127–28, 153, 165, 169, 187, 194, 200
2.17, 168–69
2.19, 98, 153, 159–60, 168–69, 188–92, 197, 201, 202n4, 213
2.20, 127, 153, 168–69, 187–94, 197–201, 203n16, 213
2.21, 98, 165, 167, 191–92, 212–13
3.1–14, 153, 169–71, 192
3.1, 190, 194, 204n25, 213
3.2, 176
3.3, 125, 168, 200
3.4, 144n56
3.5, 166, 176, 197
3.6–9, 140, 163, 169–71, 174, 201–2
3.10–11, 153, 163, 166, 169, 171
3.13, 153, 187
3.14–22, 140, 163, 170
3.14, 149, 171, 174
3.16, 170–71
3.18, 165, 167, 170–71, 212
3.19–4.7, 84, 126, *136*, 165, 212–13
3.19–4.3, 60, 150, 212
3.19–25, 125, 139–40, 152–53, 163, 170, 192, 196, 213
3.19, 49, 136, 140, 153–56, 179n47
3.21, 98, 165–69, 212
3.22, 130, *136*, 138, 140, 153
3.23–26, 149–53, 169, 192
3.23, *136*, 152
3.24, 140
3.25, *136*, 153
3.26–29, 160, 163, 170–71, 191–93, 201
3.26, 153, 169, 201

3.27, 201
3.28, 13, 200–201
3.29, 170, 201–2
4, 2, 4, 10, 18, 43, 46, 51, 67–68, 95–98, 116, 125–27
4.1–11, 153, 172, 174, 201
4.1–3, 137–40, 185n143
4.1, 79, 137, 139
4.2, 10, *136*, 138–39
4.3–9, 129, 174
4.3, 2, 6–11, 17–18, 20–21, 31, *34*, 59–60, 66, 71, 78–79, 86n5, 98, 125–30, 134–39, 145n77, 156, 160, 174–75, 189–92, 198–201, 211
4.4–7, 170–71, 192–93, 204n27, 213
4.4, *136*, 168, 187
4.5, *136*, 153, 174, 187–88, 193
4.6, 136, 153, 166, 192–93, 207n66, 213
4.7, 201
4.8–20, 191
4.8–11, 123n110, 126–27, 159–64, 168, 174, 192, 213
4.8, 14, 126, 161–62, 180n78, 200–201
4.9–10, 13, 98, 109, 161, 166, 169, 213
4.9, 2–7, 24n48, 26n85, *34*, 59–60, 86n5, 126–29, 134–36, 154–56, 161–66, 175, 191, 198–201, 206n45, 211
4.10, 6, 14, 162, 164, 199
4.12–20, 191
4.12–15, 126–27, 191–92, 213
4.12, 191, 204n18
4.13, 26n85, 60, 92n100, 126–27, 190
4.14, 49, 127, 190–91
4.15, 192, 204n25
4.19, 170, 201, 213
4.21–5.4, 171
4.21–5.1, 97–98, 172–74, 215
4.21, 171

258 *Scriptures Index*

4.23, 127, 200
4.25, *34*, 135
4.26–28, 201
4.29, 127, 200
4.30, 166, 171
4.31, 201
5.1, 152
5.2–12, 154, 159, 169
5.2, 160
5.4, 160, 166
5.5, 153, 168–71, 192, 197–98,
  201, 213
5.6, 98, 153, 160, 169–71, 187,
  192, 197, 201, 213
5.7, 154, 192, 200, 213
5.8, 153
5.13–6.2, 126, 135–38, 212
5.13–24, 150, 200–201, 213
5.13, 128, 153, 170
5.14, 153, 170, 192–93, 197, 213
5.16–25, 60, 71, 128, 140, 153,
  196, 205n41, 212–13
5.16–21, 128
5.16, 127, 134–35, 154, 168, 175,
  194–200, 205n38, 206n44
5.17, 5, 133, 135, 193–98,
  205n33, 206n44
5.18–23, 153, 171, 198
5.18, 153, 175, 193–98
5.19–21, 127, 133, 140, 194
5.21, 135, 140, 170, 197–201
5.22–6.2, 135
5.22, 168–70, 193, 197–98, 200–
  201, 213
5.23, 168–70, 197, 198, 201, 213
5.24, 75, 127–28, 132–36, 153,
  160, 175, 188–89, 192, 194,
  197, 201, 213
5.25, *34*, 134–36, 168, 188, 192,
  196–201, 213
6.5–6, 199–200, 208n86
6.6–10, 198–200, 208n86, 213
6.8, 168, 170, 197–201, 208n76
6.9, 75, 170, 200
6.10, 200–201

6.12–15, 154, 159, 200
6.12, 98, 127, 160
6.13, 127, 182n91
6.14, 98, 154, 159–60, 189–90,
  200–201
6.15, 154, 160, 168, 189, 198, 200
6.16, *34*, 134–35, 154, 189, 198–
  201, 215
6.17, 191
6.18, 204n30

Ephesians
2.3, 143n53, 146n94
4.28, 208n86
6.1, 183n122

Colossians
1.24, 144n55, 191
2, 2, 10, 46, 67
2.8–23, 215
2.8, 2–3, 10, *34*, 56n61, 211, 215
2.11–15, 202n5, 204n23
2.16–23, 102, 122n80
2.16, 180n72
2.20, 10, *34*, 56n61, 211, 215
3.5, 144n57
4.1, 183n122

Philippians
1.5, 199
1.23, 144n60
1.29, 144n56
2.10, 145n71
2.25–30, 140n3, 202n1
3.10, 132, 190
3.16, *34*, 145n71
3.19, 145n71
4.7, 151
4.11–15, 191, 199

1 Thessalonians
2.10, 170
2.14–17, 144n56, 144n60
4.5, 144n57
5.14, 140n2

Scriptures Index 259

2 Thessalonians
    1.5, 144n56
    3.11–13, 200

1 Timothy
    1.18, 208n76
    5.23, 140n3, 202n1

2 Timothy
    1.12, 144n56
    2.22, 143n53
    3.6, 143n53, 205n40
    3.11, 144n55
    3.15–17, 178n30, 183n122,
      184n125
    4.3, 143n53
    4.20, 140n3

Titus
    1.8, 183n122
    2.12, 143n53
    3.3, 143n53

Hebrews
    5.12, 7, *34*, 37

1 Peter
    1.5, 177n11
    2.11, 92n105
    4.6, 92n105

2 Peter
    1.1, 43
    3.5–13, 41–43
    3.10, *34*, 40–41, 55n44
    3.12, *34*, 41

Ancient Sources Index

Page references for figures are italicized.

DEAD SEA SCROLLS

CD
3.14–15, 182n89

1QH
4.29, 128
15.12, 128
15.21, 128
18.21, 128
18.22–23, 128

1QM War Scroll
X.11–12, 48
4.3, 128

1QS
1.14–15, 182n89
4.19–21, 128
11.9–12, 128

4QDtj
32.8, 57n71

4Q88 Psalms^f

X.5–6, 48

4Q388 Pseudo-Moses^c
1.6–7, 48

4Q390 Pseudo-Moses Apocalypse^e
1.11, 48
2.1.3–7, 48

OTHER EARLY JEWISH WRITINGS

2 Baruch
21.6, 47
48.8, 47

1 Enoch
61.10, 179n47
75.3, 48
82.4–7, 182n89
82.7–9, 14, 181n89
82.8, 48

2 Enoch

1a.5–6, 49

4 Ezra
   8.22, 47

2 Maccabees
   4.38, 92n101
   5.21, 64
   7, 87n18
   7.22–23, 63
   7.22, *35*–36, 64, 126
   10.35, 92n101
   14.45, 92n101

4 Maccabees
   1–3, 195
   12, 63
   12.13, *34*, 66

Baruch
   2.18, 127
   33–34, 48

Epistle of Jeremiah
   60, 48

Josephus
Ag. Ap.
   2.255, 117n6
   2.282, 164
Ant.
   1.p, *50*, 57n81
   1.21, 103
   1.24, 97
   1.155–156, 163
   1.158, 181n83
   2.206, 182n93
   3.91, 164
   3.120, *35*
   3.123, 118n12
   3.146, *35*
   3.159–186, 118n12
   3.159, 121n59
   3.160, 121n59
   3.164, 121n59

3.165–166, 121n58
3.167, *35*
3.168, *35*
3.172, *35*, 121n59
3.183, *34*, 39, 104
3.184, 121n59
3.185, 121n58
3.186, 121n59
8.78, *35*
8.136, *35*
11.294, 164
13.234, 164
14.264, 164
15.154, 182n93
15.413, *35*
15.415, *35*
15.418, *35*
16.312, 182n93
17.33, *34*
17.192, *34*
18.259, 97
20.267, *35*
J.W.
   1.373, 39
   1.377, *34*, 39
   2.173, *35*
   2.468, 182n93
   4.324, 104, 118n12
   4.268, 182n93
   5.131, *35*
   5.212–513, 39, 104
   5.212–218, 118n12
   5.218, 104
   5.231–237, 118n12, 121n59
   6.47, *34*, 65
   7.312, *35*

Jubilees
   1.1, 57n82
   2.1–23, 58n82
   2.1, 57n82
   2.2–20, 58n82
   2.2, 47–48
   2.8–9, 14
   2.8, 57n82

Ancient Sources Index

2.9, 181n89
2.14, 57n82
4.17, 57n82
5.20, 57n82
6.32–35, 182n89
10.24, 57n82
11.16–12.24, 113
12.16, 163
12.17–18, 163
15.31–32, 48
16, 164
48.1, 57n82
frag. a, 48
frag. a.1–23, 57n82
frag. a.20, *50*, 58n82
frag. a.24, 58n82
frag. a.113, *50*

Letter of Aristeas
99, 121n60
107–120, 88n32

Philo
Abraham
1–6, 179n65
2, 90n65
6, 112, 181n88
43, *34*
52, 112
62–80, 110
62, 113
68, 113, 123n102, 175
69, 113–14
70–71, 114
72–80, 113
78, 163
81–83, 37
81, *34*, 36
119, 123n102
162, *34*
164, 77
262–274, 114
275–276, 169
275, 114, 181n88
276, 114, 179n65

Agriculture
73–78, 195
96–97, 112
123, 90n68
136, *33*, 37
140, *35*, 53n16, 63
181, *35*, 53n16
Alleg. Interp.
1.1, 123n101
1.14, *33*, 37
1.69, 91n83, 128, 143n49
1.72–73, 195
1.72, 168
1.81, *35*
2.11, 76
2.19, 112
2.22–24, 76
2.37, 76, 90n74
2.40–41, 76
2.40, 90n74
2.45, 76, 90n74
2.49–50, 76, 91n81
2.49, 76
2.50, 76, 90n72
2.54–59, 184n125
2.70, 76
3.68, 90n68
3.75, 90n68
3.118, 195
3.121, *33*, 37
3.210, 77
3.244, 115
3.245, 115
Cherubim
1–5, 115
7, 115
8–9, 115
8, 115
21, 123nn101–2
23, 123n101
25, 123n102
88, 90n65
127, *34*, 39
Confusion
14, 123n102

21, 77
23, 90n65

Contempl. Life
3–5, 14, 124n118
3, *33*, 162
4, *33*, 64, 124n118, 162
5, 162
28, 99, 123nn101–3
66, *35*
78, 123nn101–2, 123nn104–5

Creation
1–3, 102
3, 84, 102–5, 159, 165
38, *33*, 39
52, *33*, 39
55, 100, 124n118, 180n74
58–59, 100
69–70, 134
70, 90n65
73, 179n63
77, 99
80, 90n68
84, *33*, 41
89, 65
101–116, 107
113, 101, 162
115, 101
117, 100, 113, 164
126, *33*, 37
127, *33*, 36–37
128, 107
131, *33*, 40
141, *35*
146, *33*, 40, 64, 126
147, 40
206, 180n74

Decalogue
1, 123nn102–3, 123n105
31, *34*, 39
53, 124n118, 162
54, 124n118
58, 124n118, 162
98–101, 107, 165
100–101, 107
102–105, 107

Dreams
1.14, 123n102
1.21–24, 99
1.21, *33*, 101
1.39, 40
1.102, 123n102
1.137, 55n35
1.144, 123n101
1.161, 114
1.212, *33*, 65
1.214, 118n12
1.215, 104
1.218, 123n101
2.70, 64
2.118, *34*
2.123–132, 118n15
2.139, *35*

Drunkenness
23, 179n63
85, 123n101
134, 123n101
142, 165
198, 97

Embassy
26–27, 84
80, *33*
115, 84
156, 118n15
159, 179n64
170, 179n64
256, 118n15, 179n64

Eternity
4, 56n50
6, *33*, 39, 56n50
8, 56n50
9, 56n50
21, 53n19
29, *33*, 64
46, 124n118
47, 56n50
54, 56n50
61, *33*, 39
74, *33*, 39, 64
76, 56n50
77, 56n50

78, *33*, 39
82, *33*, 39, 56n50
85, 56n50
87, 56n50
88, 56n50
89, 56n50
90, *33*, 39, 56n50
94, *34*, 145n69
95, 56n50
99, 56n50
102, 56n50
103, *33*, 39, 56n52
104, 56n50
105, 56n50
107–108, 37
107, *34*, 39, 56n50, 56n52
108, 168
109, *34*, 45–46, 56n52, 96, 211
110, 41–42
111, *34*, 39, 56n52
113, *34*, 37, 56n52
115–116, 41
116, *34*, 39, 56n52
123–129, 41
123, *34*
131, 41
135, *34*, 135, 199
143–144, 41
144, *34*, 39

Flaccus
14, 84
55, *34*, 37
92, *36*
123, 40
125, *33*, 40
156, *36*

Flight
100, 123n101
108–110, 104
108, 123n105, 123n107
184–185, 118n12

Giants
6–7, 55n35
7–8, 40–41, 48
7, *35*

8, 124n118
10, 90n65
16, 55n35
31, 184n125
22, *34*, 55n35
29–35, 141n15

God
71, 90n68

Good Person
7, *34*
43, 118n15
80, 123n101
82, 99
159, 91n83

Heir
1–129, 170
8, 170
29, *34*, 64
57, 141n15
64, 171
66, 171
69–70, 171
69, 105
76, 171
95, 169
97–99, 163
97, 114
98, 113, 163, 171, 175
102, *35*, 53n16
112, 123n101
133–134, 39, 45–46
134, *33*, 45, 96–97, 211
140, *33*, 39, 45–46, 96–97, 211
152–153, 53n19
152, *33*, 39
155, 104
175–176, 121n58
182–184, 104
184, *34*
190, *34*
196–200, 118n12
197–199, 123n101
197, *33*, 56n62, 112
199–200, 104
200, *34*, 145n69

209, *34*, 37
210, *33*, 37
213, 118n15
216–226, 118n12
217, 123n101
226–227, 123n101
226, *33*, 56n62, 104
227, *33*, 56n62
239, 123n101
268, 91n81, 141n15
276–283, 93n117
281–282, 37
282–283, 65
282, *33*, 37, 64
295, 84

Joseph
28, 123nn102–3
125, 123n102
151, 123n102
160, *36*
217, *35*

Life
113, 121n67

Migration
1, 123n101
2–3, 113
3, 64
9–12, 114
14, 114
29, 116
67, 195
83, *34*
89–93, 169
89, 105, 123n101, 123n106
91–92, 105
91, 84
92–93, 106, 123n104, 160
92, 85
93, 105, 123n101
103, 123n104
116, 84
127–128, 175
127, 114, 169
128, 114
132, 169

177–183, 124n118
178–180, 163
178, 113
179, 113–14
180, *35*, 100, 113, 162
181, 165
184–197, 163
184–195, 114
184, 114

Moses
1.78, *34*
1.96, *33*
1.97, *33*
1.155, *33*
1.156, *33*
1.216, *33*
1.289–291, 173
2.14–15, 165
2.37, 40
2.47, 84, 103, 159
2.48–53, 122n96
2.48, 103, 159, 212
2.52, 103, 107, 113, 164
2.53, *33*
2.65, *33*
2.88, *33*, 104, 118n12
2.101–124, 118n12
2.101–105, 123n101
2.101, 104
2.112, *35*
2.117–119, 121n59
2.117, 104
2.120–122, 123n101
2.121, *33*, 41
2.122–123, 121n58
2.124, *35*
2.126, 90n65, 101
2.128, 123n101
2.133–134, 104
2.133, *35*
2.135, 104
2.143, 104
2.148, *33*
2.182–185, 169
2.210–216, 165

2.210, 107
2.212–216, 107
2.212, 118n15
2.215–216, 168
2.216, 118n15
2.249, 134
2.251, *33*, *34*, 134
2.267, *33*
2.286, *33*
2.288, *34*

Names
61, *33*, 36–37
67, 123n102
77, *33*, 36–37
179–180, 134
179, *34*
217, 84
223, 98
255, 115

Planting
10, *33*, 37
12, 55n35
14, 55n35
32–36, 112
34, 64
36, 112, 123n102
52, *35*, 53n16
120, 53n19
122, 168

Posterity
5–6, 37
5, *34*, 64

Prelim. Studies
9–10, 115
11, 123n101
13, 115
18, 115
19, 115
20–21, 115
36, 115
49, 114
81–88, 173
117, *33*, 104, 118n12, 123n101
150, *33*, 37
172, 123nn102–3

Providence
2.43, 101
2.45–53, 162
2.45, *33*, 54n31, 101
2.53, *33*, 54n31, 101
2.69, 41, 109

QE
1.1, 108, 121n68, 165
2.2, 121n67
2.85, 103–4
2.109, 121n58
2.120, 121n59

QG
3.46–52, 121n63
3.47, 85, 105–6, 160, 167, 213
3.48, 106, 160
3.61, 121n63
3.62, 121n63
4 fragment 51b, *34*
4 fragment 8b, *34*, 37

Rewards
22, 169
36, 40
44, *34*
58, 113
66, 118n15, 168
93–97, 173
117, 184n125
118–124, 15, 105
119–124, 84
119–122, 17
119–120, 91n84, 171
119, 77, 91n84, 167, 212
120, 167
121–124, 77, 91n84
121–122, 167
121, 17, 77–78, 105, 212
124, 17, 77–78, 105, 141n15, 167, 212
126, 91n84, 179nn64–65
162–165, 184n125
163–167, 110

Sacrifices
14, 123n105
15, 77, 84

27, 179n63
51, 84
74, *33*, 37
108, 53n19

Sobriety
8–9, 115
9, 115
48, *34*, 145n68

Spec. Laws
1.2–7, 106, 167
1.6, 106, 160
1.8, 123n101
1.9, 85, 106, 160
1.13–16, 124n118
1.16, 100–101, 113
1.66, 103
1.84, 104
1.85–94, 118n12
1.85, 121n59, 123n101
1.86, 104, 123n101
1.92, 100–101, 113, 164
1.93–94, 121n59
1.93, 123n101
1.95–96, 104
1.97, 104, 123n101
1.149, 197
1.172, 118n12, 123n101
1.173, 197
1.175, 123n101
1.193, 207n59
1.201, 123n101
1.208, *34*
1.210, 90n65
1.264, 123n101
1.266, *34*
1.294, *34*, 64–65
1.304–305, 121n63
1.327, 123n102
1.328, *34*, 39
1.345, 98
2.1, *35*
2.31, 90n68
2.39–222, 107
2.39, 107
2.40, 107

2.45, 40
2.56–214, 207n59
2.56–175, 84, 105
2.56–139, 165
2.57–59, 107
2.60–64, 107
2.61–63, 118n15
2.62–63, 168
2.66–70, 107
2.140–144, 165
2.143, 101
2.145–161, 110
2.145–149, 108, 165
2.148, 108
2.150–161, 165
2.150, 84, 108
2.151, *34*, 39, 108
2.155–156, 108
2.158, 108
2.160, 108
2.161, 84
2.163, 104, 107, 167
2.167, 104
2.177, *35*, 53n16
2.186–192, 101
2.193–203, 165
2.194, 108
2.195, 108
2.197, 108
2.201–202, 108
2.204, 169
2.231–237, 168
2.255, *34*, 124n118
2.260, 164
2.266, 101
3.9–10, 77
3.10, 77–78, 121n62
3.111, 40
3.151–152, 40
3.162, *35*
4.79, 13, 59, 90n68
4.91–131, 207n59
4.91, 77, 90n74, 109
4.92–94, 109
4.94–95, 141n15

Ancient Sources Index

4.95, 90n68, 195
4.96, 109
4.97, 109
4.100–109, 109
4.100, 41, 109
4.110–115, 109
4.112, 123n101
4.113, 77
4.116–118, 109
4.118, 41, 109–10, 195
4.129, 41
4.131, 110
4.134, 168, 212
4.203, *36*
4.226, 168

Unchangeable
46, *34*
104, *35*
140–144, 141n15

Virtues
73, *34*, 40
178, 84
181–182, 179n63
212–216, 124n118
212, 113–14
214–215, 113, 163
214, 113–14
216–217, 169, 176
216, 114, 163
219, 114, 163

Worse
7–8, 44
7, *34*, 44
8, *34*
145–146, 84
153–155, 37
159, 113, 175

Ἀριθμῶν
4h, *34*
5a, *34*
21a, *34*
27a, *33*
73a, *33*, 36, 37
73b, *33*
74, *33*

99, *34*
103, *35*
131, *35*

Sibylline Oracles
2.194–213, 54n32
2.196–213, 54n34
2.206, *50*
3.1–92, 54n32
3.46–62, 54n32
3.75–92, 40, 42, 54n32
3.79–82, 45
3.80–86, 40
3.80–81, 211
3.80, *33*, 40
3.84–87, 54n32
5.13–15, 36
5.15, *34*
5.51–53, 36
5.115–134, 36
5.294–305, 36
5.377–380, 36
5.447–450, 36
11.15–17, 36
11.17, *36*
11.23, *36*
11.141–142, 36
11.142, *33*
11.153–154, 36
11.154, *33*
11.189–190, 36
11.190, *33*
11.195–196, 36
11.196, *33*

Sirach
1.26, 195
6.37, 195
17.17, 48
50.5–15, 121n60

Testament of Solomon
18.1–3, 50
18.1, *50*
18.2, 49, *50*

18.4–40, 50

Wisdom
6.11, 195
7.15–22, 38
7.17–19, 14
7.17, *33*, 39
11–19, 38
13.1–3, 14, 163
16.22, 38
18.21–24, 121n60
18.24, *35*
19.10, 38
19.18–20, 38
19.18, *33*, 38

ANCIENT GREEK AND ROMAN SOURCES

Alcinous
Didask.
15.1, 119n21

Alexander Polyhistor
DK
1.58b1, 102

Anon. Lond.
1–2, 133
1.27–37, 144n61
4.20–2.19, 63

Aristotle
Cael.
1.2–3, 119n21
3.2, 119n21
3.7, 119n21
De an.
1.1, 73, 89n47
1.2, 69, 88n40
2.1, 72
Eth. nic.
2.3, 212

2.3.6, 73
2.5.2, 73
2.5.4, 73
3.10–12, 212
3.11–12, 178n27
3.11.6, 83
3.12, 93n115, 212
3.12.6–8, 83
3.12.6, 73
3.12.8, 83
7.3, 205n40
7.7.8, 207n63
7.9.2, 197
7.9.6, 197
Eud. eth.
2.2–3, 89n47
Gen. an.
1.2, 119n21
3.5, 119n21
Gen. corr.
1.1, 33
2.1, 33
2.2, 62
2.6, 69
Metaph.
5.3, 32
Part. an.
2.2, 73, 89n46
2.4, 73, 89n46
Pol.
3.13, 198
Rhet.
2.12.3, 73
2.14.3, 89n49
3.11.6, 73
3.12.7, 73
4.5.3, 73
7.3.10, 73
7.7.3, 73
7.7.8, 73

BGU
3.959, 53n14

Cicero

Ancient Sources Index

Fat.
42, 90n73
Leg.
1.18, 102
2.13, 165

Diogenes Laertius
7.88, 102

Empedocles
12/6, 162
17/109, 69
62/96, 61
74/71, 61
96/105, 69, 193
98/98, 69, 126

Epicurus
Ep. Men.
127–128, 194–195

Euripides
Andr.
629–630, 75
Med.
310, 205n40

Galen
Aff. dig.
27–28, 89n48
Opt. med.
59, 88n29
PHP
3.1.10, 89n53
3.2.12, 75
4.6.8, 75, 200
4.6.10, 75, 200
4.6.35, 75
5.2.31–33, 89n53
5.3.8, 74
7.52, 75
Prop. plac.
5, 67
7, 69
15, 67–68, 78, 211

QAM
1.767–768, 68
3.777–778, 67
3.779, 67
4.781, 68, 74
5.787, 68
6.789–790, 89n42
7.791–795, 88n40, 89n46
8.801, 82, 212
9.807–808, 68, 88n41
Temp.
1.1, 67
1.510, 67
2.1, 68

Hesiod
Op.
383–384, 101

Hippocratic Corpus
Aër.
2, 61, 70, 162
24, 150, 212
5, 70
16, 70
23, 70
24, 70, 82
Aph.
3.20–23, 162
3.20, 70
3.22, 70
3.23, 69–70
Nat. hom.
1–7, 69
1, 61
3, 61
4–5, 61
4, 61
7, 61, 162

Homer
Iliad
18.108–110, 75

Longinus

272 Ancient Sources Index

On the Sublime
44.1–5, 97

Numenius
F.13, 118n13

Plato
Leg.
1.645d–e, 72
2.653b–c, 88n39
5.747c, 72, 88n41
7.789a–e, 82
7.792e, 82
7.808d–e, 82, 179n42
7.808d, 71
7.808e, 177n15
Phaedr.
245c, 72
Prot.
355a, 205n40
Resp.
3.390b, 197
4.430e, 197
4.437c, 71
4.437e, 71
4.439d, 71
4.442b, 71, 193
Theat.
201e–208c, 52n6
Tim.
27a, 126
32b–c, 62
32b, 52n6
33a, 62
37e, 121n68
39c, 121n68
42e–43b, 72
42e–43a, 62, 64, 71
43a–44c, 108
43a, 71–72
43c, 62
44a–b, 68, 71, 212
44b, 71
48b, 32
49b–c, 119n21

53a–b, 119n21
54d, 52n7
55b, 52n7
57c, 62
60a, 72
61d–68a, 88n38
62b, 88n38
65b, 88n38
70a–d, 71
70a, 71, 193
70d–71d, 71
78a, 71
82a, 62
82b, 62
86b–e, 76
86b–c, 72
86b, 72
86c–87a, 89n42
86c–e, 77
86d–e, 89n44
86d, 72, 82, 144n64
86e–87a, 72, 75, 108
87a, 72
87b–89d, 212
87b, 82
87c, 82
88a–d, 71, 82
88a–b, 71–72, 108
88b–e, 82
88b, 194
88c, 82
88d–e, 82
89d, 82, 93n109
90b–c, 82
90d, 82

PLondon
1.130, 47

Plutarch
Is. Os.
353e–f, 102
Quaest. rom.
263d–e, 102

Ancient Sources Index

Sextus Empiricus
Pyr.
    3.152, 12

Simplicius
De Caelo Comment.
    1.3.49b, 44
In Phys.
    7.10–14, 52n6

Theophrastus
Sens.
    11, 69

Zeno
Vit. philos.
    7.1.110, 74

EARLY CHRISTIAN SOURCES

Ambrosiaster
    43, 6
    46, 6, 162
    79, 6
    190, 6
    192, 6

Aristides
Apology
    3.2–3, 3
    4.1, 3
    7.3–4, 3
    7.3, 126

Athenagoras
Leg.
    16.1–5, 3
    16.3, 3
    19.4, 3
    22.1–12, 3
Resurrection
    2.5, 3

    3.2, 3

Chrysostom
Galatians
    13.41–42, 153

Clement of Alexandria
Ecl.
    26.2, 3
Exc.
    3.48, 3, 22n9
    4.81, 22n9
Paed.
    1.6.33, 66
    3.12.100, 3
Protr.
    1.5, 3
    5.65, 3
Strom.
    1.11.50, 3
    1.11.52, 3
    1.11.53, 5, 66
    2.6.31, 3
    2.11.51, 3
    4.6.32, 3
    5.8.46, 3
    5.8.49, 3
    6.8.62, 3
    6.15.117, 3
    6.148.2, 3, 22n9

Eusebius
Praep. ev.
    9.17.3, 181n83
    9.18.1, 181n83
    9.21.1–9, 122n94
    9.29.1–3, 122n94
    13.12.13, 121n71
    13.13.50, 181n83

Hermas
Vision
    3.13.3, 3

Irenaeus

274 Ancient Sources Index

Haer.
　　3.12.6, 22n10

Jerome
Galatians
　　6, 7
　　7, 7–8
　　106, 7
　　107, 6–8
　　114–115, 8
　　118–119, 8
　　180–181, 8
Vir. ill.
　　101, 7

Justin Martyr
2 Apology
　　5.2, 47
Dial.
　　62.2, 3, 126

Origen Adamantinus
Cels.
　　pref.5, 3, 7
　　4.51, 118n13

　　4.56, 3
　　4.63, 3
　　8.72, 3
Comm. Jo.
　　10.262, 3, 8
　　10.266, 8
　　13.127, 3, 8
Comm. Rom.
　　7.2, 4
Hom. Jer.
　　10.6, 4, 7, 57n65, 215n2
Hom. Num.
　　24.1.1, 4

Tatian
Ad Graec.
　　21.3, 3

Victorinus, Gaius Marius
　　138–139, 4
　　139, 5, 215
　　145, 4–5
　　165, 5
　　171, 190

About the Author

Ernest P. Clark, PhD (University of St. Andrews) is Director of Global Training with United World Mission. A Jamaican biblical scholar, his research explores the transformation of Jewish and Christian traditions as works are composed and edited in intentional interaction with other worldviews.